Women in Iran from 1800 to the Islamic Republic

Women in Iran
from 1800 to the
Islamic Republic

Edited by
Lois Beck and Guity Nashat

UNIVERSITY OF ILLINOIS PRESS

URBANA AND CHICAGO

© 2004 by the Board of Trustees
of the University of Illinois
All rights reserved
Manufactured in the United States of America
1 2 3 4 5 C P 5 4 3 2 1

∞ This book is printed on acid-free paper.

Library of Congress Cataloging-in-Publication Data

Women in Iran from 1800 to the Islamic Republic /
edited by Lois Beck and Guity Nashat.
p.   cm.
Includes bibliographical references and index.
ISBN 0-252-02937-2 (cloth : alk. paper)
ISBN 0-252-07189-1 (pbk. : alk. paper)
1. Women—Iran—History. 2. Women—Iran—Biography.
3. Women in development—Iran—History. 4. Women in politics—
Iran—History. 5. Women's rights—Iran—History.
I. Beck, Lois, 1944– II. Nashat, Guity, 1937–
HQ1735.2.W655   2004
305.4'0955—dc22   2003024078

CONTENTS

Acknowledgments   vii

A Note on Transliterations   ix

Chronology   xi

Introduction   1
Guity Nashat

1. Marriage in the Qajar Period   37
   Guity Nashat

2. Reflections in the Mirror—How Each Saw the Other:
   Women in the Nineteenth Century   63
   Shireen Mahdavi

3. The Origins and Development of the Women's Movement
   in Iran, 1906–41   85
   Mansoureh Ettehadieh

4. The Women's Organization of Iran: Evolutionary Politics
   and Revolutionary Change   107
   Mahnaz Afkhami

5. The Role of Women Members of Parliament, 1963–88   136
   Haleh Esfandiari

6. Women and Labor in the Islamic Republic of Iran   163
   Fatemeh Etemad Moghadam

7. Labor-Force Participation of Women in Contemporary Iran   182
   Amir Mehryar, Gholamali Farjadi, and Mohammad Tabibian

8. Sexuality, Rights, and Islam: Competing Gender Discourses
   in Postrevolutionary Iran   204
   Ziba Mir-Hosseini

9. Rural Women's History: A Case Study from Boir Ahmad   218
   Erika Friedl

10. Qashqa'i Women in Postrevolutionary Iran   240
    Lois Beck

Contributors   279

Index   283

ACKNOWLEDGMENTS

THIS BOOK has been in the making for some years, and the editors are grateful for the patience and steadfast support of the scholars whose contributions appear here. They also appreciate the efforts of those at the University of Illinois Press who aided the project.

Lois Beck appreciates the many people who facilitated her cultural anthropological research in Iran during the past thirty-five years, especially because her experience living among rural, nomadic, tribal, and ethnic-minority peoples has given her a wider understanding of the topic of "women in Iran" than she would have gained only by engaging in historical studies of Iran. She thanks Julia Huang for her proficiency in the use of computers and her good-humored support, and she acknowledges the aid she received from Washington University and its Department of Anthropology. Jamsheed Choksy, Layla Diba, Haleh Esfandiari, and Shireen Mahdavi offered their expertise and assistance during her work on this and the companion volume.

Guity Nashat expresses deep gratitude to her mother, Ghamar Afshar Nashat-Mirdamad, who encouraged her research and writing about women in Iran. She regrets that her mother died in 2001 before this and the previous volume were published. She thanks her coeditor and colleague, Lois Beck, for coordinating and preparing the firevision and submission of the two volumes to the press.

A NOTE ON TRANSLITERATIONS

THE SYSTEMS of transliteration used in this volume are modified versions of the format recommended by the *International Journal of Middle Eastern Studies.* The editors reluctantly exclude all diacritical marks from transliterated words coming from Persian, Arabic, and Turkish, with the exception of the ayn (ʿ) and hamza (ʾ) when they fall in the middle of a word. Confronted by the many different systems of transliteration and the amazing array of diacritical marks used by the contributors in their original submissions, we decided that a relatively uniform system was needed. Other than the issue of diacriticals, we have tried to respect the integrity of each contributor's system of transliteration and generally have not imposed a uniform spelling of certain words—for example, these and other variations occur: hijab/hejab, madrasa/madreseh, and Mohammad/Muhammad. We follow generally accepted spellings of certain other words, such as shariʿa and ulama.

Most transliterated words in Persian, Arabic, and Turkish are italicized on their first use in each chapter but not thereafter, and most such words are accompanied by short definitions in English on their first appearance. Because of their frequent use in the volume, we do not italicize the following words on first use: chador/chadur (veil-wrap), hadith (traditions of the prophet), hijab/hejab (modest Islamic dress), imam (religious and/or political leader), madrasa/madreseh (school, sometimes religious), shariʿa (Islamic law), and ulama (religious scholars).

CHRONOLOGY

Qajar Dynasty, 1794–1925

Reign of Agha Muhammad Khan (1794–97): Member of the Turkic Qajar tribe, defeats all rivals and ascends the throne in 1794, chooses Tehran as capital, and appoints his nephew as heir; he is known for frugality and austerity.

Reign of Fath Ali Shah (1797–1834): Qajar armies routed by Russian forces, causing loss of territory in northwestern Iran; shah uses polygynous marriage and concubinage as a means of consolidating control over a shaky kingdom and is known for many wives and progeny; Qajar rule acquires the appearance of an Irano-Islamic style of government; succession established in eldest son, Abbas Mirza (d. 1833), and his descendants.

Reign of Muhammad Shah (1834–48): War with Britain over Herat; Ali Muhammad proclaims himself the Bab (1844); Fatimeh Qurrat al-Ayn proclaims adherence to the Bab, harbinger of the Baha'i faith, a new religion; shah is known for piety.

Reign of Nasir al-Din Shah (1848–96): Execution of the Bab and Qurrat al-Ayn (1850); sporadic efforts to strengthen the central government; opening of first European-style school for boys; introduction of telegraph system; shah takes three trips to Europe; emergence of a small elite familiar with Europe and advocates of European-type reforms; granting of concession for building railways and developing natural resources to Baron Reuter, a British subject, and its abrogation under widespread opposition (1872–73); granting of tobacco concession to Major Talbot, and its abrogation (1892), resulting from massive opposition, including by women within the royal household; increased interest of Europeans seeking concessions from the shah and rising opposition to these efforts; heightened rivalry of Britain and Russia over extending influence in Iran.

Reign of Muzaffar al-Din Shah (1896–1907): Shah travels to Europe; beginning of accumulation of foreign debt; rising demand by disparate groups for limiting royal prerogatives results in granting of a constitution.

Reign of Muhammad Ali Shah (1907–9): Shah's suspicion of the constitution leads to bombardment of parliament; arrest and murder of some deputies; support for the constitution in several cities forces the shah to abdicate; Britain and Russia limit rivalry by dividing Iran into spheres of influence (1907).

Reign of Ahmad Shah (1909–25): Constitutional coalition fragmented but parliament passes law for universal secular education; first modern schools for girls open in Tehran; Iran invaded by allied and entente powers during World War I; British effort to turn Iran into a protectorate in 1919 rejected by parliament.

Pahlavi Dynasty, 1925–79

Reign of Reza Shah (1925–41): Reza Khan, starting as Cossack officer, minister of war, and prime minister, ascends the throne; ends sporadic civil war; creates strong central government; curbs opposition from clergy, tribal leaders, intellectuals, and others; parliament becomes a rubber stamp; shah builds a standing army; forms university in Tehran in 1935 and enrolls women; after visit to Turkey in 1937, shah bans veil for women; shah is forced to abdicate in 1941 by allied powers, which elevate his son Muhammad Reza to the throne.

Reign of Muhammad Reza Shah (1941–79): Political parties enjoy freedom; the Tudeh Marxist party becomes the party of choice among many intellectuals and university students (including women); parliament attempts to establish control over the oil industry, culminating in its nationalization and the emergence of Muhammad Musaddiq as nationalist leader and prime minister (1951–53); shah removes Musaddiq from post and places him under house arrest with support from the U.S. Central Intelligence Agency; women's organizations form the High Council of Women headed by the shah's twin sister, Princess Ashraf Pahlavi (1959); shah announces six-point program called the White Revolution (January 1963) and gives women the franchise; demonstrations against land reform and women's franchise result in the arrest and exile of clerical opposition leader Ayatullah Ruhullah Khomeini (1963); High Council of Women replaced by the Women's Organization of Iran (1966); Family Protection Law (1967, revised in 1975) passed by parliament, allows women greater rights to seek divorce and obtain custody of children and requires a husband to secure his wife's permission before taking a second wife; protests against the shah in Tehran and other cities (from January 1978) grow massive and widespread; the shah's departure from Iran (16 January 1979).

Islamic Republic of Iran, 1979–

Ayatullah Khomeini returns to Iran (1 February 1979) and gives his blessing to the formation of an Islamic government (26 February 1979); government suspends the Family Protection Law and prohibits women from assuming posts as judges; Khomeini recommends that working women wear modest dress (1979); coeducational activities in sports and education above primary levels are banned; women are encouraged to take early retirement in professions that put them in close contact with men; a new constitution is prepared and put to referendum creating the Islamic Republic of Iran (December 1979), which designates Khomeini as supreme spiritual leader; first president is elected in Iranian history (January 1980); Iran's first Islamic parliament includes 217 deputies, 4 of whom are women; Islamic dress, requiring covering the hair and body, becomes mandatory for women employees (June 1980); previously unveiled women begin to don the garb in public places for fear of being attacked by revolutionary guards; Iraq's attacks on Iranian air bases (September 1980) begin the Iran-Iraq war, which engulfs both countries until 1988; need for women's participation brings many into the labor force; death of Khomeini (1989); women supporting the regime form associations and look to original sources to learn about their rights in Islam; the cleric Muhammad Khatami, who advocates greater freedom for women, is elected president by 79 percent of the electorate (May 1997); first female vice-president is chosen; Khatami is reelected president on the same platform despite lack of endorsement from the supreme spiritual leader Ali Khamena'i (2001); women apply to run for the presidency in 2001 elections; of the first-year class in Iranian universities, 51 percent of students are female (2001), a percentage that rises to 62 in 2003; Shirin Ebadi, lawyer and former judge, is awarded the Nobel Peace Prize in 2003 for promoting women's and children's rights in Iran.

INTRODUCTION

Guity Nashat

THE REVOLUTION in 1978–79 was a watershed in the history of Iranian women. Hundreds of thousands of women participated daily in demonstrations against the regime of Muhammad Reza Shah and played a role in toppling one of the seemingly most stable states in the Middle East. The sight of many demonstrators wearing concealing black cloaks (chadurs) mesmerized many Western onlookers and Westernized Iranians who had assumed that veiled and secluded women would be fearful, apathetic, and ignorant of the outside world.

Women's roles in the revolution and subsequent gender-related policies of the Islamic Republic of Iran stimulated indigenous, scholarly, and journalistic interest in "the woman question." Until that time, few publications considered women within the context of larger developments in Iran in the twentieth century. By the early twenty-first century, we have become better informed about women's contributions to the revolution than about women's roles in any other period of Iranian history.

Studies after 1979 fall within a number of categories, only three of which are discussed briefly here. The first consists of writings influenced by Western secular feminism. The second comes from apologists for Islam. The third, emerging in Iran in the 1990s, demonstrates that Islamic teachings need not be opposed to women's rights and equality.

The underlying assumption in the first group is that Islamic teachings reinforced a patriarchal system subjecting women to inequities. While some authors concede that women's conditions were somewhat improved during the shah's regime, many assert that the Islamic Republic's policies reinforced former inequalities. Their underlying ideological approach draws them to discuss women in the twentieth century when feminist consciousness began to emerge among some Iranian women after they were exposed to modern ideas such as socialism, adopted European-style education, and witnessed the weakening of religious forces. Women's participation in the constitutional revolution of 1905–11, the revolutionary struggles of oppositional groups, and the roles of leftists in the early years of the Islamic Republic are some topics discussed in this literature. These studies pay insufficient attention to women before the twentieth century perhaps because their authors assume that seclusion and the veil rendered most women powerless, inert, and voiceless.[1] While these works contribute to our knowledge, they contain some drawbacks, including a reliance on Marxist theory and on methodologies developed for the study of women in the West, and their examples tend to draw on conditions prevailing there, which were often different from those in Iran and other Muslim areas.

Many of these studies reduce the problems that women have encountered for millennia to Islam. Blaming the teachings of Islam for difficulties that women have experienced historically, many writers reveal inadequate knowledge of Islamic history. They seem uninformed that Islamic law (shari'a) has not been monolithic or static; divergent views among the various schools of law are found on many issues, including those regarding women; and Islamic teachings adjusted to local conditions wherever they were adopted. Many practices that writers associate with Islam were fully developed before the rise of Islam and originated in the Irano-Mesopotamian values and socioeconomic conditions of pre-Islamic Iranian culture rather than in the Arabian phase of Islam. Undue emphasis on seclusion and the teachings of Islam as major causes of the inequities women experienced in the past and present prevents some scholars from discovering more fundamental causes of women's problems, in particular the underlying socioeconomic circumstances that deprive women of education, proper healthcare, and employment opportunities. Their focus reinforces the misconceptions of Westerners about women's roles in the Muslim world and about Islam's teachings on women.

Women in the Middle East have undergone a variety of inequities, as have women elsewhere in the world, although the degree of this inequity differs from place to place in the Middle East and between Middle Eastern countries and the industrialized West. The root causes of women's inequality need to be examined, rather than its symbols, which many wrongly associate with religion in the Muslim world. By using more accurate historical evidence and analyses, we could better understand women living in societies where traditional attitudes toward gender have not much changed and where opportunities that could speed up those changes are not fully available.

Contrary to the assertion of some modern apologists (the second group of writers discussed here), Islamic teachings do not place women on an equal or higher plane than men. In fact, the Qur'an places women a degree below men, an attitude that reflects Arabian views of women prevailing during the rise of Islam. It is not productive to try to mollify women by arguing that women have an equal or higher status in Islamic teachings. Where women's status decreases is in the interpretation of Qur'anic passages and in attributing practices and sayings to the Prophet Muhammad, which occurred at a later stage when many non-Arabians converted to Islam. An example is the practice of all-enveloping veiling, which became de rigueur in certain urban areas of the Islamic Middle East during the second Islamic century. The Qur'an recommends modesty to women and men but does not recommend the veil. That all-concealing attire was not intended by Qur'anic reference is suggested by the fact that during the pilgrimage (*hajj*) ceremony in Arabia, women do not cover their faces. Yet as non-Arabians converted to Islam, they began to impose what they deemed proper behavior, which included seclusion and the veil.

Another notion raised by some apologists is that Western women are treated as sexual commodities. What these authors fail to mention is that Western women have the freedom to choose any type of behavior they deem suitable for themselves and are not coerced to do so by law or fiat. Ironically, this view of women as mere sexual objects was how many Westerners described women in Iran and other Muslim areas in the nineteenth century.

In an effort to defend customary attitudes or the Islamic Republic's policies, some authors justify behavior that has little basis in the Qur'an (such as stoning women who are accused of adultery), yet they shy away from addressing more common issues (such as child marriage), and few emphasize that some early Muslim women worked outside the home, controlled their property, and participated in public life.

A more recent trend in the study of gender in Iran (the third group mentioned here) began after the death of the Ayatullah Khomeini in 1989 and flourished after the election of President Muhammad Khatami in 1997. These new writings attempt to show that Islamic teachings are not necessarily opposed to women's rights and equality. Their authors, both women and men, are committed Muslims who argue that inequities applied in the treatment of Muslim women are an aberration of Islam, and they seek to enlighten readers about Islam's teachings. Many of them use the Qur'an and the prophet's traditions (hadith) to argue that abuses are alien to early Islamic notions and practices. Their ultimate aim is to demonstrate that modern feminism and Islam are not contradictory.

Despite the light that recent scholarship sheds on some aspects of women's roles, the ideological prism through which authors approach gender-related issues often prevents them from focusing on crucial developments affecting women. Neither detractors nor defenders seem to examine the underlying contradictions in their arguments to account for the seemingly quietist attitude of women across the centuries. How could those who had been subordinated by men and treated as inferior by their religion suddenly find the courage to demonstrate on urban streets? If the teachings of Islam had made most women submissive, what prompted these same women to mount vigorous opposition to the shah's regime? If seclusion was so onerous, why did women not oppose it before? Why did they accept constraints imposed on them by an Islamic patriarchal system under which they had lived for so many centuries? If women became informed only after they encountered the teachings of Western feminism and its Iranian advocates, why did many of them favor a regime that aimed to undo laws that had benefited them? So far, few studies have raised these and similar questions or have answered them adequately.

The scholars who contribute to this and the companion volume, *Women in Iran from the Rise of Islam to 1800,* aim to provide historical and analytical perspectives to help us understand these and related issues. The first volume examines women's roles in different epochs of Iranian history and focuses on topics such as the origins of women's seclusion, impact of the Islamic conquest, consequences for women of different kinds of dynasties and ruling regimes, and attitudes toward women in chronicles, literature, and art. The present volume focuses on women since the beginning of the Qajar period in 1794 and examines factors affecting women to the present. Our aim is to consider women's actual lives (rather than idealized or critical versions of how they lived in the past) and the situations and problems they encountered. Because women's roles in the Qajar period and attitudes toward gender then have not been adequately studied, most of the discussion below is devoted to that period. We hope to bring clarity to complex questions in the chapters of this and the preceding volume.

The Qajar Period, 1794–1925

The study of women in the Qajar period presents challenges, but it also offers unique opportunities for better understanding the lives of women in the past. The Qajar dynasty stemmed from Turkic tribal groups that entered the Iranian plateau after the eleventh century. The Qajar tribe achieved historical visibility during the Safavid period (1501–1722) as part of the Qizilbash confederacy that brought the Safavids to power. Two of its branches, the Qavanlu and Davallu, emerged as contenders for the throne after the downfall of the Safavids and the assassination of Nadir Shah Afshar in 1747. Almost half a century later, in 1794, Agha Muhammad Khan, from the Qavanlu branch, became the territory's unchallenged ruler, having defeated his diverse Davallu, Afshar, and Zand rivals. He chose the town of Tehran, close to the ancestral home of the Qajar tribe in Gorgan, as his capital.

Many salient features of the kingdom that Agha Muhammad Khan came to rule were similar to those of previous Turkic kingdoms. The military was composed almost entirely of a Turkish-speaking tribal elite and its followers. Turkish was the unofficial spoken language of the dynasty's members until the end of the nineteenth century. The written language of both court and government was Persian, and civilian officials below the rank of governor were drawn mainly from Tajik- or Persian-speaking urban populations. The Irano-Islamic cultural tradition had survived in urban areas despite nearly seventy years of civil war in the eighteenth century. One factor contributing to the preservation of this culture was the imposition of Shi'i Islam on the Iranian highlands by Shah Isma'il, founder of the Safavid dynasty in 1501. The Iranian plateau was home to many people whose indigenous languages were Turkish, Arabic, and Kurdish, among others, and some were Sunni Muslims. Persian, the main medium of culture among even some non-Persian-speakers, together with Shi'i Islam, gave many people a sense of identity that differed from that of the majority of Sunni Ottomans. Among certain groups, such as the Shi'i ulama (religious scholars) and Shi'i immigrants who lived in the shrine cities of Iraq, identity was fluid and depended on a person's profession and membership in the Muslim community (*umma*). With the rise of nationalism by the end of the nineteenth century, educated Iranians and members of the Qajar dynasty identified themselves more distinctly as Iranian.

In one fundamental way, the country over which Agha Muhammad Khan ruled briefly and passed on to his nephew Fath Ali Shah (r. 1797–1834) differed from previous Turkic kingdoms that came to power in the Iranian highlands. Whereas, until the eighteenth century, Muslim states of the Middle East were on a par with their Western rivals, by the beginning of the nineteenth century, Europeans occupied positions of preeminence that could not be effectively challenged. From that point on, the balance of power was decidedly with the Europeans.

The shift in the balance of power was a result of a new world historical process empowering Europeans beyond anything the world had experienced before. This process ushered in the modern industrial age. According to Marshall Hodgson, whose account is cogent for developments in Iran and other Middle Eastern areas, this process—which he terms the Western Transmutation—was a new stage in world development comparable in significance to two earlier revolutions in world history (the inventions of agriculture and writing). It resulted from the convergence of intellectual, scientific, economic, and social developments in northwestern Europe between the sixteenth and eighteenth centuries and radiated from that area to other parts within the European cultural sphere. The Western Transmutation gave rise to a complex configuration that was for more than a century synonymous with the West.[2]

Although some components stimulating the Western Transmutation had originated in other parts of the *oikoumene* (the inhabited world), including the Nile-to-Oxus region, Europeans may not have been aware of when or how they arrived at that point, but once they became conscious of their political and social power and the wealth they were now able to accumulate, they viewed themselves, as individuals and as a group, as superior to other peoples around the globe. They believed in the preeminence of their ways of life, institutions, religion, and morality, and they measured the success or failure of other societies by how closely they approximated European standards.

Europeans who visited the Middle East came as representatives of their governments or religious institutions and as adventurers seeking lucrative concessions or pursuing romance. What most of these travelers had in common was their fascination with, sometimes combined with their condemnation of, Islam. Many viewed the way women appeared to be treated as proof of Islam's falsehood, backwardness, and moral decadence. Whereas women's freedom became the stated aim of colonial officials, rescuing women from chattel-like status and saving their souls was the stated object of missionaries. Travelers and commentators viewed the practice of bride-price (wealth from the groom's family to the bride's) as the sale of women; polygyny as proof that women were considered as property; divorce as abandonment of wives; and the veil and seclusion as signs of women's enslavement. Most Europeans, generally ignorant about women's actual status or ideologically disposed to condemn what they saw, blamed Islamic teachings. Missionaries and officials used their views to raise funds for their churches and for colonial and imperial European rule over Muslims.[3]

European travelers and officials expressed similar opinions about other aspects of Qajar society. Iranians who attended school in Europe read their books and brought them back as a novelty to their country. Iranian readers failed to realize that European observations lacked understanding of the inner workings of the societies they described and the ways of life they generally condemned. European criticism was primarily motivated by the degree of difference observers noted between these societies and their own. Post-enlightenment Europeans couched their comments in exalted language. They wrote with smug condescension about their civilizing mission to liberate Muslim women from the chains of religious and male oppression.

Lack of awareness of the gap separating industrial Europe and Iran's premodern, primarily agrarian, economy is one reason for the skewed treatment of the Qajar period by nineteenth-century Europeans. Their Eurocentric view influenced scholars who later wrote on the Qajar period; many judged Iran's conditions, including aspects pertaining to gender, through the prism of Western attitudes toward nonwestern regions. They blamed and condemned Qajar rulers for the gap that placed Iran at a disadvantage in its dealings with European states.

Many critics possessed little information about or interest in the positive aspects of Islamic teachings. Few mentioned that women had the right to inherit and to control their assets after marriage. The right to divorce, although limited for women, was preferable to not having such a right, a situation faced by many European women at the time. Polygyny was neither as widespread as Europeans claimed nor as harsh as prostitution, which was the fate of many socioeconomically deprived European women who did not find husbands; other women of more genteel backgrounds ended up in convents or depended on the kindness of male relatives. No Muslim had to kill a wife in order to marry another. Even children of temporary wives inherited from their fathers, whereas in Europe, out-of-wedlock children had no rights unless they were sired by a king or an aristocrat.[4]

Most Europeans who elaborated on these issues were merely passing judgment and were motivated by the desire to condemn the religion rather than to express genuine interest in the plight of Iranian and other Muslim women. Few Europeans who championed the cause of such women showed concern for or awareness of the difficulties experienced by many women in Europe. Many European women did not find life easy, for despite being able to mix with men, their main function was reproduction, and they were, in a way, secluded because of not being able to divorce or to hold jobs outside the home.

The Qajars had the misfortune of coming to power at this critical juncture in world history. At first Iranian leaders were little aware of changes that had taken place in their ties with Europe. Then two military defeats and loss of territory to Russia during the reign of Fath Ali Shah brought the lesson home. Abbas Mirza, the crown prince who died before ascending the throne, and succeeding Qajar rulers supported efforts to introduce European innovations, but these occurred too late and were too little. The Western Transmutation was a complex, interrelated process and could not be emulated easily or adopted piecemeal. Rulers and statesmen tinkered only superficially with some existing institutions. Advocates of European-type reforms were ignorant about the degree of financial resources, infrastructure, and knowledge that was required to effect any serious change in Iran, and the lives of most Iranians, including most women, did not alter significantly until after the fall of the dynasty in 1925.

If the assertion is that gender roles and women's lives did not undergo much change during the Qajar period, how are we justified in including any discussion of the subject in the present volume? The perfunctory answer would be that the chronological division presented here follows the standard practice of Qajar historiography. The inclusion can be justified on another ground, that of a changed perception of gender roles and a modification or replacement of traditional views by a new European-inspired paradigm among a small but growing elite. It took another century for the new paradigm to be put into practice, but it became a dividing line between those who considered themselves progressive and those who maintained earlier notions about women's traditional roles.

The new paradigm about gender roles emerged slowly. Following the discovery of how far their country had fallen behind Europe, Iranian leaders first focused on improving the military, while their faith in other institutions remained largely intact. Even contact with Europeans did not undermine pride in their culture. An English visitor to Iran relates the comments of an Iranian: "Whilst Europeans generally think them [Iranian women] treated in the most barbarous manner, with regard to their liberty and rank in society, the Persians themselves look upon their women as virtually invested with more power and liberty, and greater privileges, than women in Europe."[5] After the accession of Nasir al-Din Shah (r. 1848–96), knowledge about Europe increased; some elites traveled to Europe and learned European languages. They began to read what Europeans were writing about their country, culture, and religion. These closer contacts began to erode earlier feelings of confidence.

These highly placed individuals were awed by European achievements and overwhelmed by the material advance. The gap separating their country from Europe seemed so large that they believed the only solution was to emulate European ways. They also became more aware of the steps Ottomans and Egyptians were taking to catch up with Europeans, and they envied their seeming success in adopting European practices. They differed in opinion about how far they should imitate Europe, but few had doubts that the introduction of some aspects of European society and culture was necessary. By the end of the nineteenth century, an influential and growing segment of educated Iranians was convinced that European criticism of its society and especially its religion was accurate.

During the last decade of the nineteenth century, negative ideas about traditional society and culture began to circulate privately but more extensively. Exposure to European ideas occurred in various ways, by studying abroad, through contacts with Europeans in Iran, by reading European publications, and through greater awareness of developments in the Ottoman empire, which had begun its contact with modern Europe almost a century earlier than Iran. Iranians migrating to the Caucasus in search of work were exposed to Russian socialists exiled there, another channel of disillusionment with traditional values. Impatience with existing conditions characterized the attitude of the followers of Subh-i Azal, who were known as Azali Babis and who believed in political activism unlike most followers of Baha'ullah, who were known as Baha'is. Baha'ullah shunned politics and proclaimed himself the founder of a new religion, the Baha'i faith.

What these disparate groups held in common was a belief in the justness of European notions that Islam was "synonymous with superstition, irrationality, passivity, backwardness, theological hair-splitting, and obscurantist double-talk."[6] European assertions about women's treatment in Islam as proof of the religion's backwardness, the association of Islam with women's seclusion, and the damage that such restrictions caused women remained an enduring legacy of European contacts with Iranians in the nineteenth and twentieth centuries.

This argument was reiterated by most secular advocates of modern reform in Iran since the end of the nineteenth century. An early exponent was Mirza Agha Khan Kirmani, a leading intellectual of the constitutional period (1905–11). During his exile in the Ottoman empire, he wrote about his country's arrested development, and he included seclusion, the veil, and polygyny among its primary causes. Although he had not set foot in Europe, he imagined European women enjoying rights and freedoms that Iranian women lacked.

Another early critic of seclusion and the veil was Taj al-Saltaneh, one of

Nasir al-Din Shah's younger daughters. She studied French and music and was tutored by some of the best teachers of her day. She married the man of her choice, who may not have been her intellectual peer but who was willing to indulge her, and she controlled her own income. (In England, women acquired this right only with the passage of the Married Women's Property Act in 1870.) She divorced her husband when she became bored with him. Like other educated Iranians at the time, she accepted that the standards of civilized life were those defined by Europeans: "Alas! Persian women have been set aside from mankind and placed together with cattle and beasts. They live their entire lives in hopeless prisons, crushed under the weight of bitter ordeals."[7] Although she wrote her opinion in a private autobiography, its publication has turned her into an icon among some present-day Iranian feminists, a somewhat puzzling development since the account of her early life reveals a love of luxury, contempt for many of those serving her, praise for her own beauty and intelligence, and a narcissistic neglect of her children despite condemning her own mother for the same behavior.

The division between those who rejected the past and its ways and those who became even more adamant about protecting them in the name of religion grew as time went on. Because of their simplistic notion, which was later repeated by some intellectuals who shifted their trust from Western Europeans to socialist-type ideology, would-be Westernizers viewed those who were reluctant to accept their visions and solutions as reactionaries or as traitors motivated by self-interest. Many of those who opposed change were trying to protect their interests, but it would be naïve to dismiss their deeper reasons for fear of that change. Existing institutions, even when no longer adequate to meet the country's needs, had emerged over a long period and stemmed from the knowledge that these ways were tested; they were based on past experience and therefore less likely to fail. Throughout the Qajar period, Iran was primarily an agrarian country where most people drew income from agriculture. Like any other society in which prosperity depends on the vagaries of nature and the size of its population, its members viewed change and innovation as threatening and even dangerous and considered existing ways preferable to taking risks and experimenting with new and alien institutions.

What secularists failed to recognize was that gender roles were part of an ancient system that had emerged in response to socioeconomic conditions over the millennia. Institutions in any given society develop because they provide useful information and service to many of its members. Applied to the Iranian case, the longevity of existing institutions had bestowed on them weight and respect in the popular perception. Many people upheld them even though some past functions had become obsolete. Conditions in Qajar Iran were much closer to what had preceded this period than what emerged under the Pahlavi dynasty (1925–79) or what existed in Europe during the nineteenth century. To understand the period and its practices and value systems, we should compare the Qajar era and its institutions with preindustrial Europe. This continuity with the past can be most clearly observed in women's roles.

Such continuity has been ignored by many historians, who generally compare Iranian practices and institutions in this period with contemporary European states and find them deficient. This failure also helps to explain the condescending attitude of many Europeans who visited the country and condemned conditions that no longer obtained in Europe but that had been common a century or two earlier. Some changes did occur in this period, but it was mainly in the perception of those familiar with European critiques of their country, which blamed many ills on Islam, and in the gradual internalization of that view. Toward the end of the century, as allegiance to Islam shifted, such a perception was replaced by a sense of nationalism, which had also engulfed the Ottoman empire and Egypt.

Our understanding would be better served if we recognized continuities between the Qajar period and what came before rather than with what followed later in the twentieth century. Since changes affecting most women were minimal, greater continuity with the past enables us to discover practices affecting their lives in earlier periods. Such a perspective informs us about the lives of women, which have often been absent in official sources. Putting aside modern standards and instead using women's terms of reference and the values they upheld would provide greater understanding of their roles in and diverse contributions to society. If the grim picture of Iranian women presented in European accounts and accepted uncritically since the late nineteenth century by secular Iranians is not accurate, then what was life like for women?

Life under the Qajars

The proximity of the Qajar period to our own is one reason why material about women is more abundant than for earlier periods. Another reason is the availability of European accounts and references to women in Iranian sources as a result of European influence. Direct European sources consist

of published works and unpublished correspondence of Europeans who visited or lived in Iran in greater numbers in the nineteenth century than in the
eighteenth. Although most European visitors were men, who had little contact with women in urban areas, they left descriptions of rural women who
did not undergo seclusion as much as urban ones. Occasionally the visitor
was a woman, sometimes traveling alone. Newly created European legations
sent reports to their capitals that sometimes contained information about
women. Wives of members of the diplomatic corps had access to ruling-class
and elite households and constitute sources of information. European doctors who served Qajar rulers and the aristocracy and ran clinics inform us
about female patients. We have accounts and letters of missionaries, some
of whom were women. Despite the stereotypes that mar these works, we can
cull information about women from them if we take their biases into account.
Beginning in the last quarter of the nineteenth century, greater contact with
Europe stimulated new literary forms in Iran, including newspapers, memoirs, and journals. These sources, sometimes written by women, reveal new
perceptions about females and offer insight into their lives.

Existing sources relate mainly to a small sector of the ruling class and the
elite. The information they convey, however, sheds light on a wider sector of
urban women because some of their practices may have been similar. Visiting Bukhara in 1864, Armin Vambery was surprised to discover that the amir's
wives sewed their own clothes and served the same foods as other urban
women. Bukhara was not an Iranian city, and Iran was richer than the emir-
ate, but conditions in the two urban areas may have been alike.[8] The same
was not true of rural women, who were less secluded and played a greater
role outside the home in their community's economy. They did often lack
some amenities and the leisure available to even poor urban women, such
as visiting saints' shrines and going to baths.[9]

When the Qajars came to power in 1794, the behavior of the dynasty's
women was similar to that found among the elite of the Turkic tribal groups
that had previously ruled in the Iranian highlands. Agha Muhammad Khan,
dynasty founder, received help from two women in his family: his mother
and his aunt, who was married to Karim Khan Zand. This aunt informed him
of that ruler's death, thus giving him a chance to escape captivity before a
rival Zand prince could put him to death.[10] The authority that women wielded is also suggested by the purported advice of Agha Muhammad Khan to
his nephew and heir, Baba Khan (later Fath Ali Shah), to heal the century-
long hostility between the two branches of the Qajar tribe by having them
exchange daughters in marriage. Heeding his uncle's advice, Fath Ali Shah

encouraged intermarriage among the children of leading Qajar families. The high esteem with which some women were held is revealed in his reliance on and relationships with his daughters, such as Ziya al-Saltaneh, whom he entrusted to write his correspondence, especially confidential ones. He gave his unmarried daughters responsibilities and enjoyed watching wrestling matches between his brother's granddaughter, who had unusual physical strength, and male members of the royal family.[11]

The urban population, from which many statesmen and government officials were drawn, upheld the Irano-Islamic assumptions about women and viewed with suspicion and condemned their interest and participation in politics, which they saw as a violation of the rules of propriety. The life of Malik Jahan Khanum (1805–72), Nasir al-Din Shah's mother, exemplifies the conflict that could arise between the prevailing Irano-Islamic paradigms about women and the roles to which she and some other women considered they were entitled. She was married to her cousin Muhammad Mirza, the future king (r. 1834–48), to lessen the rivalry between the two Qajar branches. Her husband's aversion to her may be why he took a dislike to their son and heir to the throne, Nasir al-Din Mirza. Had her husband lived, he might have changed the order of succession from Nasir al-Din to a younger son, Abbas Mirza, whose mother he loved. When Muhammad Shah died, Malik Jahan was in Tehran and not with her son in Tabriz, likely in order to make her presence felt and to ensure that her son would not be bypassed during her husband's final year when his ability to govern was weakened by illness.

During the critical weeks following her husband's death, Malik Jahan, who now bore the title of the king's mother, Mahd-i Ulya (exalted cradle), presided over the state council and maintained calm in the capital and nearby provinces, which allowed her son time to reach Tehran from Tabriz where he had resided as crown prince. When the sixteen-year-old king arrived, he entrusted the running of affairs of state to Amir Nizam (later Amir Kabir) and appointed him prime minister. At Amir Nizam's suggestion, the king rarely saw his mother, and she was forbidden to have contact with the outside world. Many decades later the king related that his mentor, whom he viewed as a father figure, had advised him to shoot his meddlesome mother and claim it was an accident.[12]

The letters Malik Jahan wrote to her son during her years of banishment reveal frustration at the treatment she was receiving and anguish at being cut off from him. They also show her erudition and intelligence. She refers to her prerogative as the king's mother and the violation of that status by Amir Nizam. She joined in the efforts of unhappy courtiers who resented his control of the king and who brought about his dismissal and eventual assassination. Historians often state that had Amir Kabir survived in his post, Iran could have instituted needed reforms, and they blame Mahd-i Ulya as the main instrument of his downfall. They cite her vengefulness and desire to have her supposed lover, Mirza Aqa Khan Nuri, installed as prime minister as motivating factors for her hostility to Amir Kabir. Rarely do they credit her contributions to her son's accession, show sympathy for the indignities she suffered during Amir Kabir's ascendance, or acknowledge justice in her grievances against the statesman who treated her harshly. As a Tajik who held Irano-Islamic ideas about gender roles, Amir Kabir probably resented her aspiration to be taken seriously because she was a woman, and he may have considered her efforts to preserve her son's throne an intrusion into the male world. His neglect may indeed have brought about his downfall.[13]

Women's interest and participation in politics were not limited to members of the Qajar tribe. An example is Nasir al-Din Shah's wife, Fatimeh, better known as Anis al-Douleh. She was a peasant girl who joined the harem as a servant of Jayran, the shah's favorite wife. The shah was so touched by her loyalty to her mistress that he married her after Jayran died. Despite many other permanent and temporary wives, she became his favorite and was considered the queen by foreign diplomats. She was also the only woman who could reprimand the shah and assuage his anger. She was well informed of the realities and abuses of power in the country and tried to help the unfortunate. Her influence with the king was so great that many statesmen and his close relatives appealed to her for an audience with him.[14] In 1873 Anis al-Douleh sided with a group opposing Mirza Husayn Khan Mushir al-Douleh and demanded his resignation as prime minister for the role he had played in granting the Reuter concession. Historians often attribute her opposition to her anger at Mushir al-Douleh, who had advised the shah to send her back from Moscow instead of having her accompany him on the rest of his trip to Europe. It is more likely that she was shocked by the extensive terms of the concession granted to Baron Julius von Reuter.[15]

Another fallacy is the view that because of seclusion women had no chance to pursue an education and thus were ignorant. Even the biased observer Lady Sheil, wife of the British minister who served in Iran in the early 1850s, observed, "The interest of women only in idleness and conspicuous consumption was not due to lack of training and education. Women of the higher classes frequently acquire a knowledge of reading and writing, and of the choice poetical works in their native language, as well as the art of reading, though perhaps not understanding, the Koran. In the royal family, in particular, and among the ladies of the tribe of Kajjar, these accomplishments are so common that they themselves conduct their correspondence without the customary aid of a meerza, or secretary."[16] Education of girls was relatively common among families of the ruling class, aristocracy, high officials, ulama, merchants, and even the middle class. Initially young girls were educated along with young boys. Religious education came first, followed by Persian classical literature, and some girls wrote poetry. In the royal family, all young princesses were educated, and some were known for high achievements. Fakhr al-Douleh, daughter of Fath Ali Shah, wrote poems and transcribed popular romances.[17] Taj al-Saltaneh was highly educated as were some of her sisters. Daughters of ulama families were able to study along with male members of their households when they were young; later, they joined classes of the great religious scholars of the day by attending their lectures behind a screen.

One of the most famous educated women was Fatimeh, Zarrin Taj Baraghani, known as Qurrat al-Ayn (1814–52). She was born in Qazvin to a family of ulama. Like other girls of her class, she and her sister studied with their father before taking courses in theology from other relatives. She attained sufficient expertise in religious matters to be able to participate in theological discussions with high-ranking religious authorities, and she also taught and wrote a treatise on a religious subject. After marrying, she spent time in Karbala, a center of Shi'i learning. Eventually she became involved in the Babi movement. (In 1844 Sayyid Ali Muhammad proclaimed himself the Bab—the gate—to the long-awaited twelfth Shi'i imam and called for radical religious and social change.) The Bab's advocacy of better treatment for women may have been a reason for Qurrat al-Ayn's attraction to the new creed; once she became his follower, she began to proselytize, and in her teaching she uncovered her face before the mixed audiences who gathered to hear her. She may have played a leading role in the development of Babism.[18] She was executed along with fellow Babis in 1852 after a plot to assassinate Nasir al-Din Shah was uncovered.

Today many Iranian feminists view Qurrat al-Ayn as the first Iranian feminist. To be sure, she disregarded the conventions of her time, particularly in her refusal to cover her face in front of her audiences. But she defied prevailing conventions, including the veil, as a mark of rejecting Islam and announcing her conversion to the new religion, rather than for the sole purpose of achieving freedom and equality for women. Her steadfast refusal to recant Babism was similar to the faith of Hallaj, the first Sufi known to be killed for heresy, and other religious zealots. She was the first female Babi to be martyred for her conviction but not the only Babi woman to fight for her cause; other women were just as fearless in their refusal to abandon their faith, and many even fought alongside men until they were killed.

Urban women of the middle and upper economic levels, no matter what their status or level of education, were supposed to have as little contact with male strangers as possible. They lived in a part of the house called the *andarun* (inner courtyard). These andaruns were a far cry from the harems titillating the imagination of European artists and depicted in their Orientalist paintings. Most houses were built with an inner and an outer courtyard (*biruni*); the two parts were connected by a corridor so that no unrelated male visitor to the outer courtyard would see any women by accident. The household's men took their midday meals either in the outer courtyard or in their shops and workplaces. Men and women ate separately because unrelated women lived in most households.[19]

Despite being secluded, these urban women were by no means powerless. Running the household was left to them. They were responsible for all activities including managing the finances. Even among the wealthy, women had daily tasks. Most households consisted of extended families and included three or more generations. The wife or mother of the head of the house held ultimate responsibility for making major decisions and ensuring that all ran smoothly. The most time-consuming daily activity was preparing meals. Cooking was arduous even with servants or slaves. The female head decided what food would be served and prepared provisions for immediate and future use. Wealthy women sent servants to purchase goods, and poor women bought commodities from street vendors traveling through the quarters from door to door.

The mother was responsible for caring for children and, if the family was wealthy, hiring nannies and servants. Most boys lived in the andarun until at least the age of five, and the mother taught them the rudiments of religion. In poorer families, boys would join their fathers' work. Girls in all families were taught skills that could be used later in their own homes, such as sewing, embroidery, cooking, caring for siblings, and making small rugs. Before opportunities for employment outside the home were available to women, families viewed marriage as the best option for girls. Attitudes toward the institution were not much different from what they had been for millennia. To remain unmarried was seen as a violation of a woman's purpose in life, a message drummed into girls by their mothers from the time they were young. Early marriage may have been one reason why most girls from well-to-do families did not take education seriously.

The stereotype of the helpless oppressed woman is contradicted by European women who visited Iranian households. Lady Sheil, condescending on other issues, states, "When a woman happens to possess talent, or has a stronger understanding than her husband, she maintains her supremacy to the last, not only over her associate wives, but over her husband, his purse, and property."[20] Because women of property controlled and managed their assets, many of them were interested in developments outside the home. This experience provided such urban women, especially in Tehran, with assertiveness.

Knowledge of the outside world and confidence are reflected in the writings of women such as Bibi Khanum, who with her biting wit took men to task for their failings.[21] Western visitors made the same observation. Lady Sheil notes, "One of our neighbors was a merchant who possessed a temper that led him into frequent and noisy quarrels with his wives. The ladies seemed perfectly able to maintain their ground, as far as words went, and generally so overwhelmed him with abuse, that flight or beating used to be his common resource." Although she was wrong in her belief that most urban families were polygynous, she observes, "All classes enjoy abundance of liberty, more so, I think, than among us."[22] She adds that the veil afforded women greater freedom to remain anonymous. Carla Serena, otherwise often critical of Iranian women, claims that Iranian men lived under their wives' heels.[23]

Examples of secluded and veiled women publicly expressing anger and opposition began to be mentioned in the late nineteenth century, as historians' perceptions of women began to change. Some women protested against the injustices of governors. Others participated in the ban against the tobacco concession; smoking was forbidden in Nasir al-Din Shah's household.

What was life like for nonurban women who made up three-fourths of the female population during the Qajar period? Taj al-Saltaneh envied rural women who worked unveiled alongside men in the fields despite their difficult tasks.[24] Seclusion and the veil were not enforced to the same degree in rural areas as in urban ones, largely because of the variety of work women performed outside the home. They cooked meals, baked bread, and cared for children but also made dairy products, planted rice and vegetables, weeded crops, picked fruit, ground grain, and wove kilims, carpets, and cloth for clothes. Village houses, except for those of landowners and the wealthy, did not have inner and outer courtyards. Usually the entire family ate and slept together. In some villages, the owner and his family lived there, but their activities did not differ greatly from other villagers. Wealthier women sewed clothes of finer fabric than used by village women, their food was richer and more abundant, and they avoided contact with male strangers. Nonwealthy village women were less restricted than wealthy ones. When outdoors, they did not wear veils but sometimes covered their faces when they were not working.[25]

Maintaining a strict separation along gender lines in urban areas began to erode by the end of the nineteenth century. Roles that a few women played during the constitutional period (1905–11) demonstrate the change. Malikeh-yi Iran, one of Nasir al-Din Shah's daughters, offers an example. She was married to Zahir al-Douleh, founder of the Safi Ali Shahi order of mystics. She was a member of the order, as were her two daughters, and was known for her Sufi poetry. She joined an underground women's society (*anjuman*) created to promote a constitutional form of government and may have encouraged her young son to join the fight against the anti-constitutional king, Muhammad Ali Shah. She showed courage when the king's soldiers attacked her house to arrest her son. Not finding him, they directed their anger at her and looted her house. She escaped through the roof but not before other household members were gone and later refused assistance from the autocratic king, who wanted to compensate her for the loss of her property.[26]

Malikeh-yi Iran was one of a minority of activist women, mainly from upper- and middle-class families, including daughters and wives of prominent ulama, who during these critical years sided with the constitutionalists.[27] They made up for their small numbers by their vigor. Some used their veils as protection and acted as couriers for the transfer of messages and arms between revolutionary hideouts. They formed secret societies for enlightening other women and for generating support for the constitution and later became pioneers as founders of modern schools. Like their contemporaries in the Middle East, they had led secluded lives, and few had obtained a modern education, but that lifestyle had not made them submissive or fearful.[28] They had received a religious education, were well informed about the outside world, and ran their households efficiently. Aware of the need to assume a greater public role, they became useful agents for ending despotic government in their country. A small group among these women continued to view seclusion and the veil as the central issue even after the constitutional crisis was resolved.

The efforts of women activists during the constitutional period and the sacrifices they made did not win them the franchise or the gratitude of their male or even female contemporaries. The climate of opinion within the country toward women's activities outside the home was hostile. When a sympathetic deputy suggested giving women the vote, an uproar broke out in parliament.[29] Antagonism toward women activists was even stronger among the general public, who considered them "immoral," "wanton," "Babi," or even "apostates."

In the long run, these activists' efforts were not wasted. They learned that they could exert influence on the public sphere by combining their resources. They became aware of the need to disseminate ideas among more women. Thus, they focused on encouraging families to send their daughters to modern schools, they ran some of these schools, and they began to publicize their views by writing to reformist journals and publishing journals that catered to women. Support for modern education for girls came also from a small but influential number of secularly oriented male writers and intellectuals. Prominent poets, journalists, and authors decried attitudes that considered women inferior and their education a waste. They argued that ignorant mothers would raise ignorant sons, and the only way to improve the country and arrest its decline was to educate its women, that is, its future mothers.[30] Gradually, growing numbers of well-to-do urban families became convinced of the benefits of modern education, and more girls began to enroll in these newly opened schools.

The climate of opinion among the majority was hostile to any steps that would end seclusion and the veil, and many families viewed education in modern schools as dangerous and contrary to Islamic teachings. Serious opposition to these efforts sometimes came from the families of women activists. To overcome this hurdle, some of these women were forced to carry out their activities in secret. Despite problems they encountered, they looked back with fondness on their efforts because many students they trained in modern schools became pioneers of modern education for the next generation.[31]

Until the constitutional period, the only modern schools for girls were those opened by American missionaries in Reza'iyeh in 1835 and in Tehran in 1875. The government had stipulated that no Muslims could attend these schools, which admitted students only from Christian backgrounds. By the 1890s, a few Muslim girls had quietly enrolled in missionary schools. The first school devoted to the education of Muslim girls was opened in 1906 and was followed by the opening of several other schools in 1907. Most founders were women who had participated in the constitutional movement. To protect against charges of apostasy, the curricula of all schools included many courses on religion, which did not soften the anger of religious authorities who denounced the schools as dens of apostasy and immorality.[32] Some dedicated women founded girls' schools in the provinces but met with difficulties. Badruduja Dirakhshan, who opened the first school for girls in Isfahan in 1917, was arrested, beaten, and imprisoned. She was released only after her family promised to prevent her from reopening the school. Another school principal, Sadiqeh Doulatabadi, was forced to leave Isfahan. One of the first Iranian women to study in Europe, she went to Paris in the 1920s and studied educational psychology. After her return to Iran in 1927, she avoided wearing a veil whenever she could, such as when she visited northern Tehran.[33]

Until the outbreak of World War I, these and a few other schools in Tehran, Isfahan, and Shiraz were the only ones available for girls. Resources needed for opening more schools were limited. Levels of education among women remained low until the end of the Qajar period. The number of literate women in the country was about 2 percent in the 1920s. The number of literate men then was only 5 percent.[34] After the war, the idea of modern education for girls became more accepted. The first public school for girls opened in 1918, and gradually many private schools were incorporated into the ministry of education.

Publishing periodicals was another activity pursued by activists to widen horizons for and enlighten women. Educated women used these publications to express ideas about current events and to denounce restrictions and inequities. The first newspaper by a woman was published in 1910 but was short-lived. Several other periodicals appeared in Tehran and a few other cities after the war. Even though their circulation was small, their following was devoted, and they tried to convey the need for women to assume more public roles in society.[35]

The lives of women in towns and rural areas, as compared to those of a small minority in large cities, were hardly touched by these changes in perceptions about their roles. Iran during the first quarter of the twentieth century remained a primarily agrarian country; more than half of its population lived in rural areas.

The period of 1914–18 was disastrous for Iran. Despite its neutrality, the country was invaded by Russian, British, Ottoman, and German armies, and its political and economic affairs were severely disrupted. At war's end, the country was plunged into anarchy and chaos. Separatist movements in Azerbaijan, Gilan, Khurasan, Kurdistan, and Khuzistan threatened its survival. Most leaders and members of parliament welcomed the coup d'état in 1921 that brought Reza Khan to power.

Women during the Pahlavi Era, 1925–79

In 1925 parliament proclaimed Reza Khan king; thus began the reign of the Pahlavi dynasty. After consolidating his political power, Reza Shah initiated reforms aimed at creating a strong central government free of clerical, tribal, and foreign control. An admirer of Ataturk's reforms in neighboring Turkey, Reza Shah hoped to create Western-style institutions and practices, including active participation of women in public life. His views were organized around the ideology of forming a modern nationalist state. He used issues concerning women to bolster the state's image as modern and to undermine and discredit the ulama who believed women should be confined to domestic activities. The shah determined that women's isolation must end. He encouraged their education and workforce participation and the formation of women's societies. As he centralized power, the pace of change for women increased.

Some policies enacted by Reza Shah helped to attain the goals that women's rights activists had set for themselves. The spread of public education for girls is a case in point. Although the constitution had enshrined the principle of public education for girls in 1907, the first public school for girls did not open until 1918. It was only after Reza Shah consolidated power that the law began to be seriously implemented. Increasing numbers of secondary schools paved the way for women to enter the newly formed Tehran University in 1935. Fatemeh Sayyah became the first woman to join the faculty of Tehran University. The regime also encouraged women to take jobs in government service.

Reforms of the judicial system and civil code benefited women. The age of marriage for girls was raised to fifteen and for boys to eighteen, and registration of all marriages was required. These steps reduced the incidence of child marriage and made more difficult the practice of *mut'a* (temporary marriage, popularly referred to as *sigheh*), which allowed men to marry women for brief (or longer) periods. Some poor families offered their young daughters to older men in return for money. Many Europeans equated this type of marriage with prostitution, and most educated Iranians condemned the practice. Although the civil code did not ban mut'a relationships, requiring registration and recognizing only permanent marriages as legitimate made the practice more difficult for men. Mut'a began to be regarded as shameful even by lower-class families. The practice continued informally in provincial towns and especially in the shrine cities of Mashhad and Qum.[36]

One issue troubling Reza Shah was the veil, which for him symbolized backwardness. Despite assuming full dictatorial powers by the early 1930s, he did not assault the veil openly but proceeded with caution. At first he encouraged women to appear in public without the covering. He decreed that a few women, mainly high school teachers, form a women's center (*kanun-i banuvan*), which held lectures and exhibitions and sponsored sporting events for women for a mixed audience. A leading woman activist, Hajar Tarbiat, was chosen as the center's president. The government-controlled press published articles about the veil's disadvantages and praised its disappearance in other Muslim countries. Speakers at the center recommended that women not wear veils and encouraged them to be uncovered while attending meetings. Police protection was given to unveiled women who were harassed verbally and physically outside the center's building, not only by men but also by veiled women.[37] As rumors about the impending government decision to ban the veil circulated, signs of unrest surfaced. When people demonstrated in favor of the veil in Tabriz, they were quickly punished. The harsh reprisal seemed to put an end to further public opposition. In January 1936 Reza Shah banned the veil, one of his regime's most draconian measures.

The ban was hailed enthusiastically by many educated women as liberation from oppression and enslavement. Since the beginning of the twentieth century, leading poets and intellectuals such as Iraj Mirza, Arif Qazvini, and Mirzadeh Ishqi had denounced the veil in their poetry and writing. Some upper-middle-class women had begun to appear unveiled in private, mixed gatherings. Women activists and their male supporters had viewed the veil as the principal cause of women's low status and the symbol of their subjugation. Parvin I'tisami, the leading female poet, likened the lives of women under the veil to being held in a cage, and she called the veil the primary cause of women's ignorance. She proclaimed that the abolition of the veil "gave the women of Iran a chance to live."[38]

The number of women who praised the ban on veiling was small and consisted of upper-class and some middle-class women, mainly in Tehran and a few other cities. The majority of Iranian women were onlookers in the struggle that women activists had launched in their name. The enforced ban touched a sensitive nerve for most women who viewed the veil as a sign of propriety and a means of protecting themselves against the menacing eyes of male strangers. They considered it mandated by Islam, and its removal meant that they would be committing a sin. Many of these women chose to stay home rather than risk having their veils pulled off by police, who had orders to treat harshly any woman who dared to wear anything other than a European-style hat. Even wearing a scarf was forbidden.

While Reza Shah's policies accomplished some objectives, they also suffered serious drawbacks. The ban made it possible for a small group of women to avoid the veil, but those who were reluctant to comply with the law were punished. It created resentment among many women and their families and made them suspicious of reform and modern ideas. The repression that accompanied the enactment of Reza Shah's policies hurt the cause of improving women's position because it stifled the development of a political culture and experience among women. The fate of the Patriotic Women's League illustrates the point. It was formed in 1922 by women with socialist tendencies who had been active in the constitutional revolution. At the beginning of his rise to power Reza Shah had used various political groups to consolidate his hold over the political system, but once he established firm control, he began to disband or undercut any groups demonstrating a semblance of independence. Although the league's aim was to "emphasize respect for the laws and rituals of Islam, to encourage national industries, to spread literacy among adult women, to provide care for orphaned girls," it was forced to close in 1932.[39] Its successor, the Women's Center, came into existence by fiat in 1935, and even then it could tread only the thin line defined for it by the regime. No personal or group initiative could develop effectively under such circumstances.

Although Reza Shah's policies were welcomed by a small number of upper-class and educated women, they failed to win the support of the majority of women because such reforms were not in step with the needs and realities of Iranian society at that time. The absence of social and economic conditions that could support these changes ensured that once force was removed such policies would be abandoned. After Reza Shah's abdication in 1941, a backlash led by religious authorities, who had lost power and prestige during his reign, almost destroyed the meager gains made by women during the previous few decades.

The ulama were determined to reassert control over society by "what may be termed a Shi'i public morality or culture."[40] A quick method seemed to be reversing the ban on the veil. A repeal was not even necessary, for many women in urban centers including Tehran resumed the practice. A new style of veil, the present-day chadur, emerged; it was lighter and less cumbersome than the all-enveloping cloak and face mask of previous years. Although religious and some urban, middle- and upper-class women covered much of their face with the chadur, others did not. A more serious threat to women was the ulama's open opposition to modern schools for girls. The ulama renewed the call to close them down, and some in provincial towns and the capital were shut on minor pretexts. Emboldened by these successes, religious authorities launched a wider campaign to close the remaining schools.[41]

The ulama's efforts met with some initial success, but they were unable to reverse the clock completely for women. Several factors protected the meager gains that women had made earlier. The political freedom and ac-

tivity following the end of the severe censorship imposed by Reza Shah allowed voices of opposition to challenge the ulama's views on women. The
country's continuing increase in wealth began to affect socioeconomic conditions and provided women with better prospects in health, education,
employment, and political and civil rights.

After Reza Shah's abdication and the ascendancy of his son Muhammad
Reza Shah, one of the most active groups advocating women's rights was the
communist Tudeh party, which attracted students, teachers, and secular educated women and men. Some older women activists joined the party and
formed the Society for Democratic Women in 1949, which drew recruits and
sympathizers. The group published a periodical, *Bidari-yi ma* (Our awakening). It supported educational clubs, girls' public education, equal pay for
equal work, and women's voting rights. In 1952, on the forty-fifth anniver-
sary of the constitutional revolution, the society requested that parliament
give suffrage to women. Although Muhammad Musaddiq as prime minister
presented the request and the issue was debated, it did not pass because of
pressure from religious authorities.[42]

After the CIA-supported coup d'état in 1953 and the overthrow of Musaddiq, many of the previous decade's political freedoms were curtailed. Muhammad Reza Shah began to rule with increased authoritarianism. The Tudeh party was already banned following an attempt on the shah's life, and
the regime made it harder for opposition groups and parties to be active
openly, thus forcing some to form underground cells or move their activities to Western capitals where many students were located. In the late 1960s
and the 1970s, the appeal of radical leftist ideologies and newly formed Islamic groups threatened the regime. Despite their recent origin, Islamic parties began to attract a growing number of modern educated professionals,
intellectuals, and university and high school students. Unlike members of
radical left-wing parties who came from wealthy and even aristocratic backgrounds, Islamic groups were drawn mainly from the middle and lower-
middle classes.

To offset this threat, the shah's regime tried to co-opt less-politicized
women by supporting their aspirations for political, legal, and economic
rights. A difficulty in instituting laws that would satisfy women was the ulama's opposition. The regime did not confront the ulama directly but treated harshly only those who openly challenged its growing reliance on the
United States and its reform agenda. Ayatullah Khomeini, the most vocal
critic of the shah's policies (including female suffrage), was exiled. The se-
verity of the regime's response silenced temporarily the most radical ulama.

Small groups of reform-minded women were thus able to step up their efforts to modify some provisions of the shari'a that covered polygyny, divorce, and child custody and were disadvantageous for women. Women's organizations were tacitly aware that they had to operate within the limits set by the regime, under the supervision of Ashraf Pahlavi, the shah's twin sister, who headed many of these organizations. Despite such impediments, these women deserve credit for important measures, including female suffrage enacted as one of six initial points of the White Revolution in 1963. The regime's desire to curry favor with women and appear progressive to its Western allies and critics led in 1967 to the passage of the Family Protection Law, which enacted limited changes in marriage, divorce, and custody laws and restricted a husband's ability to prevent his wife from working outside the home.

Opposition groups on the left underestimated the significance of these laws in improving women's status. They dismissed the franchise's extension as merely giving men additional votes (on the notion that men would tell their womenfolk to vote for certain individuals or issues and that women would not make independent judgments), and they viewed the Family Protection Law as deceptive because it did not ban polygyny or give equal rights to women in divorce. Most Iranian women followed religious precepts and customs and were not affected by these laws, and only a small percentage participated in Pahlavi-era elections. Nevertheless, female suffrage was a fundamental departure from long-held perceptions about women, for it recognized them as full citizens and equal to men. Changes in family law were not as substantial as the regime's advocates claimed and were used by only a small percentage of educated women in the capital and other urban areas. Polygyny was retained; it merely required the first wife's permission. Although divorce rates had never been high in Iran, men used their total right to divorce and to gain custody of children as a perpetual threat over their wives. The new law placed decisions about custody and alimony under the control of family courts. Because these legal changes coincided with improved socioeconomic conditions during the late 1960s and especially the 1970s, they offered a real opportunity to improve women's lives. Although they did not initially gain wide acceptance, their significance to women is evident. (The Islamic Republic, branding these reforms as against divinely inspired law [shari'a], reinstated earlier conditions almost completely.)

Two related developments reinforced legal changes in women's status. Increased revenues from oil following the rise in world prices and the nationalization of that industry transformed the Iranian economy and society.

Radical political groups on both ends of the political spectrum proclaimed that the main purpose of the legal reforms was to convince Western powers that Iran was becoming a modern European-type state. They considered these changes as merely cosmetic and noted that much of the revenue was squandered on purchasing Western military technology, building palaces, and rewarding sycophants. Some oil revenue was put to good use, such as expanding educational and employment opportunities.[43]

The increase in the country's revenue and availability of jobs had a positive impact on women's education. Although the amount spent on education was only 4 percent of the gross national product in the 1970s, the quality and quantity improved. The level of literacy among women in urban areas reached 46 percent and rose in rural areas to 18 percent. Toward the end of the 1970s, many young women in upper- and middle-class families began to enter the labor force. Such participation of women did not exceed 10 percent, but increased opportunities created a more favorable climate for women working outside the home. A brighter future for women was looming.

In 1975 the shah's regime seemed to be one of the most stable in the region, backed by a strong army that could ensure stability inside the country and guard against outside aggression. Four years later the regime collapsed. Many women of varying social and educational backgrounds, including those who had benefited from recent changes, demonstrated in favor of the shah's overthrow. His seemingly progressive regime (at least in terms of women) was replaced by a religious regime that made restoring traditional gender boundaries a primary aim. Many Iranians and others had not anticipated that such developments could even be possible.

The Revolution of 1978–79

Women's participation in protests in 1978–79, combined with orders to the military not to fire on demonstrators, contributed to the success of the revolution and made it relatively bloodless. How else are we to explain the failure of many leftist and nationalist groups to bring about the revolution, for which they had worked tirelessly and sacrificed for decades? Similarly, would the revolution have occurred without the active participation of religious leaders? Actions of secular radical groups until this time had mainly served to increase the regime's resolve to be ruthless in crushing their efforts. The role that radical activists and feminists played was not surprising because many had worked against the shah's government within the country or abroad. During demonstrations, many even donned the chadur as a symbol of protest against the shah.[44]

Factors leading to the participation of urban women who wore the chadur or scarf as their customary attire outside the home have not yet received sufficient attention by scholars. Such women shared some of the objections against the regime as many other Iranians, but the call of religious leaders, particularly Ayatullah Khomeini, who equated efforts to end the shah's corrupt regime with religious duty, was also significant. Many of these women feared that the policies and pronouncements of the regime increasingly undermined the lifestyles and values that they cherished. New income, following the creation of OPEC in 1972 and the quadrupling of oil prices, went directly to the state and energized the regime's leaders, particularly the shah. He made no secret of his contempt for traditional lifestyles, which he equated with backwardness, and he expressed determination to overhaul society. The new wealth increased his authoritarianism; he no longer needed to worry about offending any particular group when he attempted to implement his plans for creating a modern, Western-style country. Such ambitions seemed to him within reach.

In its haste to attain "the great civilization" of ancient Iran, the regime emphasized Iranian nationalism and marginalized the role of Islam. Many aspects of European life were considered essential; the regime encouraged what it perceived as signs of modernity. The shah's last wife, Farah Diba Pahlavi, and many women of the upper, middle, and even lower classes adopted Western fashions. State television portrayed female university students holding hands with boyfriends, supermarkets in Tehran carried sexually explicit magazines, and movie theaters showed domestic and foreign soft-pornographic films. Makers of Iranian films containing or implying political or social criticism struggled to receive approval from the censor's office, but commercial Iranian films were allowed to portray scantily clad women playing sensual and sexual roles.[45]

The regime encouraged education and the participation of women in the workforce, developments that generally improved women's status, but it became more hostile to political dissent regardless of gender. Its disregard for political and civil rights alienated the very groups that supported state-initiated reforms and agreed with curtailing the clergy's power. Many intellectuals and opposition groups blamed the United States for keeping the shah in power and were appalled by his subservience. Despite their deep dislike for him, they seemed helpless in the face of what they believed to be an impregnable regime.

To weaken the authority of retrogressive clergymen, the regime created a religious corps to enlighten the masses in small towns and villages across the country with its version of a progressive Islam. What the shah and his modernist advisors ignored was the depth of religious feeling of many Iranians. Although perhaps not practicing religion faithfully, much of the urban population was still devout and upheld values heavily influenced by a Shi'i worldview. Its allegiance to Iranian culture was strongly tinged with religious loyalty. A charismatic and revered religious figure, Ayatullah Khomeini seemed a victim of the shah's antipathy for religion and influenced urban women who believed in his teachings.

Oil revenue benefited students from different social backgrounds, including those from lower-income families whose values tended to be traditional and religious. Although some joined radical leftist groups, most were sympathetic instead to religious leaders and intellectuals, such as Ali Shari'ati and the Ayatullahs Khomeini and Taliqani who opposed the regime. They shared the distaste of most Iranians for the shah's increasingly authoritarian rule but were also troubled by the spread of Western values that they said undermined Islamic teachings and morality.

Some young women in urban areas welcomed the freer atmosphere made possible by Western values. Marriage was still the ultimate goal, but working outside the home and alongside men, before and even after marriage, became an acceptable goal for many middle-class women and even their future husbands. Professional women such as engineers, lawyers, and physicians valued the support of their male colleagues for the useful roles they played outside the home. Other middle-class families and many lower-class ones were not as happy with the new trends. Some were reluctant to send their daughters to university for fear that they would be influenced by emerging values. Some families discarded their televisions because of what they considered was the corrupting influence of state-controlled programs.

Secular opposition groups were emboldened by Jimmy Carter's election as U.S. president in 1976, because he championed the cause of human rights. They began to denounce rampant corruption, rising authoritarianism, subservience to the United States, disregard for political rights, censorship, and the state security agency (SAVAK). Leftists played a role in the revolution, but their groups lacked programs to rally the masses behind them. The radical left in particular could not succeed without outside assistance. After the Soviet Union reached a rapprochement with the shah, its aid was no longer forthcoming. Aware of their inability to draw mass support, leftists forged alliances with clerics, whom they believed could move people to act against the regime.

Other opposition groups supported the National Front and upheld Musaddiq's secular, democratic, and nationalist ideals. They attracted educated middle-class intellectuals, university professors and students, and government officials, but they lacked a comprehensive agenda and had limited popular support. Despite their belief in secular democracy and their hatred for the shah's dictatorship, their long exposure to Marxist and socialist ideas convinced them of the need for state-sponsored leadership and reform. Anticlerical, they viewed religious leaders as reactionary and regarded Great Britain and the United States as responsible for keeping Iran undeveloped. They considered those who worked with the regime as corrupt and self-seeking. Their nationalism separated them from socialists and communists, but they shared with the left two sentiments: an abhorrence of the shah as a pernicious dictator; and an aversion for Islam, which they blamed as another cause of the country's lack of progress. They criticized the regime cryptically in their gatherings and writings, which they aimed toward the elite, not the general public.

While secular groups strove for greater political freedom and influence, more traditional groups considered themselves under siege. They believed the government was intent on wiping out their long-held religious and moral values because it launched a negative campaign against religious leaders, imprisoned some of them, banned religious gatherings, and demeaned mosques. The heightened efforts of the shah's regime to achieve its vision of a great society lent credibility to the messages of leaders such as Ayatullah Khomeini who had warned about its evil intentions to destroy Islam and undermine society. Followers included bazaar merchants, artisans, shopkeepers, those in small family-owned businesses, and government employees and were most evident in poorer sections of the capital, other large cities, and towns. Criticisms against the regime by religious leaders circulated freely among them.

The revolution started in earnest with the regime's harsh retaliation against seminary students in Qum during the religiously significant month of Muharram and with Khomeini's calls to his followers that their religious duty was to rise up against the ungodly, anti-Islamic regime of the shah. Hundreds of thousands of men and women demonstrated in the streets of major cities, especially Tehran, and unleashed their decade-long pent-up anger and feelings of humiliation.

Despite skirmishes between government forces and a growing number of demonstrators, the presence of women, sometimes carrying children, helped immobilize army conscripts, many of whom refused to shoot at women who reminded them of their own families. Soon many conscripts joined the demonstrators. Massive strikes by oil-field and other workers, government employees, and shopkeepers swelled the number of protesters to millions during the last few months of the revolution. Hoping to have his son succeed him, the shah decided to abandon the throne and leave the country in January 1979. Major bloodshed was avoided because he lacked large groups of supporters.

Women since the Rise of the Islamic Republic, 1979–

Secular opposition groups had rallied around Ayatullah Khomeini when they discovered his mass appeal. After the shah's departure, they were surprised to learn that religious leaders intended to restore the shari'a as the paramount law of the land. Through intimidation and sheer numbers of supporters, religious leaders passed a constitution in which clerics became the upholders of authority. Khomeini was designated as the country's supreme spiritual leader, a position that placed him and anyone to succeed him above the law, with the right to veto any act of parliament. Thus was born the Islamic Republic of Iran.

The new regime took steps to eliminate the more obvious symbols of the shah's time. Khomeini and other leaders viewed the restoration of traditional gender boundaries as the foundation of an Islamic society and defended these policies by reference to religious dogma and authenticity. They annulled parts of the Family Protection Law that seemed to be contrary to the shari'a, such as the high minimum age of marriage, restrictions on polygyny, more favorable division of assets in divorce, and longer periods of child custody for divorced mothers. Despite opposition from secular activists and upper- and middle-class Westernized women, religious leaders were also able to impose a type of attire (hijab) far more in keeping with their perceptions of Islamic morality. It required covering the hair and body with a hood or scarf and a long robe or chadur. They banned women and unrelated men from appearing together in public. They barred women from occupying positions such as judges and encouraged many women employed in the public sector to retire.

Many radical secular activists, some of whom had returned to Iran after the revolution, and upper- and middle-class women who had benefited from education and the country's economic growth, considered these restrictions, especially hijab, outrageous and a setback. They protested against the draconian measures affecting women by appealing to regime leaders, but they had little success in mobilizing large groups of women. Many laws enacted by the shah's regime had not affected the lives of most Iranian women, who continued to wear a chadur outdoors and to uphold traditional values.

More surprising was the reluctance of some secular men, including some on the left, to support the efforts of women against the hijab.[46] Perhaps their silence and inactivity was intended to ingratiate them with the clerical leadership, for they anticipated that clerics lacked the ability and interest to run the country for long.[47] They expected to move into positions of power when the clergy vacated them. They stirred public opinion against the United States, helped to implement anti-market programs to undermine capitalist ones, encouraged nationalization of private banks and large businesses, and supported the seizure of property of those who had "spread corruption on earth." They also tried to decimate the armed forces built up under the shah in the belief that it was created to benefit the United States and Western military industries. They feared that the military might stage a coup d'état. Then Iraqi leader Saddam Hussein attacked Iran in 1980, thus rallying much of the population.

As the clerical regime became better entrenched, it demanded greater loyalty to its brand of religion and politics. As the regime's intolerance for opposition increased, it resorted to methods of silencing dissent similar to those used by the shah. Gradually, many of those opposed to the new regime, including many leftists, fled to Europe or the United States. Ironically, few alleged socialists sought refuge in the socialist states that existed in the 1980s. One group of Islamist socialists, the Mujahidin-i Khalq, took refuge with Saddam Hussein in the hope that his victory over Iran would bring them to power.

Many women supported the Islamic Republic during the Iran-Iraq war (1980–88). Those who found the regime's policies for women's roles outside the home puzzling and even unacceptable tended to keep their misgivings to themselves and their immediate families. Simultaneously, circumstances that the regime could not control forced its leaders to change their attitudes toward women's employment outside the home. The emigration of many professionals and technocrats from the country and the massive mobilization of men during the war created a need for skilled women to fill vacancies. The regime encouraged young women to join the war effort as nurses and auxiliaries. Despite its rhetoric and initial dismissal of women from certain high positions, many women had continued to serve as engineers, doctors, managers, and office workers. This quiet change in the regime's attitude supports the notion that while ideological efforts may temporarily affect women's roles, their status ultimately depends on underlying socioeconomic factors.

After the war's ceasefire in 1988 and Ayatullah Khomeini's death in 1989, the views of religious leaders who resumed preaching that women's proper role was raising children and caring for the home began to be questioned by some educated women who found the traditional role envisaged by these leaders no longer relevant. Their rejection of the older paradigm was reinforced by the smaller size of families and their access to modern timesaving devices available even to some lower-class women. These women gradually became more vocal critics of the regime's policies, which they no longer found compatible with their aspirations.

The disaffection of many such women may seem strange in view of their earlier acceptance of household roles and their initial enthusiastic support for the Islamic revolution and its ideals. Several developments since 1979 shed light on this transformation in attitude, which reflects changes in fundamental aspects of Iranian society. Dismal economic conditions during and after the war affected many households and reduced enthusiasm for revolutionary and religious rhetoric. Women's growing loss of support was demonstrated in their votes for candidates who promised greater civil liberties and improved conditions for women. Women helped elect President Muhammad Khatami in 1997 and again in 2001 even though more conservative leaders had put forth their own candidates. A second factor in women's growing opposition was the increase in the number of women with higher education. Whereas many parents had hesitated to allow their daughters to attend or to continue with school before the rise of Islamic Republic, they trusted the new regime. In an effort to cleanse society of the corruption spread by the previous regime, the republic encouraged greater study of Islam in schools and universities. In 2001 women composed about half of the entering first-year class in Iranian universities.

During the shah's time, Ali Shari'ati had offered an earlier generation of Islamist women a revolutionary role model in Fatimeh, the prophet's daughter.[48] His radical paradigm appealed mainly to a small group of university students who resorted to acts of violence in the name of Islam. After the revolution, as new generations of women and men studied early Islamic history, they discovered that much of what they had been taught about Islam consisted of interpretations by past and contemporary religious leaders. Their study of the Qur'an and early texts revealed that early Muslim women had played more diverse and active roles than what was claimed by religious leaders. These educated young women became the vanguards of change for improved opportunities for women and led demands for greater freedom to pursue public roles. Their activism affected older women within their families and also less educated women who were exposed to their ideas.

These women were not feminists in the Western sense.[49] They accepted that men and women have different physical, psychological, and emotional constitutions, but they insisted that these differences do not imply that women should be confined to the home. Although many abided willingly by the rules of hijab, they were against coercing women who opposed the practice. They asserted that women have a religious duty to fight corruption and oppose injustice and that many laws restoring the division of society along gender lines after 1979 were no longer relevant. Despite the efforts of hardliners within the regime to silence this dissent by intimidation and imprisonment, many leaders of this new female awakening, including journalists, lawyers, professors, university students, and members of parliament, were fearless in their public criticism of the behavior of some religious leaders. They expressed their views in reformist newspapers and journals, such as *Zanan* (Women), which catered mainly to women.

The election of Khatami as president allowed greater political expression, which encouraged the activism of secular women, including women lawyers and professors, such as Shirin Ebadi and Mehrangiz Kar. They used reformist publications, especially the monthly magazine *Zanan*, and the growing international awareness of human rights to draw attention to abuses against women in the name of religion. Shirin Ebadi, who received the Nobel Peace Prize in 2003, had been a judge during the shah's regime. She was dismissed from her position by leaders of the Islamic Republic on the grounds that a female judge was contrary to the shari'a.

Despite being drawn from backgrounds where many people were sympathetic to the Islamic Republic, female members of parliament also became more outspoken in promoting laws to end discrimination against women. They succeeded in winning the support of some reformist-minded male colleagues and clerics in their demand to improve women's status under the law. Their efforts resulted in the revision of some laws that put women at a disadvantage in marriage. With some male support, they passed a proposal to improve divorce and custody laws.[50] They were among the most vocal critics of hard-line factions within the regime and publicly attacked their violation of the constitution. Leaders such as Jamileh Kadivar (who received the second highest vote in Tehran during the 2001 elections) publicly denounced the views and "despotic behavior" of the council of guardians and some judiciary members as a "departure from religious teachings" and stated that they had taken on the traits of dictatorial regimes.[51] As critics of the position of the supreme spiritual leader, they joined forces with reformist factions within parliament to amend the constitution and limit the authority of nonelected individuals and bodies that could override acts of parliament. They learned that unless the rule of law prevails, rights of both women and men can be ignored.

Unlike prerevolutionary feminists and émigré radicals who looked to the latest Western theories on liberating women, the new activists spoke a language familiar to Iranian women even in distant towns. Khatami, whose campaign in 1997 promised greater civil liberties and equal rights, received 79 percent of the vote, and most women voted for him. During the 2001 elections, many women applied to run for the post of president but were rejected by the council of guardians.

The mid-2000s will be crucial for Iranian women. Despite the difficulties many women have faced, they have become more aware of their potential, as evidenced by the high number of women who entered universities. In 2003, 62 percent of newly entering university students were women, and they constituted 50 percent of graduate students. These many educated women in the future will exert an important influence on political and economic developments that will undoubtedly affect gender roles and women's status in Iran.

The chapters in this volume shed some light on how women in Iran have reached this stage; they will help readers to understand why Iran may be in the vanguard of changes for women in countries where they are restricted in the name of religion.

NOTES

I thank Ahmad Ashraf, Lois Beck, Gary Becker, Behzad Nashat, and Djavad Salehi-Isfahani for useful comments and assistance.

1. For a review of approaches, see Parvin Paidar, *Women and the Political Process in Twentieth-Century Iran* (Cambridge: Cambridge University Press, 1995), 1–24, 30–78.

2. Marshall G. S. Hodgson, *The Venture of Islam* (Chicago: University of Chicago Press, 1974), 3:76–223.

3. For long-standing misconceptions and misrepresentations by Europeans about Islam, see Aziz al-Azmeh, *Islam and Modernities* (London: Verso, 1993), 122–45; and

Judith Mabro, *Veiled Half-Truths: Western Travellers' Perceptions of Middle Eastern Women* (London: I. B. Tauris, 1991).

4. Mabro, *Veiled Half-Truths,* 10–22.

5. James Atkinson, *Customs and Manners of the Women of Persia, and Their Domestic Superstitions* (London: John Murray, 1832), xi.

6. Ervand Abrahamian, *The Iranian Mojahedin* (New Haven: Yale University Press, 1989), 153.

7. *Memoirs of Taj al-Saltaneh,* ed. Mansoureh Ettehadieh and Cyrus Sadounian (Bethesda: Iranbooks, 1991), 98.

8. Armin Vambery, *Siyahat-i darvishi duruqin dar khanat-i asiya-yi miyaneh,* trans. Fath'ali Khwajeh-Nuriyan (Tehran: Ilmi va farhangi, 1995), 257.

9. Lady Sheil, *Glimpses of Life and Manners in Persia* (London: John Murray, 1856), 144–45.

10. John Perry, *Karim Khan Zand, A History of Iran, 1747–1779* (Chicago: University of Chicago Press, 1979), 149; Ahmad Mirza Azd al-Douleh, *Tarikh-i azudi* (Tehran: Mazahiri, n.d.), 59.

11. Azd al-Douleh, *Tarikh,* 12.

12. Dust'ali Mu'ayyir al-Mamalik, *Yaddashtha'i az zindigani-yi khususi-yi Nasir al-Din Shah* (Tehran: Ilmi, 1972), 175–76.

13. Firiydun Adamiyat, *Amir Kabir va Iran* (Tehran: Khawarazmi, 1957), 658–66; Mihdi Bamdad, *Sharh-i hal-i rijal-i Iran* (Tehran: Ilmi, 1968), 4:326–28. A sympathetic portrait of Mahd-i Ulya is in Abbas Amanat, *Pivot of the Universe: Nasir al-Din Shah Qajar and the Iranian Monarchy, 1831–1896* (Berkeley: University of California Press, 1997), 133–42.

14. Muhammad Hasan Khan I'timad al-Saltaneh, *Ruznameh-yi khatirat-i I'timad al-Saltaneh* (Tehran: Amir Kabir, 1966), 123–26.

15. He is commonly referred to in sources as de Reuter. Formerly I viewed Anis al-Douleh's opposition merely as the act of a vengeful woman; Guity Nashat, *The Beginnings of Modern Reform in Iran* (Urbana: University of Illinois Press, 1983), 91–93.

16. Sheil, *Glimpses,* 146.

17. Mu'ayyir al-Mamalik, *Yaddashtha'i,* 32–36.

18. Mangol Bayat, *Mysticism and Dissent: Socio-religious Thought in Qajar Iran* (Syracuse: Syracuse University Press, 1982), 90–91, 113–16.

19. Shireen Mahdavi, "The Structure and Function of the Household of a Qajar Merchant," *Iranian Studies* 32 (4) (1999): 560–65.

20. Sheil, *Glimpses,* 144–45.

21. Bibi Khanum, *Ruyaru'i-yi zan va mard dar asr-i Qajar du risaleh ta'dib al-nisvan va ma'ayib al-rijal,* ed. Hasan Javadi, Manijeh Mar'ashi, and Simin Shikarlu (San Jose: Jahan, 1992), 97–171.

22. Sheil, *Glimpses,* 145.

23. Carla Serena, *Hommes et choses en Perse* (Paris: G. Charpentier, 1883), 260.

24. *Memoirs of Taj al-Saltaneh,* 101.

25. C. Colliver Rice, *Persian Women and Their Ways* (Philadelphia: J. B. Lippincott, 1923), 54–55.

26. Iraj Afshar, ed., *Khatirat va asnad-i Zahir al-Douleh* (Tehran: Shirkat-i Sihami-yi kitabha-yi jibi, 1972), 357–60, 367–79.

27. Rice estimates their numbers to have been about three hundred; *Persian Women,* 270.

28. See Afaf Lutfi al-Sayyid Marsot, "The Revolutionary Gentlewomen in Egypt," *Women in the Muslim World,* ed. Lois Beck and Nikki Keddie (Cambridge: Harvard University Press, 1978).

29. Bamdad, *Sharh-i hal-i rijal-i Iran,* 3:325.

30. Hajji Mirza Yahya Doulatabadi, "Maqam-i zan," cited in Shams ul-Muluk Javahirkalam, *Zanan-i nami-yi Islam va Iran* (Tehran: n.p., 1967), 439–43.

31. Badr ol-Moluk Bamdad, *From Darkness into Light: Women's Emancipation in Iran,* F. R. C. Bagley, ed. and trans. (Hicksville, N.Y.: Exposition, 1977), 45–46.

32. Pari Shaikhulislami, *Zanan-i ruznamehnigar va andishmand-i Iran* (Tehran: Mazgraphic, 1972), 65–66.

33. Ibid., 75–88, 97. For Doulatabadi's life, see also Bamdad, *From Darkness,* 78–80.

34. Rice, *Persian Women,* 92, 107.

35. For these newspapers and the feminist movement, see Eliz Sanasarian, *The Women's Rights Movement in Iran: Mutiny, Appeasement, and Repression from 1900 to Khomeini* (New York: Praeger, 1981), 28–53.

36. Shahla Haeri, *Law of Desire: Temporary Marriage in Shi'i Iran* (Syracuse: Syracuse University Press, 1989).

37. Bamdad, *From Darkness,* 92–95.

38. Ibid., 134.

39. Ibid., 63–64.

40. Shahrough Akhavi, *Religion and Politics in Contemporary Iran* (Albany: State University of New York Press, 1980), 61.

41. Bamdad, *From Darkness,* 106; Ervand Abrahamian, *Iran between Two Revolutions* (Princeton: Princeton University Press, 1982), 336.

42. Abrahamian, *Iran,* 335–36; Akhavi, *Religion,* 63.

43. Ervand Abrahamian, "The Structural Causes of the Iranian Revolution," *MERIP Reports* 87 (1980): 21–26.

44. For the role of feminists and activists, see Paidar, *Women;* and Eliz Sanasarian, "An Analysis of Fida'i and Mujahidin Positions on Women's Rights," *Women and Revolution in Iran,* ed. Guity Nashat (Boulder: Westview, 1983), 97–108; and Azar Tabari and Nahid Yeganeh, eds., *In the Shadow of Islam: The Women's Movement in Iran* (London: Zed Press, 1982).

45. Hamid Naficy, "Women and the 'Problematic of Women' in the Iranian Postrevolutionary Cinema," *Nimeh-yi Digar* 14 (1991): 123–70.

46. Paidar, *Women,* 235.

47. For studies noting that religious leaders were prepared for running the country's affairs, see Said Amir Arjomand, *The Turban for the Crown* (Oxford: Oxford University Press, 1988); and Shaul Bakhash, *The Reign of the Ayatollahs: Iran and the Islamic Revolution* (New York: Basic Books, 1984).

48. Minou Reeves, *Female Warriors of Allah* (New York: Dutton, 1989), 113–33.

49. Ibid., 133–58.

50. "Expediency Council Expands Divorce Rights for Women," *Iran Times,* 12 July 2002.

51. "Deputy Convicted for Words," *Iran Times,* 24 August 2001; "Judges Shush Press," *Iran Times,* 31 May 2002.

1   Marriage in the Qajar Period

GUITY NASHAT

HISTORIANS HAVE PAID little attention to the institution of marriage in the Qajar period (1794–1925), although the marriages of two Qajar kings (Fath Ali Shah, r. 1797–1834, and Nasir al-Din Shah, r. 1848–96), their large households, and the lavish entertainments that some aristocratic families staged for their children's marriages have been described. One reason for the neglect of this subject is the narrow nature of the sources. Much of the available information deals with marriages of members of the royal family and the elite. Material for the study of marriage in rural areas in the middle and lower classes in cities during this period is scarce.

The constraints imposed by the sources dictate my focus in this chapter, mainly the institution of marriage in Tehran among the ruling elite. I discuss the permanent and temporary marriages of two rulers—Fath Ali Shah and Nasir al-Din Shah—to show how marriage promoted the policy needs of the dynasty. This study may encourage further efforts at detailed description and systematic analysis of marriage patterns in this period. Many families—not only the elite but also the middle and lower classes—still possess documents, such as marriage contracts, and local and oral histories of marriages could also be researched.

After Tehran became Iran's capital at the end of the eighteenth century, its population grew from 15,000 inhabitants to almost 280,000 by the end of the Qajar period.[1] Tehran's growth was the result not so much of a natural increase in the birthrate but of emigration, and practices within the capital in part represent an amalgam of what existed in some other parts of the country.[2]

Certain types of marriages were common in Iran in the Qajar period. Shiʻi Islam, the religion of the majority of the population, recognized two types of marital union: permanent (*nikah*) and temporary (*mutʻa*).[3] Most marriages were permanent, and only rulers, some princes, and some wealthy men took temporary wives. In the Irano-Islamic tradition, marriage had a dual purpose: to sanction and regulate the sexual relationship of a man and a woman and to promote reproduction. As in most premodern societies, marriage was the major option available to a woman, and her family played an important role in the choice of a husband, especially if the woman was a virgin.[4] Her seclusion, combined with the veil, and her family's socioeconomic status influenced potential suitors. The higher the status of the girl's family, the greater the degree of the family's intervention in the choice of a partner, because marriage was a means of promoting and preserving the economic wealth, authority, and prestige of all members.

Many wealthy and middle-class families in Qajar Iran lived in extended, patriarchal households. The head of the household was the oldest member, and everyone was supposed to obey his decisions. Extended households could include his sons, their wives and children, grandsons and their families, some less-wealthy widows or never-married female relatives, and wives and children of former servants. In most households the head mediated in its minor disputes. Sometimes disputes between members of two households would be negotiated by the two heads without resorting to legal or religious authorities.

In elite families, children's relationships with their parents were formal. In his private journal, Qahraman Mirza (1871–1944), Nasir al-Din Shah's nephew, refers to his parents in the most respectful manner by calling his father Shahzadeh Janam (my dear prince) and his mother Khanum Jan or Navvab-i Aliyeh (dear lady or exalted highness). He refers to his eldest brother by his official title, Imad al-Saltaneh, and reveals the same tone when he writes about his sisters.[5] Many European residents, who generally criticized Iranian practices, marveled at children's attitudes toward their parents. According to C. J. Wills, who served as a physician in Iran during the 1870s, "An undutiful son or daughter is hardly known in the country. . . . No act of serious import is ever undertaken without the advice of the mother; no man would think, for instance, of marrying contrary to his mother's advice; and by the very poorest the support of their parents would never be looked on as a burden."[6] Rulers showed the same reverence for their mothers as did ordinary subjects. When Fath Ali Shah visited his mother, he would bow to her and not sit without her permission. Nasir al-Din Shah also treated his mother with great respect.[7]

Despite the reverence a son showed his mother, in theory the father was the ultimate source of authority in wealthy, middle-class, and poor families. In the absence of the father or after his death, in most cases the eldest son assumed the position of head. Sometimes younger sons moved out of the family home and formed their own households. Family members often stayed together even when they grew wealthy enough to support independent households. Haj Muhammad Hasan Amin al-Zarb, an Isfahani merchant who moved his business to Tehran, became one of the country's wealthiest men and yet continued to live in the same house, albeit much enlarged, with his mother, wife, son, and brother's children and wife.[8]

Loyalty to the family can be partly explained by the fact that married women, whether of distinguished background or not, became members of their husband's household and family network. If they were divorced, their paternal family took care of them. Children of a temporary marriage also shared feelings of loyalty toward the family even though their mothers were generally of lower status. Such identification was prompted by the rights and privileges they received through paternal descent. An exception to this rule was the heir to the throne, whose mother in theory had to be a Qajar princess and a permanent wife.[9] The type of relationships existing within the family reflects continuity with older social practices existing in Iran before the Qajars.

During the Qajar period, the state did not play a role in officiating marriages as it did in many Muslim countries in the middle and late twentieth century. This role was played by religious figures who formed an integral part of the process regardless of differences due to sectarian affiliations of the bride and groom. A mulla drew up the marriage contract (*aqd*) legitimizing the union of a man and a woman and specifying the duties and obligations of the two partners. The most important requirement of an Islamic marriage is its contractual nature, and legitimizing a marriage contract requires the presence of the two partners or their representatives and involves an offer of marriage by the groom and an acceptance by the bride in the same session. Staging the aqd ceremony indicated that the lengthy negotiations between the families of the bride and the groom had been completed, in which the amount of bridewealth (*mahr*) was determined as well as other conditions, such as the ability of the groom to take another wife.[10]

For all women, marriage caused a fundamental change of status. Until a virgin married, she was considered the ward of her father or a male guardian, especially if she was a minor, which in Shi'i law was considered the age of nine or the attainment of puberty. Upon marriage, she achieved agency, was empowered legally, and was entitled to exercise her rights. For a wealthy woman, the most important right was economic and consisted of control of her inheritance, bridewealth, and any income generated by these resources, which were sometimes considerable.

Daughters of poorer parents viewed marriage as their best option and the major means of survival outside the paternal home. Women enjoyed few opportunities to earn income from work in the nineteenth century. In urban areas young women from low-income families could be employed as servants in the households of the rich, but rarely did they control their wages, which were given to their families, some of which may have been put aside for their trousseau. Rural women contributed to the economy of their communities but did not receive wages directly. Marriage and children did provide them with some security later in life.

Under Islamic law, a woman is subordinate to her husband, but that status does not give a husband the right to interfere with his wife's resources. Such tampering gives the woman one of the few grounds for divorce. In the Qajar period, many wealthy women protected their personal wealth and kept it separate from their husbands' assets. When Qahraman Mirza's mother bought a village jointly with her husband, she owned half of that village outright.[11] Other women used their wealth to establish charitable endowments. The bridewealth paid by the groom belonged totally to the bride. The need to provide it helps to explain the disparity in the ages of most married men and women, which was about ten years. Difference in ages partly explains why some marriages were not companionate. Men had to wait until their late twenties and even thirties to marry, but most girls married before they were twenty. Only wealthy males could marry in their teens because they could rely on their families to pay the bridewealth.[12] Bridewealth provided even the poorest woman an important asset if she became divorced or widowed. It also acted as a safeguard against divorce because a husband could not divorce his wife without its full payment. Many contemporary discussions on the subject, which equate bridewealth with the wife's purchase, miss the significance of this requirement in Islamic marriages. They ignore its importance to women in premodern societies, such as Iran, where the opportunity for earning an income outside the home was rare for most urban women. A revealing example is provided by Bibi Khanum Astarabadi, an educated and intelligent woman who commented about gender relationships in her time. Being in love with a poor man, she decided to forgo the bridewealth of four hundred tumans that was normal for a woman of her station. She later regretted her decision when her marriage almost broke up. Not having to pay the sum emboldened her husband to divorce her so that he could be with another woman.[13]

Women received part of the bridewealth at the time of marriage, but all men had to pay the unpaid portion if they divorced their wives, which may have discouraged men from taking advantage of the seeming ease that Islamic law provides them. The skewed sex ratio caused by the ability of some men at the top to have more than one wife may have been another reason why men did not rush to divorce their wives. If the divorce was irrevocable, a man could not remarry his wife unless she married another man who then divorced her also irrevocably and unless she observed the *idda*, the waiting period of three months and ten days required before she could marry again, to ensure that she was not pregnant. The ease with which divorced women found husbands within a year further confirms the availability of potential husbands and the scarcity of potential wives. To avoid payment of the bridewealth, a husband could pressure his wife to forgo it in order to get a divorce—one of the few conditions under which a woman could seek divorce.[14]

In addition to security and legal empowerment, another product of marriage was children, which enhanced a woman's prestige and her authority within the husband's family. This aspect was true for both wealthy and poor women, but its importance was greater for those in the lower economic levels who could rely on children, especially sons, to care for them in their old age. Most parents may have preferred the eldest child to be a son. Despite the negative impression that Iranian folklore and "mirrors for princes" literature (manuals of advice) may convey, having a daughter was not regarded as a calamity, at least by the well-to-do. We learn from Qahraman Mirza that ceremonies held at his parents' house to celebrate the birth of his daughter were the same as those held for his older brother's son. He repeatedly expresses pride and joy at having a girl and worries whenever she falls ill. Ceremonies for naming the child (*ismguzari*) and tying the navel (*nafbandi*), arranged by his parents for his daughter, were as lavish as those held for his nephew.[15] Fath Ali Shah and Nasir al-Din Shah favored some of their daughters as much as their sons. Ziya al-Saltaneh (light of the state) was the confidante of her father, Fath Ali Shah, and entrusted with writing important and confidential exchanges. Nasir al-Din Shah was so fond of one daughter, Fakhr al-Douleh (pride of the state), that he insisted she stay in his home twenty days per month even after she married.[16]

The favorable sex ratio may explain why some parents may not have minded having a baby girl, because they knew that getting a husband for her would not be costly. The main worry in raising a daughter was ensuring that her virginity remained intact until her marriage. Loss of virginity before marriage brought shame to her entire family.

A popular practice was marriage between paternal cousins. This preference was expressed in a widely quoted maxim in Iran and other Islamic countries that "the marriage of paternal cousins was ordained by heaven."[17] Undoubtedly, Islamic inheritance law, which entitles daughters to one-half of the share their brothers receive from their parents' estate, boosted endogamous marriages, especially among wealthy families. Because a woman would become a part of her husband's agnatic family upon marriage, she would undermine her natal family's wealth if she married someone outside the kin group. Although women in principle controlled their resources, well-to-do families, whose main source of wealth was revenue from land—villages, orchards, and real estate—tried to keep their properties within the larger group.

Although the family in the Qajar period was patriarchal, in matters relating to marriage, the mother and other women played a greater role than did men. Because of seclusion and the veil, a man in search of a wife had to rely on his female relatives for information about his future partner. That a bride became a member of her husband's household also meant that female members took interest in her choice. Because Islamic law stipulates that a woman must marry someone equal to or above her in status, it encourages marriage within the same socioeconomic group. This practice gave women a greater role because they were in a better position to investigate the background of other families through their social contacts and networks.

The Mustoufi household illustrates women's roles. Its founder, Mirza Isma'il, came from a modest family in Gorgan and entered the service of a Qajar chieftain as a young man. Later he accompanied the young Agha Muhammad Khan (r. 1794–97) before the latter ascended the throne. Yet Mirza Isma'il did not marry until the reign of Fath Ali Shah (1797–1834) when he was in his mid-forties. Such a long wait indicates that even promising government officials such as Mirza Isma'il needed to save enough to offer a generous bridewealth, buy necessary household goods, and attain a position that could support a future wife and family.[18] Perhaps not having any female relatives in Tehran to help him made it difficult for him to find the right bride.

By contrast, Mirza Nasrullah (1810–88), Mirza Isma'il's eldest son, married when he was fifteen. What made his marriage possible was his father's wealth and position at court, his own future prospects, and the network of female relatives he had acquired through his own mother and stepmother. As was customary, he joined his father in the treasury office and received training to become a *mustoufi* (accountant or treasury official). He married the daughter of another mustoufi, from whom he learned additional professional skills. His successful career, resources he received from his father, and wise investments in property made him prosperous. When his wife reached menopause, he considered her too old and decided to marry again. Despite her unhappiness, he married a younger woman. The new wife was the daughter of a rural landowning family and below him in social status and wealth. After the second wife's death, he married her sixteen-year-old niece after having negotiated with her parents and brothers to win their approval. The new father-in-law was a middling landowner. Among the concessions the elderly bridegroom made was to allow two of his new wife's brothers to join his household in the capital.[19] Mirza Nasrullah's rising position, wealth, and age did not match the status of the women he married. His first wife came from a background similar to his, but his second and third wives, who were younger, came from progressively less distinguished rural backgrounds. The older he became, the higher the demands of the bride and her family. His marriages also reveal that a man could marry at any age, while a woman was considered old when she reached menopause.

As the family grew, Mirza Nasrullah enlarged his living space by buying and renovating adjoining properties in order to have the children from the three wives he married over a fifty-year period live in the same compound. By the time of his death in 1888, he was an important state official, second only to Mustoufi al-Mamalik, minister of finance. Mirza Nasrullah was also a wealthy man and tried to preserve the family's wealth by encouraging his children to marry within the now-larger kin group. Many of his descendants married their relatives. These marriages ensured that control of the extended family's assets could be maintained within the same family to offset the impact of Islamic inheritance laws.

Islamic inheritance laws may have fostered endogamous marriages among the wealthy, but such marriages offered another advantage. Most urban families had better knowledge of their own relatives than of outsiders. Many brides and grooms in extended families had seen one another as children, had studied in the same informal schools the wealthy held in their households, and may have continued to associate with one another during adolescence. Despite laws of seclusion, enforced mainly in urban areas, future partners were often mutually acquainted.

Since men and women, including husbands and wives, lived in separate worlds, approval of the household's women about marriage choices helped to preserve its peace and harmony. If the wife of a sibling or cousin was troublesome, the problem could draw other members into conflict. In the Mustoufi family, a younger son of the patriarch, Mirza Mahmud, left the paternal compound due to disputes with his oldest brother, aggravated by rivalry and animosity between his wife and her sisters-in-law.[20]

Relying on the judgment of female relatives for choosing a wife continued beyond the end of the Qajar period even among those who had received a modern education and knew Europe firsthand. Continuity is suggested in the way Abdullah Mustoufi, Mirza Nasrullah's son from his third wife, chose his bride. He was one of the first graduates of the political science school in Tehran and served in St. Petersburg for five years. When he returned to Tehran, he was ready to marry. His stay in Europe had convinced him that "even the most beautiful woman after a year or two becomes ordinary in her husband's eyes." In his view, happiness in marriage depended on shared values and background. Because women were still secluded, he relied on his mother to find him such a wife. The search fell on a distant relative. The marriage produced several children and outlasted the Qajar dynasty by several decades.[21]

Women, even those who had never married before, had some say in the choice of spouse. Bibi Khanum was a memorable satirist who left a biting critique of contemporary men. She tells us that her guardian, a maternal uncle, was opposed to her marriage to a poor man she loved, but her mother's support finally brought her uncle around. A younger girl may have lacked the stamina to resist her family's wishes as did Bibi Khanum, who was in her mid-twenties when she married.[22]

We know less about marriage among the middle and lower classes during the Qajar period. Most likely the geographical and social backgrounds of people in search of a bride limited their possibilities. Most parents preferred that their daughter marry a relative or acquaintance, and they were suspicious of a young man who could not find a suitable wife from among his own relatives. Tehran's population had been growing throughout the nineteenth century, and older inhabitants viewed the new arrivals with suspicion. While searching for a young woman she could introduce to her husband in the hope that he would take her as a temporary wife, Bibi Khanum encountered a woman from Rasht who claimed to have been abused by a former employer. Bibi Khanum had given birth to six children in nine years of marriage and longed for a respite from conjugal duties. She hired the woman as a maid and hoped to interest her husband. Before long, Bibi Khanum's relationship with her husband began to deteriorate, and she returned to her mother's home. She was surprised to learn that the Rashti woman had been the instrument of her troubles with her husband, who had indeed taken her as a temporary wife, and that the new wife was pressuring her husband to choose between them. What saved the breakup of her marriage was the discovery that the woman had fabricated the story of abuse by the former employer and that she had deceived him also. Although xenophobia may not have been the moral Bibi Khanum wanted to convey to her readers, nevertheless she reveals the danger of trusting strangers.[23]

In some cases, an unmarried girl's family might seek help in finding a suitable groom, either because it did not approve of an available male relative or because the daughter was passing the accepted age of marriage. To avert disaster, her family would resort to different methods, such as referring to a female broker or matchmaker (*dallaleh*), appealing to saints and talismans, and even visiting Christian churches to improve her chances. A broker's help was usually sought by families that had recently moved to the capital and had limited social networks or did not know any suitable candidate among their own kin and acquaintances. The rules of seclusion created the opportunity for some widows and older women to act as go-betweens and render useful services to upper- and middle-class women, such as being agents for the sale of small luxury items, fabrics, and jewelry and finding nannies, servants, and cooks. Their access to the women's quarters (*andarun*) of their customers allowed them to observe all family members and learn about girls of marriageable age. The groom's family turned also to a broker for help in finding the right bride. The dallaleh played a role in the proceedings before female members of either side became directly involved. She acted as a mediator for the bride's or the groom's family and tried to acquire information on each to ensure that neither side lost face in upcoming negotiations. She would visit the other family and also inquire about the individual in question from neighbors and acquaintances before the family itself paid its first visit. Another source for locating a suitable bride was the bathhouse masseuse (*dallak*). The laws of purity in Islam require frequent bathing, and female dallaks were considered knowledgeable about the physical attributes of young women.[24]

Marriage Ceremonies

Once a candidate was located, female kin of the groom would request a visit to the prospective bride's house. Custom required that the bride-to-be not appear when the visit began but join the company after the two sides had established some rapport. The girl would enter the room accompanied by a female relative or friend. If the groom's family liked her, they would investigate her character from neighbors and acquaintances. The girl's family would do likewise by looking into the groom's family background and learning about him. They might go incognito to his workplace, if he worked in the bazaar, to see if he flirted with female customers. They might also bring the young woman along so that she could see the groom herself. Sometimes a man would bribe the matchmaker to inform him in advance if the girl was going out so that he could see her height and the way she walked. The period of investigation was prolonged because marriage was considered a serious affair. If both sides determined that they had found the right person, then the groom, accompanied by a few respected male relatives and friends, would visit the bride's father or male guardian to ask for her hand.[25]

The next stage among all families, wealthy or poor, entailed negotiations to determine the bridewealth. The meetings were generally conducted by fathers or older men if the girl was a virgin and the groom had not married before or was young. In lower- and middle-income families, the bridewealth consisted of clothing, shoes, and some payment in cash. Wealthy families would also demand some property and cash for the bride, depending on her socioeconomic background, age, and appearance. The girl's family could include additional provisions to protect her welfare, one of the most important being the ability to divorce if the man married another wife, because under Islamic law only the man has the absolute right to divorce and a woman's right to appeal for divorce is restricted.

Once negotiations were completed, female members of the groom's family would send the customary gifts of cones of sugar, sweets, and shawls wrapped in expensive cloth to the bride's house to inform her family of their intention to visit later that day. During this visit, a younger member of the groom's family would place a ring on the girl's finger to indicate that the couple was engaged.

Then came the marriage contract (*aqd-i nikah*), the actual contractual part, and it required serious preparations. The two families would determine the day of the ceremony and the number of guests to be invited, and the two sides would send separate invitations to male and female relatives and friends. This ceremony took place in the bride's residence and was held during the day, except during the month of Ramadan, when it occurred after breaking the fast. The groom would provide the bride all the necessary accoutrements, including fabric for the wedding dress and other clothes, shoes, head coverings, outerwear, underwear, a large mirror, and two candelabras. Preparing for the upcoming event took several days, from sewing the wedding dress and the special veil to preparing at least two rooms, one for men and another for women. Virgin brides were allowed to pluck facial hair, use facial cosmetics, and arrange their hair on that day.

The ceremony required the presence of one or two mullas (religious figures), depending on the status of the two families, because males and females would congregate in separate rooms. At this stage all the terms negotiated and accepted by the groom's and bride's families were written down in the marriage contract. The groom and bride both had to announce audibly their willingness to form a marriage; rules of propriety required that the woman express her acceptance only after the mulla had repeated the formula several times. Women from the bride's family performed customs that they believed would ensure her future happiness and make her acceptable to the groom's family. Those who were lucky in marriage would hold a white cloth over the bride's head while another would grate two sugar cones over it to sweeten her married life. Another popular custom was sewing a piece of fabric with a threaded needle to silence any future opposition to the bride from her mother-in-law. Although the man and woman would be considered husband and wife under the law, they would still not be considered fully married until their union was consummated after the nuptial ceremony (*arusi*). In religious families the groom would not be allowed to see the bride until that stage. In other families the groom would go to the bride's chamber, which was filled with female family members and guests. Custom required that he offer her a present, generally a piece of jewelry, on this occasion. While awaiting the completion of preparations for the arusi, the groom would pay occasional visits to the bride in her parents' house, but the couple would not be left alone.[26]

The wedding ceremony was the final stage when the bride was transferred from her parental home to the groom's. The period between the two stages could vary depending on the bride's age and status. Two daughters of Nasir al-Din Shah, whose aqds were held when they were twelve, waited until they were in their late teens to move to their husbands' houses. When brides were older, the period between the aqd and arusi was much shorter.[27]

The trousseaus of most women, even from poor families, consisted of furnishings for one or more rooms. A middle-class family provided its daughter with at least one carpet, a mattress and quilt, cushions, a chest, sheets and towels, a brazier, a samovar, serving trays, and cooking utensils. The bride's family also sent the groom and his close relatives gifts, which included a turban or hat, shirts, socks, footwear, and fabric for a suit. The trousseau along with the presents the bride received from the groom were carried to the groom's house the day before the actual wedding day. A few older female relatives accompanied the furnishings to help prepare the nuptial room.

The bride spent one or several days preparing for the event, which included an elaborate bathhouse ceremony where henna was applied to her hands and feet and all bodily hair was removed. In wealthy families she would be joined by relatives and perhaps some female singers while she was washed. On the day of the arusi, special attention was paid to her hair, face, and general appearance. By the time she was ready to leave the parental home, a wealthy bride was adorned with jewelry from head to toe. She walked or rode the distance on a mule or horse, depending on how far she had to travel and the status of the two families. Fath Ali Shah's daughter rode an elephant to her new abode. Carriages began to be used in the late nineteenth century. Male and female relatives and musicians would accompany her, but neither parent would join the procession. As the bride neared her final destination, the groom would exit the house to greet her. He had also prepared himself by taking a special bath, which might have required applying henna and color to his beard if he was graying, and by dressing in his best wardrobe. His relatives would welcome the bride and offer her gifts, which could include pieces of property. Before entering her new abode and as a good-luck gesture, she threw a fistful of raw rice on girls who were not married.[28]

The bride was led to the nuptial room, and women would begin the festivities. Some would dance, others might sing, and occasionally professional musicians would enliven the merriment. After dinner, which always included sweet rice (*shirin pulou*) and many other dishes, the groom's father would enter the room, place the bride's hand in his son's hand, and say, "I entrust him to you." As he left, the women there followed his lead, and the groom and bride were left alone. The night was important for them; she had to prove her virginity and he his virility. Once the girl had joined her husband's household, she would not return to her parents' house for forty days in order to acclimatize herself to the new life. Her father and mother treated the first visit (*pagusha*) as a major celebratory event.[29]

The advantages of marriage for middle-income and poorer women were so great that most sought it. Young girls could usually find husbands before they reached twenty, divorce was rare, and divorced women could remarry within a year. The ability of a few men whose wealth and/or high position allowed them to have more than one wife increased the sex ratio of the unmarried in women's favor; more men were looking for wives than the numbers of women still available.[30]

Polygyny and Temporary Marriage

Despite widespread perceptions that most marriages were polygynous, the evidence reveals a different picture. With the exception of rulers and the wealthy, most marriages were monogamous. Even when a small percentage of men married more than one wife, this shifted the sex ratio and helps to explain why historically in Irano-Islamic society unmarried women were the exception rather than the rule.[31] Polygynous marriages even among the well-to-do were rare but were not unknown. Men took second wives when their first wives were barren or reached menopause. The prospect of sharing a husband with another woman was still a threat hanging over the heads of many wives.

Although Shi'i religious law sanctions taking more than one wife, we have little evidence that most men in fact took advantage of it. Many members of the aristocracy and royalty, such as Kamran Mirza (Nasir al-Din Shah's son) and Amin al-Sultan (later Atabak A'zam), had only one wife. The shari'a injunction that permanent wives be treated equally may have discouraged the pious from taking more than one. No such requirement existed for temporary wives, which may explain the reason for the popularity of this type of marriage.[32]

Of pre-Islamic Arabian origin, temporary marriage (*mut'a; sigheh* in Persian) was banned in Sunni Islam, even though most Sunni scholars attributed the ban to Umar (r. 634–44), the second caliph, and not to the Prophet Muhammad. The ban may have been imposed later, which may explain why early Shi'is, who were mainly an Arabian minority and closer in attitude to practices of the prophet's time, rejected it by considering it an innovation and a departure from the ways of the prophet and the Qur'an. Equated by many Westernized Iranians in the twentieth century with prostitution, temporary marriage has been condemned in many literary works. After 1979 the Islamic Republic tried to revive this form of marriage as a way of alleviating the desire of young people for companionship with the opposite sex.[33]

A temporary marriage required a contract, the terms of which were defined before it commenced. The woman—rather than her family—negotiated for the bridewealth she received and the marriage's duration. At the termination of the bond, the woman had to observe the waiting period (idda) to ensure that she was not pregnant. If she was with child, the man could renew the marriage with her or walk away.[34] Men may have chosen to renew the bond or even turn the marriage into a permanent one, because having a child was highly regarded.

Early theologians banned mut'a marriage in part because it empowered women; it gave them the right to choose a husband, the amount of bridewealth, and the duration of the tie. Non-Arabian theologians, instrumental in the development of the shari'a in the second century of the Islamic era, considered unacceptable and disturbing any practice that gave women these rights.

Temporary marriage was popular in the Qajar period. Anecdotal evidence suggests that many sons of well-to-do families in the nineteenth century began their sexual experience with a temporary wife. Qahraman Mirza mentions that his mother suggested to him that he marry as a sigheh the daughter of their gardener. The reason he does not elaborate on this experience is perhaps the low status of her family.[35] She continued to live in his parents' household, even after he married Galin Khanum, daughter of the court architect, whose background was similar to his own. Elite families contracted a sigheh marriage for their adolescent sons to try to prevent them from having sexual contact with servants or relatives within the household.[36] In some cases taking a temporary wife served the purpose of having children, because child mortality was high.[37] When Kamran Mirza, Nasir al-Din Shah's third son, lost his only child, a son, he took several temporary wives in the hope that one of them would produce a son. Most women who became temporary wives derived from a lower social background than their husbands and entered such marriages because they could acquire some wealth. The granddaughter of a servant in the Mustoufi household became a temporary wife of a wealthy notable and accumulated assets. Such wealth enabled her to marry as a permanent wife a man of higher status.[38] Permanent wives were not always threatened by temporary wives, perhaps because of their lower status. This notion is implied in the episode narrated earlier about Bibi Khanum, whose anger was aroused by the woman's duplicity and not by her becoming a temporary wife.

Marriage within the Dynasty

Qajar rulers had many more wives in their households than even the wealthiest men in the realm. Having a large harem in Irano-Islamic society was a sign of wealth and esteem rather than insatiable sexual appetite. Fath Ali Shah's many marriages were a means of enhancing his authority and his and the dynasty's legitimacy. The institution acted as a double-edged sword because these marriages produced a proliferation of princes, many of whom could challenge the heir apparent or the sitting ruler's claim to the throne.

Before coming to power, Qajar leaders followed tribal traditions in marriage, which was monogamous and conducted with a simple ceremony. Once they were firmly established, they adopted practices of former dynasties and held elaborate wedding celebrations to impart the aura of royalty to these events. They also used marriage to cement alliances and cultivate friends, a policy Agha Muhammad Khan elaborated. He tried to end the century-long hostility between the Qavanlu and Davallu branches of the Qajar tribe by having Baba Khan, his nephew and heir, marry a Davallu woman even though the treachery of this clan's leader had contributed to the death of Agha Muhammad Khan's father. He also advised Baba Khan to have his descendants marry women from the rival branch.[39]

Agha Muhammad Khan was assassinated in 1797 before he could consolidate his hold over his newly established kingdom; his nephew Baba Khan succeeded him as Fath Ali Shah. The new ruler faced many challenges, but he lacked his uncle's energy, bravery, and resolve. To neutralize the main external threat from the Russian empire, he eventually ceded some territory to it. To overcome internal threats to his legitimacy from members of his own tribe and from rival dynasties, he resorted to manipulation, co-optation, and appeasement whenever he could not handle opposition by force of arms. He was careful to maintain a balance of power within rival factions to ensure that no group acquired too much power that could displease another group or undermine his own authority. One of the policy instruments he used to weaken internal opposition was marriage.

In keeping with shari'a injunctions, three of Fath Ali Shah's permanent wives were daughters of important Qajar chiefs; the fourth permanent wife was the daughter of the most important Zand pretender. Fath Ali Shah tried to lessen the pain he and his uncle had inflicted on their defeated rivals by taking their daughters as temporary wives. The names of his many temporary wives reveal that they were daughters of Qajar tribal grandees, provincial strongmen, Zand and Afshar pretenders, provincial notables, and high officials of state, who had sided with him or his uncle during the civil war. To maintain order and minimize rivalry among the wives, Fath Ali Shah instituted a system of receiving his wives in the outer courtyard (*biruni*) after he ended the day's official duties. They would line up on the basis of their families' rank. The Qajar wives stood on one side, the non-Qajar ones on the other, headed by the Zand permanent wife. The mother of the crown prince,

Asiyeh Khanum, from the Davallu branch, stood at the head of the Qajar line. The ruler's cousin, Badran Khanum, also a permanent wife but childless, was so angered by having to stand behind a Davallu that she moved to a private residence outside the harem so as not to have to suffer that affront.[40]

Despite the many women filling his harem, Fath Ali Shah favored one wife over all others. Maryam Khanum, a woman he seems to have loved passionately, was a great beauty who had been married to Agha Muhammad Khan. Fath Ali Shah married her after his uncle's death even though the marriage created a feud between him and his brother who was equally besotted by the woman. Another early favorite was Nushafarin Khanum, daughter of a Zand rival his uncle had defeated.[41] The ruler also married temporary wives whom he respected for their honesty and efficiency. The most famous was Gulbadan Baji (later Khazin al-Douleh), his mother's slave. When Fath Ali Shah's mother, Mahd-i Ulya, died, his wives could not decide on a successor, and they requested that Gulbadan Baji be left in charge of running the household because she was familiar with the ways of her mistress.[42] By choosing her, they would not be perceived as favoring one wife over another. After a while, the ruler was so impressed by her performance that he married her as a sigheh. Even after marrying the shah and giving birth to two sons, she continued to manage efficiently the harem's affairs and finances. At Nouruz (beginning of the New Year) and other occasions, she chose gifts for the harem residents, princes, and notables including governors of provinces. She kept a detailed list of all expenditures and incoming and outgoing presents. Another wife, a female secretary, and several female scribes assisted her in her work. She was trusted by many within and outside the harem. Merchants sent her "thousands upon thousands" in merchandise without the slightest anxiety.[43]

Fath Ali Shah's soul mate was a temporary wife. Tavus Khanum (later Taj al-Saltaneh, crown of the state) came from a distinguished Shiraz family and was known for her erudition, intelligence, and love of learning. After marrying the ruler, she decided to resume her studies with a leading scholar of the day, Abd al-Wahhab Nishat I'timad al-Douleh, with whom she had studied before marriage. She was proficient in the art of calligraphy and was an accomplished poet. She rose rapidly in the shah's favor, and he built her an elaborate residence with its own inner and outer courtyards (andarun, biruni). Two ministers, one male and one female, and many pages, grooms, slaves, and servants staffed her residence. Her establishment was so large and her prestige so high that the entire harem visited her during Nouruz. The ruler's affection grew so strong that he offered to change her status to that of a permanent wife. She refused, saying the change might tamper with the auspicious moment of her aqd.[44]

Fath Ali Shah also used his children's marriages to improve ties with members of the Qajar tribe and notable families. He required that all his sons marry as their first wife a woman from the Davallu branch, and he paid for such weddings from his private purse. He applied the same rule to his daughters, who were also required to marry members of the dynasty. He fostered the marriages of his children and grandchildren to important personages of the realm in order to improve his standing with those families. The first time one of his daughters married the son of a non-Qajar grandee, many of his relatives took offense because they believed royal daughters should marry only Qajar men.[45]

First-rank princesses were able to maintain their independence and refuse to marry. Some retained their virginity after marriage. One of Fath Ali Shah's daughters, Fakhr Jahan Khanum (later Fakhr al-Douleh, meaning pride of the state, a title and name used often by the Qajars), married her cousin and lived with him for nine years, but she returned to her father's home still a virgin. She and her sister, Ziya al-Saltaneh, who did not marry until after her father's death, provided aid to him. The first was entrusted with running the harem treasury; the other served as his private scribe. Some of Nasir al-Din Shah's daughters, such as Fakhr al-Douleh and Taj al-Saltaneh, married men of their own choice.

At other times a princess was forced to marry a much older man or to divorce a husband if he fell from favor. Such was the fate that befell Malikzadeh (later Izzat al-Douleh), Nasir al-Din Shah's sister, who was given in marriage to Amir Nizam (later Amir Kabir) when he was in his fifties and she was only thirteen. Fortunately for her, she developed great love for her husband and had two daughters with him. After his fall from power, she insisted on accompanying him to exile in Kashan, and she was deeply grieved by his murder. She felt differently about the next husband whom she was forced to marry, despite her protests. He was the son of the new prime minister, Mirza Aqa Khan Nuri. When this prime minister lost favor with the ruler, she was free to divorce. Her next two marriages seem to have been more to her liking.[46]

Marrying one of the ruler's daughters or sisters opened the door to visits to the shah's andarun and brought prestige and advantage to families who won such a privilege. The men who became royal in-laws were occasionally great officers of state, such as Amir Nizam. Some were so wealthy that their

marriage ceremonies became legendary for their opulence, such as the wedding of Dustmuhammad Khan Mu'ayyir al-Mamalik and Ismat al-Douleh,
the daughter of Nasir al-Din Shah.[47] Wealthy families offered the king and
many of his close relatives gifts as a sign of gratitude for the honor bestowed
on them. Such marriages imposed other costs on the groom. He had to divorce all other wives before marrying an important princess. Such divorces
could undermine the reputation of an impeccable statesman. A newly appointed prime minister, Amin al-Douleh, arranged a marriage between his
son and Fakhr al-Douleh, daughter of Muzaffar al-Din Shah (r. 1896–1907)
and yet another woman holding the name. Many contemporaries who had
considered Amin al-Douleh an honorable man lowered their opinion of him
because his son was already married to the daughter of his father's best friend,
and the son had to divorce this wife to marry the shah's daughter.[48]

Fath Ali Shah died at the age of seventy in 1834. Although his marriage
policies consolidated his authority and averted some conflicts, the many
children these marriages produced contained the seeds of trouble for his
successors. One hundred of his three hundred children survived him. He had
decided to have Muhammad Mirza, son of the crown prince Abbas Mirza
(who had died a few months before his father), succeed him. Later, some older
princes refused to acknowledge the legitimacy of their nephew, who ascended
the throne as Muhammad Shah (r. 1834–48). This ruler's religiosity, poor
health, and short rule; the challenges he faced from his own family; and his
death at an early age may have all contributed to the small size of the family
he left behind—five sons and three daughters.[49]

Nasir al-Din Shah's marriages were motivated by a policy similar to that
of his predecessors, but he did not marry as many wives as his great-grand-
father, Fath Ali Shah. His permanent wives were prominent Qajar relatives,
but the need to marry daughters of important members of the dynasty and
notable families subsided during his rule. Although at the beginning of his
reign he was challenged by members of his family, the dynasty's legitimacy
became firmly established. During the second part of his rule, he took many
temporary wives.

Nasir al-Din Shah's favorites were temporary wives just as his great-
grandfather's had been. His early favorite was Jayran (later Furugh al-Saltaneh), daughter of a royal gardener. Her eyes captivated the shah, but she
was also intelligent and excelled in horse-riding and shooting. She accompanied the shah on his hunting trips, and when riding she would wrap her
face-cover (*ruband*) around her head in order to expose her face. He was so
enamored of her that he decided to change the rule of succession, which re-

quired the crown prince to be both of Qajar descent and the son of a permanent wife, so that her sons could succeed him. Although his immediate family was unhappy, the ruler was determined to have the sons of his favorite wife follow him. The divorce of a permanent wife turned Jayran's status to that of permanent one, but overcoming the other requirement was more difficult until the court historian devised an ingenious genealogy. He traced Jayran's descent to the Mongols, with whom the Qajars claimed some affinity.[50] To the relief of those who had opposed the idea, both heirs and their mother died well before Nasir al-Din Shah, who reverted to the established practice by appointing Muzaffar al-Din, son of his permanent Qajar wife, as crown prince. But he mourned Jayran's loss and wrote elegies expressing his love for her. This affection did not wane with the passage of time, and he was attracted to other women who reminded him of her. He was fatally shot near her grave by an assassin, and he was buried next to her in the shrine of Shah Abd al-Azim.[51]

After Jayran's death, Nasir al-Din Shah turned to Anis al-Douleh, who had begun service as Jayran's maid and who became his temporary wife. Some contemporaries were puzzled by his attachment to her. "She has no beauty, no charm, no [knowledge of] reading, no writing! Nothing!" said one.[52] The shah may have been drawn to her because of her loyalty to her late mistress, and gradually he began to love her for her intelligence, common sense, and honesty in criticizing his ways. Many foreign representatives viewed her as the queen, and she received their wives during official holidays such as Nouruz. She was the only wife allowed to sit with him during dinner and share his meals occasionally. She remained his favorite until the end. Her company must have given him comfort because he spent every night with her, even though other women might visit his bedroom beforehand. Her influence with the shah prompted courtiers to seek her aid and advice, as did many of the shah's children.[53]

Another wife Nasir al-Din Shah trusted implicitly was Amina Aqdas, a Kurdish peasant, who rose from being a maid to a temporary wife to a supervisor of the entire harem. Her relationship with the ruler seems to have been prompted by her devotion to him and the affection he grew to have for her nephew, Malijak (later Aziz al-Sultan, beloved of the king), who eventually became the shah's son-in-law. When she developed an eye disease, he sent her to Europe and was distressed by her death.[54]

The increase in the number of Nasir al-Din Shah's wives was not entirely his doing. The mystique of kingship was a magnet for many families who wanted him to marry one of their daughters, and the benefits that accrued

to humble families from being related to the ruler were great. Jayran's brothers, despite being illiterate peasants, became governors of small cities, and
Nasir al-Din Shah favored the nephew of Amina Aqdas more than his own
children. Elite parents may have disliked the ruler's growing preference for
young peasant girls and may not have wished to have a daughter join his
harem as a temporary wife, but the competition among many rural and urban families to attract the king's attention to their daughters was fierce. When
rural parents learned that Nasir al-Din Shah would be passing by their village, they would line up their daughters along the road in the hope that he
would take notice. Sometimes the shah chose one and had her brought to
the harem if she struck his fancy.[55] Various quarters of Tehran also competed to have one of their residents augment the number of royal wives.

Nasir al-Din Shah's desire to be surrounded by women increased with
age, and he would lose his heart to a newly acquired beauty, who would then
be elevated to the status of a temporary wife. Occasionally he became infat-
uated with one of his temporary wives, which made him an object of scorn
to courtiers and relatives and caused him pain and inconvenience. He developed an attraction for the sister of a new temporary wife, Fatemeh (also called
Bashi), daughter of a gardener. When Bashi learned of the shah's feelings for
her sister, she asked her to leave the andarun immediately. Bashi, to whom
the shah was also attached, refused to accept the gifts the king offered as
enticements to have the sister allowed back for visits. She would yell at any
courtier who dared intercede on the king's behalf, and her shouting matches with the ruler became a legend in the court and capital. The ruler appealed
to an older, respected wife to intervene, and she said, "I obeyed the shah's
command, and I went to see Bashi that afternoon. Whatever I brought up,
she responded like a learned *mujtahid* [religious scholar]. Her answers were
very convincing but I did not mention them to the shah." Bashi refused to
visit the shah in his bedroom until he granted permission to her sister to
marry someone else.[56]

Another advantage in being married to the ruler was that if the wife bore
a child, her future security would be most likely ensured. Since many major
princes were assigned to lucrative posts, such as governors of provinces and
cities around the kingdom, and princesses married prominent and wealthy
men, the mothers would join the households of sons or daughters after the
king's death. Even if wives had no children, they would receive stipends if they
chose not to marry after the ruler died.[57] Most were treated with respect by
the new ruler, in any case, and would be able to live within the royal house-

hold if they had no one else to join. Some former wives chose to move near Shi'i shrines, especially those in Najaf and Karbala.

At Nasir al-Din Shah's death, he left eighty-five wives behind but only twenty children. This number suggests that rumors about his impotence may have had some merit. Perhaps this condition explains his increasing need to prove his masculinity during the last year of his life, when he spent every Friday with newly chosen temporary wives (none of whom bore him children).

The wives and all female members of the royal household lived in the harem, a large one a sign of prestige and an indication of majesty. Agha Muhammad Khan, despite being castrated as a young boy, established a harem and married a few women. Fath Ali Shah emulated his uncle and created the kingdom's largest harem. During Nasir al-Din Shah's long reign, he expanded the harem's size. Not all the women who lived there were the ruler's permanent or temporary wives; some were slaves and maids, and others were daughters of the king or his unmarried close relatives and their attendants. Such a situation may account for the discrepancy in the number of wives attributed to Fath Ali Shah and Nasir al-Din Shah by many European visitors to Iran in the nineteenth century.[58]

Life within the harem was organized according to rules of seniority, except that the king's favorites had high status regardless of the length of their marriage. Important and favorite wives and unmarried daughters of the king lived within large establishments and received high salaries; lesser wives and their attendants resided in smaller apartments. The king's mother held the highest rank within the harem. After her death, the king's favorite wife usually filled the position. The older and more efficient wives performed supervisory functions there.

Some men—agents, eunuchs, guards, and servants—were also listed on the harem's payroll, but the majority of those serving the royal household were women. Favorite wives were often powerful, such as Jayran, Anis al-Douleh, and Amina Aqdas, who exerted enormous influence within and outside the harem walls. Although they were temporary wives, many statesmen, princes, princesses, and lesser wives paid them homage, tried to enlist their support for particular issues outside the harem, and appealed to them to intervene on their behalf with the ruler.

The impression of foreign visitors and contemporary observers is that many wives of rulers considered themselves fortunate compared to other women because those who joined the harem enjoyed opportunities.[59] If they

chose, wives and princesses could lead idle lives, which may have rendered
some of these women as objects to be pitied.[60] Some wives became rivalrous
about status or their husband's affection, but other women formed close and
rewarding bonds. We encounter women such as Tavus Khanum, who devoted
herself to intellectual and poetic pursuits. Many princesses used their privileged position in the same manner, exemplified by Ziya al-Saltaneh (Fath Ali
Shah's daughter) and Fakhr al-Douleh (Nasir al-Din Shah's daughter). The
latter is credited with leaving behind some literary works. Some wives pursued an interest in sports and went horseback riding in the royal estates near
the capital. Some women, including Nasir al-Din Shah's mother and an influential wife, took advantage of the anonymity offered them by the veil to
leave the harem in order to play pranks on shopkeepers or attend mosques.
During Nasir al-Din Shah's last years, Tehran was rife with rumors that some
younger wives bribed the harem eunuchs and visited their lovers regularly.

How did these rulers regard their large harems and many wives? Evidence
from Nasir al-Din Shah's period suggests that occasionally the rivalry of wives
undermined his peace of mind. His frustration is revealed by his nephew, who
recounts that on meeting a religious scholar who had several wives, the shah
asked how he managed. The mujtahid, renowned for his sense of humor, shot
back, "Tell me how you manage!" The shah laughed and said, "Very hard, with
great difficulty, and many headaches."[62] After Nasir al-Din Shah, the next
Qajar rulers began to limit the number of wives they took. The last Qajar
ruler, Ahmad Shah, had only one wife, which possibly reveals the spread of
European influence among the royal family and the ruling class.

Although Qajar rulers were surrounded by many wives, they often seemed
devoted to one particular woman. For example, Fath Ali Shah expressed deep
love for Tavus Khanum, and Nasir al-Din Shah's emotional needs were met
by Jayran (Anis al-Douleh). This situation is also true of many other men
who left records of their lives. Although contact with European society meant
more frequent mention of women in publications appearing toward the end
of the nineteenth century, private correspondence between husbands and
wives from the earlier part of the century reveals that high government offi-

cials and other elites relied on their wives for support and information. When Farrukh Khan Amin al-Douleh went to France to negotiate the Anglo-Iranian peace treaty in 1856–57, he relied on news from his wife about developments in Tehran.[63] Even more remarkable are the letters exchanged between Zahir al-Douleh and his wife Malikeh-yi Iran (Nasir al-Din Shah's daughter) during the critical years between the accession of Muhammad Ali Shah in 1907 and his abdication in 1909. Although their son, Zahir al-Mulk, was a revolutionary whose arrest was demanded by the ruler, it was her husband's security that worried her. The exchanges also reveal the respect that the husband held for his wife.[64]

The journals of Qahraman Mirza, Nasir al-Din Shah's nephew, shed light on the daily activities of an aristocratic couple. He revealed his affection and concern for Galin Khanum, his wife, because she suffered from chronic eye disease. He did not join his mother, sisters, and brother on a trip to Kerbala because she could not go along. Instead, he took Galin Khanum to Ask near Damavand for two weeks of relaxation. During evenings at home, she read poetry to him; he recorded some verses in his journal.[65] Even royal princes worried about offending their wives. Qahraman Mirza expressed concern about Galin Khanum's reaction when he returned home after spending a few days with his parents. Her response was so fierce that he wrote, "May God not let it happen again." Galin Khanum was not a cipher. Once, when Qahraman Mirza's father asked him to go to Alamut on family business and tried to change his plans for a trip to a saint's shrine with Galin Khanum, she insisted on going by herself. He recorded his fights with his wife on this occasion, and on her return she continued to scold him.[66] Also revealing the strong bond between husbands and wives is the love that Ihtisham al-Saltaneh, Fath Ali Shah's grandson, expresses for his wife. He states that when his father ordered him to divorce his wife in order to marry the crown prince's daughter, he felt compelled to disobey his father. "This was the only instance I disregarded his wish. I apologized to him because I was satisfied with my wife and loved her more than anyone."[67]

Conclusion

The institution of marriage showed great resilience during the Qajar period and continued to function as it had before because many people considered that it worked well. What the continuity in marriage practices suggests is that institutions in a society often change if they no longer serve their purpose.

Even by the end of the Qajar period, despite change in the political system and the introduction of a constitutional form of government, no demand to change the familiar way people chose partners had yet emerged. Because seclusion was still a fact of life, and men could not get to know women intimately before they proposed to them, the qualities that female relatives, with experience handed down through the generations, looked for in prospective brides remained unchanged.

The marriages of Fath Ali Shah and Nasir al-Din Shah, allegedly the two most lascivious Qajar rulers, show that many of their marriages were prompted by the need to enhance their legitimacy and authority. While both appreciated beauty in a woman and sometimes chose temporary wives merely for their appearance, each of them was steadfast in his relationship with one particular wife and put his trust in only one or two women as friends and confidantes.

NOTES

I thank Lois Beck and Shahla Haeri for reading the manuscript and offering invaluable comments.

1. George N. Curzon, *Persia and the Persian Question,* 2nd ed. (London: Frank Cass, 1966), 1:303, 333; *Encyclopaedia Britannica,* 11th ed., s.v. "Persia," 194.

2. Mahmud Katira'i, *Az khisht ta khisht* (Tehran: Danishgah-i Tehran, 1348/1979). His material covers a broad segment of Tehran's population and not merely wealthy families.

3. Shi'i Islam was proclaimed the state religion by the founder of the Safavid dynasty, Shah Isma'il (1501–24).

4. Abdullah Mustoufi, *Tarikh-i Qajar ya tarikh-i ijtima'i va idari-yi doureh-yi qajariyyeh,* 3 vols. (Tehran: Zavvar, n.d.), 1:100–101.

5. Qahraman Mirza Salur, *Ruznameh-yi khatirat-i ayn al-saltaneh,* 7 vols., ed. Iraj Afshar and Mas'ud Salur (Tehran: Asatir, 1374/1995), 1:430, 420, 441.

6. C. J. Wills, *The Land of the Lion and the Sun* (London: Ward, Lock, and Co., 1891), 314.

7. Ahmad Mirza Azud al-Douleh, *Tarikh-i azudi,* ed. Husain Kuhi-yi Kirmani (Tehran: Mutahhari, n.d.), 91; Dust'ali Mu'ayyir al-Mamalik, *Yaddashtha'i az zindigani-yi khususi-yi Nasir al-Din Shah* (Tehran: Ilmi, 1351/1972), 172.

8. Shireen Mahdavi, "The Structure and Function of the Household of a Qajar Merchant," *Iranian Studies* 32 (4) (1999): 559–60.

9. Nasir al-Din Shah ignored this practice when he appointed the children of his favorite wife Jayran as heirs; Mu'ayyir al-Mamalik, *Yaddashtha'i,* 15.

10. For discussion of laws regulating various types of Shi'i marriage, see Shahla Haeri, *Law of Desire: Temporary Marriage in Shi'i Iran* (Syracuse: Syracuse University Press, 1989), 30, 36–37.

11. Qahraman Mirza, *Ruznameh,* 1:339.

12. Mustoufi, *Tarikh-i Qajar*, 1:153.

13. Bibi Khanum Astarabadi, *Ma'ayib al-rijal dar pasukh-i ta'dib al-nisvan*, ed. Afsaneh Najmabadi (Chicago: Midland, 1992).

14. Katira'i, *Az khisht*, 101–7.

15. Qahraman Mirza, *Ruznameh*, 1:573, 576, 691, 871; Katira'i, *Az khisht*, 54–58.

16. Azud al-Douleh, *Tarikh-i azudi*, 10–11; Mu'ayyir al-Mamalik, *Yaddashtha'i*, 36.

17. Mustoufi, *Tarikh-i Qajar*, 1:210.

18. Ibid., 1:3, 40.

19. Ibid., 1:199, 216.

20. Ibid., 1:189.

21. Ibid., 2:420–21.

22. Bibi Khanum, *Ma'ayib*, 85.

23. Ibid., 90–93.

24. Katira'i, *Az khisht*, 90–112.

25. Ibid., 123–25.

26. Ibid., 133–50.

27. Qahraman Mirza, *Ruznameh*, 1:112–15, 529; Mustoufi, *Tarikh-i Qajar*, 2:79.

28. Katira'i, *Az khisht*, 186; Qahraman Mirza, *Ruznameh*, 1:884–85; 893.

29. Katira'i, *Az khisht*, 128–204; Qahraman Mirza, *Ruznameh*, 1:920–22.

30. Katira'i, *Az khisht*, 118.

31. Yakub Idvard Pulak, *Safarnameh-yi pulak, Iran va iranian*, trans. Kaykavus Jahandari (Tehran: Khwarazmi, 1368/1989), 145.

32. Docteur Feuvrier, *Trois ans a la cour de Perse* (Paris: F. Juven, n.d.), 183, 188.

33. Haeri, *Law of Desire*, 19.

34. Ibid., 49–73.

35. Qahraman Mirza, *Ruznameh*, 1:143, 819.

36. Ibid., 1:548–49.

37. Lady Sheil, *Glimpses of Life and Manners in Persia* (London: John Murray, 1856), 149.

38. Qahraman Mirza, *Ruznameh*, 1:830; Mustoufi, *Tarikh-i Qajar*, 1:157.

39. For pre-dynastic wedding ceremonies and use of marriage as state policy, see Azd al-Douleh, *Tarikh-i azudi*, 6, 44.

40. Ibid., 4.

41. Ibid., 5–6.

42. The practice of calling the king's mother Mahd-i Ulya (sublime cradle) was copied from the Safavids by Agha Muhammad Khan, who gave the title to Baba Khan's mother because his own mother was dead when he ascended the throne; Azd al-Douleh, *Tarikh-i azudi*, 91.

43. Ibid., 10–11.

44. Ibid., 6–7.

45. Ibid., 30–34.

46. Abbas Amanat, *Pivot of the Universe: Nasir al-Din Shah Qajar and the Iranian Monarchy, 1831–1896* (Berkeley: University of California Press, 1997), 107–8, 324.

47. Mu'ayyir al-Mamalik, *Yaddashtha'i*, 7–8.

48. Mihdiquli Khan Hidayat, *Khatirat va khatarat* (Tehran: Zavvar, 1344/1965), 1:143.

49. Jahangir Mirza, *Tarikh-i nou*, ed. Abbas Iqbal (Tehran: Ilmi, 1327/1947), 312–15.

50. Amanat, *Pivot of the Universe*, 324.

51. Mu'ayyir al-Mamalik, *Yaddashtha'i*, 46–51.

52. Qahraman Mirza, *Ruznameh*, 1:678.

53. *Encyclopaedia Iranica*, s.v. "Anis al-Dowla," 74–76.

54. *Encyclopaedia Iranica*, s.v. "Amina Aqdas," 954–55.

55. Qahraman Mirza, *Ruznameh*, 1:593, 823.

56. Ibid., 1: 881–82. According to Islamic law, a man could not marry two sisters at the same time.

57. Azd al-Douleh, *Tarikh-i azudi*, 84–89.

58. For example, see Curzon, *Persia*, 1:410–11.

59. See Taj al-Saltaneh, *Growing Anguish*, 130–32; Mu'ayyir al-Mamalik, *Yaddashtha'i*, 38–43, 113. With firsthand knowledge of life within the harem, these authors present a positive, lively picture of life there.

60. Pulak, *Safarnameh*, 164.

61. Azd al-Douleh, *Tarikh-i azudi*, 9.

62. Qahraman Mirza, *Ruznameh*, 1:810.

63. The growing interest in issues relating to gender may result in the publication of more private letters by women. For example, see Farrukh Khan Amin al-Douleh, *Majmu'eh-yi asnad-i Farrukh Khan Amin al-Douleh* (Tehran: Tahqiqat-i Irani, 1358/1979), 3:354–55, 361.

64. Iraj Afshar, ed., *Khatirat va asnad-i Zahir al-Douleh* (Tehran: Sihami-yi kitab-ha-yi jibi, 1351/1972), 357–60, 367–79.

65. Qahraman Mirza, *Ruznameh*, 1: passim.

66. Ibid., 599–601.

67. Sayyid Muhammad Mihdi Musavi, ed., *Khatirat-i Ihtisham al-Saltaneh*, 2nd ed. (Tehran: Zavvar, 1367/1988), 1:41–43.

2 Reflections in the Mirror—How Each Saw the Other: Women in the Nineteenth Century

SHIREEN MAHDAVI

HISTORY IS NOT BUILT of events and descriptions of institutions but of varying perceptions of them. In analyzing these perceptions, an element of the concept that Giambattista Vico calls *fantasia* or imagination has to be exercised.[1] Once this concept is applied to historical writing, the certainties of events and functioning of institutions described dissolve into multiple possibilities of alternative narrations as seen through different eyes and differing prejudices. This notion applies to the position of women in the nineteenth century in general and to that of Middle Eastern women in particular. A vast gap separated the reality of women's situation in the East and the West and the preconceived notions that each held about the other. Western women were not totally emancipated nor Eastern women totally enslaved. Gray areas fell between the two perceptions, and women's position in both regions differed between urban and rural areas and among socioeconomic classes. In this chapter I analyze how each saw the other, what their channels of communication were, who their intermediaries were, and how their perceptions of each other differed from reality.

People in the West had been fascinated by and had contact with the Middle East long before Muslims, including Iranians, took any interest in events in the West. Contact was limited to some adventurous travelers and a few ambassadors whose view of life and ideas left little impact.[2]

The primary impact of the West on the world of Islam, including the Ottoman empire and Iran, was as a result of military defeats. These defeats, which in the Ottoman empire happened earlier and in Iran later, were the cause of a new attitude on the part of Muslims toward the West. Previously,

Muslims living in a relative state of isolation kept aloof and hence were out of touch with the scientific revolution and the resulting growth of economic and military power. Military defeats made them acknowledge the West's military superiority and attempt to discover the key to its secret. By seeking military knowledge, engaging Western military advisors, and sending students to be educated in the West, Muslims became familiar with the ideas of the French revolution.

Following the French revolution in the late eighteenth century, Europe in the nineteenth century was the setting for the industrial revolution, rise of nationalism, and beginning of colonialism, all of which affected Iran directly or indirectly. Among the egalitarian ideas generated by the French revolution was the equality of women. In 1793 the Marquis de Condorcet proposed conferring political rights on women. In England in 1792, Mary Wollstonecraft wrote *A Vindication of the Rights of Women*.[3] After the publication in 1869 of John Stuart Mill's essay "The Subjection of Women," ideas about women's equality took the form of a political movement.[4] Ideas of and hopes for political and legal equality permeated the minds of many Western women throughout the nineteenth and into the twentieth century. At the same time, merchants and other people from the East started traveling to the West. They returned with impressions of Western ways including the apparent freedom of Western women. These travelers and the foreign women who were in Iran either in their own right or as wives became the channel through whom Iranian women became acquainted with Western women and their ways.

Foreign women were also employed in the Qajar court as tutors and translators as early as the reign of Fath Ali Shah Qajar (r. 1797–1834), and Iranian women witnessed Western ways and heard about Western women through them. One of the first was Madame de la Marininere, a French woman who came to Iran in 1810 and was a French tutor to the children of Abbas Mirza, the crown prince (*vali ahd*) in Tabriz.[5] In the court of Muhammad Shah Qajar (r. 1834–48), another French woman was Madame Abbas or Gulsaz (flower maker), the second name referring to her profession of flower-making. Although she had come to Iran as Hajj Abbas Shirazi's wife and a specialist in artificial flower-making, her influence extended far beyond that. She not only tutored the future king Nasir al-Din Shah but was a close confidante of Mahd Ulya (queen mother), and when Nasir al-Din Shah assumed the throne he appointed her as the official interpreter of the *andarun* (women's quarter).[6] (Royal palaces and houses of people of wealth were divided into the outer section [*biruni*] for men and male servants and the inner section [andarun] for women, children, and maids. The same division was created by the use of a curtain among less affluent people.)

The first group of students from Iran was sent to the West in 1811, and successive groups followed them. Aside from bringing back Western skills, some students also returned with Western wives. One of the first students, Muhammad Ali Chakhmaq Saz, married an English girl, Mary Dudley, daughter of his landlady in England, and brought her to Tabriz where she was apparently an habitué of the andarun of Abbas Mirza and introduced Western manners such as eating with cutlery to members of the andarun and to the local inhabitants. Muhammad Ali is the first known Iranian to have married a European woman.[7] Another was Mirza Riza, who after finishing his medical studies in Paris in 1861 returned with a French wife. Later he became the private physician of Prince Zill al-Sultan. Both he and his wife were the prince's French tutors.[8]

In seeking military and scientific knowledge, the first secular institution of higher learning in Iran, the Dar al-Funun, was established in Tehran in 1851 by the reformist prime minister Amir Kabir. That institution employed some European teachers, some of whom came to live in Tehran with their foreign wives and families.[9] Two other students who returned from Europe, Hidayat al-Allah Khan and Hajji Muhammad Khan, married the daughters of Constant, the painting teacher at Dar al-Funun.[10]

Wives of members of the diplomatic community were also among the early group of foreign women to live in Iran and have contact with members of the royal harem and the andarun of prominent people. For instance, Munir al-Saltana, one of Nasir al-Din Shah's wives, annually gave a party on the birthday of Fatima, the Prophet Muhammad's daughter, to which wives of the diplomatic corps were invited. Further, grandees such as Amin al-Dawla and Amin al-Sultan held balls, mixed dinners, and lunches at their houses where guests danced and wives of diplomats socialized with men. News of these events and the participants' behavior must have permeated through servants to the andarun's members.[11]

Another group of Western women who came to Iran consisted of missionaries as teachers or medical assistants in their own right or as spouses. American and British missionaries reached an agreement among themselves to divide the country in two spheres of interest: Americans in the north and British in the south. Although they did not convert many people to Christianity, their influence on Iranian women was far-reaching through the schools they established. In 1835 Americans established an elementary four-grade school in Urumia for Armenian girls and boys.[12] Eventually they established schools in other towns including one in Tehran to which girls were admitted in 1875 with Nasir al-Din Shah's permission. The French sisters of Saint Vincent de Paul also established a school for girls, which some Muslim girls attended on the condition that the sisters refrain from interfering with religious beliefs.[13] Some female doctors were among American missionaries.[14] Finally, a small group of female travelers, alone or with their spouses, also came.

Although Iranian women did not travel to the West in the nineteenth century, they were able to see some European women shopping in the bazaar, visiting andaruns, and riding sidesaddle through the countryside wearing habits and hats. The questions to consider are what they thought of each other and whether or not they held any preconceived notions.

The nineteenth century was the height of Europe's fascination with the Orient. By that time many men had written travel accounts describing women's veiling, seclusion, and activities inside the harem (although none had ever visited one).[15] The prevalent preconceived notion of Muslim women was of erotic exotic beings languishing within an enclosure where sexuality was rampant. Writers gave no consideration to the fact that only a few such establishments existed exclusively for the wealthy or that women within them could be preoccupied by anything but sex. Male travelers expressed two attitudes toward women's veiling and seclusion: fascination and repulsion. Sir John Malcolm who went to Iran at the beginning of the century describes both attitudes well: "In Persia the lower classes deem females important in proportion as they are useful in domestic life; the higher consider them as born for their sensual gratification. Women have, in fact, no assigned place, but are what their husbands, or rather lords, may choose to make them."[16]

Lady Sheil, who came to Iran in the mid-nineteenth century accompanying her husband the British minister, left one of the earliest accounts of a European woman's impressions. She appears to have been an intelligent woman who wished to give an objective account of Iranian women's lives, yet two factors intervene to prevent her from doing so. She brought preconceived notions with her from travelers' accounts, and she used her own culture as a superior standard by which to judge what she saw. As a result we get contradictory statements: "A Persian woman of the upper class leads a life of idleness and luxury, though rather monotonous according to our ideas of existence."[17] And then, "I found the few Persian women I was acquainted with in general lively and clever; they are restless and intriguing and may be said to manage their husband's and son's affairs. Persian men are made to yield to their wishes by force of incessant talking and teasing."[18] She shows

A Tipsy Lady. Signed by Mirza Baba. Possibly Tehran, dated A.H. 1215/ A.D. 1800–1801. Oil and metal leaf on canvas; 57½ × 37 inches (146 × 94 cm). Collection of Mrs. Eskandar Aryeh.

that her criterion for judging Iranian women is a belief in the superiority of Western women in remarks such as, "I do not think a Persian woman ever feels the same affection for her husband as some Europeans do." Or, "Persian women seem to have no idea of a calm, tranquil life. Novelty, or whatever causes excitement, is what they seek. . . . They have not strong religious or moral principles."[19] Her wish to be objective emerges in many instances. She distinguishes between the lifestyle of urban and rural women by saying, "The lot of women among the tribes, and among the peasantry, is not, from all I hear, an unhappy one. Their interests are identified with their husbands; divorce is rare; and the number of wives does not often exceed one."[20] She concedes that women in the andarun have preoccupations beyond eating sweetmeats and applying cosmetics: "Women of higher classes frequently acquire a knowledge of reading and writing, and of the choice poetical works in their native language, as well as the art of reading, though perhaps of not understanding, the Koran."[21] She shows a lack of bias in seeing that veiling may have some advantages as a form of a convenience. "All classes enjoy an abundance of liberty more so, I think, than among us. The complete envelopment of the face and person disguises them effectually from the nearest relatives, and destroying when convenient, all distinction of rank, gives unrestrained freedom."[22]

Despite the preconceived notions with which Lady Sheil arrived in Iran, her account is the most impartial and observant of the female travelers. The

Woman with a Veil.
Attributed to Muham-
mad. Iran, circa 1845.
Oil on canvas; 58 × 32½
inches (145 × 81 cm).
Hashem Khosrovani
Qajar Collection.

same cannot be said of Carla Serena, who apparently traveled to escape the boredom in her own life. Her account depicts the first attitude of travelers, that of fascination with a fairy-tale existence of exotic beings. She is invited to spend the day at the andarun of the shah's daughter. Passing through the biruni (men's quarters) and entering the andarun she describes the scene awaiting her:

> I was astounded and amazed by the magical scene which I beheld. We have all in our own theaters been witness to the group of dancing elves and fairies attired in glittering costumes. In these scenes which are very artistically arranged the director has to devise the lighting in such a manner so as to be able to depict the vivid colors of the Orient. Upon entering the andarun from the biruni [there was] a picture so delectable, so indescribable, under the radiant rays of the sun in the golden sky, of the princess surrounded by one hundred women which dazzled and amazed me. After leaving total loneliness [in the biruni] suddenly I found myself in a brilliant environment glowing with life. I had no doubt that up to that moment a plain curtain of green [that between the biruni and the andarun] had separated me from an extremely happy environment. This scene reminded me of Calypso [a nymph in Greek mythology] in the midst of water and wood fairies. The group of women who surrounded the princess were just as fascinating and magical.[23]

In giving these descriptions, Serena does not seem to take into account the fact that she is not witnessing an everyday occurrence, that the event was organized as a form of entertainment for her, and that normal daily life could be quite different.

A Frenchwoman, Jane Dieulafoy visited Iran in 1881 accompanying her husband who was an archeologist. She dressed as a man and collaborated with him in photography. She left an astute and observant account of her visit. During her time in Iran, she visited many andaruns and came into contact with women from different walks of life, but her accounts of their lives are absolutely neutral. She is critical of the government, administration, rampant corruption, and Islam but never passes judgment on the condition or status of Iranian women. Such a stance is remarkable because Dieulafoy was a feminist par excellence. In her own country, she agitated for women's rights, yet as far as Iranian women are concerned she remains only an observer.[24]

The history of women in general and of Iranian women in particular is that of the inarticulate. It is difficult to explore the world of women who left few direct accounts of their lives, thoughts, and feelings. It is here that the element of fantasia has to be exercised in how Iranian women saw the foreign women with whom they came into direct contact. Two Iranian women from different backgrounds who met two European women from equally dissimilar backgrounds could well have written the following letters based on accounts of their meetings. (These are imaginary letters composed by the author but based upon actual events.)

A Qajar princess who was present at the meeting of Lady Sheil with Mahd Ulya, mother of Nasir al-Din Shah, might well have written the following letter to her sister in Shiraz:[25]

> A new British minister has come to Tehran. His wife was not able to pay her respects to Mahd Ulya due to the months of mourning [a feature of Shi'i Islam], but Mahd Ulya finally received the minister's wife last week, and madame was there to interpret. I am writing because I thought you would like to hear an account of her looks and the stories she recounted. Her clothes were most interesting and appeared uncomfortable. Her dress had an open neckline, the bodice went down to an abnormally narrow waist, the skirt was in the shape of a bell, and the whole thing was trimmed in much lace. She was wearing a poke bonnet on her head, and her hands were covered with gloves. Later I discovered that they wear something underneath like a cage [corset] with bones in it to make their waists narrow. In reality they are prisoners in their costumes. I asked her how she could sleep at night in that attire, and she told me about another strange custom. Imagine, they take off all their clothes before they go to bed at night and put on a long white dress called a night dress. In fact from what she told me they have different costumes for different occasions and different times: a dress for walking, another for riding, a dress for morning, another for evening, and a court dress. When Mahd Ulya asked the minister's wife to tell her about the English queen and her court, the woman responded that the queen was a happy person with her fine husband and sons and the amount of power she has. Not only are their clothes and behavior different from ours but so are their court ceremonies. Apparently their a'yan [nobles] and ashraf [notables] are not automatically accepted in "society" until they are presented to the queen in a ceremony called "the drawing room." She holds many of these every year in the throne room at Buckingham Palace. One of the many extraordinary aspects of it is the timing which is at three o'clock in the afternoon when we would be resting rather than receiving people. Both men and women have to wear special court costumes. The women's court dress consists of a petticoat, bodice, and train four zars [zar: approximately a meter] long! Their headdress has to have exactly three feathers and a veil of white tulle. Their gloves, shoes, and fans have to be white, and they must carry bouquets of flowers. They talk of the freedom people have in Europe, yet it seems to me that they lack any because

so many rules and regulations exist for eating, drinking, dressing, sleeping, and even just existing. I do not have time to tell you of the order of precedence and the number of positions held by people at court, but all that is equally complex. Anyhow, after everyone has arrived and is waiting, the queen comes accompanied by members of the royal family and sits on the throne. Then someone called "lord chamberlain" calls out the names of people to be presented, and they go toward the throne and bow; some are allowed to kiss the queen's hand and others are not, and after that they become a member of "society." It is lucky for us that we do not need any of this rigmarole because we already know who everyone is, and if we do not know them it means we do not need to.[26]

After meeting Jane Dieulafoy, the wife of Kashan's governor might have written the following account to her sister in Tehran:

The other day an interesting and unusual thing happened which I thought you would like to hear. We were coming back to town from the village, and in passing through the bazaar I heard a commotion and noticed the footmen pushing someone aside. When I arrived home I discovered that the cause of the commotion in the bazaar was a foreign woman dressed as a man who takes photographs. You can imagine how impatient I was not only to meet such a creature but also to have my photograph taken, but as you can also guess my husband would not agree. So secretly I sent my maid to this foreign woman with a message first apologizing for the footmen's rudeness and then asking her to meet me at the house of the *imam jum'a* [Friday prayer leader] whose wife as you know is my close friend. She agreed to come. When I saw her I was astounded by the way she looked. She had cut off her yellow hair completely, wore no makeup, and donned masculine clothes, trousers, and jacket. These foreigners are so peculiar. She told us that she was the court photographer and that she had to work for a living. We are so lucky that our husbands do not make us work. The wife of the imam jum'a who knows nothing about Europe was even more astonished when I explained to her that women over there are not as lucky as we are, that some are secretaries and teachers, that the daughter of the Russian shah is a general, and that a female shah reigns in one of their countries. The imam jum'a's wife wanted to know if the female shah had many husbands but the woman photographer assured us that she did not. Still, we must be grateful for our lot because it is so much better than theirs. And now to family news . . .[27]

Despite the governor's wife stating she was lucky, there is no doubt that Iranian women were veiled, secluded, and in general excluded from decision making, public and private.[28] Exceptions did occur in the limitations of wom-

Ladies around a Samovar. Isma'il Jalayir. Tehran, third quarter of the nineteenth century. Oil on canvas; 56½ × 78½ inches (143.8 × 195 cm). Victoria and Albert Museum, London.

en's power because those who wished to do so could influence their husbands from behind the scenes. A powerful woman behind the scenes of Qajar Iran was Anis al-Dawla, Nasir al-Din Shah's favorite wife. She was able to organize opposition to governmental policies with which she disagreed and to individuals whom she disliked.[29] She dared to express her opinions to the shah frankly. I'timad al-Saltana relates that on one occasion when someone unsuitable was petitioning to be given the post of "master of the horse," which was for sale like all other positions in Qajar Iran, the shah related the story with amusement to Anis al-Dawla, who retorted, "It is not surprising that he wants to become master of the horse; with your love of money you will give anything to anyone. You would even give me away if they paid you enough for it."[30] On another occasion when the shah was considering replacing his brother Rukn al-Dawla as governor of Fars, she wrote a secret letter to the shah saying, "I have just heard that you have once again changed the governorship of Shiraz. By God it is astounding. Having sustained all that loss [in purchasing that post], Rukn al-Dawla has been gone for only seven months. If it is *pishkish* [tribute] you desire, get it from the prince himself and let him stay. Otherwise in this way the wretched people get ruined and drained. The governor does not provide it [the money] out of his own pockets. It is unjust. In every way they [the people] are depleted."[31]

Another example of a capable woman active both privately and publicly is Furugh al-Dawla, Malika-yi Iran, daughter of Nasir al-Din Shah. She was married to Ali Khan Davalu Zahir al-Dawla, himself a Qajar prince. She belonged to a darvish order, and both she and her husband were patriots and supporters of the newly won constitutional system.[32] Her story is worth describing in some detail. Her nephew, the reigning monarch Muhammad Ali Shah (r. 1907–9), opposed the constitutional movement and was organizing a counter-revolution to reinstall absolute monarchy. He ordered the bombardment of the *majlis* (parliament) building in 1908 and the destruction of Malika-yi Iran's house. Her letters to her husband, who at this point was governor of Gilan province along the Caspian sea, contain detailed accounts of these destructions, the arrest and imprisonment of constitutionalist sympathizers, and other events in the capital on the eve of the arrival of the constitutionalist forces, who finally succeeded in defeating and deposing the shah. Her letters written in impeccable prose are valuable historical chronicles of the momentous events she witnessed. On a personal level, her description of the Cossack attack on her house, in the absence of her husband, and the incredible feats of bravery through which she rescued her children and the women of the household is a testament to her courage. The letters throw a special light on the cowardice of members of the royal family and bear witness to the political acumen and patriotism of Malika-yi Iran.[33] In a letter to her husband, who was by then governor of Kirmanshah province, she describes Muhammad Ali Shah's flight with family members to the Russian embassy and the flight of others to the Ottoman embassy. Of herself she says:

> Yesterday morning, after the shah went to the embassy, Azud al-Dawla, the shah's master of the horse, came here to the door of the andarun to see how I was. He sent a message saying that since his excellency is not here and you do not have a man in the house, I am at your command; but I think it would be advisable for you to go either to the Russian embassy or to Kamraniyya [a royal summer palace outside Tehran]. How can you risk sitting here so fearlessly? I sent a message back thanking him and saying that I am neither going to the embassy nor to Kamraniyya nor do I fear anyone. He then said that he would go and bring an Ottoman flag and raise it atop Sahibqaraniyya [another royal summer palace outside Tehran, where they were then in residence]. I told him it was not necessary. He persisted but I would not accept. . . . After his departure I called the deputy of Sahibqaraniyya and told him

to go to the storage room and bring the large Lion-and-Sun [national] flag of Iran and hoist it up on the pole above the big hall. What pleasure it gave me when the wind blew at our own flag and waved it in the breeze above my room![34]

This act was particularly courageous in the midst of the prevailing anarchy and when the terrifying experience of Malika-yi Iran is remembered after her house was plundered and destroyed.

Another woman who in the absence of her husband not only ran the household and took care of family finances but also kept a watchful eye on her husband's political career is Gulrukh Khanum, wife of Farukh Khan Amin al-Dawla, close advisor to Nasir al-Din Shah and a diplomat.[35] In 1858–59 when he was ambassador in Istanbul, his wife became aware that the prime minister, Mirza Aqa Khan Nuri, who feared Farukh Khan's influence with the shah and thought he had ambitions to replace him as prime minister, was not only keeping him out of Iran purposely but was also intriguing against him with the shah. After giving news of various family members, she says,

> But we are out of our minds concerning you due to reports we hear from people. Each of the women who comes to the house speaks of the prime minister's enmity with you. Reliable sources say that the prime minister will never consent to the return of Farukh Khan from Istanbul and will daily find something for him to do there. This is the rumor circulating among everyone and must therefore be true that the prime minister will not let you return from Istanbul. . . . Do not wait for horses and servants to be sent . . . if you wait for them and the prime minister's permission, it will be a great mistake. Travel by post. You are in the shah's good graces. He will not mind you traveling by post and will not let the prime minister finish you off. . . . You must come. All that I have written is the truth. There is no mistake. Under no condition prolong your stay in Istanbul. Come. Come.[36]

These letters reveal women who are a far cry from the passive, lazy women who, as seen through Western eyes, were illiterate, unintelligent, and uninvolved in their husbands' affairs. Furthermore, literacy was not limited to royal women such as Malika-yi Iran or upper-class women such as Gulrukh Khanum. The ulama and merchants who were not members of the aristocracy sent their daughters to girls' *maktab*s (elementary schools).[37] An example of this class is the wife of Mirza Riza Kirmani, the assassin of Nasir al-Din Shah.[38] She wrote a petition, asking for financial aid, to Hajj Muhammad Hassan Amin al-Zarb in 1890–91: "I am the wife of Mirza Riza Kirmani who is in prison in Qazvin. I have a son who is like an orphan without his father. I wish for him to join the ranks of the followers of the messenger of God [the Prophet Muhammad] and to circumcise him. I have no money. Be kind enough as to make a donation."[39] This woman's sister, Mirza Baji, was not only literate but was also secretary to one of Nasir al-Din Shah's wives, Amin Aqdas, and conducted correspondence on her behalf with notables.[40]

Aside from these individual women, of whom far too many examples exist for the scope of this chapter, many examples are available of women during the struggle for the attainment and preservation of the constitution who demonstrated in public in support of the constitutionalists.[41] But these were individual voices and scattered incidents dependent and conditional upon enlightened men in the family. In general, from the point of view of most men, the "ideal type" of woman under the Qajars was a submissive being. This type is well described in an anonymous treatise of advice for women, *Dar bayan-i ta'dib al-nisvan* (Statement concerning the proper upbringing of women), written in 1891. According to this work, the family is an important unit in which the father is the all-powerful patriarch and the wife and children are obedient servants. The rules of marriage imply the wife's total obedience and servitude. The author admonishes women: "The satisfaction of the husband is the satisfaction of God, and the wrath of the husband the wrath of God. The Tuba tree [in paradise] is the reward of the woman with whom her husband is satisfied." The wisest act, according to this treatise, is for women to obey their husbands and after that to spin cloth. "A woman who provokes her husband to anger . . . on the Day of Judgment her tongue will be pulled out from the back of her head, [she will be] beaten by chains of fire, and fire will be in her mouth." The reward of the woman who serves her husband well is in paradise.[42]

This attitude is challenged by Bibi Khanum, an educated woman from a traditional nonwealthy background. In a treatise, *Ma'ayib al-rijal* (Shortcomings of men), not only does she respond to the above author point by point by exposing the defects of Iranian men but she also expounds her views on women in the West:

> What is even stranger is that this ignoramus considers himself educated according to Western tradition and sees himself as civilized and a follower of European teachers. It is apparent that he is not even "semi-vilized." . . . All inhabitants of Europe consider women as flowers. . . . They [the men] are at their [women's] service. . . . The respect in which women are held is greater than that of men. . . . It is extraordinary that the writer of *Ta'dib al-nisvan*

considers himself and men in general to be gods and women to be slaves and servants. . . . Does he not know that in the West they look after women like "bouquets of flowers"? According to geography, history, and travelers' accounts, in the West all aristocratic educated women are learned in many subjects, sit at the table with unfamiliar men, and when dancing hold hands and dance together. But the customs of the Muslim religion are different. The women of Iran are all occupied with housekeeping and housework, especially peasant women. . . . Yes, we women are deprived of work, business, and learning.[43]

Bibi Khanum's husband, Musa Khan Mir Panj, was a *ghulam* (mounted messenger) at the British embassy in Tehran, so some of her information concerning European women may have come from his accounts of life there. She did not have a happy marriage, about which she says, "My beloved companion became a snake, my home a cave, and my days dark as nights." She later founded an elementary school for girls in 1906, which became the subject of much protest by the ulama.[44]

Another woman from an entirely different background who was obsessed by the West was Taj al-Saltana, daughter of Nasir al-Din Shah. She was born in 1883 and brought up in the royal harem. She had a private tutor, learned French, was instructed in the ideas of the Naturalists, and read European novels.[45] She started rejecting Iranian customs and ideas while she adopted European ones. Subsequently she wore European clothes and went bareheaded when women wore veils according to religious injunctions. She was so influenced by her Western education that she abandoned Muslim prayers and drank wine. She became consumed with the thought of a trip to Europe. In her memoirs she expresses herself strongly: "I wanted to go to Europe madly. This desire gained such strength that it caused me to divorce my husband [who presumably would not allow her to travel]."[46] She does not hide her love for another man whose "eyes full of love and affection went through me like a flame of fire. I never feared looking at this youth. A strike of lightning and a storm enveloped the whole of my being."[47]

In adopting "naturalistic" philosophy and abandoning traditional religious views, Taj al-Saltana began questioning the political and social status quo. Her primary concern was the position of Iranian women. "I am sad and depressed that members of my sex, the women of Iran, are not aware of their rights and are not fulfilling their duties as human beings. In complete futility and void of purpose, they sit in the corners of their houses and spend all the hours of their life acquiring bad habits."[48] She writes poignantly in her

Portrait of Princess Taj al-Saltana, 1884–1936. Artist unknown. Tehran, circa 1910. Oil on canvas; 35 × 27 inches (88.9 × 68.6 cm). Collection of Mohammad and Najmieh Batmanglij.

memoirs about her fate and that of Iranian women compared to Western women's. "Women in Iran have been separated from the human race, placed in an enclosure with animals and beasts. From morning to night they lead a wretched, hopeless existence in prison cells. This group either watches from afar or reads in newspapers how European women are defending their rights and fighting for them. They have been demanding the right to vote, to enter parliament, and to have a voice in political affairs, and they are succeeding. In America they have obtained all their rights and are diligently working. The same is true of London and Paris."[49] Taj al-Saltana wished she could travel to Europe and address her counterparts in the following words: "While you, in the midst of good fortune, are honorably defending your rights and are victorious in your objectives, throw a glance at the corners of Iran and observe . . . [women] in chains of bondage." Then she exclaims, "Are these women too? Are those women too?" (meaning, if they are women, how can we be women too?).[50] Her views on women's position reflect her notions on social and political problems while expressing her reformist ideas. She indicated that if women were able to enter the political arena, not only would they be more aware of people's needs and therefore rule better but also they would be less corruptible than men.[51]

Although written a century ago, Taj al-Saltana's views echo those of today's feminists regarding women's qualifications for political life.[52] Her account of the condition of Iranian women is corroborated by descriptions of a contemporary English female missionary. Taj al-Saltana's voice finds an echo in this woman's words: "Ought not the cries of distress and agony from the poor women of Persia so to arouse us, their sisters in England, that we shall determine to do all that lies in our power to lighten their burden and to bring some rays of light into the dark lives of our Eastern sisters?"[53] But the women of England were dealing with their own problems and were not able to go to anyone else's aid.

The contrast between women in Iran and in Europe in the mid-nineteenth century is provided by a brief comparison of the nature of the rebellion of two contemporaries, Tahira Qurat al-Ayn (1817–52) and George Sand (1804–76).[54]

Tahira was born to a distinguished family of Shi'i ulama. Through her upbringing in this family, she was learned in Persian and Arabic literature, jurisprudence, theology, and Qur'anic interpretation. Her education and knowledge were most unusual among women of her time in Iran. She defied her father and uncle (who was also her father-in-law) in converting to Babism, considered a heresy of Islam, and became a fearless champion of that faith. She appeared in public places, unveiled, proselytizing. She died a martyr to her cause at the age of thirty-five, executed in the general massacre of Babis in 1852. She left behind some scattered writings and a substantial body of poetry.[55]

Despite the difference in background between the two women, some similarities are found. They were feminists and writers who left their husbands and defied conventional modes of dressing. But Tahira left her husband because of religious differences, while Sand left hers to have tumultuous affairs. Tahira stopped wearing the veil, whereas Sand wore masculine attire and smoked cigars in public. Sand espoused free love and humanitarian reforms in her writings, while Tahira's poetry consists mainly of spiritual invocations and mystic poetry. Sand already possessed those advantages that Tahira still lacked, so Tahira's defiance had to take a different form.

Women were indeed clamoring for their rights in Europe, but their position was neither the romantic one depicted by Bibi Khanum nor the powerful one portrayed by Taj al-Saltana, and they did not obtain full rights until well into the next century. In the nineteenth century, women in England and France lacked legal rights. Under English common law and the new Napoleonic code, married women were virtual nonentities. According to the common law, a married woman could not legally own property, not even if she inherited or earned it herself. All her worldly goods belonged to her husband. She could not sue anyone or be sued in a court of law. The education, upbringing, and residence of children was the sole prerogative of the father. In France the situation was only slightly better because certain kinds of property were sometimes protected under marriage contracts (as was also the case in England but to a lesser degree). Under the Napoleonic code, a wife had to obey her husband in return for his protection and had to live wherever he wished. She was not permitted to enter into any commercial or legal transaction without his permission. As in England, the husband had full control of the children, and even widows who wanted to remarry had to obtain permission from the dead husband's relatives as far as child custody was concerned. Female-initiated divorce was virtually nonexistent in both countries; in England men could divorce their wives on the grounds of adultery, but the reverse was not possible. From the mid-nineteenth century onward, various changes beneficial to women took place in family law although their pace and substance varied from one country to another. By the end of the century, women could control property and inherit from their husbands and have custody of children. In England women obtained the right to vote in 1919. Divorce legislation was slower to follow, and it was not until 1923 that the same grounds for divorce for both sexes were granted. In France radical revisions to the Napoleonic code took place as late as 1930, and female suffrage was not obtained until 1944.[56]

The reality for Iranian and Western women in the nineteenth century was that both were oppressed but to varying degrees and in different forms. If Western women could not own property, Muslim women could and had control of it. If Iranian women were secluded, so were Victorian women. The ascendant bourgeois ideology dictated that the newly rich should emulate the upper classes by building villas where their women were secluded and occupied with learning female accomplishments and receiving a limited education with the objective of making them good wives and mothers.[57] The boredom of their lives is portrayed in many novels of the period. Some female travelers who came to Iran and passed judgment on the dullness of Iranian women's lives were escaping from the monotony of their own lives. The same ethos prevented middle-class women from working and often motivated them to became missionaries to escape the restrictions of their home life.

Although the working classes in both societies suffered many disadvantages, in general the lot of women in Iran was relatively better, for the unwritten Islamic ethos of the man taking pride in being the sole breadwinner prevented him from sending his wife out to work. In comparison it was incumbent upon her European counterpart from an early age to be a wage earner in domestic service or, with the advent of the industrial revolution, in factories.

The idealized monogamous marriage in the West was based on a sexual double standard by which women were considered as passive and men active, and female passivity was the domain of only upper- and middle-class women. Working-class women provided an outlet for male sexuality in the form of prostitution. At least in Iran, the children of polygynous marriages were acknowledged and women provided for.

Thus, it can be seen that neither was quite as the other saw her. A vast gap existed between a woman's realized and idealized life in both Iran and the West, and each had to strive to overcome her predicament. Just as the forms of oppression and subjection differed, so did the rebellions against them. Actual or imagined, fact or fiction, reality or fantasy, it was the romantic vision Iranian women had of European women being "bouquets of flowers," promenading in parks, dining with men, dancing at balls, and obtaining their legal rights that in the final analysis fired their imagination and inspired them to strive for similar status.

NOTES

1. See Isaiah Berlin, *The Crooked Timber of Humanity: Chapters in the History of Ideas* (New York: Alfred Knopf, 1991), 64–65.

2. For a distinction between contact with the West and the impact of the West, see A. K. S. Lambton, "The Impact of the West on Persia," *International Affairs* 33 (1975): 12–25.

3. Mary Wollstonecraft, *A Vindication of the Rights of Women* (1792; reprint, London: Everyman's Library, 1970).

4. John Stuart Mill, *The Subjection of Women* (1869; reprint, London: Everyman's Library, 1970).

5. Husayn Mahbubi Ardakani, *Tarikh-i mu'assasat-i tamadduni-yi jadid dar Iran* (Tehran: University of Tehran, 1978), 1:238–39; Huma Natiq, *Iran dar rahyabi farhangi: 1834–1848* (London: Payam, 1988), 158.

6. Ardakani, *Tarikh*, 1:187–88. Also Abbas Iqbal, "Madame Hajji Abbas Gulsaz," *Yadigar* 3 (6–7) (1947): 106–9.

7. Denis Wright, "Memsahibs in Persia," *Asian Affairs* 14 (1983): 8. Also Mirza Salah Shirazi, *Safarnama,* ed. Isma'il Rain (Tehran: Davarpanah, 1968), 379, 386.

8. For more on Mirza Riza, see Mahdi Bamdad, *Tarikh-i rijal Iran: Qurun 12–13–14* (Tehran: Zarvar, 1970), 5:97–98; Mas'ud Mirza Zill al-Sultan, *Tarikh-i Mas'udi* (Tehran: Yasavoli, 1983), 62, 85–86, 91, 194.

9. Monica Ringer, *Education, Religion, and the Discourse of Cultural Reform in Qajar Iran* (Costa Mesa, Calif.: Mazda, 2001). For a list of foreign teachers employed at Dar al-Funun, see Faraydun Adamiyat, *Amir Kabir va Iran* (Tehran: Offset, 1969); and Husayn Mahbubi Ardakani, *Chilil sal tarikh-i Iran,* ed. Iraj Afshar (Tehran: Asati, 1989), 1:403–4.

10. Adamiyat, *Amir Kabir,* 332.

11. For more on Mirza Ali Khan Amin al-Dawla, see Bamdad, *Tarikh-i rijal,* 3:354–66. For more on Ali Asghar Khan Amin al-Sultan, see ibid., 387–425. Munir al-Saltana was the mother of Kamran Mirza Na'ib al-Saltana. For accounts of the entertainments, mixed or not, see Muhammad Hasan Khan I'timad al-Saltana, *Ruznama-yi khatirat* (Tehran: Amir Kabir, 1971), 454, 620, 702, 852. Isabella Bird among others gives an account of a mixed breakfast party; see her *Journeys in Persia and Kurdistan* (1891; reprint, London: Virago Press, 1988), 1:206.

12. Justin Perkins, *Residence of Eight Years in Persia* (New York: M. W. Dodd, 1843), 497; and Natiq, *Iran.*

13. Jane Dieulafoy, *La Perse, La Chaldée, La Susiane, relation de voyage,* trans. Farahvashi (Tehran: Sa'idi, 1982), 118–19.

14. S. G. Wilson, *Persian Life and Customs* (1900; reprint, New York: AMS Press, 1973), 310.

15. For extracts from some of these accounts, see Judith Marbo, *Veiled Half-Truths: Western Travellers' Perceptions of Middle Eastern Women* (London: I. B. Tauris, 1991). An exception to this fact is Gaspard Drouville, who spent time in an Iranian household and mingled freely with women there; *Voyage en Perse fait en 1812 et 1843* (Paris: Librairie Nationale, 1825), iv, v, 24.

16. Sir John Malcolm, *The History of Persia* (London: John Murray, 1829), 2:425.

17. Lady Sheil, *Glimpses of Life and Manners in Persia* (1856; reprint, London: John Murray, 1973), 145.

18. Ibid., 134.

19. Ibid., 144.

20. Ibid.

21. Ibid., 146.

22. Ibid., 145.

23. Carla Serena, *Hommes et choses en Perse,* trans. Ghulam Riza Sami'i (Tehran: Naw, 1984), 276–89.

24. For more on Dieulafoy, see Eve and Jean Gran-Aymeric, *Une vie d'homme* (Paris: Perrin, 1991).

25. For a short biography of Malik Jahan Khanum, who carried the title Mahd Ulya, see Bamdad, *Tarikh-i rijal,* 4:326–29; also Abbas Amanat, *Pivot of the Universe: Nasir al-Din Shah Qajar and the Iranian Monarchy, 1831–1896* (Berkeley: University of California Press, 1997).

26. Based on Lady Sheil's account of her meeting with Mahd Ulya and one of the shah's sisters. See Sheil, *Life and Manners,* 130–34, 204. For details on Victorian clothes, see Doris Langley Moore, *Fashion through Fashion Plates, 1771–1970* (London: Ward Lock, 1971); François Boucher, *20,000 Years of Fashion* (New York: Harry Abrams, 1967). For details of Queen Victoria's drawing room, see Barry St. John Neville, *Life at the Court of Queen Victoria, 1861–1901* (Exeter: Webb & Bower, 1984), 104–5.

27. Based on Jane Dieulafoy's account of her meeting with the wife of the governor of Kashan; see Dieulafoy, *La Perse,* 203–7.

28. For women's position under the Qajars, see Shireen Mahdavi, "Women and Ideas in Qajar Iran," *Asian and African Studies* 19 (1985): 187–97. For the origins of that position in Shi'i Islam, see Shireen Mahdavi, "The Position of Women in Shi'a Iran: Views of the Ulama," in *Women and the Family in the Middle East,* ed. Elizabeth Fernea (Austin: University of Texas Press, 1985), 255–68.

29. The two women closest to Nasir al-Din Shah, his mother Mahd Ulya and his wife Anis al-Dawla, were instrumental in the removal from office of his two reformist prime ministers, Amir Kabir and Mushir al-Dawla. Anis al-Dawla was also a major figure in the organization of the opposition to the abortive Reuter concession; see Amanat, *Pivot,* 436–37.

30. I'timad al-Saltana, *Ruznama,* 841.

31. Bamdad, *Tarikh-i rijal,* 3:315. For a short biography of Anis al-Dawla, see ibid., 317.

32. Ali Khan Davalu Qajar Zahir al-Dawla belonged to the Ni'matullahi darvish order and was head of a constitutionalist secret society called Ukhuvat (brotherhood). For more on Zahir al-Dawla, see Bamdad, *Tarikh-i rijal,* 2:367–70.

33. Malika-yi Iran's letters to her husband are published in *Tarikh-i vaqayi-yi mashruta-yi Iran,* ed. Jahangir Qa'immaqami (Tehran: Tahuri, 1969). For an account of the plunder and bombardment of her house, see 57–67.

34. Ibid., 112.

35. For the correspondence of Farukh Khan Amin al-Dawla, see *Majmu'a asnad va madarik-i Farukh Khan Amin al-Dawla,* ed. Karim Isfahanian, 5 vols. (Tehran:

Tehran University Press, 1979). Although Gulrukh Khanum herself was not of royal birth, she was connected to the royal family because her sister Khatun Jan Khanum was a wife of Fath Ali Shah, and her niece Shams Khanum by that marriage was a princess.

36. Isfahanian, *Majmu'a asnad*, 3:362–64.

37. A maktab was a nongovernmental school run by mullas in which Persian, some Arabic sufficient for reading the Qur'an, and sometimes arithmetic were taught.

38. For more on Mirza Riza, see Huma Natiq, *Karnama va zamana-yi Mirza Riza Kirmani* (Bonn: Hafiz-Verlag, 1984).

39. Ibid., 10. The letter is in the Mahdavi Archives in Tehran. For more on Amin al-Zarb, see Shireen Mahdavi, *For God, Mammon, and Country: A Nineteenth-Century Persian Merchant* (Boulder: Westview, 1999).

40. Amin Aqdas was one of the shah's favorite wives. She was held in such esteem that the shah sent her to Vienna for treatment when her eyesight was failing. She was the aunt of the boy Malijak, Aziz al-Sultan, to whom the shah was irrationally and excessively attached. Mirza is a Persian title that at the beginning of a name means an educated person, a scholar, or a scribe. It was usually reserved for men.

41. See Ahmad Kasravi, *Tarikh-i mashruta-yi Iran* (Tehran: Amir Kabir, 1977), 69, 180, 315, 344.

42. *Dar bayan-i ta'dib al-nisvan*, 1891, unpublished manuscript, Central Library (Kitabkhana-yi markazi), University of Tehran. An edition of *Ta'dib al-nisvan* is published; see *Ruyaru'i-yi zan va mard dar asr-i Qajar*, ed. H. Javadi, M. Mar'ashi, and S. Shukrlu (San Jose: Cypress, 1992).

43. Bibi Khanum Astarabadi, *Ma'ayib al-rijal*, 1895, unpublished manuscript, University of Tehran Library. Two published editions of *Ma'ayib al-rijal* are H. Javadi, *Ruyaru'i-yi zan*; and Afsanah Najmabadi, ed., *Ma'ayib al-rijal dar pasukh-i ta'dib al-nisvan* (Chicago: Midland, 1992).

44. Abdul Husayn Nahid, *Zanan-i Iran dar junbish-i mashruta* (Saarbrücken, Germany: Nawid, 1989), 19–23.

45. Naturalist philosophers of the Enlightenment held up nature as a model of conduct.

46. Taj al-Saltana, *Khatirat*, ed. Mansoureh Ettehadieh (Nezam Mafi) (Tehran: Tarikh-i Iran, 1982), 110. It is translated into English; *Taj al-Saltana: Crowning Anguish*, trans. Anna Vanzan and ed. Abbas Amanat (Washington: Mage, 1993). See Shireen Mahdavi, "Taj al-Saltaneh: An Emancipated Qajar Princess," *Middle Eastern Studies* 23 (1987): 188–93. All translations are my own.

47. Taj al-Saltana, *Khatirat*, 40.

48. Ibid., 12.

49. Ibid., 98. Taj al-Saltana was not correct about the position of women in Europe and America.

50. Ibid., 99.

51. Ibid., 98.

52. Certain scholars question the authenticity of these memoirs. As far as I am aware, the manuscript's date is not suspect. Whether written by Taj al-Saltana or another woman or even a man, the memoirs express surprisingly progressive views. There is also no doubt that Taj al-Saltana's lifestyle was unusual for her time, and

she was well known to have taken lovers and to have associated freely with men, as attested to by the poetry of Arif (Ghulam Husayn Arif Qazvini, known as Arif). For an example of this poetry, see Shireen Mahdavi, "Taj al-Saltaneh."

53. M. E. Hume-Griffith, *Behind the Veil in Persia and Turkish Arabia* (Philadelphia: Lippincott, 1909), 103.

54. For an account of George Sand's life, see André Maurois, *Leila: The Life of George Sand,* trans. Gerard Hopkins (London: Jonathan Cape, 1953).

55. For more on Tahira's life, see Bamdad, *Tarikh-i rijal,* 1:204–9, and 3:453. For further discussion of her life, sources, and selections of her poetry, see A. A. Mushir-Salimi, *Zanan-i sukhanvar,* 3 vols. (Tehran: Ilmi, 1956). Also E. G. Browne, *A Traveller's Narrative of the Bab* (1891; reprint, Cambridge: Cambridge University Press, 1975), 309–16.

56. For an overview of the situation of European women, see Patricia Branca, *Women in Europe since 1750* (New York: St. Martin's, 1978).

57. See J. Mourdaunt Crook, *The Rise of the Nouveaux Riches* (London: John Murray, 1999).

3   The Origins and Development of the Women's Movement in Iran, 1906–41

MANSOUREH ETTEHADIEH

THE ORIGINS AND DEVELOPMENT of the women's movement in Iran go back to the early twentieth century when the constitutional revolution of 1906 was in the making.[1] The movement grew after the granting of the constitution and progressed on its own until the change of dynasty in 1925. It was a dynamic and spontaneous movement unparalleled until the Islamic revolution of 1978–79. The new Pahlavi dynasty under Reza Shah (r. 1925–41) set up a strong modernizing dictatorship that controlled many aspects of life. Henceforth, women's issues became central to the country's overall political orientation and have remained so into the twenty-first century.

Women's movements in Iran and many Middle Eastern countries were broadly similar because of their common religion and similar experiences vis-à-vis the West and imperialism.[2] Of course, different local practices existed due to varied customs and divergent interpretations of Islam. The basic laws governing women's position before the modernizing process began in the nineteenth century were the Islamic legal code (shari'a) and the hadith (the Prophet Mohammad's traditions). According to some historians and social scientists who consider women's place in Islam, one set of laws is ethical and spiritual and regards women as equal to men, and the other is legalistic and social and regards women as second-class persons.[3] This duality of perception allows women leverage to change to their advantage some laws and practices that have emerged over time.

In Iran women were considered as weaklings. Many of them led strictly secluded lives, and their world was limited to the claustrophobic atmosphere of the home and centered on caring for their husbands and children. A woman was considered as half a child who needed to be looked after all her life.[4] Girls were often illiterate or able only to read, lest they write love letters, despite the Qur'an stipulating education as a duty of both Muslim men and women.

Lower-class urban women performed some work in society, as indicted in censuses in 1856 and 1900. Besides serving as domestic slaves, servants, and wet nurses, women worked as bath attendants, midwives, teachers of small children, and petty traders.[5] In Tehran a woman dispensed eyedrops, another walked geese, and others (*mulla baji*) offered some religious teaching. In general, poor women's jobs were menial, and women were maltreated in a society that gave them no protection.[6]

Men possessed the right to divorce their wives, polygyny was accepted, men had custody of children in case of divorce, men's share of inheritance was twice that of women, and wives did not have custody of their children when the husband died. Killing a woman suspected of adultery was acceptable. Of course, there were positive sides to the shari'a with regard to women, as in the case of ownership and control of property.[7]

By the beginning of the nineteenth century, Iran came into contact with the West. This contact grew with time, and by midcentury it began to affect the political, economic, social, and cultural life of the country. Iran's intellectuals and politicians, aware of Europe's progress, began to discuss ways to achieve reform by emulating European models of political, legal, educational, and social reforms.

Mirza Malkam Khan, a foremost reformer of the time, left an indelible mark on more than one generation of Iranian liberals. He believed that it was not productive to attempt to create indigenously the laws, institutions, and inventions that already existed in Europe and that it was better to copy them outright.[8] Women's education attracted little or no attention at the time, although Malkam mentioned the need. It was not long before some women were vocal themselves, as evidenced by the writings of Taj al-Saltaneh (daughter of Naser al-Din Shah) and Bibi Khanum.[9] They were both critical of women's status in society and advocated their education and social rights.

The constitutional revolution in 1906 triggered a spontaneous and intense women's movement. A response to widespread dissatisfaction throughout Qajar society, it was a liberal, Western-looking movement aimed at establishing a parliament (*majles*), limiting the shah's powers, enacting constitutional laws, and ending foreign dominance. Most ulama (religious scholars) joined the ranks of the constitutionalists, but when the ulterior aims of the revolutionaries, such as secularizing legal and educational systems, became apparent, an internal conflict developed, one group siding with the shah and the constitution's enemies and the other with the parliament.[10]

Eventually constitutional laws gained legitimacy and became nonviolable, although parliament never had the power to implement them fully. These laws indirectly affected women, or it should be said that women took advantage of them. Constitutional laws and the supplementary fundamental laws granted freedom to organize political societies and the freedom of the press. They also made government-funded education compulsory.[11] Women were denied the vote along with criminals and the insane, and the parliament refused women's request to organize a political society, but they were inspired by revolutionary fervor, supported by intellectuals, led by women activists, and participated in the revolution as ardent nationalists. Their activities did not always meet with social approval, and they emphasized that their aims were strictly Islamic, honorable, and patriotic. When the newspaper *Iran-e now* published information about a conference held by women to collect money to aid a government loan, it reiterated that those who attended were Muslim, nationalistic, virtuous, and knowledgeable.[12] Even the names women chose for schools they founded showed their purpose: Namus (virtue), Pardegian (veiled), Masturat (the clad), Mokhadarat-e eslami (Muslim women), Afaf (virtue), and Hejab (veil).

Some of the revolution's leaders, popular poets, intellectuals, and newspaper editors encouraged women to act by trying to indoctrinate them and by pointing out their illiteracy, ignorance, and superstitions. They reminded them that society considered them worthless. This kind of concern and support was particularly forthcoming from socialists and liberals. Newspaper such as *Sur-e esrafil, Iran-e now, Majles, Habl al-matin, Now-bahar,* and *Ra'ad* all discussed women's issues and problems.[13] In the second phase of the revolution, *Iran-e now* particularly supported women's education, encouraged and propagated their cause, and gave them information about women's movements in other countries.[14] Women were aware of women's conditions elsewhere and were no doubt inspired by them. They knew about schools opened for Armenian, Chaldean, Zoroastrian, and Jewish girls and their advances in education.[15]

Women expressed no political demands for themselves initially and envisaged no fundamental change, but they did not remain indifferent to the nationalist wave sweeping the country, and they gave their support to men. The evils of polygyny and child marriage and the question of the veil were mentioned much later. Some women demanded equal human rights and parity with men.[16] Despite women's awareness of the need for discretion, the women's movement had many enemies. Perhaps for this reason the greatest emphasis by women was on education, which was more justifiable on religious grounds. Nonetheless, education too met with opposition, and teachers and pupils were pelted with stones and accused of corruption and being a threat to society. Sometimes opposition came from the women's own relatives.[17] Men's opposition did not deter women from the goals they had set for themselves, and they often faced their opponents courageously.

Women who became involved in women's affairs were in general daughters, sisters, and wives of well-known constitutionalists. Others came from less prominent backgrounds and were just as active, and many remained anonymous. Some signed their names as "the homeland's servant" (*shams al-nesa*), "headmistress" (*om al-maddares*), or "daughters of Shams al-Maʻali" (the doctor of Naser al-Din Shah, whose daughters established three schools for poor girls). Most women who were active at the time were like their male counterparts, from educated middle-class families. Upper-class women or women from the aristocracy did not usually take much interest in these matters. On one occasion a woman complained that rich women contributed nothing.[18] Principals of girls' schools made efforts to interest richer women in these institutions.

In a study of the women's movement in Iran, Eliz Sanasarian lists twelve women who were active in this period. They were from wealthy families and were well educated.[19] Eight were educated at home with private tutors, eleven had educated fathers, most married young, five came from provincial towns and others from Tehran, and some held more than one job at a time. The women's movement was an urban phenomenon limited to a few cities. The majority of women in the country led sheltered lives, unaffected by or unaware of such matters. When the unveiling of women became government policy much later on, provincial governors in charge of implementing the policy reported on the outcome of their undertaking. Their reports provide, probably for the first time ever, a picture of the lives of the majority of women in Iran in the early twentieth century and illustrate how little the questions discussed in the capital and other major cities affected the lives of women in the countryside (see below).

Nonetheless, eagerness and enthusiasm emanated from those women who were finding, for the first time during the revolutionary era, a kind of freedom to work and express themselves. A touching letter written by a woman to a newspaper reads, "I regret that I am not a man to say what I wish and do what I want and to shed my blood to the last drop in the cause of my country."[20]

Women were discovering for the first time that they belonged to a single social class and experienced common problems. They were, as they expressed themselves, compatriots (*khaharan, madaran-e vatani*) with a common cause. Women began writing to newspapers complaining of their miserable lot, illiteracy, weakness, ill health, and general dissatisfaction. One woman mentions that even respectable women saw themselves as less than animals.[21] They claimed they were now awakened and wanted to take matters of concern into their own hands, because neither men nor the government took action to alleviate their situation. Furthermore, they began to take part in political activities.

The attention paid to the women's movement during the constitutional period by historians such as Ahmad Kasravi, Mehdi Malekzadeh, Moham-mad Nazem al-Eslam, Morgan Shuster, and correspondents of the *Times* newspaper illustrates its importance. Demonstrations by women were not unheard of, for previously women had protested in times of scarcity or fam-ine, but now women agitated for a political cause. When the ulama took sanc-tuary in the Shah Abd al-Azim shrine, women stopped the shah's carriage and beseeched him for the return of their religious leaders.[22] According to Kasravi, when the ulama left Tehran for Qom, one woman was seen bran-dishing her headscarf on a pole and crying that henceforth the Belgian E. Joseph Naus would have to perform marriage ceremonies for their daugh-ters because they had no ulama to do so. When merchants took refuge in the British legation, some women demanded to be admitted as well but were refused entry by the British chargé d'affairs.[23]

Women threatened the shah, and one woman shot a mulla who was preaching against the constitution.[24] Women who wanted to participate in the civil war in Tabriz were turned back; bodies of twenty women wearing men's clothes were found among the fallen.[25] From Qazvin a woman wrote offering to send money to the national bank and said that another woman wanted to send goods to the parliament to be auctioned in favor of the loan.[26] Shuster too wrote that during the Russian ultimatum in 1911, when people feared the parliament's closure, women demonstrated in front of the parlia-ment building, made pro-constitution speeches, and boycotted Russian goods.[27]

Following the example set by men, women organized political societies, despite the parliament refusing their request.[28] One such organization was the society for women's freedom, founded in 1906. It met secretly twice a week but was discovered, and women barely escaped before being attacked by a mob. Another society was the revolutionary, secret women's association that

aimed at Iran's independence.[29] Some societies organized conferences where
tickets were sold in support of charities and adult education for women.
Healthcare was another topic of interest to women. The charitable society
of Iranian women asked the health department to oversee women's condition, especially in connection with childbirth, and requested that midwives,
wet nurses, and bath attendants who acted as midwives should not be allowed
to practice before being instructed by a teacher and passing an examination.[30]
The patriotic women's organization was founded in 1922 by Mohtaram
Eskandari, a woman from an aristocratic family related to the Qajars and
whose brother was the head of the Democrat party. The ulama condemned
the society, and she was arrested and her house burnt. This society also published a newspaper. Zandokht Shirazi, another woman activist, organized the
women's revolutionary association and published the *Dokhtaran-e Iran*
magazine.

Although women were officially barred from political activity, they nonetheless showed interest in it. For instance, a meeting was organized at a school,
and the wife of Yeprem Khan, the Armenian police chief, spoke about freedom.[31] Some principals and teachers advertised meetings at their schools and
invited women to attend and listen to speeches on nationalism.[32]

The interest shown by newspaper editors to women's issues no doubt
encouraged women to write to newspapers, which must have been a stimulating outlet, for the number of letters is considerable. Themes varied, but
the main topic was education as the key to development. One woman wrote
an illuminating letter in this vein:

> You think that we are ignorant or unconscious, have no initiative, and have no
> share of human rights. If we are women we are not foolish. We watched every
> effort and service the nationalists performed and all the pain they suffered. But
> we had no remedy. Some of us patriots celebrated the day the constitutional-
> ists were victorious and felt happy, and when bad fortune struck, we wept, but
> we were allowed in no gathering or meeting. . . . God knows how on those dark
> unforgettable historical days we burned for the fallen youth of Azerbaijan and
> how during the long nights we roared like whales as their sisters. We threw salt
> on our bleeding hearts and wore no new clothes or drank clear water nor did
> we caress our children, but we lamented until dawn and thought of a way to-
> ward salvation and freedom, so that we too might lift a thorn from the path of
> our fellow men and serve the children of the fatherland.

That was the reason, the writer added, that women concluded that the best
solution was to found schools for girls, for they were the first teachers of men.

Each family would have an educated head who would know all that was necessary for running the home. "From her breast the newborn would suck the love of the fatherland, so that when necessary he would lay down his life."[33]

The arguments put forward by women in most of their letters to newspapers and the justifications they gave for the schools they founded were that they were doing it for their country. Not until women were educated would Iran advance. They usually blamed men in strong language for not letting women study.[34] One woman wrote that they should blame women's ignorance for their condition, and another wrote that they should expect nothing from men.[35] They repeated that the prophet himself had made it the duty of men and women to study, that all philosophers emphasized it, and that the past greatness of Iran was owing to its educated women.[36]

In a letter to *Iran-e now,* a woman who signed her name as Tayereh (servant) made a passionate plea: "Do you know how many children die or become blind because they are not cared for and because women are not educated and are ignorant? . . . Oh you brave brothers who are keepers of virtue . . . why is it that you think we are unworthy? How many schools have you founded for us oppressed women? How many teachers have you appointed for us . . . that convinces you we are unworthy and have no aptitude? Why is it you want comfort, pleasure, travel, and science for yourselves and deprive us of their benefits and say that in our country women are unworthy of education? . . . Come brothers, undo the oppression of the women's race, and let us obliterate the shame our civilized neighbors blame us for." She mentioned the evils of polygyny and was outspoken in her accusation against men who oppose women's education.[37]

Women took advantage of the supplementary fundamental laws that granted freedom of the press. They began to publish their own newspaper, which was not distributed by street vendors as men's newspapers were but was available only through subscription. One woman said it would increase the paper's sale if it was sold on the street like men's papers.[38]

Appearing in 1910, the first newspaper, *Danesh* (Knowledge), was published by a doctor's wife and was written for women.[39] It was followed by *Shokufeh* (Blossom), founded in 1912 by Mozayan al-Dowleh who was also the founder of three schools, one of them vocational.[40] *Shokufeh* was entirely dedicated to the question of women's education; it was outspoken and often attacked the ministry of education outright for neglecting girls.

Another important women's newspaper, later a magazine, was *Zaban-e zanan* (Mouthpiece of women) founded by Sediqeh Dowlatabadi in 1919 in Isfahan. More outspoken than other women, she openly criticized the veil

and women's general condition. She was interested in politics, and her paper included many articles on the parliamentary election, the question of the
northern oil agreement, and the 1919 agreement between Iran and Great
Britain, but she never forgot that her primary concern was women. She wrote
that if women had the right to vote they would never elect the type of people men elected, people of the upper classes who worked only for their own
interests.[41] Dowlatabadi was also the founder of Kanun-e banovan, a woman's committee, which later played a prominent role in women's unveiling
during Reza Shah's reign. She contributed widely to other newspapers and
wrote on diverse topics, including the freedom women gained in other countries and the difficulties of modern marriages.[42]

Jahan-e zanan, Alam-e nesvan, Jam'iyat-e nesvan, and *Nameh-ye banovan*
were some of the other newspapers and magazines published by women in
this period. They familiarized women with European culture, history, and
literature and discussed health, childcare, and cooking. They encouraged
women to write to them. A regular correspondent was Shahnaz Azad from
Shiraz, who later founded her own paper, *Nameh-ye banovan,* in 1921.

From the end of the revolutionary era around 1914 to the change of dynasty in 1925, the women's press placed less emphasis on the question of
constitutionalism and patriotism and more on women's issues. Women began to write to newspapers from the provinces, and they translated biogra-
phies as well as articles and books on manners, childcare, health matters, and
home economics. Some wrote short stories to ridicule society's customs. They
paid attention to the development of the women's movement in Europe and
to the West's educational system. Men also wrote on women's issues.[43] These
articles were more Western-oriented than before, and references to European and American men and women abound.[44]

The scope of women's interests had expanded to include discussion of a
wider range of subjects such as child marriage and the need to support home
manufacturing, close cafés where opium was smoked, have medical examinations before marriage, and send women to study midwifery abroad. The
rights and legal status of women were discussed, especially in the magazine
Jam'iyat-e nesvan headed by Molouk Eskandari. One article announced that
women's equal rights had been declared in the world and that women had
entered every kind of high-level job in Europe because they studied the same
subjects as men. This path was impossible for Iranian women, prohibited by
the veil from pursuing the paths taken by men. The veil and the disadvantages it imposed on women were mentioned more frequently. In one issue
the magazine declared that nothing would detain women from seeking their

rights and their equality.[45] A particularly Western-oriented paper, *Alam-e nesvan,* was published by graduates of Tehran's American School. It often made comparisons with women's status in other countries. In a humorous article about the veil, it said that women in Iran could never become ministers or lawyers if they wore the covering, and if women in Europe wore the veil they too would not become lawyers or occupy other professions. In a contest to describe the ideal girl, someone wrote from Hamadan about a mother who asked her daughter what she wished to do after she graduated from school. The girl replied that she wanted to go to Luristan (a socioeconomically disadvantaged region) to help people. The writer commented that she was the ideal girl, with the strength of Voltaire and Rousseau, the love of mankind like Sayyid Jamal al-Din Asadabadi, and the fearlessness of Joan of Arc.[46]

Foreign missionaries founded the first school for girls, and it was attended mostly by religious minorities. Mirza Hasan Roshdiyeh, a famous educator and the founder of modern schools for boys, founded a girls' school in 1903 but had to shut it immediately because of opposition. Hostility was persistent in the case of the modern boys' schools as well.[47] At the beginning of the constitutional revolution, Bibi Khanum Vaziroff founded a girls' school but had to close it on the advice of the minister of health.[48] When Nazem al-Eslam, a revolutionary leader, broached the question of a girls' school, Ayatollah Tabataba'i opposed it on the grounds that it was unsafe for girls to go out.[49] Shaikh Fazlallah Nuri, a staunch anti-constitutionalist, also voiced strong opposition to schools for girls.[50] Opposition was not only toward female education but also to the general advancement of women. A certain stigma remained attached to schoolgirls during this period.[51]

Despite persistent opposition, women founded schools on their own initiative, and *Iran-e now* and later *Shokufeh* contained many announcements about school openings and graduation ceremonies to which women were invited to see the progress girls were making. Some efforts were also made to this effect in the provinces.[52] Syllabi in these schools were not uniform. Newspapers mention such subjects as Arabic, geography, natural science, arithmetic, and languages. The vocational school of Mozayaniyeh had carpet-weaving classes, sewing, and sock weaving, and another school had a midwifery class.[53]

Although the government took no steps toward girls' education until 1918, it appointed women inspectors.[54] *Shokufeh* wrote that school examinations in 1913 were performed in these inspectors' presence.[55] But all was not well with these private schools, especially because they did not have uniform programs and were not government-supervised. The ministry must have approved a certain syllabus but apparently not all schools complied. Some papers included advertisements that certain schools were teaching the ministry's program. One woman complained that many people were satisfied with only a school's name and were unaware of actual conditions. Another wrote that no one cared about or thought what was best for women and founded schools for personal or financial gain. Some women expressed disappointment with their work's outcome.[56] Gradually it became obvious that conditions would not improve unless the government took action.

For a long time, the government did nothing for girls' education, despite criticism in the papers. Boys' education was also neglected partly because of political upheaval and lack of funds after the revolution. In the case of girls, the task was doubly difficult because of many opponents. During the second parliament in 1911, further legislation was enacted emphasizing that education was to be compulsory for everyone and providing the means for the implementation of compulsory primary and secondary education for boys. Still no step was taken to ensure the same for girls. It was only in 1918 that at last the government provided funds to establish ten primary schools for girls.[57] In the same year, a teacher-training college for women was also opened, no mean achievement considering the opposition's strength, and it was no doubt owing to the persistent efforts of these pioneering women. The government made no provision for secondary education, and women were far from reaching equality with men.

Women pointed out the disparity between the status of men and women. One woman wrote in 1921 that the education of boys and girls was unequal, especially in the country's south, that permission had not been granted to open girls' schools, and that permission to publish a newspaper for women was given only with difficulty.[58] In 1913 *Shokufeh* published a list of twenty-five private schools for girls, with a total of 890 students, in Tehran. By 1922 Tehran had fifty-one girls' schools with 2,978 pupils and 79 teachers, whereas there were sixty schools for boys with 8,955 pupils and 441 teachers.[59] Progress had been made, and the government had assumed responsibility for girls' education.[60]

The circumstances inspiring women to act involved feelings of nationalism and enthusiasm engendered by the idealism of the constitutional revolution. Women emphasized their weakness, powerlessness, and inferiority, but they were vocal as a class for the first time and took advantage of the political circumstances to make themselves heard. The fact that the government did nothing to help at the movement's beginning gave special impetus to women's efforts despite many obstacles.

Gradually revolutionary fervor subsided, and a lull in the women's movement occurred. Sediqeh Dowlatabadi wrote that when the women's movement started with such ardor, someone pointed out that if women did not have the stamina to persist in the work they had begun, they should not start.[61] Another woman commented that women had lost their enthusiasm.[62] But women continued to work in their chosen fields, despite difficulties. The government began to take matters concerning education and health in hand, no doubt because of the efforts of these pioneering women. By emphasizing their rights and giving vent to their wishes, women created the women's question, and henceforth the government had to consider women's problems and needs.

The first phase of the women's movement was spontaneous, inspired by feelings of nationalism and democracy. The second phase, beginning with the dynastic change in 1925, was ordered from above and fitted into a general policy of government centralization.

Overthrowing the Qajar dynasty, Reza Shah was a nationalist whose aim was Iran's modernization and Westernization. He nevertheless ruled as a dictator and abolished many of the freedoms won during the revolution. Many reforms sought by constitutionalists and nationalists were implemented at the cost of democracy, the ultimate goal of nationalists. Part of the policy of modernization concerned women's position, although no substantial social or political reform or emancipation was envisaged. Nothing was done to safeguard women's interests in the case of divorce or polygyny. The shah himself had four wives. Some minor improvements were made; marriages were registered, and a minimum marriage age was imposed.

The most important improvement was in education, where genuine and lasting efforts were made to increase the opportunity for girls to study. Besides the founding of secondary and vocational schools for girls, women were admitted to Tehran University in 1936, a year after it opened. Women were also encouraged to participate in charitable works and join the newly founded Red Lion and Sun Society. The first school of nursing was founded at this time under the auspices of the shah's daughter. Efforts made in the field of education did not solve the problem of illiteracy among the majority of women and did not penetrate the country at large. Education was limited to cities and towns, and villages and tribal areas did not benefit from the educational system as such, thus making it more difficult to influence women there. The government's policy of unveiling depended on schools and government officials, and in the absence of such entities in villages, it was left to the police to put the policy into practice.

The government's most important policy with regard to women concerned their clothing, especially the veil.[63] This policy was presented as the emancipation and modernization of women, and it was decreed that it should now be called "the opening of the veil" (*kashf-e hijab*). In 1927 Reza Shah had already obliged men to discard their traditional attire and headgear in favor of Western coats and hats. Clothes worn by tribesmen and various classes of people were presented as backward, and the policy to change them was enforced rigorously and brutally in many instances with varying degrees of success. Gradually the issue of the veil, which was a more delicate question, was also raised.[64]

Tentative mention of women's unveiling and the advantages of the policy appeared in newspapers, especially in women's newspapers, even before the dynastic change in 1925, and examples demonstrated that women in Europe and the United States were advanced because they were free.[65] From 1925 rumors circulated about the imminence of unveiling, but no action was officially taken. No doubt encouraged by the government, some women dared to appear in public unveiled, the first one being Sediqeh Dowlatabadi.[66] At the time, controversy emerged about whether women should discard their black veils for lighter attire, uncover their faces, or unveil totally. When the shah's own wife and daughters uncovered their faces at the holy shrine of Qom, Muslim clergy considered the act as tantamount to being unveiled and were critical. The shah's reaction was immediate and hostile.[67]

Many people opposed the unveiling of women, and perhaps that was the reason the government proceeded discreetly and by decree rather than by enactment of law.[68] The example of Afghanistan and the uprising there in 1929 is another reason for the government's cautious approach to its policy.[69] The main opposition came from the ulama. For this reason and the more general one of weakening the ulama's power, Reza Shah undermined their freedom, privileges, and prerogatives by turning them into state servants and limiting their numbers. Clerics had to pass state examinations, and if they opposed government policy their licenses to preach could be removed or they could be exiled or accused of corruption. Some clergymen were forced to comply and support the government's policy, but in general they remained silent.[70]

In Qom and Mashhad, two important religious centers, the ulama's opposition was the most ardent. In Qom, when girls were required to attend school unveiled, the ulama encouraged parents to remove their daughters from school. Women teachers refused to teach and were made to comply under threat.[71] In Mashhad the situation was worse. When girls were forced to go to school unveiled, an *alim* (religious scholar) who denounced this measure was arrested. Ulama in Mashhad sent an emissary to Tehran in 1936 to negotiate with the government, and he was arrested. Thereupon the ulama of Mashhad and men and women gathered in the mosque of Goharshad to demonstrate against the government's action. Many lives were lost when the army fired on the crowd. Several prominent religious leaders were deported or arrested, Mashhad was placed under martial law, and the keeper of the shrine, a layman, was executed.[72]

Magazines and newspapers carried articles by men and women in support of freeing women from their "black prisons" and allowing them to advance along the road to civilization and progress.[73] A women's committee, Kanun-e banovan, was organized with branches in major provincial cities under the auspices of the government and the shah's eldest daughter, Shams Pahlavi, and under the directorship of Sediqeh Dowlatabadi, herself a staunch supporter of unveiling. This committee unified the various women's organizations under government supervision and prepared women for unveiling. The activity gave women an opportunity to meet, especially in major cities and smaller towns.[74]

In 1932 the second Congress of Women of the East was organized in Tehran, and women activists from Lebanon, Egypt, India, and Iraq were invited. The presidency was bestowed upon Princess Shams, and Dowlatabadi was the secretary.[75] Topics discussed included the legal status of women and emphasized women's backwardness in society and the wish to be equal to women in Western countries. No mention of the veil was made.

Reza Shah's visit to Turkey in 1935 served as a catalyst for his developing notions about modernization. He was an admirer of Kemal Ataturk and while in Turkey was apparently impressed by his programs, particularly by the advances made by women in the field of education.[76]

Since 1933 female teachers in Iran had been encouraged to unveil, and in 1935 the government decided to start the policy of unveiling girls in school. It was the duty of the ministers of education and the interior to implement the policy in three stages: primary schools were to be made coeducational, and children would be taught by women teachers; children were to wear simple uniforms, thus abolishing the veil for girls; and women were to organize conferences in girls' schools where women teachers wearing special uniforms were to attend. Women of good families would be invited with their husbands to be present, and lecturers and knowledgeable people were to be asked to talk about healthcare, home economics, and the usefulness of thrift. Girl students were encouraged to make speeches on such occasions.[77]

By 1936 preparations were considered sufficient; it was time to announce the policy of unveiling officially.[78] Orders were issued by a secret decree from the prime minister to provincial governors to prepare the ground for unveiling, and the police were ordered to cooperate.[79] The occasion chosen for the policy's official declaration was 8 January 1936 at the graduation ceremony of the girls' college where the shah's own wife and daughters appeared completely unveiled for the first time in public. The queen handed out diplomas, and Reza Shah spoke about half of the population being disregarded. He asked women to work in education and reminded them that the country's future happiness was in their hands. Some women when they unveiled wore Western hats, and others went bareheaded. Some women had prepared hats and special clothes for the occasion, and just before the event two hairdressers appeared at the school to arrange women's hair.[80]

The degree of popular acceptance was mixed. In general, the upper classes, especially the younger generation, welcomed the law. These women possessed more knowledge of the West, and many intellectuals had discussed the question for some time. In Tehran and some larger cities, unveiling was mostly successful. For students and the wives of government officials, merchants, teachers, and army officers, the policy was easier to impose because of pressure applied, although it still needed constant supervision.[81] Enforcing this policy was a different matter when it concerned women whose husbands held no official position and women living in small towns, villages, and border areas. The press was strictly censored, and all news about this event stressed its success, but people in the 1990s still recounted stories about the anguish of their parents and relatives. Reports of provincial governors, who had to demonstrate success in carrying out the government's orders, often admitted failure despite the possibility of reprisal or dismissal.[82] These reports not only show the difficulties encountered by local authorities who tried to execute the government's orders but also reveal widespread civil disobedience and nonviolent resistance at all levels of society, especially among the poor, elderly, peasants, and middle class without government jobs. Resistance was the more remarkable because of the fear in which the government was held and the constant vigilance of its spies.[83] Disobedience and defiance broke out throughout the country. For provinces such as Kermanshah, Gilan, and Mazandaran, the reports seem to be more positive, but they too recount the same tale of general failure.

Provincial governors were impeded by their understanding of local situations and the difficulty of enforcing the government's strict injunction.[84] They had photographs taken to show how positively women greeted the policy, and they organized festivities and lecture series for towns.[85] Governors repeated with frustration that they needed more police reinforcement and even the army's help if the policy was to succeed.[86] Whenever governors were unsuccessful, they contemptuously blamed local people as "backward, wild, unintelligent, barbarous, and dirty" and said that they were unappreciative about what was being done for them and understood only force.[87] Qa'enat's governor wrote that people were so used to being beaten on the head that no amount of force was effective.[88] Sometimes influential people were blamed for encouraging women to disobey. Some raised the possibility of extortion, and others complained that they had been unjustly treated.[89]

In provincial towns, the example of unveiling was supposed to be set by wives of government officials, local dignitaries, and influential people, who did not always obey.[90] These were the easiest people to coax, but some resisted the pressure. Many local officials did not take their wives to public functions on the pretext that they were pregnant or sick.[91] A year after the decree about unveiling, many reports were issued about the policy's failure. For a celebration in Damghan, only two of the invited men came with wives. In Sabzevar the names of those who had not brought their wives were recorded to be reported later. In Gonabad, officials who came without wives to a school's graduation ceremony were rudely told to leave.[92]

The government was at times at a loss about how to proceed and gave contradictory or ridiculous orders.[93] It often reported that no violence was to be used, but it did not reprimand the use of force and police brutality. The coercion and violence were probably the policy of local authorities rather than government orders, but because the shah would not tolerate exceptions, local authorities must have been obliged to use force. In Saveh two hundred scarves and veils were pulled from women's heads in one day. In Sabzevar women were forbidden to raise their coat collars. In Bojnurd women did not leave their houses to fetch water. In Gonabad women walked over rooftops to visit the bathhouse. Whole families from Khorramshahr took refuge in neighboring Iraq. Many complained that women refused to leave their homes. Kalat's governor wrote that in twenty days he had not seen twenty women. In Qom a woman died who had been beaten by the police wanting to remove her veil.[94]

Threats, deportations, punishments, dismissals from work, and extra pay for police were some means by which the government tried to oblige people to comply. Usually men were punished for their wives' noncompliance. Three years after the announcement of the unveiling policy, a plea was made to allow men who had been deported to return.[95] Shopkeepers were asked not to sell goods to veiled women, bus drivers were not to permit them to ride, bath attendants were not to admit them, and government officials were not to allow them to enter offices.

Both men and women suffered, but the brunt of the policy was borne by women who for the first time were made to appear unveiled, in the company of men, and often did not know how to behave or what to wear.[96] In Torbat-e Jam peasant women unaware of this movement came to town veiled, and when policemen pulled off their veils, their attire underneath was inadequate for public places.[97] Sometimes women who unveiled were ridiculed, threatened, or attacked. Until some influential people were exiled as punishment, this behavior did not cease. The voices of many of these women were not heard, at least in the surviving public record. Probably because of their husbands' positions, their own jobs, or their beliefs, some women made speeches in favor of unveiling.

One way to discern the opinion of women who opposed unveiling is to judge their behavior, as reflected in documents, or their reaction immediately after Reza Shah was forced to abdicate. Some women complained to the government, and the ulama came out in full force against unveiling.[98] The *fatwas* (religious decrees) of well-known figures such as Ayatollah Kashani gave the necessary backing to women, which the government, with many problems on its hands, was reluctant to combat.[99] Many women throughout Iran resumed wearing the veil. Some officials half-heartedly tried to continue the old policy but were unsuccessful. Some women complained that they were attacked because they were unveiled now, and several schools were closed in Yazd and Qom.[100] Women working in the civil service and as nurses and teachers did not don the veil again or did not wear it at work. Most upper-class women discarded it for good, except for some older women. Women of the lower and middle classes and peasant women chose to cover their heads. Henceforth, the veil become a sign of class distinctions.

▧ ▧ ▧

The women's movement in Iran began during the constitutional revolution, and its undisputed area of success was education, the basic demand of these pioneering women. Women also demanded government supervision in health matters, and positive changes in that field were also made. These reforms were not evident except in major cities for a long time to come, and the majority of women were left unaffected, illiterate, and without access to proper healthcare. Little demand was made for legal or political rights during the constitutional period and in the stronger government of Reza Shah. The women's movement not only lost its impetus but was taken over and controlled by the government. Henceforth, the government decided women's issues.

From the outset, the women's movement faced many obstacles. Women's inexperience, illiteracy, lack of social cohesion, and economic dependence were major stumbling blocks as were men's obscurantism, bigotry, and fanaticism. Ambiguity in Islamic laws with regard to women was another deterrent. The major obstacle to the movement's fundamental development was that the women's question was politicized and subsumed as government policy by the modernizing Iranian state.

NOTES

1. Eliz Sanasarian states that by 1920 a women's movement existed in Iran having all the characteristics inherent in a social movement. "The movement comprised middle and upper class women, from the capital and other major cities of Iran. It had a loose structure and a limited scope of operation"; "Characteristics of the Women's Movement in Iran," in *Women and the Family in Iran,* ed. Asghar Fathi (Leiden: E. J. Brill, 1985), 105.

2. In the Ottoman empire, the progressives argued that in order to create responsible citizens it was necessary first to educate women. From 1868, women's voices were heard deploring women's conditions and making a plea for education. Women saw their liberation and progress in education. The same kind of argument was put forward by women in the West a century earlier. The same trend of development occurred in Egypt. During the first decades of the twentieth century, feminism became visible intellectually, organizationally, and politically. At the beginning of the century, women began to contribute to newspapers. Societies for the intellectual improvement of women were founded, and women began to participate in political agitations against the British occupation of Egypt. None of these developments escaped the notice of women activists in Iran. See Nukhet Sirman, "Feminism in Turkey: A Short History," in *New Perspectives on Turkey* (1989), 3:1–33.

3. Leila Ahmed, *Women and Gender in Islam* (New Haven: Yale University Press, 1992), 65–67.

4. In letters by Naser al-Din Shah to two of his daughters, Tuman Agha and Turan Agha, both highly literate, he used playful, indecent, and obscene language exactly as if addressing a half-child, half-grown woman. In two censuses prepared in 1853 and 1900, those women named are obviously poor women or prostitutes. Others are mentioned as wives, sisters, or mothers of someone. Rich or aristocratic women are usually named; *Amar-e dar al-khalafeh-ye Tehran, asnadi az tarikh-e ejtemaʻi-ye Tehran dar asr-e Qajar,* ed. Sirus Saʻdvandian and Mansoureh Ettehadieh (Nezam Mafi) (Tehran: Tarikh-e Iran, 1368/1989).

5. There are 3,525 women servants and 2,525 women slaves listed for Tehran in 1869. The total number of women listed is 46,603. Tehran's population at the time was 147,256; *Amar-e dar al-khalafeh,* ed. Sa'dvandian and Ettehadieh, 346.

6. Sometimes newspapers carried news about poor women. For instance, in 1907 *Sur-e esrafil* wrote about the sale of girls in Quchan to Turkmans and campaigned on their behalf until those responsible were brought to trial. *Iran-e now* also dealt widely with the plight of poor women. *Sur-e esrafil,* no. 4, 8 Jamadi al-Awal 1325/1907; *Iran-e now,* nos. 45, 46, year 1, 1327/1909; no. 49, year 2, 1328/1910; and nos. 44, 47, 68, year 3, 1329/1911.

7. It is difficult to measure women's wealth during the nineteenth century. In the 1853 and 1900 censuses, there are references to a few *hajjieh,* women who had made the pilgrimage to Mecca, and there are some endowments (*vaqf*) made by women. As far as property ownership is concerned, in 1853 only 1 percent of houses and shops in Tehran were owned by women, and in 1900 only 3.5 percent; *Amar-e dar al-khalafeh,* ed. Sa'dvandian and Ettehadieh, passim.

8. Malkam Khan, *Majmu'eh-ye asar-e Mirza Malkam Khan,* ed. Mohammad Tabataba'i (Tehran, n.p., n.d.), 10–12, passim.

9. *Khaterat-e Taj al-Saltaneh,* ed. Mansoureh Ettehadieh (Nezam Mafi), 2nd ed. (Tehran: Tarikh-e Iran, 1371/1992), 5–12, 98–99. *Ruyaru'i-ye zan va mard dar asr-e Qajar, do resaleh, ta'dib al-nesvan va mo'ayeb al-rejal,* ed. H. Javadi, M. Mar'ashi, S. Shekarlu (San Jose, Calif.: Cypress, 1992), passim.

10. Mansoureh Ettehadieh (Nezam Mafi), *Peydayesh va tahavol-e ahzab-e siyasi-ye mashrutiyat* (Tehran, 1362/1983), 199–225.

11. *Majmu'eh-ye mosavvabat-e majles-e showra-ye melli, dar chahar dowreh-ye taqniniyeh* (Tehran: National Parliament, n.d.), 4–35.

12. *Iran-e now,* no. 148, year 1, 1328/1910.

13. Mohammad Sadr-e Hashemi, *Tarikh-e jarayed va majellat-e Iran,* 4 vols. (Isfahan, 1363/1984), passim. *Iran-e now* was the organ of the socialist Democrat party. This paper was edited by Mohammad Amin Rasulzadeh who had come from Baku and was the party's theoretician. The views of the Democrats and *Iran-e now* about women followed socialist ideology and advocated women's emancipation. They had to be careful lest they were accused of being non-Islamic. Ettehadieh, *Peydayesh,* 199–225.

14. *Iran-e now,* for example, took pains to let Iranian women know about the suffragette movement in Britain; nos. 5, 26, 31, year 1, 1327/1909; no. 32, year 2, 1328/1910.

15. Ibid., no. 34, year 1, 1327/1909.

16. *Shokufeh,* no. 9, year 1, 3 Jamadi al-Awal 1331/1913; also *Jam'iyat-e nesvan-e vatankhah,* no. 2, 1332/1914.

17. Eliz Sanasarian, *Women's Rights Movement in Iran: Appeasement and Repression, 1900 to Khomeini* (New York: Praeger, 1982), 33.

18. *Shokufeh,* no. 7, 21 Rabi al-Awal 1331/1913.

19. Sanasarian, *Women's Rights Movement,* 42–44.

20. *Sur-e esrafil,* no. 11, 12 Rajab 1325/1907.

21. *Shokufeh,* no. 21, year 2, 20 Zihajeh 1332/1913.

22. Mohammad Nazem al-Eslam Kermani, *Tarikh-e bidari-ye Iranian,* ed. Sa'idi Sirjani, vol. 1 (Tehran: Bonyad-e farhang-e Iran, 1357/1978), 361.

23. Joseph Naus was the Belgian director of customs and minister of post and telegraph. Unpopular, he was suspected of carrying out the wishes of the Russians. Ahmad Kasravi, *Tarikh-e mashrutiyat-e Iran* (Tehran: Amir Kabir, 1369/1970), 107.

24. Mangol Bayat-Philipp, "Feminism and Nationalist Politics in Iran, 1905–1911," in *Women in the Muslim World,* ed. Lois Beck and Nikki Keddie (Cambridge: Harvard University Press, 1978), 295–306.

25. Kasravi, *Tarikh-e mashrutiyat,* 698.

26. *Ruznameh-ye majles* (newspaper), no. 44, year 1, 1324/1906.

27. William Morgan Shuster, *The Strangling of Persia: A Record of European Diplomacy and Oriental Intrigue* (London: Fisher and Unwin, 1913), 176–77, 183–89; and *Cuttings from The Times* (newspaper), U.K., 7 December 1911.

28. Janet Afary, "Grassroots Democracy and Social Democracy in the Iranian Constitutional Revolution, 1906–1911," Ph.D. diss., University of Michigan, 1991, 224; also her *The Iranian Constitutional Revolution, 1906–1911: Grassroots Democracy, Social Democracy, and the Origins of Feminism* (New York: Columbia University Press, 1996).

29. Afary, "Grassroots Democracy," 232; Sanasarian, "Characteristics of the Women's Movement," 98. One must not overrate the extent and repercussions of this movement, as its achievements at best must have been limited.

30. *Iran-e now,* no. 5, year 3, 1329/1911.

31. Sanasarian, "Characteristics of the Women's Movement," 98.

32. *Iran-e now,* no. 128, year 2, 1328/1910.

33. Ibid., no. 166, year 1, 1326/1908.

34. Ibid., no. 19, year 1, 1327/1909.

35. *Jam'iyat-e nesvan-e Iran* (sometimes also called *Jam'iyat-e nesvan-e vatankhah,* the society founded by Mohtaram Eskandari), no. 1, year 1, 1302/1923.

36. *Majles,* no. 6, year 1, 1324/1906.

37. *Iran-e now,* nos. 65-92, year 1, 1327/1909.

38. *Shokufeh,* no. 14, year 4, 18 Rabi al-Awal 1334/1915.

39. Sadr-e Hashemi, *Tarikh-e jarayed,* 2:266–67.

40. Ibid., 3:80–81.

41. Sediqeh Dowlatabadi's life and work are revealing in this respect. She came from a religious family from Isfahan but had been allowed to study dressed as a boy. She founded a girls' school in secret at age fourteen but was apparently found out, and it was closed after three months. Sanasarian, *Women's Rights Movement,* 32–34; and Sadr-e Hashemi, *Tarikh-e jarayed,* 3:6–11.

42. *Dokhtaran-e Iran,* nos. 1, 2, 3, year 1, 1310–11/1931. Dowlatabadi wrote an elegant obituary in *Jam'iyat-e nesvan* (nos. 5, 6, year 1, 1302) on the occasion of the untimely death of Mohtaram Eskandari. On another occasion she wrote a bold letter to *Dokhtaran-e Iran* (no. 2, year 2, 1310) about the evils of polygyny.

43. Sadr-e Hashemi, *Tarikh-e jarayed,* passim.

44. *Dokhtaran-e Iran,* nos. 1, 2, 6, 7, year 1, 1310–11/1931.

45. *Jam'iyat-e nesvan,* nos. 1, 2, year 1, 1302/1922.

46. *Alam-e nesvan,* no. 1, year 11, 1309/1931. Also no. 1, year 2, 1300/1921.

47. *Savaneh-e omr,* ed. Shams al-Din Roshdiyeh (Tehran: Tarikh-e Iran, 1362/1981), 32, 148.

48. Afary, "Grassroots Democracy," 234–35.

49. Nazem al-Eslam, *Tarikh-e bidari*, 1:244.

50. Shaikh Fazlallah Nuri, an opponent of the constitutional revolution, opposed girls' education and indeed all modern education. *Rasayel, elamiyehha, maktubat-e shaikh-e shahid, Fazlallah Nuri,* ed. Mohammad Turkman (Tehran: Rasa, 1363/1984), 68–70, 262. Sayyid Hasan-e Moddares, a more liberal-minded religious and political leader and head of a political party called Elmiyeh, also appears to have opposed girls' education. In 1915, when discussion began in the third parliament about the government's policy of reforming primary education and the founding of a teacher-training college for women, Elmiyeh opposed it on the grounds that the time was not yet right. See *Mozakerat-e majles-e sevvom,* 20th session, 12 Jamadi al-Awal 1333/1915.

51. *Dokhtaran-e Iran,* no. 5, year 1, 1311/1931. The same paper stated that the reason men did not marry was because they could not tolerate illiterate, ignorant women anymore, but they could not trust educated schoolgirls either; ibid., no. 4, year 1, 1311/1931.

52. Some school principals advertised that the methods they taught were in accordance with Islam, and some announced that they accepted poor girls without charge. The principal of Namus school organized religious ceremonies on holy days to demonstrate that it was an Islamic institution. The Mokhadarat-e Eslamiyeh school invited literate, well-educated women of Tehran to attend the second-year examination. *Iran-e now,* nos. 5, 19, year 1, 1327/1909; nos. 17, 41, year 2, 1328/1910; nos. 46, 71, year 3, 1329/1911; and *Shokufeh,* no. 22, year 2, 1332/1913; no. 8, year 4, 1334/1915.

53. *Iran-e now,* no. 17, year 2, 1328/1910; no. 46, year 3, 1329/1911; and *Shokufeh,* no. 11, year 1, 1331/1913; no. 19, year 2, 1332/1914. The Mozayaniyeh dar al-elm va sanaye and other vocational schools were also founded, such as the Dabestan-e sanaye-e mokhadarat where embroidery and knitting were taught.

54. The chief school inspector was Nur al-Dojay, daughter of Emam al-Hokama; she was a graduate of the American School; *Shokufeh,* no. 19, year 2, 1322/1914.

55. Ibid., nos. 10, 15, year 1, 1331/1912.

56. *Iran-e now,* nos. 33, 34, year 1, 1327/1909; also *Ra'ad,* no. 3, 5 Moharam 1332/1913; *Shokufeh,* no. 8, year 2, 1332/1914.

57. *Salnameh-ye vezarat-e mo'aref va farhang va oqaf* (Tehran: Ministry of Education and Culture, 1336/1918), 76. Also *Majmu'eh-ye mossawabat,* 425–28.

58. *Jahan-e zanan,* no. 5, 1 Mizan 1300/1340.

59. *Iran* (newspaper), no. 902, 16 Ramazan 1339/1921; and *Ra'ad,* Sha'ban 1334/1916.

60. *Majalah-ye ta'lim va tarbiyat,* no. 9, 1304/1925.

61. *Dokhtaran-e Iran,* no. 1, year 1, 1310/1931.

62. Ibid., no. 5, year 1, 1311/1932.

63. Sanasarian, *Women's Rights Movement,* 59–60. A precedence existed for political interference with women's clothes. In 1918 Malek al-Sho'ara Bahar wrote an article, "What Is Demagogy," and explained how in 1912, during the regency of Naser al-Molk, to make people forget his autocracy, the government gave strict orders to curtail the women's movement and to specify their attire; *Now bahar,* no. 101, 9 Jamadi al-Awal 1336/1918.

64. Two books published by two government organizations contain 797 documents about the policy of unveiling. They cover the period from the winter of 1936, when the

first decrees were issued, to about two years after the shah's abdication in the autumn of 1941. These reports were mainly secret and coded and show the importance the government attached to this policy and the way it implemented it. They further illustrate people's conditions and the way they reacted to the policy. *Vaqa'eh-ye kashf-e hejab, 1313–22/1934–43* (Tehran: National Archives, 1371/1992); and *Khoshunat va farhang asnad-e mahramaneh-ye kashf-e hejab* (Tehran: National Archives, 1371/1992).

65. *Alam-e nesvan*, nos. 1–6, year 2, 1300/1921; *Dokhtaran-e Iran*, no. 4, year 1, 1311/1932.

66. Badr al-Moluk-e Bamdad, *Zan-e Irani az enqelab-e mashrutiyat ta enqelab-e sefid* (Tehran: Ibn Sina, 1347/1968), 51.

67. Peter Avery, *Modern Iran* (London: Ernest Benn, 1965), 288.

68. The queen of Afghanistan who appeared unveiled on a state visit to Iran with her husband was criticized. In Shiraz some women who wore light-colored veils were attacked by a mob.

69. Avery, *Modern Iran*, 291.

70. *Khoshunat va farhang*, doc. nos. 38, 43, 119, 148, 188, 240, 467. It is possible that documents about the ulama's cooperation have been removed from this collection because only a few are recorded in both volumes. Reza Shah's regime had undermined the ulama's power and prestige for some years prior to this.

71. Ibid., doc. no. 387.

72. Vahed-e Sina, *Qiyam-e Goharshad* (Tehran, n.p., n.d.), 37–38.

73. Bamdad, *Zan-e Irani*, 89–91.

74. In a city such as Isfahan, the organization of meetings was not difficult because many convenient places such as the Chehel Sotun (where a garden party was held), a factory, a conference hall of the department of education, the municipality, a house of a rich merchant or official, and a school were available. It was more difficult to find places suitable for meetings in smaller towns. In Bojnurd and Qa'enat, it was said that there was nowhere to hold a meeting. *Khoshunat va farhang*, doc. nos. 92, 93, 94, 174, 263.

75. *Iran*, no. 39, 1311/1932; also *Alam-e nesvan*, no. 1, year 13, 1311/1932.

76. Reza Shah emulated Ataturk in more ways than one. Although Ataturk was opposed to the veil, it was never abolished as brutally as it was done in Iran. In fact, a 1935 proposal to ban women's veils in Turkey was never implemented.

77. *Khoshunat va farhang*, doc. nos. 2, 3.

78. Hesam al-Din Ashna, "Kashf-e hejab dar ayneh-ye asnad," *Ganjineh*, no. 1, 1370/1991.

79. *Rastakkhiz*, no. 511, 1355/1976. Also Ashna, "Kashf-e hejab."

80. *Khoshunat va farhang*, doc. no. 6.

81. Ibid., doc. nos. 261, 410, 416. In Ferdows women had taken to wearing their old chadors as soon as the governor left on leave; ibid., doc. nos. 82, 285, 445, 446.

82. In Kalat someone asked to make an exception for older women, but the request was refused. From Isfahan the governor wrote that the city was conservative, that even carriage drivers wore turbans, and that it would take a long time to undo the habit of centuries. In both cases no exception was allowed. From Gilan it was reported that women were too poor to afford new clothes, and the government was asked to advance two months of salary for municipal employees; ibid., passim.

83. Ibid., doc. nos. 106–7, 84, 301, 452.

84. Ibid., doc. no. 293.

85. Ibid., doc. nos. 58, 355, 354, 388, 409.

86. Ibid., doc. nos. 453, 287.

87. Ibid., doc. no. 261.

88. Ibid., doc. nos. 132, 261, 263.

89. Ibid., doc. nos. 391, 206, 216, 229.

90. Ibid., doc. nos. 97, 59, 240.

91. Ibid., doc. no. 228.

92. Ibid., doc. nos. 316, 190, 191.

93. Ibid., doc. nos. 257, 279.

94. Ibid., doc. no. 244.

95. Ibid., doc. nos. 32, 44, 45, 261.

96. A man recalled that he realized his wife was beautiful once he saw other women unveiled. See also Baba Safari, *Ardabil dar gozargah-e tarikh* (Tehran: Danishgah-ye azad-e Ardabil, 1370/1991), 2:23–25.

97. *Khoshunat va farhang,* doc. no. 180.

98. Some women wrote to parliament complaining that many pregnant and sick women had lost their lives as the result of police brutality and that large sums of money had been extorted from them. The government of Yazd replied in answer to an inquiry from Tehran that it could not ascertain who had written the letter and that it suspected that one author was a local religious leader. Ibid., doc. nos. 568–70.

99. Ibid., doc. no. 49.

100. *Vaqaʻeh-ye kashf-e hejab,* doc. nos. 196–99; *Khoshunat va farhang,* doc. nos. 570, 139.

4 The Women's Organization of Iran: Evolutionary Politics and Revolutionary Change

MAHNAZ AFKHAMI

THIS CHAPTER IS AN ACCOUNT of the women's movement in prerevolutionary Iran. The focus is on the activities of the Women's Organization of Iran (WOI) and its interactions with the government, royal court, and clergy and other conservative forces during the two decades preceding the Islamic revolution in 1978–79. Much of the discussion, particularly where the story of WOI is concerned, is based on the author's personal knowledge and experience as WOI's secretary-general between 1970 and 1978. WOI was a link in a chain of events that began with the first progressive impulses in Iran's recent history. It is important to place it in historical perspective on issues of culture change, political power, socioeconomic development, and institution building.

The dynamics and contradictions of political, economic, and social factors that allowed the Iranian women's movement to go forward despite strong and seemingly immovable historical and traditional obstacles are not only of historical interest but also relevant to the condition of women in other contemporary developing countries. The history of Iranian women's struggle for rights shows that changing cultural nuances differentiate societies and often alter the balance of values in the same society over time. The process of differentiation makes language and behavior deceptive when encountered out of context. Words such as *freedom, equality, equity,* and *justice* connote differently in different settings. As Iranian society moved through the twentieth century, it became increasingly multicontextual. Different social sets saw reality through different lenses that often reflected varied and sometimes contradictory images and made it difficult to reach consensus. Varieties of conflicting political forms of modernity such as democracy, socialism, communism, and fascism clashed not only with each other but also with different manifestations of traditionalism, including religious reaction to modernism regardless of its form or substance. Under these circumstances, for most groups that sought to influence society, options were limited to either using force or seeking a balance among various interests. The story of WOI is best understood if we keep in mind the need for balance.

In Iran, as in other parts of the world, women have always had to fight for their rights. But different women—and the same women at different times in their personal development—understood the meaning of "rights" variably according to the society and culture of their specific environment at the time. Clearly, at any given moment only certain groups of women possessed the opportunity to participate in the political processes we associate with women's human rights. The activist woman belonged by definition to a minority of her gender, regardless of her social status. The problem she faced was how to reconcile her ideals with the inertia marking the larger patriarchal society and culture that surrounded her. Men were only one component of the patriarchal order; the other, more complex and difficult to bring into the balancing act, were women belonging to the majority who, deeply inundated in the patriarchal society and culture, were at once preservers of the old order and objects as well as subjects of the activists' political struggle. Thus, depending on the historical moment, the successful woman activist moved carefully within a range of options defining the limits within which she could communicate with the larger society without betraying her ideals.

Because the combined forces of men and women who supported the patriarchal order were inordinately strong, women activists have always resorted, consciously or not, to a variety of devices depending on the society's place on the scale of change. In Iran, as this short history of the women's movement indicates, the device used at the turn of the twentieth century was sporadic demands for the education of girls. Seemingly innocuous, the demand nevertheless elicited ferocious opposition. In fact, girls' education did not materialize on any socially meaningful scale until decades later when it was buttressed by the state's power. But the state was also patriarchal. It could not accept education for girls and women as a human right. Rather, it saw it as a mechanism to equip women with the intellectual means necessary for bringing up males capable of serving the state. In time, the ideology of development took root, and the state began to eye women as "manpower" for development. Now women assumed value also in their own right, not only as nurturers of sturdy, serviceable boys but also as agents of socioeconomic development. The tempo of women joining the rank of the minority accelerated. As women became active on the socioeconomic scene, they began to affect men, transforming some of them into agents of struggle for women's rights. These men, inside and outside the government, were critical for the success of the women's cause. They became bridges that initially connected women to political and economic power.

The state, of course, was never feminist. In Iran, women always had to fight an uphill battle. The converted men in the government were useful, but they rarely occupied positions directly related to women's rights, particularly in the realm of law. Nor would they spearhead change if not spurred by women. The history of WOI's relationship with the state is in part a history of women mobilizing converted men in the government to help convince others, notably Muslim clerics, that women's demands were not only good for modernization and development but also socially and culturally innocuous. In time, women were able to talk directly to the unconverted, but by then WOI had achieved significant power in its own right.

The source of this power was organization. The function of organization was to interconnect many small groups of women leaders who were scattered across the country working at the grassroots level, usually in poorer districts of cities and small towns. Together these women constituted a mutually empowering system forcing society and government to pay attention at both the center and the periphery. This chapter demonstrates how the process of mutual empowerment among women was begun in Iran and how it developed.

In modernizing patriarchal societies, international connections and support are particularly relevant in promoting women's human rights. In WOI's case, international connections proved critical. Iran played a major role in formulating concepts and policies that became the World Plan of Action adopted by the United Nations First World Conference on Women in 1975 in Mexico City. The WOI then used the world plan to formulate and implement a National Plan of Action that allowed WOI to become an integral part of the political decision-making process, not only in matters that were traditionally considered women's issues but in all government decisions that had an impact on women's lives. This feat was until then unmatched anywhere else in the world.

The Women's Organization of Iran was established and grew in size, membership, and function during a period of rapid economic and social development. It was sometimes said that WOI was an arm of the government and the shah, but women's roles in the subsequent revolution belie this statement. We will take up this issue when we discuss the reasons why women, many of whom were WOI members, participated and were able to do so in great numbers in the revolution. Iranians and others who write about Iran often mention Mohammad Reza Shah Pahlavi (r. 1941–79) as if he were omnipotent—a notion more imagination than rational discourse. He was in many ways, formally and substantively, the point of convergence of decisions about broad policy. The state acted in his name; he gave the commands; hence he was assumed to be always the mover. In reality, for the shah to support any social-policy proposal, sufficient social pressure from various power groups within and outside the government had to occur in order to convince him that a manageable convergence of opinion existed in favor of the move. It was up to WOI and its allies to lobby the government and other loci of political power to produce the conditions in which the convergence could be perceived. Whenever women failed to elicit this perception, they also failed to mobilize the state's support in favor of their demands.

The women's movement in Iran must also be studied in the perspective of history if it is to be understood at all. We must look at women's place in Iranian society before the modernizing process began, develop a theory of social change in relation to women and modernization, and devise a model that best corresponds to the social facts and events as they existed and oc-curred in real time and space. Only then can we come close to appreciating differentially the challenges that Iranian women faced and their successes and failures before and after the revolution. I expand on these points by discuss-ing briefly change in the social conditions of Iranian women and their strug-gle for rights in the first half of the twentieth century; WOI's organization, membership, and activities; and Iranian women's achievements before the revolution.

A Half Century of Struggle for Rights

The life of the Iranian woman at the turn of the twentieth century was a maze of regulations and limitations meant to keep her cloistered existence beyond the reach of any but her immediate kin. As an infant, her birth brought dis-appointment to all, even the midwife who lost the gift coin that a boy's birth would bring her. As a child, she was told to move quietly, sit demurely, keep her eyes downcast, and not speak unless spoken to. She was taught—if she belonged to the privileged classes—to read the Qur'an and recite from the great poets. At the age of nine, she was considered mature. Security tightened around her. In more affluent urban settings, she resided in the *andarun* (inner house) with other women of the family. She would not leave this space or go outside the high walls of the courtyard unless she attended the public bath or paid an occasional visit to a relative's or friend's family in the andarun of another house.

As soon as possible, a marriage was arranged for her with a man whom she had never seen but whose female relatives had briefed concerning her physical attributes, which they had studied in the women's bath. Following negotiations over her *mahriyeh* (bride-price) and *jahizyeh* (dowry), in which she could not participate, the wedding took place.

Sometimes she found herself one of two or more wives whose competitive struggle to retain their place and security within the household would include elaborate intrigue and intricate maneuvering. She would also have to accept direction from and domination by her husband's mother and criticism from his sisters. The in-law behavior pattern would become a model for her to follow in later years when she gained a similar position of power and prestige in the household of her married son. Her public presence was limited to appearances on the streets only to perform necessary missions related to religious or family duties. Bundled in a black shroud, her face covered except for holes in the eye area to permit vision, she was allowed on one side of the street while men walked on the other. If it became necessary to cross the street, she would have to receive permission from a policeman. Horse-drawn carriages, the only means of transportation, were rigidly segregated by sex. Drivers were required to raise the carriage hoods when carrying women.

Despite these circumstances some women demonstrated extraordinary independence, courage, and initiative and, at times, even struggled to assert their will in social and political matters.[1] Women's participation in the revolution of 1905–9 is on record.[2] Once the constitution was in place and the parliament (*majlis*) began the work of governing the nation, however, women's roles in the revolution were ignored. Although the original document did not place a limitation on political participation on the basis of sex, the electoral laws of 1911 specifically barred women from the political process.[3] The first two decades of the new century brought other developments that helped provide the necessary foundation for the eventual participation of women in the country's sociopolitical affairs. The first girls' schools opened in Tehran and a few other cities, paving the way for the establishment of a teacher-training college in 1918, which in turn provided trained teachers for the expansion of secondary education for women. During the same period, periodicals were published by and specifically for women. These early stirrings among women met with extreme antagonism whenever they gained public notice.[4]

Women's situation changed significantly during Reza Shah's reign (1925–41). More women were admitted to schools and government service, the latter particularly in the fields of education and health. The state policy of unveiling (1936), although resented and opposed by traditional urban men and women and controversial among the rest, proved nevertheless the single most important step toward ending the segregation of women in society. Many educated women wished to unveil, and after Reza Shah's abdication in 1941 these and other women continued to appear unveiled in public and to work in government and private offices.

The 1940s saw a heightened consciousness of women's roles in society. The clash of ideas in the free-for-all political arena led to an effervescence of ideological and utopian thinking. The prevalent ideologies rarely emphasized women's issues, but they did allow women a freedom of expression that enhanced their consciousness. In this process the Tudeh party played a particularly important role by enlisting young women from student and other social groups at various organizational levels. Tudeh publications pointed to existing prejudices against women and promised a bright future under socialism, but the process was handicapped by the systematic and persistent subordination of women's political, economic, and social rights to the demands and priorities of ideology.

During the 1950s the now much larger group of educated women, increasingly aware of women's progress in other countries, began to form various organizations to improve women's condition in Iran. One of the first of these organizations was the Rah-e No (new path) organized by Mehrangiz Dowlatshahi in 1955. Another organization, founded by Safieh Firouz in 1956, later known as the Women's League of Supporters of the Declaration of Human Rights, actively sought equal political rights for women. The central committee of this organization had an audience with the shah in 1956. "The Shah, who was impressed with their request for political rights, promised three seats in the [Tehran] municipal council. Immediately a delegation of over eighty mullahs warned His Majesty against taking any favorable action for the women, saying 'if you act, you may not be here to carry out the action.' The Shah did not act."[5]

After several attempts to unify the women's movement and various experiments in creating a federation of women's organizations, women leaders, seeking high-placed support in their efforts to gain the franchise, asked

Ashraf Pahlavi, the shah's twin sister and a powerful personality in her own right, to lend support to the movement. In response, the princess commissioned a fifty-member organizing committee to prepare the articles of association for a new federal body called the High Council of Women's Organizations of Iran. The high council came into being formally in 1959 with a membership of seventeen organizations interested in women's issues. It concentrated its efforts largely on gaining the franchise.[6]

Despite progress made in the preceding three decades, Iranian women in the early 1960s were still deprived of some basic legal, social, and political rights. They could not work outside the home or travel without their husband's written permission. They could not initiate divorce proceedings except in extreme cases of the husband's illness, insanity, imprisonment, or desertion. They could not become guardians of their children even after the father's death, when, according to the law, a paternal grandfather or uncle took precedence over the mother. Women could not serve as judges or become career diplomats. They could not transfer their citizenship to their children; indeed their citizenship was in jeopardy if they married a non-Iranian. They inherited from a father's estate only half of what their brothers received and from a husband's estate only one-fourth when there were no children and one-eighth if there were children. They could be divorced by their husband with or without their knowledge by a simple unilateral statement, or they could be faced with the presence of a second, third, or fourth wife in their home at any moment. Forced by economic need and patriarchal fiat, they could be contracted in a *mut'a* (temporary) marriage for periods ranging from hours to years in exchange for a fee for their sexual services with no enforceable rights for themselves or any children resulting from the union.

The ability of Iranian women to control their lives at mid-century was conditioned by the strong, deep-rooted, and systematic opposition of the conservative Muslim clergy and other conservative forces, many within the government, to their efforts to gain rights. The clergy's attitude about women's rights was also a key factor in its persistent opposition to the Pahlavi regime's modernization policies. But women's objective situation had significantly changed by the 1960s, even though their rights and responsibilities appeared to be the same in the shari'a (Islamic law) and in law books. The work of educating and organizing, which had begun before the constitutional revolution of 1906, had accelerated and expanded, to produce a larger number of qualified women committed to change. These developments in turn provided the infrastructure without which the rapid transformation of women's roles in the following years would have been unlikely.

By the 1960s women had become more organized and politically vocal, capable of lobbying the shah, the government, and the more moderate members of the clergy. A culture of development, which included the idea of women's participation in social affairs, had taken stronger root, and the shah, a believer in modernization, had become more powerful politically.

On 26 January 1963 Mohammad Reza Shah's six-point reform program (later dubbed the White Revolution), which included the revision of the electoral law to grant women the right to vote, was approved in a national referendum. In February parliament formally ratified the revision. Some members of the clergy, including Ayatollah Khomeini, who led a series of uprisings in Qom and Tehran, reacted violently. The government withstood the pressure against reform, and following bloody clashes between the army and the demonstrators Khomeini was exiled to Turkey. The subsequent election of six women to parliament (including Hajar Tarbiat, an early leader of the women's movement) and the appointment of two women to the senate brought further encouragement and optimism. Equally important, the reforms were followed by an important change in the composition of the cabinet. With the appointment of Hasan Ali Mansur as prime minister in March 1964, a relatively younger group of men, soon to be joined by a woman, entered the cabinet. Younger, more educated men and women assumed leadership positions in ministries related to economic, social, and cultural affairs. These changes affected the relationship between women activists and government leaders. Whereas in the past the government's initial reaction to women's demands was invariably negative and cautious, now a positive, although still cautious, attitude of cooperation emerged. Similar attitudinal changes in the now-expanding modern private sector produced a rudimentary political synergy in favor of women. It had now become easier for women to organize and to communicate their needs and demands.

The rapid expansion of the women's movement and the growth of the organizational capability of the various affiliated groups in the High Council of Women in the next few years led to a reorganization of the umbrella body. In 1966 the high council initiated, organized, and supervised the election of a five-thousand-member assembly of women representatives from all regions of the country. The assembly met in Tehran on 19 November 1966 and eventually approved the charter creating the Women's Organization of Iran.[7] Fifty-five existing women's associations affiliated themselves with the newly created body. Other associations, including women lawyers and university women whose members were actively involved with WOI, chose to remain autonomous.

Women's Organization of Iran: Organization and Evolution

The Women's Organization of Iran was a nonprofit institution working mainly through volunteers. Its basic unit was a branch formally established in any locality where thirty women gathered in a general assembly to elect a seven-member board of directors, who then chose one of their members to act as secretary of the branch. The average branch member was a woman in her late twenties or early thirties, usually an elementary-school teacher or low-level government worker and sometimes a homemaker. Each branch sent elected representatives to the national general assembly, which met annually to set goals and establish guidelines for the organization's activities. Between meetings of the general assembly, a council of eleven members met weekly in its place to manage the organization's general affairs. Initially five members of the council were elected by the assembly and six, including the secretary-general, were appointed by the honorary president. The appointment powers of the president were used to include members of religious minorities as well as academics in the policy-making processes of the organization.[8]

The WOI budget was initially provided by local charitable contributions, national fund-raising, and five rials (approximately seven cents) per elementary-school textbook donated by the Offset Printing Press (affiliated with the imperial organization for social services and producer of school texts for the ministry of education). The cadres worked on a voluntary basis, except for some forty women employees at the headquarters who were paid through funds from the printing company. During my tenure (1970–78), we developed and implemented the concept of women's centers to help women achieve, among other things, economic self-sufficiency. The centers required paid professional staff. The budget for the centers was raised through a variety of means. The actual physical premises were sometimes built using funds donated by individuals, groups, or local councils. Sometimes they were old rented houses in underprivileged neighborhoods. As the educational, legal, family-planning, and job-oriented programs of the centers grew, WOI was able to convince relevant government agencies that each function performed at the centers satisfied a specific national need. Eventually WOI convinced the government that its services were necessary for national development and that the government was obligated to assist the organization in the best possible manner. Women deserved and had a right to receive their fair share of the common patrimony that the government controlled and appropriated as income from the sale of oil and other nationalized resources. By the late 1970s, WOI had some two thousand paid specialists in its legal, childcare, and family-planning sections in 120 centers throughout the country. The budget of the organization had grown tenfold, not counting volunteer services and in-kind and charitable contributions of members. The plan and budget organization suggested and parliament approved the amount of support provided the centers based on their review of the centers' work in the areas of literacy, general education, and vocational training.

Learning from the Grass Roots: Concept of a Family Welfare Center

Initially WOI focused on establishing contact among women belonging to different social strata in various geographic areas. Members agreed from the outset that neither Western models nor traditional Iranian concepts about the proper role of women offered a satisfactory conceptual framework for the Iranian women's movement. Western concepts presupposed historical conditions as well as sociocultural structures not existing in Iran. Traditional Iranian concepts, based on patriarchal structures, established a context too narrow to allow for women's most rudimentary rights, let alone full participation in society. Clearly, we needed to develop concepts and strategies to enable us to build and successfully cross a bridge linking legal and political conditions largely wedded to local traditions with aspirations emerging mostly as a result of changes related to global history.

Women were drawn together at this stage by a common belief in the unsatisfactory and unfair state of their condition. Women leaders—including secretaries of WOI branches, members of central and provincial councils, heads of organizations, and other prominent women associated with WOI—began a dialogue with a wide variety of individuals and groups in order to explore women's priorities and identify goals appropriate for the movement. They believed that without some sort of consensus among women it would not be possible to establish an efficient national organization with truly effective programs.

The initial contacts and discussions throughout Iran expanded WOI's organizational network and helped clarify some immediate demands of the majority of women activists. In every forum and discussion, the recurring theme was the need for economic self-sufficiency. The primary means to achieve this goal was education, in most cases involving simple literacy skills followed by vocational training in fields where a scarcity of skilled labor occurred. The organization's main concern soon became the teaching of literacy and job-oriented skills. The classes, becoming the nucleus of WOI centers, were designed to meet the requirements of the job market. Two limiting factors existed: lack of trained teachers in some fields in parts of the country and the reluctance of some women to participate in classes with an "unfeminine" image. No matter how lucrative the result and how simple the training, most women hesitated to take part in certain courses on the grounds that such training would reduce their chances for marriage. "What man would want a carpenter/plumber/electrician for a wife?" they asked. Considerable consciousness-raising was necessary before nontraditional courses would meet with any degree of success.

Around the classes grew other subsidiary services required by the exigencies of women's living conditions. The necessity of providing care for the trainees' children brought to classes made childcare facilities a standard feature. It soon became apparent that unwanted pregnancies curtailed life planning for women and stopped their training and professional development. Distribution of family-planning information and, where possible, advice and services became a function of WOI centers. Job counseling and placement services, a needed outgrowth of the training courses, soon expanded to include family and legal counseling.

By 1975 WOI had built a network of 349 branches and 120 centers and had reached an understanding of the problems and demands of different groups of women. Experience showed that to gain maximum results the centers must remain an integral part of the community, that neither size nor appearance must differ markedly from the surrounding architecture, and that small centers, each within walking distance of neighboring homes, were more inviting than larger, more elaborate structures. The centers developed and expanded in number and quality but not in individual size. Twelve centers were located in impoverished areas of south Tehran. WOI's school of social work, which trained employees selected from across the nation for work in the centers, was in Naziabad, south of Tehran, one of the country's poorest communities. Young women chosen for this course were given two years of training before returning to their towns and villages. Schooling was kept at a minimum so that ties between the young women and their home network and lifestyle would not be permanently altered by long stays in Tehran.

Research on Women

While new centers were created locally throughout Iran, WOI's center for research on women was conducting studies on women in various socioeconomic and geographic sectors and identifying ways of finding solutions to their problems. Various studies pointed to the interrelationship of the status of women and general improvements in society as a whole. Although changes in women's status were shown to improve their situation in the family and society, the reverse was not necessarily true. Improvements and development in various sectors of the economy did not automatically improve women's position. In some cases, such as the mechanization of agriculture, women's status was lowered and their participation in family financial and material affairs was decreased substantially because learning new methods was largely limited to men while women were consistently left with the more menial and unrewarding tasks. Four of the center's studies that significantly affected WOI policy are mentioned here.

A Comparative Study of the Socioeconomic Situation of Working Women in Tehran, Qazvin, and Kashan, conducted in 1974–75, investigated the working conditions, social awareness, and degree of independence of women workers in these cities.[9] The study showed that the best means of reaching these women was the radio (41 percent referred to it as their sole means of gaining information), that lack of efficient WOI contact with these women was due to the almost exclusive reliance of the organization on printed material (only 25 percent knew of the organization and its activities), that they perceived themselves as having little freedom of choice (only 30 percent thought they were the final source of decision making on matters of personal and social concern to them), and that they were religious but their religious attitudes were at best full of ambiguities (83 percent said they followed all religious rules and practices, yet only 12 percent considered a "good" person to be a "religious" person). Additional information was gained regarding these women's attitudes toward family planning, health practices, and social activities. This study helped shift WOI's attention to the use of the radio as the primary means of communication and reemphasized the provision of childcare services as the prerequisite for women's participation in the workforce.

A study of Qashqa'i tribal women conducted in 1974 and published as *The Status of Women in Tribal Society* supplied information on women's roles in the Qashqa'i social order, their tasks, assigned roles within the family, differences in attitude and lifestyle in various tribal strata, and customs regarding marriage, childcare, and divorce.[10] It revealed that in Qashqa'i society, women's rights were based on tribal customs and traditions rather than on Islamic or state law. The attitude of women toward life was reflected in their stated aspirations regarding their children's future. Of all the women interviewed, no one chose farming, gardening, or shepherding for her child. Nomadism had come to be perceived as an inferior lifestyle by these women. When women were asked about the preferred place of residence for their children, the majority stated that cities were, if appropriate jobs were available there. This study helped WOI to understand better the problems of Qashqa'i women. It brought greater sensitivity to the preparation of material for an elementary course in women's studies at Shiraz's tribal teacher-training school. It also helped WOI clarify its position on the question of the settlement of nomads.

Images of Women in Elementary-School Textbooks charted out the recurrence of certain concepts and images of men and women in texts that led to the inevitable conclusion that women's roles in society were limited in type and variety.[11] It proved that even when pictured within the home, women's activities and impact were portrayed within traditional areas of nursing and household duties and not in supervision, organization, and decision making. The tone of schoolbooks was completely masculine.

> The texts under study reflect male and female roles in a rigid and unexchangeable fashion. . . . The roles assigned to men and women are always and without exception assigned to men and women according to sex, and exchange of roles does not occur. . . . For example, the role of women in the family has always been shown to be cleaning, cooking, and so forth, and the responsibility of men is always financial support. Never does it occur that a man is either cooking or helping his wife in the process of food preparation. The reverse is also true—that is, a woman is never seen as a scientist or writer. It is as if the social role, like biological roles, is unexchangeable. The only role assigned to both sexes is that of teacher. Not only are the roles assigned to women limited, but little variety occurs in them, so that the only atmosphere for self-expression for a woman is that of the family. . . . In contrast, the roles assigned to men reflect a considerable variety. A man has a foothold within the family and status and responsibility in society. All scientific, literary, and artistic creation is his, and he governs all productive social activity. The number of references to the role of women in the books is negligible compared to the frequency of references to men.[12]

Aside from the unequal treatment of men and women, the general value system imparted to schoolchildren through books was slanted and less than wholesome because relationships based on "expression of power, command, and pity and acts of assistance and generosity have been mentioned or imparted as unilateral and one-sided actions, and concepts such as cooperation, joint effort, mutual trust, and values such as attention to human worth have been understated."[13] This study resulted in the creation of a committee composed of representatives of WOI and the ministry of education to study and revise elementary schoolbooks to eliminate sexist attitudes and images.

Urban Design and Women's Lives presented specific suggestions to promote community cooperation and services to assist working mothers through urban planning and community development projects that provide for the needs of working women facing loss of support from the extended family.[14]

A series of legal research projects focused on a comparative study of the laws of Iran and the U.N. Convention on the Elimination of Discrimination against Women. These provided detailed information on the shortcomings of existing laws and for the preparation of proposals for revision of these laws.[15]

The most significant undertaking of the center for research and one with the most impact was the Saveh functional literacy project cosponsored by UNESCO in 1973–75.[16] Its purpose was to experiment with the best methods to increase the literacy rate among village women in Iran. The project included seventeen villages near the town of Saveh in Central province. It viewed the problem of literacy as an aspect of the life experience of rural communities and approached it within the framework of nonformal education and in harmony with the social, cultural, religious, and economic fabric of each community. It prepared teaching material and took into account the general learning needs of the community, including teaching basic literacy and mathematics, agricultural instructing (such as growing nutritionally consequential products), preparing more marketable designs and dyes for carpet weaving, and setting up cooperatives for the production and sale of handicrafts.

The inclusion of these activities in the experimental project spurred interest and guaranteed the continued attendance of women participants. The teacher-training program taught methodology to thirty-five village women and six supervisors from WOI's research center. The project provided the first instance in Iran where the task of literacy training for village women was undertaken with the participation of women in villages. Adjunct activities included printing the monthly publication *Zan-e dana* (Wise woman), written and produced with the help of participants in the classes.

The project reconfirmed some basic assumptions with which it had begun. It proved that a successful literacy program for women in rural Iran must be multipurpose and take into consideration the social context of the village women's lives in each locality, interrelatedness of the program with other existing educational programs, inclusion of classes for men within the literacy project, recognition of the villagers' religious beliefs, concentration on moral and spiritual as well as material benefits of literacy, and exclusive employment of local teachers. Such a program was thought necessary for an all-encompassing nationwide system rather than a series of sporadic, isolated projects.

The project was given over to the national committee for world literacy program, which incorporated its findings into the national program and was able to institute similar programs in more than seven thousand villages throughout Iran, administered on a decentralized organizational basis through local groups and committees.

From Man's Complement to Complete Woman: Gradual Transformation of WOI's Mission

In the 1940s, 1950s, and early 1960s women's groups were for the most part engaged in welfare and charity projects in which more privileged women tried to help and comfort the underprivileged. They also emphasized education by arguing that it would make women better wives and mothers. As more women were educated and sought employment, the rhetoric changed to stress women's ability to carry both the burdens of homemaking and professional responsibility while remaining good mothers, good wives, and pleasant companions for their mates. Women's education and professionalism, it was stressed on every occasion, would in fact allow them at once to help with family finances and raise their children better. Rapid changes in women's condition, especially an increasing number of trained and educated professionals entering the workforce, made it apparent that to carry the double burden of home and profession without changes in men's behavior or in society's structures and attitudes would be well nigh impossible for a majority of women. The ideological turning point came at the 1973 general assembly, which led to the amendment of the WOI constitution.

At the assembly's opening session, some activists spoke about the beneficial effects of women's education and employment for the family and women's proven ability to perform as traditional mothers and wives and simultaneously as modern professionals. A member of the central council argued that the role of woman was complementary to that of man, using the image of an apple—the woman being the half that completes the whole. I walked to the podium after my colleague. I looked at the gathering and wondered if I had sensed its feelings correctly from our conversations and debates during exploratory sessions made in preparation for the assembly. I said, "Sisters, it is time to name our problem and its solution. We know that we are not all superwomen. It is unfair to expect us to be superwomen. No one can function in so many different and demanding roles. We ought not to be asked to accept total responsibility for the home while holding a full-time job outside the home. Women should not be asked either to do both jobs or to give up life outside the home. We are each a whole human being, complete in ourselves. We are half of nothing and no one." After a few seconds of silence, applause broke out and then shouts and the loud ululations of our colleagues from Iran's south. We had reached a point where we were able and willing to express our thoughts freely and to insist that our condition, roles, and needs had changed. We no longer begged for a chance to do everything under rules that were not of our making. We demanded that society's structure and relationships among family members change so that an equitable distribution of rights and responsibilities would occur. We were challenging the political structure of the family unit as well as the social hierarchy of which it was the nucleus.

After the initial exuberance and enthusiasm, reality set in. We were concerned about how our discussions would be reflected in the press and how the public and the authorities would react. But there was no turning back. The assembly proceeded to take appropriate measures, including amending the constitution. The major change involved part of article one, which had defined the organization's goal as "assisting women in performing their social responsibilities and also in performing their important role as mother and wife within the changing Iranian family." The revised constitution made no mention of women's role in the home and split rights and responsibilities into two separate articles with rights appearing two paragraphs above responsibilities. The goal now was "defending the individual, family, and social rights of women to ensure their complete equality in society and before the law." The other significant change in the constitution involved the election of members of the central council. In the previous constitution, half of the council was elected while the other half was appointed by the honorary president. In the new constitution, all members were elected.

International Activities

One of WOI's instruments of pressuring the government was the relationship it established with women's organizations in other countries. Contacts with women's groups in countries with diverse sociopolitical systems such as the People's Republic of China, France, Iraq, Pakistan, and the Soviet Union were established through exchange of delegations. These contacts facilitated comparative research and provided information on issues of priority to women, which was used in support of changes sought in Iran. International women's organizations also provided moral support as well as ammunition in the national struggle. International appeals were particularly effective in countries sensitive to international public opinion and actively interested in improving their image. Thus Iran, whose leadership was highly responsive to international media and opinion, was particularly affected by the interaction of Iranian and international feminist leaders. WOI joined the activities of the International Women's Year in 1975 with enthusiasm. With its strong national network, its third-world Muslim society and culture, and potential financial support from the government, WOI was in a highly favorable position to play a leading role in the International Women's Year conference. The consultative committee producing the draft of the World Plan of Action for the improvement of women's status was chaired by Princess Ashraf Pahlavi, head of Iran's delegation to the conference. During the conference in Mexico City, the main resolutions, which committed member nations among others to a mid-decade world conference to monitor national progress and to establish the International Research and Training Institute for the Advancement of Women (INSTRAW), were initiated by Iran. Iran was to host the mid-decade conference in 1980 and to provide a permanent home for INSTRAW. The final draft of the World Plan of Action adopted by the U.N. General Assembly in 1975 reflected many of the ideas researched and tested in Iran and was based essentially on the following concepts: (1) regardless of sociopolitical, cultural, and economic differences among nations, similarities in the situation of women are found throughout the world; (2) problems of development cannot be solved efficiently and in any real sense without a thorough change in women's status in developing countries; and

(3) involvement of governments and their total commitment to initiate, implement, and monitor change are essential in bringing about women's full participation.

The National Plan of Action

Once the World Plan of Action was adopted by the U.N. General Assembly, WOI began preparing the National Plan of Action (NPA) for the improvement of the status of women in Iran. Ostensibly, NPA was a response to the U.N. call on member states to give priority, over the ten-year period of 1975–85, to policies and actions designed to achieve the objectives of the U.N. decade for women. WOI used the international decree to pressure the government to allocate necessary resources to improve women's status in all social sectors. Real change in women's status, however, involved such drastic alterations in the infrastructure that it could not possibly be attained without a convergence of opinions on priorities, values, and needs of women; a realistic appraisal of available resources; and women's ability to engage government organizations in problem solving and policy implementation.

To achieve a consensus among women, more than seven hundred panels, organized and financed locally by WOI chapters in 1976 and 1977, debated relevant issues. The panels were followed by statewide seminars in each province and provided opportunities for further and more comprehensive discussion and dialogue. Out of hundreds of hours of deliberation by thousands of women across the country, a preliminary draft plan of action was produced.

The next step was to involve the government in the process of planning in order to take advantage of its information resources and, more important, to mobilize its machinery in support of WOI's goals. After much lobbying, WOI succeeded in establishing a high council for cooperation—composed of eight cabinet ministers; directors of national Iranian radio and television, the civil service commission, and the national committee for world literacy program; and the Women's Organization—to support women's goals. The special committees charged with preparation of policies and programs of the sixth development plan and the national council of provincial governors general were persuaded to allocate special sessions to the plan's discussion. Each series of suggestions emanating from these discussions was studied at WOI meetings, and certain adjustments were made in the draft. To test popular reaction at the grassroots level, the final draft was placed on the agenda of each town and village council. The resulting document, more conservative in certain areas but immeasurably more radical in implementation potential, was approved by a national congress of ten thousand women delegates in Tehran in January 1977.

Following lengthy negotiations, the cabinet finally approved the document in May 1978. In its final form, the document stipulated not only basic goals and broad guidelines for improving women's status but also mechanisms for implementation, evaluation, and monitoring. This process was a prologue in Iran to one that in later decades became known as "gender mainstreaming," which emerged as a primary goal of development programs internationally. Iran's cabinet decreed that the high council for cooperation (including twelve ministries and national organizations) be formally responsible for reviewing the status of women under its jurisdiction, identifying resources, creating viable programs, drafting necessary legislation, and evaluating improvements in women's status. The prime minister chaired the annual meeting of ministers, and the minister of state for women's affairs chaired the monthly meetings of senior deputy ministers, which were held in the prime minister's office. The momentum achieved through widespread consultation and interaction among women and between government participants and nongovernmental organizations changed what would have otherwise amounted to no more than a plea of a pressure group to an essential part of the national agenda. As such, it became the most important accomplishment of the women's movement in Iran. If the failure of the political system in Iran had not made it irrelevant, Iran's experiment in the interaction of the women's movement and the national decision-making apparatus could well have provided a model for many developing (and perhaps other) countries.[17]

WOI and the Government

To transform the condition and role of Iranian women, WOI was faced with the task of mobilizing national and international resources on a scale hitherto unknown in Iran. Contrary to revolutionary rhetoric that portrayed WOI as a propaganda tool used by the shah to support his modernization efforts,[18] Iranian women had to fight for every improvement in their lives. A political leadership committed to modernization helped. Whatever measure was deemed necessary for socioeconomic development, such as full literacy, better health and nutrition practices, and training of skilled workers to make possible rapid industrialization, could be easily tied to the necessity of achieving full participation for women. The presence of a network of active women throughout the country, however, was the most important prerequisite for serious consideration of the arguments of women activists by the government. WOI's successful project implementation provided it with credibility. The rest involved a blow-by-blow battle in an ongoing struggle that succeeded when the goals of national development and of women activists could be effectively shown to correspond and that often failed when women's goals reflected gender-related concepts and behavior dealing with interpersonal and family ties. Thus, a quota system to encourage women to participate in technical and engineering fields was achieved almost without a struggle, while the effort to eliminate the husband's permission for women to acquire a passport cost the activists one of their two seats in the senate by bringing about the resignation of Senator Mehrangiz Manouchehrian and a barrage of conservative propaganda accusing WOI of espousing loose moral standards and policies that would weaken family ties.[19]

The shah himself was not a supporter of feminism. His role as the king of kings represented the essence and personification of patriarchy. He stood as the archetypal father figure for the family and nation. But he, as well as many other government leaders, was conscious of and fully accepted women's argument that development was impossible without the full integration of women and a complete change in their status. "Women constitute half of the population of the world. They make up a great workforce whose effective participation in activities is an essential requirement for all development and progress. . . . Let us not forget that problems such as human rights, population, family planning, campaign against illiteracy and poverty, on which the fate of the human race depends, cannot be resolved without the complete and effective participation of women."[20]

Farah Diba Pahlavi, Iran's queen, became a feminist in the early 1970s through a process of delicate consciousness-raising. Her support was sought on issues as diverse as the amendment of the penal code and the revision of elementary-school textbooks to eliminate sexist images. She was often under pressure to formulate her role as the archetypal mother figure for the nation and to serve as an example of a responsible professional woman. On a trip to towns near the Kavir desert, she was brought a chador (veil-wrap) to wear so that she could enter a saint's tomb. A companion gently reminded her that as a role model she ought not to allow herself to be photographed wearing a chador. The mullas present and the local authorities stood by with raised eyebrows. She finally donned the chador but folded it in half to look like a scarf—a sincere attempt at compromise that pleased neither group.[21] Princess Ashraf Pahlavi was a valuable ally whose blunt and straightforward statement of issues in the occasional high-level meetings with government officials was an effective lobbying mechanism that set the tone and pace for actual negotiations later followed by women activists.[22]

Still, suspicion and distrust of any program of organized activity involving women was a great hurdle to overcome. Many men resented any attempt to draw women out of the home and into society. Much work had to be done to convince people that the goal was indeed to strengthen the family. Changing the name of the centers from "houses of women" to "family welfare centers" was an aspect of this campaign. In many locations, drawing influential women into the centers' activities helped to gain trust and prestige. In Qom, for instance, the participation of Ayatollah Shariatmadari's daughters was key to the center's viability. By consciously seeking the participation of female members of the families of the leading clergy in the centers' activities wherever necessary, and by including religious instruction and the reading of the Qur'an in special classes in some areas, WOI minimized confrontation with the clergy, whose overt opposition would have drastically curtailed the expansion of the network.

Another ongoing task was mobilizing government financial support for projects while controlling government interference. The plan and budget organization held certain preconceived ideas about the size and specification of buildings and personnel qualifications that often did not meet needs and possibilities in distant towns and villages. Clashes occurred between WOI secretaries who were familiar with the needs and priorities of underprivileged communities and the plan organization's rather rigid and sometimes unrealistic standards. For example, WOI insisted on keeping the childcare facility in tune with the children's atmosphere and lifestyle. WOI suggested a large, multifunctional space where children played and ate and where cushions were stacked in a corner and then spread on the floor for naps. Most underprivileged children were unfamiliar with beds, mattresses, and chairs. Standards upheld by the government sometimes became not only costly but also alienating to the users. Another problem with which WOI had to cope was the speedy urbanization of young women who came to Tehran to be trained for work in provincial centers. They often sought to further their education and not infrequently preferred to seek employment in Tehran.[23]

Rapid economic growth and the government's modernization philosophy supplied strong arguments for women leaders to seek government support and assistance for programs related to women's participation in the development process. Other programs were presented to government agencies as specific projects addressing particular national, regional, or provincial problems. WOI's successful project implementation and network expansion gradually elicited cooperation from government agencies. The ministry of labor, for example, agreed to supply equipment and teachers wherever necessary when it became clear that women could take on jobs that would otherwise go to foreign workers, thereby eliminating problems of linguistic and cultural adjustment created by imported labor. The ministry of health agreed to provide nurses, midwives, and medical supplies for birth control when it was shown that women would take advantage of a clinic in a women's center much more readily than one in a government institution. Thus, WOI's project-by-project mobilization of government resources resulted in a considerable increase in its capabilities with a minimum negative effect on the autonomy of its volunteer-powered, decentralized organization.

Iranian Women and the Religious Establishment

As WOI became stronger and more influential, opposition to its efforts became stronger and more overt. Leftist opponents of the regime disparaged the movement because, in their strategic thinking, acknowledging its impact would have been tantamount to recognizing the regime's success in an important area of social policy.[24] Religious fundamentalists opposed WOI because its activities conflicted with their version of Islam and, perhaps even more important, because, largely due to WOI efforts, much of their power and authority was lost when a whole set of juridical issues in family interaction was removed from clerical jurisdiction and became a matter for the family courts to decide.

As a matter of routine policy throughout the 1970s, WOI did its best to avoid confrontation with religious authorities. It acknowledged Islam's progressive, egalitarian concepts and its underlying motive of justice for all. Quotations from the Qur'an were used in support of women's rights—for example, lines from the verse (*sura*) Nisa, "Who so doeth good works, whether male or female, and he [or she] is a believer, such will enter paradise and will not be wronged by the dint [blow] of a date stone." Existing role models among the prophet's kin were adopted as heroines of the movement, among them Zainab, whose heroic speech to her family's enemies is an eloquent testimony to a woman's courage. The prophet's wife, Khadija, who was the first to follow him, was mentioned often and honored. Where direct references in the Qur'an related to specific legal arrangements regarding women, care was taken to consult enlightened religious personages so that formulas would be found to skirt direct conflict in legal revisions. For example, the revision of the Family Protection Law in 1975 was so worded that the matter of divorce, which is the unilateral and absolute right of the man in a male-defined Islam, was given by him to his wife as part of the marriage contract. Whenever possible, *fatwas* (religious rulings) were sought from religious leaders on various changes in the laws.[25] In cases such as inheritance, where, aside from the impact of formal statements on the subject in the Qur'an, the economic interests of believers were very much at stake, the issue was left in the background until more immediate and readily attainable goals were achieved. This approach to Islam was based on respect for the opinion of the majority of Iranian women, including many leaders of the movement, who fervently wished to remain within the spiritual guidelines of Islam yet also allow themselves possibilities of growth, change, and progress. The movement's spokeswomen often pointed out that the sacred texts of other religions also placed severe limitations on women's role, a fact that can be understood within the context of the historical conditions in which religious ideas were initially formed. An analogy was often made to the institution of slavery for which all great religions of the world originally made legal provisions. These conflicts were seen to be resolvable without placing a woman in a position of having to make a choice between her religious beliefs and her belief in a progressive modern society.

Little support, however, could be expected from conservative religious authorities, who at best would refrain from outright attacks on WOI. The more progressive Islamic figures such as Ali Shari'ati, whose sermons became popular among certain intellectuals and young university students in Iran, also did not present an egalitarian or, unlike the more conservative clerics, a well thought-out concept of the role of Muslim women in modern society. Shari'ati praised Islam for its realism in upholding mut'a (temporary marriage) on the grounds that "if it [Islam] didn't accept it, it would happen anyway, but out of reach and control. But now having accepted it as a natural and inescapable fact, it makes it a legal and religious fact . . . and frees the conscience of men and women from a feeling of sin."[26] In his famous treatise on women, *Fatemeh Is Fatemeh,* except for generalities focusing on Fatemeh's relationship to her father, the Prophet Mohammad, little information comes through about Fatemeh herself, who is posited as the appropriate model for modern Muslim womanhood. Of all that could be selected for emphasis in such a woman, Shari'ati chooses only one specific act, namely

Fatemeh's washing the blood-stained sword of her husband Ali, who, having returned from killing the enemies of Islam, orders her "in a proud and epic voice, 'Fatemeh, wash my sword.'"[27]

WOI always understood that to promote women's human rights in the existing Iranian society, it needed to account for the social disposition of power and influence. The clerical establishment wielded significant influence on various social strata and therefore needed to be counted in any policy calculation. WOI also understood that to achieve human rights for women, it needed to transcend the discourse of the "value of the woman in Islam" and reach for some rendition of global feminism that accommodated the cultural and religious disposition of Iranians.[28] Given the history of the development of feminist thought in Iran and abroad, WOI concluded that although one could justifiably and comfortably be a Muslim and a feminist striving to achieve full human rights, one could not achieve rights within the context of "Islamic feminism" without either subordinating them to Islamic prescriptions or rendering meaningless the Islamic adjective defining feminism.[29]

Women and the Revolution

Women's massive participation in the 1978–79 revolution was in part a result of the mobilization efforts of various women's organizations in the preceding decades, especially WOI's activities in the late 1960s and the 1970s. The recurrent theme in all group sessions, conferences, and discussions was the need for women to assert themselves, participate, state their demands, and make their presence felt. Women, having gained consciousness of their own collective political power, marched not in defense of retreat or regression but in support of a freer, more egalitarian government. The fundamentalist revolutionaries misrepresented the aims of the revolution by avowing their support for "freedom" and "equality" of women and denouncing the treatment of women as sex objects, while carefully avoiding concrete statements on the substance of their agenda for women. Whenever women activists asked for clarification of positions on specific issues of women's rights and status, they were accused of introducing secondary issues and admonished to maintain the unity of rank and purpose against the regime.[30] The mobilization efforts launched by women activists in the preceding decades combined with the revolution's misleading assertions about women's status were instrumental in drawing women to the demonstrations. A sadly humorous but telling comment in clarification of this point was made by the secretary of the Kerman branch at a prerevolutionary meeting of WOI's provincial secretaries. When queried about the identities of the veiled women who had led demonstrations in her city the week before, she responded, "They are our own members. We kept saying, 'Mobilize the women.' Now they're mobilized, and they shout, 'Down with the regime!'"[31] It was their newly gained organizational experience added to their political awareness that enabled women to march in hundreds of thousands in the front lines of the demonstrations.

Conclusion

In 1978, a mere fifteen years after women had left the company of minors, criminals, and the insane in Iranian law, and a little over a decade after the creation of the Women's Organization of Iran, women were working as judges, diplomats, cabinet officers, mayors, governors, and policewomen and in the health and education corps. In the area of education, the focus of the literacy campaign had shifted to women. Some 12,403 women in the literacy corps taught in villages. By 1978, 39 percent of all females aged six and above were literate. The percentage of girls in primary schools had increased from 34 in 1966 to 42.5 in 1977.[32] At the university level, women made up 30 percent of the student population. They were encouraged to take part in technical and scientific fields through the provision of special scholarships. A quota system was established to give preferential treatment to eligible girls who volunteered to enter technical fields or fields traditionally closed to women. More women than men were accepted after university-entrance examinations for the field of medicine. In the area of employment, special programs had been established to prepare women for higher-paying jobs through training classes in various areas of semiskilled and skilled work. All labor and employment laws had been reviewed to ensure equal pay and comparable benefits for comparable work. A package of proposals aimed at ensuring increased and continuous participation of women in the workforce was approved by the cabinet. One part of the package made possible part-time work for working mothers up to the third year of a child's life, the three part-time years to be considered equivalent to full-time work in terms of seniority and retirement benefits. Providing childcare facilities in the vicinity of factories and offices became obligatory by law. A joint effort of WOI and various ministries made possible the establishment of childcare facilities for approximately one-third of all the children eligible in a period of less than two years after the regulation's passage. The centers were subsidized by the government and supervised by a committee of mothers working in each office. Maternity leave was extended to allow a mother up to seven months' leave with full pay. All regulations regarding housing, loans, pensions, and other job benefits were adjusted to eliminate discrimination.[33]

In the area of women's legal rights within the family, the Family Protection Law, as revised in 1975, gave women the right to ask for divorce on the same grounds and conditions as men, left decisions regarding child custody and alimony up to a special family court, recognized the mother as her child's legal guardian in case of the father's death, practically eliminated polygyny by stipulating exceptional conditions, limited legal marriages to a second wife only with the permission of the first, and increased the minimum age of marriage to eighteen for women and twenty-one for men. Abortion was made legal with the husband's consent. Unmarried women could have abortions on demand up to the eighth week of pregnancy.[34]

In the area of political participation, all local panels reviewing the qualifications of candidates for political office were required to include a member of WOI. The secretary of WOI in each provincial capital was appointed special advisor for social affairs to the province's governor.

Iranian women's experiences in the twentieth century, particularly in the two decades prior to the revolution in 1978–79, suggest the following:

First, Iranian women achieved rights primarily through their own hard and persistent efforts. It took them almost a century to move from near-total public invisibility to a position of visible political, economic, and social presence.

Second, to achieve widespread effect, women's movements must find ways and means of connecting with the grass roots. In the Iranian case, the family welfare centers played a pivotal role as a bridge connecting national and provincial women leaders and grassroots women in cities and villages. In 1976, the last year before political tensions altered normal life patterns throughout the country, more than a million women participated in one or more of the centers' activities. Through the challenges and problems emerging in the work, the centers provided a framework for general consciousness-raising for all concerned—men and women of each neighborhood as well as workers and volunteers of the branches and committees of the organization. The centers were seen as a means and not as the goal of the organization. They made it possible to organize women throughout the country by providing much needed services. These services, selected through a participatory decision-making process, allowed WOI to receive funds from the government for specific projects according to WOI priorities while avoiding government control. Most important of all, by creating accepted, noncontroversial functions, the centers built legitimacy for the organization at the grassroots level and within communities where problems of illiteracy and strict control of women's movements outside the home made other methods of reaching out to the masses of women impractical.

Third, without the support of the modernizing state and its political organs, which were controlled by men, meaningful progress in women's rights would have been unattainable in Iran's conservative patriarchal society. The law as the expression of the state's will was indispensable to securing women's rights. The state, however, was a reflection of the patriarchal order. An important function of the women's movement was to use the modernizing impulses of the political leadership in favor of women's projects despite the ruling elite's essentially unsympathetic attitude to women's rights.

Fourth, Iranian women achieved rights mainly outside the sphere of traditional Islam and against the will of conservative religious leaders. They strove to transcend the traditional Islamic discourse, which means they had to internalize and implement values that were exogenous to their traditional culture. They had to reconcile these values with Islamic prescriptions if they were to communicate successfully with the masses of women in villages and small towns and to enlist the support of at least a part of the political leadership.

And fifth, consciousness of rights creates new historical conditions that are not easily reversed. This situation is clearly demonstrated by the way Iranian women reacted to fundamentalist Islamic injunctions after the revolution and, conversely, by the Islamic Republic's seesaw politics vis-à-vis women's rights at home and in the workplace. The first Iranians who demonstrated in the Islamic Republic in defense of their rights were women. After the revolution, women worked actively to support their families in the fields and factories. They achieved success in the arts, literature, and politics. They were forced to observe hijab (modest Islamic dress) in offices and public places; in turn, they forced the government to backtrack in many areas. They made it impossible for the Islamic Republic to sustain changes in policy and law demanded by its ideology and constitution.[35] Most important, they placed the role of women in society at the center of the ongoing debate on the nature of Islamic governance.

NOTES

The author would like to thank G. R. Afkhami, Shahla Haeri, and Seyyed Vali Reza Nasr for their helpful suggestions.

1. See Guity Nashat, "Women in Pre-Revolutionary Iran: A Historical Overview," in *Women and Revolution in Iran,* ed. Guity Nashat (Boulder: Westview, 1983), 5–35; Pari Shaykh-ul-Islamzadeh, *Zanan-i ruznamehnegar va andishmand-i Iran* (Tehran: Mazgraphic, 1972), 85–86.

2. M. Malikzadeh, for example, describes the march of hundreds of women on the parliament, clad in veils and carrying revolvers and threatening to kill their own husbands and brothers if they gave in to the constitution's enemies; *Tarikh-i inqilab-i mashrutiyat* (History of the constitutional revolution), 2 vols. (Tehran: n.p., 1949). See also Badr ol-Moluk Bamdad, *From Darkness into Light: Women's Emancipation in Iran,* ed. and trans. F. R. C. Bagley (Hicksville, N.Y.: Exposition Press, 1977), 25–41; and Mangol Bayat-Philipp, "Women and Revolution in Iran, 1905–1911," in *Women in the Muslim World,* ed. Lois Beck and Nikki Keddie (Cambridge: Harvard University Press, 1978), 295–308.

3. Janet Afary, *The Iranian Constitutional Revolution, 1906–1911: Grassroots Democracy, Social Democracy, and the Origins of Feminism* (New York: Columbia University Press, 1996).

4. Sheykh-ul-Islamzadeh, *Zanan-i ruznamehnegar,* 109. See also the contribution by Mansoureh Ettehadieh in this volume.

5. Ruth Francis Woodsmall, *Women and the New East* (Washington, D.C.: Middle East Institute, 1960), 74.

6. See oral history memoirs, Farangis Yeganegi and Mehrangiz Dowlatshahi, Oral History of Iran Archives, Foundation for Iranian Studies, Washington, D.C.

7. See Elaheh Hasanli, Masudeh Khalifi, and Fereshteh Qaem-maqami, *Tarikhcheh va fa'aliatha-yi sazeman-i zanan-i Iran* (History and activities of the women's organization of Iran) (Tehran: Daneshkadeh ulum va irtebatat-i ijtima'i, n.d.).

8. During WOI's history, Mehri Rasekh, a prominent member of the Baha'i community, and Shamsi Hekmat, a Jewish educator, were members of the central council of WOI. Farangis Shahrokh (Yeganegi), a prominent Zoroastrian feminist, was appointed first secretary of the high council and later deputy secretary-general of WOI. Other appointed members were university professors Parvin Buzari, Fakhri Amin, Vida Behnam, and Nikchehreh Mohseni (a Baha'i).

9. Cyrus Elahi, *A Comparative Study of the Socioeconomic Situation of Working Women in Tehran, Qazvin, and Kashan* (Tehran: WOI, 1977), 9–15.

10. Sekandar Amanolahi, *The Status of Women in Tribal Society* (Tehran: WOI, 1977). See also Lois Beck's chapter on Qashqa'i women in this volume.

11. Nikchehreh Mohseni, *Images of Women in Elementary-School Textbooks* (Tehran: WOI, 1976).

12. Ibid., 49.

13. Ibid., 51.

14. Moira Moser-Khalili, *Urban Design and Women's Lives* (Tehran: WOI, 1976).

15. See Mahnaz Afkhami, ed., *Women and the Law in Iran, 1967–1978* (Bethesda, Md.: Women's Center of the Foundation for Iranian Studies, 1994).

16. Parviz Homayounpour, "The Experimental Functional Literacy Project for the Social and Economic Promotion of Rural Women" (Tehran: WOI, 1976).

17. Mahnaz Afkhami, "Iran's National Plan of Action: Ideology, Structure, Imple-

mentation" (Tehran: WOI, 1978); manuscript prepared for publication for the center for research.

18. See Afsaneh Najmabadi, "Hazards of Modernity and Morality: Women, State, and Ideology in Contemporary Iran," *Women, Islam, and State,* ed. Denise Kandiyoti (London: Macmillan, 1991); Parvin Paydar, *Women and the Political Process in Twentieth-Century Iran* (Cambridge: Cambridge University Press, 1995).

19. "An Interview with Mahnaz Afkhami," *Women, State, and Society in Iran, 1963–1978,* ed. Gholam Reza Afkhami (Bethesda, Md.: Foundation for Iranian Studies, 2003).

20. Speech by Mohammad Reza Pahlavi, *Proceedings of All-Iran Women's Congress* (Tehran: WOI, n.d.), 11.

21. The author accompanied Farah Diba Pahlavi on this trip.

22. Princess Ashraf Pahlavi's interests as head of the Iranian delegation to the U.N. General Assembly and her brother's emissary to foreign heads of state were mainly in foreign affairs. Occasionally she agreed to help WOI projects when her presence at meetings was necessary to ensure better attendance by high-level personalities.

23. For further details, see the oral history memoirs of Mahnaz Afkhami, Maryam Chamlou, Fereshteh Shahrokhi, and Ezzat Aghevli, Oral History of Iran Archives.

24. For a critique of the left and women during the 1978–79 revolution, see Hammed Shahidian, "The Iranian Left and the 'Woman Question' in the Revolution of 1978–79," *International Journal of Middle East Studies* 26 (2) (1994): 223–47; Haideh Moghissi, "Feminism-i populisti va 'feminism-i islami': Naqdi bar girayesh-ha-yi muhafizikar dar mian-i feministha-yi danishgahi," *Kankash* 13 (1997): 57–95.

25. Ayatollah Kho'i's advice was sought in particular on the Family Protection Law. Ayatollah Shariatmadari was regularly consulted on various legal matters pertaining to women and the family.

26. Ali Shari'ati, *Fatemeh Is Fatemeh* (Tehran: n.p., n.d.), 64.

27. Ibid., 202.

28. See Mahnaz Afkhami, "Towards Global Feminism: A Muslim Perspective," in *Radically Speaking: Feminism Reclaimed,* ed. Diane Bell and Renate Klein (North Melbourne: Spinifex Press, 1996), 525–27.

29. For a critique of Islamic feminism, see Hammed Shahidian, "Feminism-i islami va junbish-i zanan-i Iran," *Iran Nameh* (16) (4) (1998): 611–39.

30. Oral history memoir, Maryam Chamlou, Oral History of Iran Archives, 26.

31. "An Interview with Mahnaz Afkhami."

32. *Economic Report of the Central Bank of Iran* (Tehran: Government Printing Office, 1978).

33. *Report of the Ministry of Science and Higher Education* (Tehran: Government Printing Office, 1978).

34. For the text of these laws, see Afkhami, *Women and the Law in Iran,* 351–74.

35. See *In the Eye of the Storm: Women in Post-Revolutionary Iran,* ed. Mahnaz Afkhami and Erika Friedl (Syracuse: Syracuse University Press, 1994).

5 The Role of Women Members of Parliament, 1963–88

HALEH ESFANDIARI

IN FEBRUARY 1963 a royal decree gave Iranian women the right to vote and to be elected to parliament. In September 1963 six women were elected for the first time in Iranian history to the *majlis* (lower house), and two were appointed to the senate by Mohammad Reza Shah. This chapter examines the context in which Iranian women were granted the vote and the role women members played in the majlis and senate in 1963–67 and 1967–71. It also discusses briefly the role women deputies played in the first two parliaments of the Islamic Republic of Iran, in 1980–84 and 1984–88, and it adds some comments about women's political activity through 2000.[1]

The Iranian women's movement achieved many milestones during the Pahlavi dynasty (1925–79). Earlier, in 1918, the government had announced the opening of a teacher-training college for women and ten primary schools for girls. For Iranian women the era of change started in the 1920s under Reza Shah (r. 1925–41). Iranian society underwent considerable transformation during that period, and Iranian women did not sit on the sidelines. Educated activist women leaders sought the removal of restrictions imposed on them and pushed for the expansion of educational opportunities for girls. The number of girls' schools increased rapidly despite obstacles imposed by some members of society.

In 1935 when Tehran University opened its door, twelve women were admitted.[2] These women found themselves at odds not only with their male professors but also with their male classmates, who did not know how to behave in such close proximity with women. One member of that class, Badr ol-Moluk Bamdad, remembers that girls "usually stayed together in a corner to avoid glances. The boys mostly seemed ill at ease in the new situation. While the girls had deliberately and prudently prepared themselves for entry, the boys were completely disconcerted. For most of them, mixing with girls was something quite unforeseen. They therefore avoided talking to the girls or even answering them, and if there was no escape they blushed from ear to ear and stuttered. At the lectures, wherever a girl sat, the bench on each side of her stayed empty."[3] By the time these women entered university, the ban on the veil (chador) had been in effect for over a year.

One of Reza Shah's most daring reforms was the abolition of the veil in 1936. This decision came as a surprise to the majority of Iranians. For some women activists, the announcement that Iranian women could appear in public unveiled and that the government would protect them was the culmination of a long struggle. The royal decree was enforced brutally and created mental and financial hardship for families and also for the central and provincial governments that had to enforce the law.[4]

Some changes in women's legal status were introduced under Reza Shah. Although these were not of major importance, they laid the foundation for significant changes in women's legal status in the 1960s and 1970s.

The Iranian constitution of 1907 did not grant women the right to vote or to be elected to parliament. On the few occasions when the possibility of female suffrage was brought up in parliament, the majority of deputies refused even to discuss the issue.[5] Over the years women in various women's organizations discussed the question of women's suffrage. They argued that women had the right to vote not only in most Western countries but also in some Islamic ones. The government was aware of the clergy's opposition and did not react to such demands. In the late 1940s, the Tudeh party introduced a bill in the majlis that called for the right to vote and other improvements for women. It came to a vote three years later, during the premiership of Mohammad Mosaddegh but failed to pass because of opposition from the clergy and other majlis conservatives.[6] The clerical establishment voiced its opposition every time the idea of granting women the vote was raised. Clergymen wrote books and articles, petitioned the government, and urged the public to oppose the idea.

In a collection of essays published (probably in the very early 1960s) under the title of *Women and Elections,* a group of clerics opposed female suffrage on religious grounds and predicted the collapse of public morality if women were granted political rights. Nasser Makarem-Shirazi wrote the introduction, and clerics including Ali Hojjati-Kermani, Mohammad Shabestari, and Hossein Haqqani contributed essays, although they were not individually signed. All contributors were students at seminaries in Qum. In his introduction, Makarem-Shirazi criticizes the Westernized elements of Iranian society who argued for women's participation in all areas of social life. In passages meant to be ironic, he writes, "Let us have a few women dressed in the latest fashion sit next to men in our offices, and tomorrow they will sit in the majlis and town councils in order to make up for our backwardness. This way we will be able to count ourselves among the civilized nations and rescue ourselves from savagery and primitiveness."[7] He suggests that the handful of women who insisted on gaining such rights did not speak for Iran's ten million women or the majority of the population, who were against women's participation in elections. He asserts that Iranians respected Islam, and the constitution forbade laws contrary to the religion. He notes that people learned their religious duties from the ulama and the *marjas* (sources of emulation). "Has . . . [the government] once . . . asked their opinion on the problem of women's participation in elections?"[8]

The author of the essay "The Participation of Women in Elections from the Viewpoint of Islam" criticizes ignorant people who tried to argue that Islam and the Qur'an grant women political rights. Just because women hold positions in government in other Islamic countries, he writes, does not mean the Iranian government should imitate them. If one day Iranian women hold legislative and judicial office, this does not mean that other Islamic countries should follow suit.[9] In the book's concluding pages, the authors collectively predict the downfall of the country, honor, and the family if women who seek equal rights succeed.

This book must have appeared before Asadollah Alam's government promulgated a new law for local councils in October 1962, which allowed women to vote in their elections. The new law created hope among women, who saw it as a first step perhaps leading to full suffrage. The local-councils law, however, aroused strong clerical opposition. Reacting in a speech in Qum, Ayatollah Ruhollah Khomeini describes granting voting rights to women as promoting immorality and lewdness. "We do not object to women's progress. We are against this prostitution. We object to such wrongdoing. Do men in this country have freedom, that women should have it?"[10] In the same speech, he describes the law as violating Islam and the constitution and asks, "Is progress achieved by sending four women to the majlis? Have the men who up to now were there brought you progress so that your women should bring progress? We say sending these [women] to these centers is nothing but corruption."[11] In 1978, having witnessed the mass participation of women in demonstrations leading to the Islamic Republic's formation, Ayatollah

Khomeini not only reversed his previous stand but asked women to take part in great numbers in the referendum to decide Iran's future government. In a speech on the eve of the referendum, he said, "Islam has observed the rights of women more than the rights of men. Women have the right to vote. This is more than the rights women have in the West. Our women have the right to vote and to be elected."[12]

In 1962 clerical leaders not only opposed women's participation in local-council elections but also objected that the law did not require candidates or those elected to be Muslims. The clerics rightly interpreted the oath-taking requirement—electees to take the oath of office on a "holy book" rather than specifically the Qur'an—as opening the door to the election of non-Muslims including Baha'is. Clerical leaders sent cables to the prime minister and the government expressing their opposition to this measure. The government faced several days of street demonstrations and protests and was finally forced to rescind the law. Once more it became clear that in order to secure the right to vote, either women had to gain the clergy's acquiescence or Mohammad Reza Shah had to make the decision.

In January 1963 the shah announced a referendum (held on January 26) to endorse his White Revolution, a package of reforms including land distribution and a share for industrial workers in factory profits. Women were not officially allowed to vote, but at the suggestion of the minister of agriculture, Hassan Arsanjani, who was helping organize the referendum, women set up their own balloting centers and ballot boxes, voted, and announced the results, thus for the first time expressing their opinion on a national question through the ballot.

Mehrangiz Dowlatshahi, a woman activist, participated with several other women, on the eve of the referendum, in a debate with Arsanjani broadcast on Iranian television.[13] She told the minister that women were part of the Iranian nation, wanted to participate in the referendum, and needed to know how to go about it. The minister agreed that peasant women were hardworking people and should have the right to vote. He promised to present this matter to the cabinet that same evening. Dowlatshahi and some other women activists took that as approval for women to vote the next day.

Radio Tehran and the small-circulation morning newspapers carried a report on Arsanjani's suggestion. (Tehran's large-circulation newspapers, *Kayhan* and *Ettelaat,* came out in the afternoon.) It was left to women themselves to notify one another by word of mouth the morning of the referendum. Hajar Tarbiat, a woman activist, recounts that when women heard on the radio that they could cast votes, they telephoned one another, organized, and went in groups to vote. Shokat Malek Jahanbani, a school principal and activist, recalls that women, excited by the opening Arsanjani suggested to them, went to balloting centers and voted in large numbers. Nayereh Ebtehaj-Samii, another woman activist, remembers that "women from all the various women's organizations took to loudspeakers. I even remember that Hajar Tarbiat took a loudspeaker and went to the south of Tehran and other parts of the city and urged the people, the women, to come out of their homes and go to the ballot boxes and not lose this opportunity."[14] Dowlatshahi recalls that in some provinces where no ballot boxes existed, women cast their votes in garbage containers. She did not see any men objecting. "For example, taxi drivers, orange sellers, and the shopkeepers on Istanbul avenue seemed very happy. They congratulated us. When we asked them whether they approved of this measure, they answered, 'Yes, you are our sisters. Why should you not have the right to vote? Why should you educated women not have the right to vote?'"[15]

Many thousands of women voted in the referendum. That same evening the minister of interior, Amir-Azizi, announced that the government would not officially recognize votes cast by women. Nevertheless, the tradition of excluding women from voting was broken. Women had gone to the ballot boxes and made a political statement.

Women's participation in this referendum, although informal and unofficial, encouraged the shah to act on their behalf. In February 1963, during an address to an economic conference in Tehran, he announced that he was extending to women the right to vote and the right to be elected to parliament. He said he was acting by virtue of the powers vested in him by the constitution. Later, the import of this royal decree was incorporated into law. In fact, all that was required was to strike the word "women" from clauses in laws specifying those barred from voting and from standing for parliament.

In his speech from the throne to the twenty-first parliament in September 1963, the shah described the White Revolution and the granting of suffrage to women as an Islamic act: "This authentic revolution, which fortunately is the reflection of the spirit and the divine meaning of the holy religion of Islam, namely justice, equity, equality, and defense of the right of the deprived, is unique in the several thousand years of Iranian history."[16] In the same speech, he reminded the deputies that by giving women the right to vote, "we rendered obsolete the shame that had denied half the people of our country their legitimate rights and participation in the course followed by the world's free and civilized communities."[17]

In September 1963 six women were for the first time elected to the majlis, in large part because of the all-out effort of newly enfranchised women.

At the same time, the shah named two women to serve as senators. (The senate was composed of sixty members, half elected and half appointed by the shah.) The six women who entered the twenty-first majlis that autumn were Farrokhru Parsa, Mehrangiz Dowlatshahi, Nayereh Ebtehaj-Samii, Hajar Tarbiat, Showkat Malek Jahanbani, and Nezhat Nafisi. Shams ol-Moluk Mosahab and Mehrangiz Manouchehrian were appointed to the senate.

Parsa, Tarbiat, and Jahanbani were elected from Tehran. All three were educators and had spent their careers teaching and running girls' schools. Elected as a deputy from Kermanshah, Dowlatshahi came from a prominent Kermanshahi family and had studied in Germany. Elected from Rasht, Ebtehaj-Samii was a member of a well-known family there and was one of the first women graduates of the American School in Tehran. Nafisi was a deputy from Baft, a town near Kerman. She belonged to a prominent Kermani family and at the time of her election was married to the then-powerful mayor of Tehran, Ahmad Nafisi. Mosahab and Manouchehrian were among the first group of girls to graduate from Tehran University. Both went on to get their doctorates. Mosahab was an educator and well-known literary figure. Manouchehrian studied law and became an ardent advocate of changing existing laws pertaining to women's rights. She was later forced to resign from the senate because of her unequivocal stand on these issues.

The two women senators and five of the six women members of the majlis had dedicated their lives to girls' education and improving women's legal status. (Nafisi had been only marginally involved in women's issues.) Their candidacies and election to parliament were not accidental. They were neither hand-picked puppets of the regime nor imitations of Western women.

These women were all born and brought up in traditional Iranian families but had enlightened fathers who provided them with educations. Some had gone abroad for further studies. Because of their family backgrounds and their lifelong struggle for women's rights, these women were familiar with the restrictions Islamic law imposed on women's participation in society. They always found it necessary to describe the changes they sought in the law as falling within the boundaries set by Islam for women.

Once women received the right to vote and run for parliament, women leaders started mobilizing and lobbying. Dowlatshahi and Ebtehaj-Samii decided to run from their native provinces, namely Kermanshah and Rasht. Although a native of Tabriz, Tarbiat stood as a candidate in Tehran because she feared that religious-minded Azerbaijani voters would find it difficult to vote for a woman. (Over time attitudes toward women underwent a marked change. In 1975, still under the monarchy, Fahim-Azar was elected as a majlis deputy from Azerbaijan. More than a decade later, in parliamentary elections under the Islamic Republic in 1992, Ghodsieh Alavi was elected to the majlis from the holy city of Mashhad.) Parsa and Jahanbani were candidates from Tehran. Both women ran girls' schools. Parsa was the daughter of an early Iranian feminist who was exiled from Mashhad because of the progressive content of the women's magazine she was publishing. Parsa's mother was pregnant with Farrokhru when she was exiled to Qum. Not only was Farrokhru Parsa among the first women elected to parliament, she also later became deputy minister of education and the first woman to hold a cabinet position in Iran. In 1968 she was appointed minister of education.[18] Jahanbani came from an established family. She founded a girls' school in a poverty-stricken neighborhood of south Tehran and thus made it possible for many girls to become educated who otherwise would never have had access to proper schooling.

The women deputies in the twenty-first majlis and the two women senators spoke primarily during the time allowed to pre-agenda speeches, which enabled them to address a wide range of topics. They devoted themselves to problems of their constituency—Iran's women. They focused on education and especially on problems women and girls encountered in attempting to secure it. They spoke on women's legal status and the legal disabilities they suffered. They used every occasion—a royal birthday, commemoration of the veil's abolition, or a religious holiday—to remind parliament that Iranian women still had a long way to go to obtain equal rights with men. They attempted to show that the rights and changes in social status they sought for women were in accordance with Islam. Thus, they quoted the Qur'an and cited as models for emulation the Prophet Mohammad's family and paid special attention to Fatemeh, Mohammad's daughter and the wife of Ali, the first imam in Shi'i Islam. They praised the progressive outlook of Islamic law on women's issues. They also reported to parliament on their various activities in Iran and abroad on various women's issues.

The two women senators used the pre-agenda speeches to discuss matters relevant to women's education, women's rights, and existing social problems. They demanded explanation and clarification from the government and criticized it for its slowness in implementing existing laws. They raised people's complaints and dissatisfactions with the way the government was operating. While the two women senators were more outspoken, the women deputies did not differ greatly from their male colleagues. Some spoke frequently and boldly; others hardly participated in debates. They were more outspoken in the early years when official tolerance for loyal dissent was greater. When discussion in parliament became less critical because of government pressure, women deputies, along with their male counterparts, grew more restrained.

In the early 1960s, it was still possible for members of parliament to criticize the government in public session. In the late 1960s, as the shah grew more autocratic and more sensitive to criticism, the government sought to project a picture of a harmonious family in which government, parliament, and the loyal opposition worked hand in hand to further the goals of the White Revolution, a program identified with the shah and the shah alone. Thus, all significant discussions and parliamentary debates occurred in committees and behind closed doors. When a bill reached the majlis floor it generally received rubber-stamp approval.

The women deputies reacted to these restraints much like their male counterparts. Nevertheless, they found opportunities to make themselves heard and to speak on issues important to their constituency. They were articulate and experienced and had little difficulty in voicing women's grievances when they enumerated the inadequacies of the educational system, described working-class poverty and the hardships imposed on women, and detailed the inefficiencies of government agencies, especially those providing important services to women, such as the ministries of education and justice, municipalities, and health-delivery organizations.

Working-class poverty and problems of housing, sanitation, air pollution, healthcare, and sewage in the urban slums of Tehran were a particular focus of attention for these deputies. Jahanbani was familiar with conditions in poor districts in southern Tehran because the school she ran was located there. She spoke on many occasions about the plight of that district's inhabitants. Standards of living, she reported, were low; no piped water, sewage system, or schools were to be found; some people still lived in huts. She described the misery, poverty, and lack of facilities. She spoke of Tehran as a city of contrasts—hovels in the south and modern apartment buildings in the affluent north. She expressed anger that the municipality spent large sums on the north and little in the south. While the neediest area had few schools, the government built luxurious ones in north Tehran. Claiming a lack of garbage trucks, the municipality did not collect refuse in south Tehran. Open water canals, which for some inhabitants were a source of drinking water, were a health hazard. The brick kilns in south Tehran emitted air pollution. She received letters from constituents complaining that they and their children became sick from the fumes; yet the municipality did nothing. "The more they try and beautify north Tehran," she said, "the more the ugliness of the south will show itself."[19]

In the senate Mosahab took the municipality to task for waste and neglect and asked the government for a complete report. The minister of interior, Mehdi Pirasteh, under whose jurisdiction the municipality functioned, explained that the government intended to set up city and town councils and let people run their own affairs and that in all but 50 cities (out of 390) councils had been established. Two hundred Tehran municipal employees who were found to be on the payroll without performing work had been immediately dismissed. Mosahab was not satisfied with this explanation and wanted to know why these people were simply dismissed and not brought to court. The minister of interior, she noted, acknowledged the poor condition of asphalt on city streets yet did nothing about it. Why did the government not prosecute the responsible contractors? "This can't go on. When one goes out into the streets one is bound to stumble. . . . You no sooner pull your foot out of a ditch than you fall on your head into a pothole."[20]

In the same speech, Mosahab criticized the minister of justice, Baqer Ameli, for admitting that there were people on the municipal payroll thanks to string-pulling but claiming that such people could not be prosecuted for lack of a relevant law. "It is sad that the minister of justice accepts and admits that [municipal] money is expended on the bases of friendship, position, and bribery," she said. "What sort of law is that?" she asked. "This is lawlessness."[21]

Mosahab was a relentless critic of the government and various ministries. She brought to the attention of other senators the contents of letters of complaint she received from people. For example, she criticized driving conditions on Tehran streets and the main roads outside the capital. She asked why no traffic police stood at crossroads to direct cars. She reminded the senate that although one of the people's few recreations was to drive to the Caspian sea, the road was so treacherous that people were often killed. "These are not problems without solutions,"[22] she said. Roads could be widened and curves improved so that drivers could see other cars coming.

In another speech Mosahab complained that no matter how many times she reminded the government of its shortcomings, her remarks were either ignored or she was told that she was not aware of even worse problems. She said this attitude reminded her of a story about Molla Nasreddin, an endearing character in Iranian folktales. "When Molla Nasreddin was told that his hands were dirty, he answered, 'You should thank God that you can't see my feet. They are much dirtier.' Now when we tell a civil servant that a certain waste occurs, he replies, 'Be grateful to God that you are not aware of even more waste.'"[23] Mosahab also urged the government to end favoritism and open its doors to men and women seeking employment but lacking political connections.

Mosahab took the plight of prisoners' families to the senate floor. She told heart-wrenching stories about destitute families and about abandoned children whose parents were in jail. She said she received letters from prisoners and their families who needed help. She gave the example of four hundred prisoners in Khuzestan charged with drug trafficking who wanted someone to examine their long-pending cases. She said that the major drug traffickers were not in jail and that they not only lived well but "they have a position in society and are respected. . . . Only the small-time drug peddler or the young boy or the woman, whose father and family bread-winner is in jail and who makes a meager living from selling this poison, is in trouble."[24] A year later she was still pursuing the plight of prisoners' families. She told the senate of a letter she received from a woman who had repeatedly asked the authorities to examine her case but without any result. Mosahab said that a person needs to have "the patience of Job" given the indifference of the authorities. She was angry at a government agent who told her that people who wrote these letters did not have anything else to do. "What sort of talk is that?" she asked. "This type of thinking must change. One has to deal with people's complaints."[25]

The women deputies also spent time discussing problems in the educational system: the difficulties teachers faced, lack of teachers' health insurance, shortage of schools, poor quality of schoolbooks, and overall inefficiency of the ministry of education. These were problems with which women deputies, most of whom had spent a lifetime in education, were closely acquainted. Moreover, they not only described the educational system's inadequacies but also suggested policies and legislation for dealing with these problems.

Tarbiat took the government to task for spending millions of tumans on a research program at the faculty of letters at Tehran University but little on building schools in rural areas. Mosahab took up the same topic in the senate. Nine million Iranians did not speak Persian, she said, and had to be taught to speak, read, and write the language. Educational reforms needed long-term planning, yet each newly appointed minister of education undid his predecessor's policies and programs. "They should know that education belongs to the country and is not a private fiefdom. The ministers are not so superior in knowledge and learning as to introduce any changes they want without any previous studies."[26] Jahanbani focused on the shortage of schoolbooks, a problem she said plagued parents and schools at the beginning of every school year and was more severe in remote rural areas. Progress in the educational field was agonizingly slow, she said, "yet this is no longer the century of the [horse-drawn] cart and the camel litter."[27]

Mosahab was critical of the rapid increase in the number of private schools that charged high tuition without providing children with a proper education and were not better equipped than government schools. She complained that her numerous queries to the ministry of education about the

criteria under which these schools operated were ignored. The senator did
not approve of foreign schools operating in Iran, especially because their
curricula were not compatible with those of the ministry of education. "For
example, they don't pay much attention to Iranian history and geography,"
she complained.[28]

Parsa reminded parliament that while the literacy rate among men was
18 percent, among women it stood at only 9.5 percent. She argued that the
government did little to inform women of the availability of adult literacy
classes. Mosahab noted that not only was there a shortage of schools but also
inadequate opportunities for young people to pursue higher education in the
country, thereby forcing them to go abroad for university studies. The for-
eign-study scholarship program was full of loopholes. A student with a high
school diploma in literature secured admission to a college abroad to study
medicine, went abroad, and returned a few years later with a certificate in
radio repair—all done on government scholarships.

Other areas of concern for these deputies were the general plight of wom-
en and their disadvantaged legal and social status. Once the euphoria over
obtaining the vote had subsided, women deputies began to push for legislation to improve the legal status of women and children. Time and again, they
stressed the lack of legal protection for infants and children and the necessity for changing laws pertaining to women's rights in marriage, divorce, child
custody, spousal financial support, and travel. Not surprisingly, they insisted that the changes they sought could be encompassed within the provision
of Islamic law.

Tarbiat prefaced a call for divorce and financial-support rights for wom-
en by asserting that the prophet made no distinction between men and wom-
en or black and white; he valued those who were the more pious. All laws
should be based on justice and equality, she said; protecting the rights of
women and children would strengthen, not weaken, the family. Like Tarbiat, Dowlatshahi argued that the necessary legislation to improve women's
position could be introduced within the framework of Islam. In its attitude
to women, she suggested, Islamic law was more progressive than European
law. Islam gave women economic independence; women in Europe did not
have such rights.

Among the women representatives, Manouchehrian was the most ardent
proponent of women's and children's rights. By the time she was appointed
to the senate, she had written and spoken at great length about the necessity
of revising existing laws. She was a lawyer by training and an advocate of legal
reform. In her maiden speech in the senate, she criticized the government

for not even once referring to the need to "coordinate the laws in order to give equal rights to women."[29] She explained that granting equal political rights to women would not be enough as long as parts of the penal code, citizenship law, and civil code remained unchanged. She specifically referred to divorce law. She said a woman had no security in her husband's home. A woman enjoyed no rights over her children or part of the family wealth: "She can be thrown out of the house at any moment."[30] The government was duty-bound to empower the courts to rule on child-custody and divorce cases. In the majlis, Dowlatshahi complained about discrimination in child-custody cases: "Why, even after the father's death, is the mother not given guardianship over her children, and why is the paternal grandfather given precedence over the mother?"[31]

Manouchehrian expressed puzzlement at the justice ministry's reluctance to review laws pertaining to women's rights and suggested that members of the senate and majlis should themselves propose legislation for improving women's legal status rather than wait for the government to do so. Existing laws "give such a power to men, they turn them into monsters. Men can divorce their wives, marry several wives, and take children from their mother."[32] She criticized the ministry for not giving women the opportunity to serve as judicial experts, let alone become judges.

Manouchehrian was also bothered by the existing passport law. She wondered why it was necessary for a woman to have her husband's written permission in order to acquire a passport. She told her fellow senators that when a woman needs to go abroad for medical treatment, pilgrimage, or just enjoyment, "once more the husband appears as the angel of torture because the passport office requires the husband's permission to issue her a passport. Has anyone ever asked the office whether it requires the wife's permission when a married man abandons his wife and children to travel abroad for fun?"[33]

While pursuing the same goals, Mosahab tried to calm the anxiety of men who thought that equal rights for women meant the disruption of society. She noted that equality for women does not mean "lining up against men" or "limiting men's rights." She criticized those who believed that women should work only for female employers and wondered why women could not serve the country as free persons. Women needed the government's and men's help to overcome existing obstacles. "Women have political freedom, but they still don't have any security in the family, and sometimes a woman's destiny depends on the whim and desire of her spouse who can disrupt their life together as easily as he drinks a glass of water."[34]

Both Mosahab and Manouchehrian in the senate and their counterparts in the majlis kept pushing for a revision of laws pertaining to marriage, child custody, and divorce even while they expressed satisfaction about the political rights given to Iranian women. In her maiden speech in the senate, Mosahab recounted a discussion on a women's issue she had had five years earlier with a well-known politician. She was expecting him to introduce the issue before the majlis. But the politician told her that "to bring up this matter is not only very difficult, it is also dangerous. If someone else raises this issue, not only will I not participate in the discussion, I will shut my ears."[35] Such was the attitude of men, she added.

Dowlatshahi recalled mentioning to the shah in 1958 the obstacles women faced regarding divorce and child custody. Sharif Emami, later president of the senate, interrupted her to tell the shah that the existing laws were fine. She thought that the shah was worried about the clergy's reaction to changes in family law. In those years it seemed as if no one wanted to take up the cause of women's rights, for fear of the clerical community's reaction.

These women never gave up. Manouchehrian in the senate and Dowlatshahi in the majlis took the government to task for not joining international conventions on women's rights. Dowlatshahi reminded parliament that Iran had not yet acceded to International Labor Organization accords requiring equal pay for equal work or to various other international conventions setting a minimum age for marriage and requiring the registration of all marriages. She urged that Iran follow the practice of Pakistan, another Islamic state, where laws required legal cases regarding divorce, polygyny, and other family matters to be referred to special family councils.

Two months after her arrival in the senate, Manouchehrian asked the ministry of foreign affairs why Iran had not signed the convention on political rights for women approved by the United Nations in 1953 and the convention for children's rights approved in 1959. The foreign minister replied that in 1953 the government was not ready to join the convention on women, but that Iranian women had obtained political rights and the government had instructed its U.N. mission to investigate the feasibility of Iran's ratifying the convention. He promised that his ministry would soon submit the convention text to parliament. Manouchehrian was not satisfied with his reply and was puzzled that a government ratifying the international convention on human rights hesitated when it came to women's rights. She was pleased that the government voted for the convention on children's rights and suggested that once parliament ratified it, the convention might be applied to child-custody cases in family disputes.

A year later Manouchehrian submitted to the senate a bill, co-signed by nineteen senators, on reforming juvenile courts. She told the senate that the existing law treated crimes committed by children as adult crimes, and the government bore a responsibility to rehabilitate and retrain these juveniles. Her bill stipulated that private institutions and groups should be invited to help the government in setting up reform homes and to assist families whose children were involved in crime. She argued that because in most cases parents were responsible for their children's delinquency and that existing laws did not provide preventive measures, her proposed amendments to the law offered measures to prevent young people from becoming juvenile delinquents.

Manouchehrian found in Farah Diba Pahlavi, Iran's queen, an ardent supporter for the reforms she said were necessary in family law and children's rights. The queen provided a direct channel for conveying these proposals to the shah. She recalls her horror in learning from Manouchehrian that children were brought to adult courts and given adult sentences: "It was important to protect the rights of children. I did not want to become openly involved in controversial issues, but children's rights were not controversial."[36] The queen cautioned Manouchehrian and other women about religious and cultural sensitivities and obstacles when they raised the issue of women's rights with her. Through the queen, the women deputies reassured the shah that the changes they were promoting were not contrary to Islamic law. "It was a very delicate matter," remembers the queen. "I believed it had to be done in the context of our cultural and social conditions. I was worried that too much pressure from our side would create a lot of antagonism. Our society was male-dominated. I used to receive thousands of letters: women complaining about their husbands' divorcing them with no alimony, women losing their children to their husbands, and women being thrown into the streets by their husbands. I wanted change, but I believed in moderation and a step-by-step approach."[37]

Various women's groups had been working on a family protection law. The Rah-e No organization, of which Dowlatshahi was a founder, had spent three years preparing a draft of a family law. The Iran Novin party was also working on a similar draft. Manouchehrian's group, the organization of women lawyers, prepared a revision of articles in the civil code pertaining to women's rights in family law. All these groups moved cautiously.

Manouchehrian presented to the senate a bill on family law, sponsored by sixteen senators. The bill caught the other senators by surprise and caused panic in the shah, government, majlis, and senate about the clerical community's reaction. Dowlatshahi remembers hearing the shah telling prime minister Amir Abbas Hoveyda that he had received calls from clerical leaders in

Qum declaring Manouchehrian to be an infidel and demanding she be expelled from the senate. "Is this woman mad?" the shah asked Hoveyda.[38] Manouchehrian circulated copies of her bill among the press. Newspapers that evening carried parts of the proposed bill under sensational headlines. "I was a troublemaker," Manouchehrian said.[39] She remembers being visited by a secret-police officer who wanted to know what foreign group was behind the bill. "I told him I had asked different embassies for their respective family laws. I had studied the laws of seventy-two countries. I showed him my annotated copy of the Iranian civil code. He took it with him."[40] Sharif Emami, the senate president, who was reprimanded by the shah for permitting the bill to be tabled, managed to postpone discussion of the bill and finally to have it filed away indefinitely. No senator, not even those who cosponsored the bill, protested, Manouchehrian recalls.

It nevertheless fell to women deputies in the majlis to put to rest the anxiety expressed by certain elements of society regarding changes they sought in women's legal status. These deputies took the position that their approach to women's rights was shaped by the teachings of Islam and by national customs and traditions.

Once the uproar over Manouchehrian's proposed bill died down, the ruling Iran Novin party organized a seminar and circulated a draft proposal to amend existing family laws in the interest of women and minors. A committee was subsequently formed in the ministry of justice to examine the feasibility of new legislation that would strengthen women's rights in marriage, divorce, and child custody without conflicting with Islamic law. Anticipating clerical opposition, the minister of justice, Javad Sadr, took the draft proposal for endorsement to Ayatollah Hakim in Najaf, then the most eminent source of emulation in the Shi'i world.[41]

The Family Protection Law was presented to the majlis in March 1967. According to Dowlatshahi, it had taken the legislative branch more than three years to develop it. The law established new family courts to handle disputes regarding marriage, divorce, and child custody. Husbands could no longer divorce their wives by unilateral repudiation and now were required to obtain the court's permission. Although a man was not barred from taking a second wife, he needed his first wife's permission, which was to be given in court. The marriage age was raised to fifteen for girls and seventeen for boys. In case of divorce or the father's death, the court would decide issues of child custody. In the debate that followed the first and second readings of the bill, women members of the majlis and ministry of justice officials argued that the bill was in total accordance with Islamic law and principles, standards of social justice, and interests of the family. It was voted into law in June 1967.

All women deputies voted for it, except for Nafisi who was opposed because it was silent on women's right to travel abroad. Manouchehrian had raised the issue in the senate on many occasions (and it later led to her resignation).[42]

Manouchehrian was not happy with the Family Protection Law as it was passed in parliament. As far as she was concerned, vesting authority in the courts to permit a man to take a second wife was tantamount to having the judge sanction and justify the "prostitution of men or to act as a pimp for men." She wanted total equality between men and women. The queen (Farah Diba Pahlavi) remembers the controversy generated by the Family Protection Law and the debate over the passport law: "I wanted all these changes, but I believed in moderation. The Family Protection Law was a first but important step. Because of my position I could not openly support the law, but in private I pushed for it."[43] Dowlatshahi states that had women not been elected to parliament, the Family Protection Law would never have been discussed, let alone approved. Once it passed, women deputies started explaining to other women, especially those in villages and provincial towns, the new law's significance.

During the twenty-first majlis, the government also submitted a bill proposing a constituent assembly to amend the constitution to permit the queen to be appointed vice-regent should the crown prince succeed to the throne while still a minor. Manouchehrian used the opportunity to remind the senate that under the Daylamid dynasty during the high Islamic period, the mother of Majd ed-Dowleh Daylami had served as vice-regent. She praised the current queen for her abilities and tried to assure her colleagues that becoming the vice-regent did not mean becoming the ruler. The queen herself was taken by surprise when she learned of the proposed amendment to the constitution. "I believe His Majesty, by appointing me to the vice regency, wanted to show the importance he felt for Iranian women," she noted many years later. "He saw how much I worked and how active I was and that I was worthy of such a trust. As a mother I would never betray my son."[44]

In the twenty-second majlis (1967–71), Sadr al-Malek Bozorgnia replaced Nafisi as deputy from Baft. Parsa became deputy minister (and later minister) of education and was replaced in parliament by another women, Nayereh Saidi. The other four deputies and the two senators were returned for a second term. The women deputies and senators continued to focus on the educational, legal, and social problems of women. Because the ruling Iran Novin party (of which most women deputies were members) enjoyed an unchallenged majority in parliament, issues brought up in the legislature were generally those that the party had sanctioned.

Among the important bills passed during the twenty-second majlis was the law on women's social services enabling women to participate in the literacy corps and the health corps. The law made national service in these corps a requirement for female high school graduates but gave married women an automatic exemption if they desired it. (Up to that time, national service was a requirement for men only.)

Having supported the passage of the Family Protection Law, the women deputies and senators pushed for its enforcement. Mosahab believed that people's lack of education and awareness was a further problem. She related a newspaper article about a son who killed his mother because she left the house without his permission. She argued for improved opportunities for women to become economically independent so that they would not be faced with poverty and destitution after divorce.

Time and again Mosahab reminded her fellow senators that present changes in the law regarding women's political and family rights were based on the teaching of Islam, articles of the constitution, and economic and social justice. She recalled a time when women did not have the right to walk in the streets or express interest in attending school—a situation difficult to understand at the time she spoke.

Manouchehrian once more took the government to task for not signing the convention on political rights for women. When the deputy foreign minister told her that the government was still studying the convention, she expressed hope that this study would be completed during this century. Muslim countries, including Pakistan, Turkey, Afghanistan, and Indonesia, had already ratified this convention, she pointed out.

Tarbiat focused her attention in the majlis on the notorious article 179 of the criminal code, according to which a man who caught his wife in bed with another man could kill her and suffer no punishment. A man who found his sister or daughter in bed with a man other than her husband could kill her and receive as punishment only eleven to sixty days in prison. The law presumably regarded such killing as a crime of passion or as justified in order to restore family honor. In underlining the law's absurdity, Tarbiat recounted the case of "a man who strangled his wife and, when asked why, said she was ill-tempered."[45]

Women deputies and senators used every opportunity to remind Iranian women, especially the younger generation, of the progress they had made in the sphere of women's rights and encouraged them to cherish these rights and prove themselves worthy of them. During the twenty-second majlis, Parsa was appointed as Iran's first woman minister of education. According to Mosahab, the importance of granting Iranian women political rights was not that a few women reached prominent positions in the government but that it removed existing obstacles.

Women deputies and senators in the twenty-second majlis were less active in parliamentary debates than in the twenty-first session. Because the government was identified with the shah, it became more difficult to take the government to task for its shortcomings. Parliament increasingly became a rubber stamp for government programs and bills. Women deputies in parliament acted no differently than their male counterparts in this regard.

A major shift in the center of gravity of the women's movement took place in the 1970s. Leadership passed to a younger generation of women. The main impetus for the movement shifted from parliament to the Women's Organization of Iran (WOI). The Family Protection Law was revised in 1975. Women started serving as judges. (One early judge, Shirin Ebadi, won the Nobel Peace Prize in 2003 for her efforts to promote the rights of women and children.) Maternity leave for women was extended. The WOI launched an all-out effort to attract women to adult literacy classes, established vocational-training classes for women, and pressed the government and the private sector to appoint more women to senior managerial and decision-making positions.[46]

Behind these efforts was the idea that women of all classes should acquire the means for economic independence. During these years virtually all areas of employment opened up to women. In 1978, on the eve of the revolution, women were found at all levels and in most professions in the public and private sectors. The floodgates blocking women's presence in all parts of society had opened, and women from all classes pushed for improvements in their existing status.

Many young people raised in traditional families had a chance in these years to enter schools and universities, go abroad to study, and enter the job market. These women and men were looking for ways to reconcile Islam with modernity. Some found answers in the writings of the lay Islamic thinker Ali Shari'ati and the cleric Morteza Motahhari. Both men asserted the compatibility of Islam and women's rights. These and other Islamists who wrote in a similar vein provided powerful evidence that the changes in women's status had taken root, appealed to middle- and working-class women as well as elites, and could no longer be reversed.

On the eve of the revolution, women looking for a way to reconcile religion and their newfound aspirations thus had ample reason to believe that an Islamic government would not stand in the way of women's progress and would even accelerate the movement toward improved rights. Hundreds of thousands of women joined demonstrations in 1978–79 that led to the overthrow of the Pahlavi regime. Representing the full political spectrum, women of all ages, socioeconomic classes, and statuses participated in the mass protests. They joined men in strikes in public and private domains. Women organized protest groups, ran first-aid centers, made fiery speeches, and donated blood. Ayatollah Khomeini, directing the revolutionary movement from abroad, encouraged the full participation of women. He criticized Iranian women who imitated Westerners, but he emphasized that an Islamic government would grant women all necessary rights on the basis of Islamic law.

Ayatollah Khomeini made his triumphal return to Iran in February 1979. The monarchy collapsed, and a revolutionary government of his choosing took power. In those heady days after the revolution, hundreds of Iranian men and women every day visited the school where Khomeini resided to pay their respects. Discussions were meanwhile under way among Khomeini's close associates regarding the shape and policies of the revolutionary government, including the policy the new government would adopt on women, an issue raised repeatedly. The massive presence of women in the revolutionary movement and the enthusiasm women showed for the revolution's leader proved to be the decisive factor in causing Khomeini to overrule those of his lieutenants who wanted to relegate women to their homes.[47]

Women soon discovered that the revolutionary council did not include a single woman. Nor did the government of Mehdi Bazargan, the Islamic Republic's first prime minister, have a single woman minister or deputy minister. Although some women stood as candidates for the assembly of experts that was to draft the new constitution, only Monireh Gorgi, a schoolteacher, was elected to the seventy-three-member assembly. She made it clear from the beginning that she would promote laws regarding women's rights only within the framework of the teaching of the Qur'an and the shari'a.[48]

Shortly after the revolutionary government came to power, and in reply to a written inquiry submitted to Khomeini's office, the government announced the suspension of the Family Protection Law. Women discovered that the new constitution, approved in December 1979, was ambiguous on the issue of women holding the office of president. It barred women from becoming judges, although they were free to study law. They did not have to wear the chador, but in government offices they had to observe an Islamic dress code, namely a concealing robe and scarf. In the civil service, some women (like some of their male counterparts) were purged, dismissed, or pressured into early retirement.

Men were once again able to divorce their wives without going to court.

Child custody was automatically granted to men. The newly approved law of Islamic punishments specified lashing and even stoning for women found guilty of violating Islamic concepts of decency.

It was against this background that four women were elected to the first majlis (1980–84) of the Islamic Republic: Azam Taleghani, Mariam Behrouzi, Ateqeh Rajai, and Gowhar Sharieh Dastghaib. In the second majlis (1984–88), three of the four women were reelected, while Marzieh Dabbagh replaced Taleghani.

Previous to their election, these women were not much exposed to women's issues. Once in the majlis, they were flooded with complaints from women, especially about the suspension of the Family Protection Law. Because most educated, emancipated, middle-class Iranian women did not consider these women as their representatives, it was less-affluent women who turned to the women members of parliament with their problems. It was precisely this category of women that had benefited most from legal changes and new educational and economic opportunities under the previous regime. These women wrote letters, complained in person, and demanded that women deputies take up their cause. They expected that within the newly established Islamic Republic their fundamental rights would be observed.

The issues taken up by the women deputies in the first and second majlis under the Islamic Republic once more centered on women's rights, education, part-time work, extension of maternity leave for women civil servants, and hijab (Islamic dress)—issues strikingly similar to those that concerned their predecessors under the monarchy.

Spokeswomen for an Islamic revolution and serving under an Islamic republic, these women deputies emphasized that legislation relating to women's rights had to be compatible with Islamic law, but they differed from their male colleagues on the law's interpretation. When the government presented a bill to the majlis regarding half-time work for women in the civil service, women deputies fully supported it, but some male colleagues argued against the presence of any women in the workplace. Men argued that women would render better services to society by staying at home. Behrouzi reiterated the view that women were a beneficial force in society and that the country should make full use of them. The bill, she explained, was in conformity with the constitution. It gave women the chance to work and also look after the family. The bill was enacted into law in November 1983, a year after it was presented to the majlis.

Women deputies did not always agree with one another on legislation before the majlis. When the ministry of education presented a bill extending maternity leave for women teachers from three to nine months, some male deputies like their female colleagues regarded the bill as discriminatory toward other women civil servants. Behrouzi described the bill as unfair and even cruel to other professional women. The bill was rejected by the majlis after lengthy debate. One male deputy wondered why men should defend the bill when women deputies were against it.

In the second majlis, a bill regarding government funding for students going abroad to study contained a controversial clause specifying that only married women accompanied by their husbands could benefit from the legal provisions. Once more it was Behrouzi who insisted that in Islam women and men were equal and that approval of such a law discriminated against women. Dastghaib asked why the "marriage clause" should not apply equally to both male and female students. This bill was passed with the controversial clause intact.

When it came to women's rights, women deputies were concerned about the lack of legal recourse for women in cases of divorce, child custody, and polygyny. Without ever mentioning the suspended Family Protection Law, they complained about male-dominated courts that granted men divorce on demand. Taleghani was disturbed by the increasing number of women being divorced and abandoned with their children. Dastghaib complained about courts that issued divorce decrees without even requiring the requisite evidence from two witnesses familiar with the case. She said any two men could be called in from the street and asked to act as witnesses for the man seeking a divorce.

Behrouzi and Taleghani spoke of the humiliating treatment women suffered in the workplace. They complained about the blatant effort to force women from their jobs and the insults women had to endure on the street and at work. Behrouzi blamed such behavior on men "distant from Islam, who humiliate women, compensate for their own lack of personality by trying to portray women as lacking in character, and empty all their complexes on the heads of women."[49]

The reintroduction of hijab after more than four decades surprised many women who had grown up not covering their hair. Both Gorgi in the constituent assembly and her women colleagues in the majlis, although wearing the chador themselves, had to deal with this problem continuously. They complained about the harassment of women by vigilante groups in the streets of Tehran. Revolutionary guards stopped women who showed a strand of hair and took them to neighborhood revolutionary committees to be reprimanded or punished. Following the enactment of the law on Islamic punishments, women were given up to seventy lashes for exposing their hair. Women deputies under the Islamic Republic defended the requirement that women observe the hijab. As far as Dabagh was concerned, hijab was "God's command." For Behrouzi, it was an expression of "independence." Taleghani referred to it as a form of "liberation" but was against women being punished for not observing Islamic dress. Women, she said, should be educated in the benefits of Islamic dress.

The first and second parliaments of the Islamic Republic had to handle many laws enacted under the monarchy that the new men in power believed needed to be changed or rewritten. Among these were laws pertaining to women's rights. Soon after the suspension of the Family Protection Law, Khomeini explained that women could stipulate the right to seek a divorce by writing it into their marriage contracts. This measure proved insufficient to protect women. In the absence of family courts, any notary office could issue a divorce decree on demand to the husband. It was left to women deputies to push for the passage of bills that, within the constitution's framework, ameliorated problems women faced in their daily lives.

Women outside the majlis exerted pressure on the women deputies and demanded the reintroduction of the Family Protection Law, end to divorce on demand by men, reversion of child-custody rights to mothers, and lifting of barriers to women in certain fields of study. Women in parliament became spokespersons for average Iranian women. When daycare centers were shut down, it was lower-class and lower-middle-class working women who found they lacked a place to leave their children and were forced either to stay at home or to take their children to work with them.

The four women deputies in the first Islamic majlis took an active part in debates, some more than others. They made pre-agenda speeches on general topics. They took a sympathetic, less-conservative position than most male deputies on questions of women's rights. They came to parliament with little or no experience in the area of women's rights. They responded to developments and events as they occurred. They were the beneficiaries of the progress that women had made in the decades preceding the revolution. Unlike their predecessors under the monarchy, these women had not devoted many years to the struggle for women's rights. By contrast the first women elected to the majlis under the monarchy and who sat in the twenty-first and the twenty-second parliaments had devoted their professional lives to working on women's issues, including access to education, economic independence, and equality before the law. Although they came from an affluent class, these deputies argued for rights beneficial to all Iranian women. The Family Protection Law for the first time gave Iranian women recourse to and protection in the courts in matters of marriage, divorce, and child custody. Taking a second wife was more common among families lower on the socioeconomic ladder and among traditional bazaar families than among the upper class. It was working-class women who wanted to work in factories and earn salaries and who, along with women in the civil service, needed daycare centers. Under the monarchy, women from lower socioeconomic levels gradually became aware of opportunities that were opening to them and their daughters.

This awareness and the desire to gain greater freedom and independence generated in women high expectations about the revolution. Women from less privileged and traditional backgrounds wrote letters to women deputies in the first Islamic majlis to complain about mistreatment they experienced in the courts and their exclusion from the job market. Even if women deputies dismissed similar complaints from Westernized upper-middle-class women, they could not ignore this constituency, religious women from the underprivileged classes, and women deputies expressed a responsibility to address their grievances.

The massive presence of women in the activities of daily life, their resistance to being relegated again to their homes, and their participation in Friday prayers and in street demonstrations forced the government to acknowledge that it had a "women's problem" on its hands. The government sought to accommodate some of their demands. As a result, some laws pertaining to women's rights were reluctantly reintroduced. Laws were approved granting custody of children to women widowed by the Iran-Iraq war (1980–88), allowing women in the civil service to work half-time, and providing financial aid for women and children who lacked means of support. At the same time, a proposal to permit single girls to study abroad on government scholarships was rejected. The third majlis (1988–92) passed bills whose effect was to reintroduce a new version of some provisions of the Family Protection Law, including establishing special civil courts to hear family disputes. Although women could not sit as judges, they started serving as special advisors in courts dealing with family disputes. In 1998 the government appointed four women as investigative magistrates. They still could not issue any rulings, but they acted as advisors to clerics presiding over family courts. Women lawyers represented both men and women plaintiffs in civil and family courts. On the eve of the fourth majlis elections in 1992, the third majlis established a parliamentary committee on women, youth, and family affairs. It also enacted a law providing a divorced woman with monetary compensation. A husband who sought a divorce when the woman was not at fault was required to pay his wife a cash settlement based on the number of years she worked as housewife and mother in the conjugal home.

Over the years the number of government-sponsored organizations dealing with women's affairs steadily increased. These included the sociocultural council for women, the international office for women in the ministry of foreign affairs, and offices for women's affairs in other key ministries such as education, health, labor, justice, interior, and Islamic guidance. Provincial governors were instructed to set up special offices for women's issues. A bureau for women's affairs was established in President Rafsanjani's office and was maintained by his successor. The number of women elected to parliament steadily increased. Nine women were elected to the fourth majlis (1992–96), fourteen to the fifth (1996–2000), and thirteen to the sixth (2000–2004).[50]

In 1997 President Khatami replaced Shahla Habibi, the first special advisor to the president on women's affairs, with Zahra Shojai. Unlike her predecessor, Shojai sat in on cabinet meetings where she was joined by Masoumeh Ebtekar, the first woman vice president in charge of the environment. In 1999 Zahra Rahnavard was appointed as president of Al-Zahra University, the first woman ever to hold such a position. That year Fatemeh Hashemi (daughter of President Rafsanjani), Zahra Mostafavi (daughter of the late Ayatollah Khomeini), Fatemeh Karrubi (member of the fourth majlis and wife of the former speaker of parliament), and Azam Taleghani (daughter of the late Ayatollah Taleghani) each headed a different women's organization.

Women's magazines became more outspoken on issues pertaining to women's rights, needs, and problems. *Zanan* (Women)—a progressive, even feminist, women's magazine—routinely published articles arguing for expanded women's rights, new interpretations of Islamic law, and removal of obstacles that women faced daily. The magazine was run and edited entirely by women. The ministry of Islamic guidance, annoyed in 1994 by the contents of *Zanan*, stopped providing newsprint at the government rate to the magazine, thereby forcing it to appear every other month instead of monthly. Denial of government advertisements also forced the magazine to stop printing colored pictures. Faezeh Hashemi, member of parliament from Tehran, launched the newspaper *Zan* (Woman), but it was banned in 1999. Ashraf Geramizadegan, former editor of *Zan-e rouz* (Today's woman), launched a magazine, *Hoquq-e zanan* (Women's rights), which concentrated on issues of women and the law.

The most dramatic manifestation of the growing visibility of Iranian women took place during presidential elections in 1997. Women and members of the younger generation were decisive in the election of the more moderate candidate, Mohammad Khatami. During the presidential campaign, Khatami promised more opportunities for women and talked about equality under the law for men and women. After he was elected, women enjoyed somewhat greater freedom in matters of dress, presence in public, and intermixing of the sexes. In 1998 parliament passed a bill requiring that the *mahr* (fixed sum of money promised to a woman by her husband in the marriage contract) be recalculated to reflect the rate of inflation.

Conservatives, who continued to control a near-majority in the majlis, pushed for legislation restrictive against women. Two of these bills were particularly controversial. The "picture bill" in 1999 made it punishable under law for newspapers and magazines to print pictures exploiting women or encouraging women to ornament themselves. A second bill, pending in 1999, made it difficult for male doctors to treat women or women doctors to treat men. Parliament also failed to raise the marriage age for girls (which still stood at puberty), to grant married women the right to choose where they and their husbands would live, or to allow women the right to travel abroad without their husband's permission. Temporary marriage remained on the books, as did the law of retribution. In 2003 parliament raised the marriage age for girls to thirteen.

Every year conferences were held in Iran on women's position in an Islamic society. Female Iranian delegates participated in many international conferences dealing with women's status. An Iranian delegation took part in the U.N. World Conference on Women in Beijing in 1995. Women at these conferences addressed the progress women in Iran had achieved and the barriers and impediments they continued to face.

Changes in the Islamic Republic since 1979 were further evidence that women as a group would resist attempts to deny them the substantial gains they had achieved in the 1960s and 1970s. More than twenty years after the Islamic revolution, the women's issue remained at the center of political debate. The government recognized that it could not easily relegate women to their homes, control their appearance no matter how harsh the punishment, create a segregated environment for women, or eradicate Western influence in the younger generation. It had not yet devised viable guidelines that were in keeping with a conservative interpretation of Islamic law and that also satisfied the aspirations of modern Iranian women.

NOTES

This chapter is a revised, expanded, and updated version of my essay "Women and Parliaments under Monarchy and Islamic Republic," *Princeton Papers in Near Eastern Studies*, no. 2 (1993): 1–24.

1. For discussion of debates on women's issues in the first and second parliaments under the Islamic Republic, see Haleh Esfandiari, "The Majles and Women's Issues in the Islamic Republic of Iran," in *In the Eye of the Storm: Women in Post-Revolutionary Iran,* ed. Mahnaz Afkhami and Erika Friedl (London: I. B. Tauris, 1994).

2. Shams ol-Moluk Mosahab and Mehrangiz Manouchehrian were among the first twelve women to enter Tehran University. In 1963 Mohammad Reza Shah appointed them as the first women ever to sit in the Iranian senate.

3. Badr ol-Moluk Bamdad, *From Darkness into Light: Women's Emancipation in Iran,* trans. and ed. F. R. C. Bagley (Hicksville, N.Y.: Exposition Press, 1977), 98–99.

4. See *Violence and Culture: Confidential Records about the Abolition of Hijab, 1313–1322,* Iran National Archives (Tehran, 1371/1992). See also Morteza Jaafari et al., *Vaghe-ye kashf-e hejab: Asnad-e montasher nashodeh az vaghe-ye kashf-e hejab dar asr-e Reza Khan* (Tehran: Sazman-e madarek-e farhangi enqelab-e Islami, 1371/1992).

5. For example, in 1911 the Hamadan deputy, Vakil ol-Ro'aya, introduced the idea of equal rights for women. His speech created such an uproar that the speaker was obliged to strike the speech and the resulting debate from the record.

6. Hammed Shahidian, "The Iranian Left and the 'Woman Question,'" *International Journal of Middle East Studies* 26 (2) (1994): 224.

7. Nasser Makarem-Shirazi et al., *Zan va entekhabat* (Women and elections) (Qum: Elmiyeh, n.d.), 8.

8. Ibid., 11.

9. Ibid., 55.

10. "Nazar-e be vaz-e zanan Iran az enqelab-e mashrutiyyat ta asr-e velayat-e faqih" (Examination of the conditions of Iranian women from the constitutional period to the era of the vice-regency of the jurist), *Iran Nameh* 3 (1985), 316.

11. "Sima-ye zan dar kalam-e Imam Khomeini" (Women as depicted in Imam Khomeini's words) (Tehran: Ministry of Islamic Guidance, 1369/1990), 20.

12. Ali Akbar Sedaqat, *Zan dar Islam: Payamha mossahebeha va gofteguha-ye Imam Khomeini darbar-e zan* (Women in Islam: messages, interviews, and sayings of Imam Khomeini) (Qum: Ruh, 1360/1981), 53.

13. Interview with Mehrangiz Dowlatshahi, Oral History of Iran Archives, Foundation for Iranian Studies, Washington, D.C.

14. Interview with Nayereh Ebtehaj-Samii, Oral History of Iran Archives.

15. Dowlatshahi, Oral History.

16. Speech from the throne, 1342/1963. Text in bound volume of majlis debates, opening of twenty-first majlis. See *Mozakerat-e majlis-e showra-ye melli* (hereafter, *Majlis Proceedings*), sessions 1–38, bound volume in Princeton University Library.

17. Ibid.

18. The revolutionary government charged Parsa with "corruption on earth," "spreading prostitution," and "warring against God." She was executed by firing squad in December 1979 in Tehran.

19. *Majlis Proceedings,* 8 Ordibehesht 1345.

20. *Senate Proceedings,* n.d. (probably Bahman 1342).

21. Ibid.

22. Ibid., 4 Khordad 1343.

23. Ibid., 18 Ordibehesht 1344.

24. Ibid., 12 Esfand 1343.

25. Ibid., 17 Khordad 1344.

26. Ibid., 11 Khordad 1343.

27. *Majlis Proceedings,* 19 Khordad 1343.

28. *Senate Proceedings,* 27 Khordad 1347.

29. Ibid., Aban 1342.

30. Ibid.

31. *Majlis Proceedings,* 19 Esfand 1343.

32. *Senate Proceedings,* 9 Esfand 1344.

33. Ibid.

34. Ibid., 14 Dey 1345.

35. Ibid., 1 Aban 1342.

36. Personal interview with Farah Diba Pahlavi, Greenwich, Connecticut, May 1994.

37. Ibid.

38. Dowlatshahi, Oral History.

39. Personal interview with Mehrangiz Manouchehrian, Tehran, June 1994.

40. Ibid.

41. For a description of the meeting between Sadr and Hakim, see Haleh Esfandiari, "Women and Parliaments."

42. In an interview with the author in Tehran in June 1994, Manouchehrian said that when the passport bill was being discussed in the senate, she once more objected to the article requiring a husband's permission for a wife to travel abroad. She argued that this stipulation was not acceptable socially or from a religious point of view. If a woman wanted to go on a pilgrimage (*haj*), her husband did not have the right to stop her. The speaker of the senate, Sharif Emami, interrupted her to tell her not to talk "nonsense." Manouchehrian left the speaker's stand and walked out of the senate. She said that Sharif Emami later came to her house to apologize, but she insisted that a political apology must be public. He refused, and she sent her resignation to the imperial court.

43. Personal interview with Farah Diba Pahlavi, Greenwich, Connecticut, May 1994.

44. Ibid.

45. *Majlis Proceedings,* 18 Azar 1348.

46. See Mahnaz Afkhami's chapter on the Women's Organization of Iran in this volume.

47. Personal interview with an associate of Ayatollah Khomeini, who wished to remain anonymous.

48. For a discussion of issues pertaining to women's rights in the assembly of experts, see Haleh Esfandiari, "Majles and Women's Issues."

49. *Majlis Proceedings,* 2 Mordad 1363.

50. Twelve women were elected to the seventh parliament (2004–08).

6 Women and Labor in the Islamic Republic of Iran

FATEMEH ETEMAD MOGHADAM

IN THIS CHAPTER I examine female labor in the Islamic Republic of Iran and attempt to place the subject in a conceptual framework. I use a comparative historical approach to assess the performance of the Islamic Republic in relation to two major feminist questions: the treatment and compensation of female labor at home, and the emancipation and participation of women in the labor market.

I demonstrate that the treatment of female labor has been subject to three distinct gender policies in the recent history of Iran. During the 1960s and 1970s, the government pursued an explicit policy of recognizing the productivity of female labor outside the home and attempted to emancipate women and use their labor. It also modified certain aspects of the gender gap in spousal personal legal rights in marriage in favor of women but did not explicitly recognize the productivity of female labor at home. During the first decade after the Islamic revolution, the 1980s, the government attempted to reverse these policies. Except for such professions as teaching and health-related services that were crucial to the state's policy of sex segregation, the state attempted to drive women from the labor market. Women also lost all the improvements in spousal rights that they had achieved earlier. Some recognition of the productivity of female labor at home was seen, however. During the 1990s the government explicitly recognized such labor productivity and the need for its compensation. It also modified obstacles to women's work outside the home. Nevertheless, the state continued to regard the allocation of time to household activities the primary responsibility of a Muslim woman and that to the labor market secondary. In the labor market, certain occupations were deemed suitable for women, and others were reserved for men. Thus, the state continued to support the patriarchal structure of the family and pursued a policy of occupational segregation.

Conceptual Framework

Mainstream economists were historically preoccupied with male labor-market participation and did not recognize female household labor as productive activity. Many critics of mainstream economics also treated household labor as nonproductive. Marx argued that family labor could not be analyzed in the scientific terminology of "value."[1] Veblen considered it wasted effort used in serving the master of the house.[2] Marx and Engels, however, recognized the productivity of female labor in the market and considered labor-market participation a positive contributor to women's emancipation.

In what has come to be known as "the new home economics," Gary Becker distinguishes between two types of productive female labor: allocation of time to household activities and allocation of time to the labor market.[3] He explicitly recognizes the productivity of female labor at home. Household labor, however, is not channeled through the market system and is unpaid. In his model, he assumes that the male head of household is altruistic, and thus all members share family resources. Becker's feminist critics argue that his assumption of altruism conceals the possibility of selfishness and that his choice-based behavioral model overlooks issues such as dependence, interdependence, tradition, and power.[4] Despite the controversy, the basic concept of the division of female labor time and the recognition of the productivity of household labor has now become a standard approach in studying female labor.

Current debates among feminist economists focus on the two aspects of female labor and argue that in both, women are unfairly treated. One body of feminist thought emphasizes the devaluation of and low material rewards accorded to activities and traits that traditionally have been deemed appropriate for women. Child rearing and household work are not viewed as contributing to "the wealth of nations." A second body of thought emphasizes women's exclusion from traditionally male activities and institutions. Thus laws, cultural beliefs, and other discriminatory practices exclude women from politics, religious leadership, military positions, and traditionally male crafts and professions within paid employment. These exclusions have important implications for women because activities traditionally regarded as male are those associated with the largest rewards of honor, power, and money.[5]

With an understanding that fundamental methodological differences exist between economic theory and socioeconomic, traditional, and legal treatments and perceptions of female labor in Iran, I attempt to find parallel categories. I make the case that the postrevolutionary regime in Iran (1979–) recognizes three legal categories of female labor: marital duties (*vaza'if-e zanashu'i*) (activities directly derived from female sexuality including reproductive labor), household labor, and participation in the labor market. With the exception of the treatment of spousal sexual relations as a contractually binding marital service in the first category, the first two categories combined correspond to Becker's allocation of time to household activities. The adequacy and fairness of compensation to female labor in Iran is controversial. Nevertheless, legal provisions allow for material compensation in the form of entitlement and wages to all three categories. They are all paid labor. Iranian law as of 2001 maintains and reinforces the patriarchal bias in men as heads of households and their legal authority to exercise power over women. As justification, the ulama (religious scholars) argue that Islam requires men to be just (*adel*). This assumption bears resemblance to Becker's "altruism" and can generate similar feminist criticisms. The first two categories of labor are perceived to be the primary duties of a woman. Thus, allocation of time to the market is secondary. In general, certain occupations are considered suitable for women, and others are reserved for men only, hence an explicit policy of occupational segregation.

Background

Family law in Iran has evolved from medieval Islamic law (shari'a). Legally a woman's entitlement in marriage includes her dower (*mahriyeh*) and upkeep (*nafaqeh*). From a legal point of view, a Muslim marriage contract (*aqd*) is essentially a sale contract, and the object of sale is female sexuality and reproductive labor. Thus, mahriyeh is compensation for the sale and nafaqeh for the maintenance of female sexuality in marriage.[6] Qur'anic provisions indicate that a woman is not required to breast-feed her child, and if she does so she can expect wages from the man, which can be interpreted to mean that women can expect payments for child raising.[7] Furthermore, the advice that men who can afford it should hire domestic help for their wives may be interpreted to mean that women are not required to perform housework in marriage. With the possible exception of the legal profession, no explicit Qur'anic rules prohibit women from participating in the labor market.[8] Indeed the Qur'an is clear about the entitlement of working women to fair wages.[9] The lives of the Prophet Mohammad's first and highly revered wife Khadijeh, a merchant, and his granddaughter Zeinab, who showed extraordinary courage and publicly challenged the caliph Yazid, can be used as examples indicating that Islam allows for women's involvement in the market and other domains of public life.

While medieval law did not negate these provisions, and Islamic jurists expressed respect for the above-mentioned women, the law did not focus on these labor-related aspects. This law, the requirement of veiling, and the socioeconomic and political conditions of medieval Iran created a situation in which women in urban areas were secluded in their private quarters, did not participate in public life, and received no explicit compensation for their household labor.

Many of these legal, socioeconomic, and ideological characteristics have persisted in modern Iran. An important development of the modern era, however, is a growing tendency to perceive women as agents whose potential or actual labor contributes positively to society. For example, at the turn of the twentieth century, advocates of women's education stated that educated women were better mothers.[10] The underlying assumption in this argument is that female labor productivity in childbearing and raising is positive and can be increased through education. Similarly, advocates of the veil's removal argued that seclusion kept women away from public life and was a factor contributing to Iran's backwardness. Thus, women were perceived as having the potential ability to contribute positively to public life.

This perception of women as productive labor was most pronounced in the 1960s and 1970s when the government aimed to bring rapid growth and industrialization to Iran. Official government documents explicitly referred to women as "a relatively untapped supply of labor" that should be used in the labor market for economic development. The underlying strategy for women's emancipation appeared to be the removal or modification of traditional barriers to women's participation in education and the labor market.[11] The government also undertook policies to reform family law. These policies aimed to modify the gender gap in the personal rights of spouses in matters such as polygyny, divorce, and child custody. According to these reforms, a man seeking to marry a second wife could not do so without the approval of the first, a man could no longer unilaterally divorce his wife, the issue of divorce had to be settled in civil courts, divorce could be initiated by a woman as well as a man, a woman could seek custody of her children after divorce or her husband's death, and the issue of custody was to be resolved in civil courts.[12] These reforms did not address the allocation of female time to household labor. The implicit assumption was analogous to that of a Marxist position: only participation in the labor market constitutes productive labor, and labor-market participation is a prerequisite for women's emancipation.

Postrevolutionary Ideology and Allocation of Time to Household Activities

Postrevolutionary ideology and the legal system sanction traditional Islamic law and the legal commoditization of female sexuality. Thus, the Family Protection Law (first passed in 1967 and revised in 1975) was suspended. In contrast to medieval law, postrevolutionary reforms in family law focus on the productivity of female labor at home. The advocates for these reforms argue that the traditional marriage contract compensates only female sexual services and reproductive labor and does not account for other types of labor at home and that Islam emphasizes complementarity of the sexes and in contrast to Western liberalism aims to maximize family rather than individual welfare. Household activities take precedence over participation in the labor market and constitute the primary responsibility of a Muslim woman. Marriage is viewed as quasi-employment, and women's economic rights at the termination of marriage become a central issue.

Postrevolutionary reforms stem from a legal distinction between two categories of female labor at home. The first category is referred to as marital duties (vaza'if-e zanashu'i), activities directly derived from female sexuality and an inalienable part of a marriage contract. A married woman is contractually bound to submit to her spouse and bear his children. Female sexuality is in essence sold to the husband upon marriage. The product of the marriage, the children, belong to the husband. Thus, in divorce the man has the right of child custody. In return for his wife's duties, the husband is legally obliged to provide full financial support (nafaqeh) for the wife. Nafaqeh is not a minimum support but the maintenance of a living standard compatible with the woman's status and the man's income. It is payable irrespective of the wife's personal wealth or income. Another financial obligation is the dower (mahriyeh), which is legally due when the marriage is consummated but in practice is demanded by women at divorce. A law passed in 1996 requires cost-of-living adjustments for the payment of mahriyeh at divorce. The proponents of this law argued that the stipulation of a monetary value in a marriage contract should be interpreted as the specification of real purchasing power at the time of marriage. Therefore, necessary adjustments for inflation should be made at divorce.[13]

The second category of household labor is child raising and production for family consumption. Historically women have performed these tasks, but a marriage contract does not legally bind women to do so. This legal aspect is used for most financial reforms in the divorce law. In 1984 the Islamic regime introduced a new standardized marriage contract. Among other conditions, this contract provides for an equal division, at divorce, of the wealth accumulated by the man during the marriage. Legally a woman's personal wealth and income are not shared in a Muslim marriage. The husband's acceptance of this provision is voluntary and applies only if a man is unilaterally divorcing his wife. The idea is widely advertised, and many couples accept this provision.[14] For justification, the ulama argue that women perform household labor that is not covered by nafaqeh and mahriyeh. Reform of the divorce law in 1991 includes another clause based on the same idea. If a marriage contract does not include a provision of wealth sharing, a man who unilaterally divorces his wife has to pay the wage equivalent (*ojrat olmesl*) of household labor performed during the marriage.[15] This idea is used in yet another way. If a divorced woman does not have a paying job and if her husband has unemployment insurance, by law she becomes eligible for one-third of her husband's insurance benefits accumulated during the marriage.[16]

These reforms were in part attempts by the government after the revolution to ameliorate the deterioration in the rights of women in marriage. The introduction of a new marriage contract in 1984 was a response to bitter complaints of women, many of whom had actively participated in the revolution, about the suspension of the Family Protection Law. The ruling clergy argued that this law was un-Islamic because it applied indiscriminately to all couples. They argued that a woman may include favorable conditions in her marriage contract as long as the man voluntarily accepts them and if the conditions are not contrary to the essence of an Islamic marriage. Thus, postrevolutionary contracts include a long list of conditions, each of which should be negotiated and signed separately by the man. The 1991 and 1996 reforms in divorce law were a response to rising divorce and the growing number of women and children with no financial support. After the revolution, men could unilaterally divorce their wives not only in civil courts but also through notary publics where they were not required to justify the divorce. Furthermore, rampant inflation had made the prerevolutionary mahriyehs, usually expressed in nominal monetary terms, nearly worthless. Thus, divorce became easy and low cost for men. According to discussions held in parliament about the passage of the 1991 law, during the first ten years of the Islamic regime only 15 percent of divorces were decided by civil courts and 85 percent were issued by notary publics. In comparison to the prerevolutionary period, divorce increased by 200 percent in Tehran. Many men did not pay nafaqeh, a woman could be divorced in absentia, and notary publics sometimes took the law into their own hands and did not honor conditions included by women in their marriage contracts.[17] It was argued that an Islamic country could not remain indifferent to the suffering of women and children and that the provision of a minimum welfare for the growing number of poor women and children was too costly for the government.[18] These reforms were also used as a justification for the law requiring the husband's permission for married women who wish to work outside the home. It was argued that women receive nafaqeh and ojrat olmesl, and a married woman's allocation of time outside the home should be approved by the husband.[19] Thus, the reforms were intended to reinforce the family's patriarchal structure and to emphasize the secondary aspect of female labor-market participation.

Published data pertaining to the actual impact of these reforms are not available. Various reports in the widely circulated women's magazine *Zan-e rooz* (Today's woman), as well as statements by women lawyers, indicate that many legal loopholes create obstacles for the realization of these changes. For example, the condition of division of wealth at divorce is applicable only if a man is unilaterally divorcing his wife. Such a man is likely to plan for divorce and its timing. In the absence of a developed system of income and wealth taxation, it is possible for the man to change the composition of his wealth and to conceal it at divorce. Legally the husband owes mahriyeh to his wife. It is a form of debt. If he proves unable to pay, if he is bankrupt, he can escape paying it. When women wish to divorce or are trying to obtain child custody, they often forgo their mahriyeh or other financial benefits. Problems concerning the measurement of ojrat olmesl also exist. In practice its value is determined arbitrarily on a case-by-case basis by the relevant judge.[20] The woman has to prove that she did not agree to perform these labor services free of charge, and she cannot ask for ojrat olmesl if she initiates divorce.[21] A significant gap exists between the entitlement and the actual re-source shares of women at divorce. In the absence of data, it is not possible to measure the extent of the effectiveness of the legal recognition of the productivity of household labor and the need for its compensation. Nevertheless, the legal entitlement of women to material resources for household labor is a significant development, at least symbolically. The issue generated new discussions and controversies that have the potential to create future reforms.

A debate is ongoing concerning additional entitlement to household labor. Some high-ranking clergy have proposed that the concept of nafaqeh has broad implications, that it means the provision of an adequate living standard for women. Thus, it could include insurance for divorce as well as old-age pensions for women. A man could open a pension fund for his wife at the beginning of a marriage, and the woman would be entitled to the proceeds at divorce or old age.[22] Advocates of women's rights argue that ojrat olmesl is based on the category of household labor that is not contracted in marriage and should be payable upon demand and irrespective of divorce.[23] It is further argued that in cases in which a working woman quits her job to allocate time to housework, the wage equivalent should be calculated on the basis of the forgone wages. These and similar issues are debated in seminars, newspapers, and the parliament. The issue of a woman's economic and other rights in an Islamic marriage has become highly politicized, and new reforms are likely to result from discussions.

Labor-Market Participation

Although government policy and ideology are likely to have a significant impact on labor-market participation, a host of other socioeconomic and cultural factors also affect participation. Thus, an evaluation of labor-market participation is complex. Global studies have found significant relationships with the following variables: education, fertility, age of marriage, growth and structural changes in the economy, urbanization, growth of service and industrial sectors, and changes in the agricultural sector.[24] The following factors have positive impacts on employment: increase in the level of educational attainments of women, decline in fertility, and increase in the age of marriage for women. The latter two variables reduce women's domestic responsibilities, and an increase in education raises the possibilities for employment and the earning power of women outside the home, thus increasing the attractiveness of wage labor. In the case of developing countries, increase in the years of schooling may initially cause a decrease in the participation rate because a larger percentage of young women will attend school instead of participating in family or low-wage labor. The impact of economic growth on participation is less clear and is not always positive, and no clear consensus on trends associated with development in women's labor-market participation exists.[25] While sluggish growth may contribute to a decrease in the relative share of female employment, empirical findings are not conclusive.[26] Although the overall performance of an economy should be considered in an examination of labor participation, its significance should not be overemphasized.

Many studies on third-world countries emphasize the significance of cultural factors, the legal status of women, and government policy.[27] The extent and type of patriarchal domination differ by culture, and these differences affect the extent and type of participation of women in the labor force. A government's gender policies are likely to have a pronounced impact in an oil-producing country such as Iran in which public policy strongly affects the economy.

In this chapter I use changes in the level and structure of the Iranian economy, education, fertility, age of marriage, cultural and legal factors, and government policy as factors affecting women's employment. I argue that postrevolutionary changes in fertility, age of marriage, legal status of women, access to higher education, and emphasis on traditional cultural values are part of a broad gender ideology and that the ideological factor was more pronounced during the early years after the revolution. Thus, a distinction should be made between the earlier period ending with Ayatollah Khomeini's death in 1989 and the subsequent years. In the earlier years, attempts were made to undermine female participation, while a comparatively moderate approach was adopted in the 1990s. The situation with respect to labor participation is also dynamic and subject to controversy and open debates.

The empirical evidence presented here is based on data from population censuses and sample surveys that date as far back as 1956. The last census was carried out in 1996.

Overview

The following general assessments can be made from the data. The percentage of active women in the total female population of ten years and older increased during the period 1956–76 and was 12.93 in 1976, three years before the revolution. This rate declined to about 8.2, 8.7, and 9.1 for 1986, 1991, and 1996, respectively.[28] Female labor as a percentage of the total active labor declined from 20.3 in 1976 to 10, 11, and 13 for 1986, 1991, and 1996, respectively.[29] Despite possible methodological differences, a comparison with other countries of the Middle East can be useful in understanding the extent of the problem. By 1976 women comprised about 20 percent of the total active labor in Iran. While this share was lower than that of Israel (39 percent) and Turkey (36 percent), it was high for the Middle East as a whole. The share of women in total active labor was 7 percent in Egypt (1976), 17 percent in Iraq (1977), 13 percent in Kuwait (1980), and 4 percent in Pakistan (1981). In 1986 this percentage had declined to 10 percent in Iran and was lower than the comparable shares in all of the above-mentioned countries.[30]

Since the revolution the economy has been generally stagnant, although its worst performance was during the first half of the 1980s. Society and culture in Iran are patriarchal, and legally and socially men are expected to provide for their families. It is likely that stagnation contributed to increased discrimination against and marginalization of women.

Ideology and Government Policy

Comparisons of pre- and postrevolutionary labor laws pertaining to work at night, maternity leave, breast-feeding rights, and daycare facilities indicate marginal changes in positive as well as negative directions. For both periods, labor laws are generally protective. The law is explicit in the entitlement of women to equal wages for equally productive work.[31] Changes in the dress code for women were legalized. During the earlier postrevolutionary years, considerable rhetoric concerning moral standards applied to women and their proper place in society. Shortly after the revolution, many conservative traditionalists argued that women's labor should be spent exclusively in the family. Such moral campaigns dissuaded many families from allowing their wives and daughters to work outside the home. Leftist and populist groups advocated improvements in female labor laws, which would increase the cost of female employment. Although such changes did not materialize, these advocates were likely to have dissuaded many employers from hiring female workers.[32] Thus, different and sometimes opposing ideological rhetoric had negative implications for women's employment.

One stated objective of the revolution was to end what the clergy perceived as the un-Islamic and "morally decadent" public appearance and position of women as found under the Pahlavi regime and to return to "true Islamic values" that would "elevate" women's social and moral position. The government undertook a campaign to expel women from work outside the home and to purify government offices and factories. Early retirement incentives were also used to persuade women to leave the job market. According to a new law, workers could ask for early retirement after fifteen instead of twenty-five years of service. Although the law included male as well as female workers, it persuaded more women than men to retire.[33]

In accordance with early Islamic practices, the legal age of eligibility of girls for marriage was reduced from eighteen to nine years, provided that the girl had reached puberty and a special court and the girl's guardian approved the marriage. These courts are lenient in giving permits. On the average each court takes a few minutes to ask the girl if she is voluntarily getting married and then issues the permit.[34] The percentage share of married girls in the age category of ten to fourteen was almost zero in 1976. This share was nearly 2.5, 2.2, and 2.2 percent for 1986, 1991, and 1996, respectively. In general, the age of first marriage declined for 1986, a factor contributing to a decline in labor participation. In comparison to 1976, the data for 1991 and 1996 indicate a significant decline in the percentages of married young women in the age category of fifteen to twenty-four, reflecting a general increase in the age of first marriage.[35] The law concerning child marriage was not reversed for many years, but parliamentary deputies who were elected in 2000 intended to change the minimum age to fifteen. In 2003 they voted to raise the minimum age to thirteen.

Fertility is another factor affecting female employment. Population-growth figures averaged about 2.7 percent annually for 1966–76.[36] For 1976–86, the average annual growth was estimated to be 3.9 percent.[37] For 1986–96, population growth was estimated to be just under 2 percent; for 1991–96, it was 1.5 percent.[38]

These changes reflect a change in government policy. After the revolution, abortion became illegal, and other measures of population control were considered immoral, against the principles of an Islamic society, and an attempt by Western countries to reduce the number of Muslims in the world.[39] Supporters of the revolution vowed to protect the "oppressed" (*mustaz'afin*), promised free urban housing to the poor, and offered precedence to families with many children. In mosques and through the media, the clergy urged people to marry and have children. But an explosive population growth alarmed the ruling clergy. In 1989, just before his death, Ayatollah Khomeini

made a religious declaration that considered use of contraceptives and ster-
ilization of men and women acceptable. Through the 1990s the government
pursued an aggressive policy of population planning, accompanied by distribution of free contraceptives in health clinics as well as active use of
mosques, the media, and educational institutions to persuade people to have
fewer children.

Officially abortion continued to be illegal in 2001. In practice, legal loopholes and clerical interpretations made abortion highly accessible and free
of charge in government hospitals and clinics. According to the law, abortion can be performed if pregnancy is harmful to a woman's health. The law
uses the word "harm," and not "endangerment," thus making it easy for
physicians to issue medical attestations. In practice, such attestations were
regularly signed. According to clerical interpretations, if an abortion takes
place during the first 120 days, before the fetus acquires a soul, it is not a crime.
The person who performs an abortion has to pay a penalty to the lawful heirs
of the fetus, the parents. After that period, it is a crime, and more blood
money should be paid to the heirs of the fetus. This interpretation is a guar-
antee for physicians that the potential penalty does not include imprisonment. According to doctors and nurses, abortion was frequent, and no one
heard of a single case of a doctor being reprimanded.[40]

In the 1990s government policy concerning subsidies underwent change.
In 1991 it was declared that only the first three children in each family were
eligible for food and other subsidies.[41] In the 1990s the entire policy of food
and other subsidies was reexamined.

Since the early 1990s, the work environment has become more friendly
to women.[42] In contrast to the earlier period when daycare facilities in some
government institutions were closed, in recent years many workplaces have
established such facilities for their employees.[43] A law passed in 1990 allows
women to retire after twenty years instead of a minimum of twenty-five years
in government service. While this law shows a pattern similar to earlier policies of keeping women at home, it was a response to the demands of wom-
en workers in the public sector and recognized the double burden of wom-
en. The law explicitly states that no woman should be coerced into retirement
and that the law is applicable only if a woman voluntarily asks for early retirement.[44] Women fought to have this law passed by parliament.[45]

During the 1990s, despite significant modifications in ideology and in the
treatment of working women, the regime continued to consider household
labor the primary occupation of a Muslim woman and regarded certain jobs
in the labor market such as teaching and health-related occupations suitable

for women. Women in growing numbers challenged the requirement of a husband's permission for a woman to work outside the home. In response to these demands, a parliamentary deputy argued that women have the right to work as well as not to work. Since they receive nafaqeh, their work outside the home should be with the husband's permission.[46] The issue is dynamic and surrounded by controversy, and not all religious leaders agree. According to Ayatollah Borujerdi, a man cannot prevent his wife from pursuing work outside the home, and the law requiring the husband's permission is an incorrect interpretation of Islamic jurisprudence.[47] These and other legal and ideological issues were challenged and debated by women's groups and publications and by women parliamentary representatives.

Education

The percentage of female students in the postrevolutionary years increased, a trend consistent with that of the prerevolutionary period. The percentage of female students in the population of ten years of age and older rose from about 15 percent in 1976 to 17, 22, and 27 percent for 1986, 1991, and 1996, respectively. This increase in part explains the decline in women's labor participation, especially that of teenage girls. The combined percentage shares of female students and active female labor for 1976 (33 percent) is larger than that of 1986 (29 percent) and indicates that factors other than the increased share of women students account for the decline in female labor participation. For 1996, this combined share (36 percent) shows an increase over 1976.[48]

During the 1980s higher education was characterized by a gender-based discriminatory policy that aimed at segregating men and women and that reflected an ideological perception of proper occupations for women. In general women were considered suitable for teaching professions and health-related services. Such fields as engineering were considered to be against women's nature. Despite a significant growth in secondary education from 1975 to 1986, the level of higher education for females remained constant. The closing of coeducational technical schools meant that women could no longer have access to technical education. Although special female technical schools were established, they were limited to the fields of hygiene, first aid, sewing, cooking, and knitting. For 1984–85, 91 fields of study (54 percent) out of 169 areas offered by some 120 institutions of higher education were not available to women, mostly in technical and scientific fields. In other areas maximum quotas ranging from 20 to 50 percent were applied to women students. In

1989 certain modifications were introduced that increased the areas open to women by about 10 percent.[49] Further changes in 1994 allowed women to participate in all fields of higher education, which marked the end of discriminatory policy in higher education.

Agriculture and Manufacturing

Employed women in Iran are largely clustered in agriculture, manufacturing, and services. Since rural women were not an ideological target of the Islamic regime, changes in their labor participation were due to structural and economic changes. Because serious measurement problems pertain to women's work in agriculture in Iran, I state simply that a large percentage of active women are in agriculture. The government's census and other data certainly underestimate their participation in this sector.[50]

In 1986 the absolute number of women in manufacturing had declined to one-third of its 1976 level. In comparison to 1986, the number had increased in 1996, but this absolute number was less than that of 1976. A substantial part of the decline in 1986 was in unpaid family labor, and the share of these female workers in total manufacturing declined from 21 percent in 1976 to 4 and 8 percent in 1986 and 1996, respectively. This decline was largely due to economic stagnation and the general decline of the activities of small family workshops (making carpets and other products). A similar pattern is observed in male employment in this category. In 1986 female wage labor in manufacturing also declined to one-third of its 1976 level, and its share in total active labor in manufacturing dropped from 10 to 4 percent. For the same period, male wage labor rose, and its share in total active labor increased from 43 to 52 percent. In comparison to 1986, the 1996 figures indicate an increase. Nevertheless, both the absolute number and the percentage share in total manufacturing are lower than in 1976. Women have not regained their share in manufacturing wage labor.[51]

Traditionally the textile industry has been the largest employer of female labor in Iran. The number of women employed in this industry declined by 419,000 in 1986 and accounted for 97.4 percent of the total decline in manufacturing. General economic stagnation and rural-urban migration explain the closing of many small carpet workshops that were predominantly located in rural areas. For the same period, male employment in the textile industry declined by only 16,000.[52] During the period 1976–86, no significant changes in technology and use of machinery took place in these industries. Thus, the decline was not due to job obsolescence resulting from technological change. Government policy and ideology were also important factors. After the revolution, the number of cooperatives in the textile and apparel industries significantly increased. In these cooperatives male workers joined as own-account workers, and thus reorganization of factories resulted in job loss for women. During the early postrevolutionary period, many large textile factories came under public control. In addition to early-retirement incentives, another law entitled the husbands of women who resigned from factory jobs to a lifetime monthly salary increase of 10,000 rials (roughly $100 at the time of the law's passage). During the 1980s this law persuaded many poor working women to resign.[53]

Other Structural Characteristics of Female Labor

The number of women employed in the category of public, social, and private services rose for both 1986 and 1996. For 1986, the increase is largely due to the increase in the number of women teachers and to a lesser extent women health-service providers. In 1986, 42 percent of employed women worked for the public sector, in contrast to 30 percent in 1976. About 83.2 percent of women employed by the public sector were teachers, and 8.9 percent participated in health-related services. The evidence for 1996 suggests greater diversity in the employment of women in the public sector.[54]

For 1986, a slight increase in the total number of women also occurred in the category of administrator, manager, and executive, from 1,356 in 1976 to 1,534 in 1986.[55] Nearly all women in this category are school principals, and the number of women in any other managerial category is near zero. It should also be noted that on average the women employed by the public sector were better educated than men; thus the difference is not due to differences in human capital but rather to other factors such as discrimination based on ideology and culture, probably the main contributors. In 1996 the absolute number and its share in total for this category rose substantially. The evidence also indicates significant diversity in the positions occupied by these women.[56] The debate in 2001 was ongoing, and many women's rights activists were challenging the existing discriminatory system.

Conclusion

The findings of this chapter suggest that the Islamic Republic recognizes three legal categories of productive female labor. The first is marital duties, activities directly derived from female sexuality and reproductive labor and an inalienable part of a marriage contract, which is in essence the sale of female sexuality and reproductive labor. In return women are entitled to mahriyeh and nafaqeh. The second category is child raising and household labor. According to legal interpretations, this aspect of female labor is not compensated by mahriyeh and nafaqeh and should be compensated separately. For this category, the law provides other types of entitlements for women at divorce. The third category is participation in the labor market. According to the ideology of the Islamic Republic, as well as aspects of the law such as the requirement of a husband's permission for a married woman to work outside the home, this category of female labor is subordinate to the first two categories.

In the 1990s the government introduced several legislative reforms concerning women's entitlement in marriage and household labor. While it is not certain if these reforms have contributed to significant financial gains for women, at least they are important symbolically. This is especially notable in terms of the explicit recognition of the productivity of female household labor and its entitlement to monetary rewards.

NOTES

When used in this chapter, the present tense refers to 2001. An extended version of the conceptual argument presented here appears in Fatemeh E. Moghadam, "Iran's New Home Economics: An Exploratory Attempt to Conceptualize Women's Work in the Islamic Republic," *Research in Middle East Economics* 4 (2001): 339–60.

1. Nancy Folbre, "Socialism, Feminist and Scientific," in *Beyond Economic Man: Feminist Theory and Economics,* ed. Marianne A. Ferber and Julie A. Nelson (Chicago: University of Chicago Press, 1993), 94–110.

2. Thorstein Veblen, *The Theory of the Leisure Class: An Economic Study in the Evolution of Institutions* (London: Macmillan, 1899).

3. Gary S. Becker, "Human Capital, Effort, and the Sexual Division of Labor," *Journal of Labor Economics* 3 (1985): 533–58.

4. Rebecca M. Blank, "What Should Mainstream Economists Learn from Feminist Theory?" in *Beyond Economic Man: Feminist Theory and Economics,* 133–43.

5. Paula England, "The Separative Self: Androcentric Bias in Neoclassical Assumptions," in *Beyond Economic Man: Feminist Theory and Economics,* 37–53; Lourdes Beneria, "Accounting for Women's Work: The Progress of Two Decades," *World Development* 20 (11) (1992): 1547–60.

6. Fatemeh E. Moghadam, "Commoditization of Sexuality and Female Labor Participation in Islam: Implications for Iran, 1960–1990," in *In the Eye of the Storm: Women in Post-Revolutionary Iran,* ed. Mahnaz Afkhami and Erika Friedl (London: I. B. Tauris, 1994), 80–97; Shahla Haeri, *Law of Desire: Temporary Marriage in Shi'i*

Iran (Syracuse: Syracuse University Press, 1989); Ziba Mir-Hosseini, *Marriage on Trial: A Study of Islamic Family Law: Iran and Morocco Compared* (London: St. Martin's, 1993).

7. *Qur'an-e Majid* (The Holy Qur'an), trans. (Arabic to Persian) Abdol-Majid Ayati (Tehran: Soroush, 1988), verses 2:233, 65:6.

8. In court, two female witnesses are considered equal to one male, which can be interpreted to mean that women are not qualified for the legal profession.

9. This point was elaborated in an interview with Ayatollah Mohammad Moosavi Bojnurdi, *Zan-e rooz*, no. 1432, 28 Aban 1372 (1993), 13.

10. Janet Afary, *The Iranian Constitutional Revolution, 1906–1911* (New York: Columbia University Press, 1996), 177–207.

11. Kaveh Mirani, "Social and Economic Change in the Role of Women, 1956–1978," in *Women and Revolution in Iran,* ed. Guity Nashat (Boulder: Westview, 1983), 69–86; Moghadam, "Commoditization of Sexuality," 80–97.

12. Mirani, "Social and Economic Change."

13. For discussion of this interpretation, see the interview with Ayatollah Bojnurdi, *Zan-e rooz*, no. 1444, 2 Bahman 1372 (1993), 14–16.

14. This information is based on personal interviews in 1997 with three notary-public managers and three women lawyers in Tehran as well as an examination of postrevolutionary marriage contracts.

15. Law concerning the reform of regulations concerning divorce approved by parliament in 1992; *Zanan* 2 (9) (1993).

16. *Zan-e rooz*, no. 1216, 30 Ordibehesht 1368 (1989), 2–30.

17. In addition to the above-mentioned reforms, the 1991 law returned divorce cases to the courts.

18. *Zan-e rooz*, no. 1246, 25 Azar 1369 (1990), 15.

19. Interview with Amid-e Zanjani, parliamentary deputy; *Zan-e rooz*, no. 1440, 4 Day 1372 (1993), 14–15. Also, an interview with Ayatollah Yazdi; *Zan-e rooz*, no. 1407, 18 Ordibehesht 1372 (1993), 4–6.

20. Personal interview with three women lawyers in Tehran in 1997.

21. *Zanan* 2 (9) (1993).

22. *Zan-e rooz*, no. 1443, 26 Day 1372 (1993), 10–13.

23. *Zan-e rooz*, no. 1439, 27 Azar 1372 (1993), 19.

24. Among other sources, see Gary S. Becker, *A Treatise on the Family* (Cambridge: Harvard University Press, 1991), 54–56; Francine D. Blau and Marianne A. Ferber, *The Economics of Women, Men, and Work* (Englewood Cliffs, N.J.: Prentice-Hall, 1986), 120–22.

25. T. Paul Schultz, "Women's Changing Participation in the Labor Force: A World Perspective," World Bank Working Paper, December 1989, WPS 272, 6; Ester Boserup, *Women's Role in Economic Development* (New York: St. Martin's, 1970), 53.

26. Schultz, "Women's Changing Participation," 6–9.

27. See Sharon Stichter and Jane L. Parpart, eds., *Women, Employment, and the Family in the International Division of Labour* (Philadelphia: Temple University Press, 1990), 1–9.

28. For statistics and sources, see Moghadam, "Iran's New Home Economics," 359.

29. Based on empirical evidence from many developing countries, economists

argue that female labor participation is U-shaped. During the early years of development and industrialization, the participation rate declines because many young women attend school instead of working in agriculture and/or urban workshops. During the later years, participation goes up because of higher education and lower fertility. See Nilufer Cagatay and Sule Ozler, "Feminization of the Labor-Force: The Effects of Long Term Development and Structural Adjustment," *World Development* 23 (11) (1995): 1883–84. Iran appears to be an exception to this pattern. During the 1960s and 1970s, the participation rate rose and then started falling. Survey methods in Iran have consistently underestimated women's work in agriculture. Thus, the extent of decline in agricultural labor is also underestimated. Furthermore, the government policies and rapid growth of the 1960s and 1970s, as well as the ideological changes of the 1980s, appear to have overshadowed other factors.

30. *ILO International Labor Statistics.*

31. Mehrangiz Kar, "Yek gozaresh darbareh hoquq-e kar-e zanan" (Report on female labor laws), unpublished, 1992.

32. Ibid.

33. Mitra Baqerian, "Bar-rasi-ye vijegihayi-ye eshteqal-e zanan dar Iran, 1355–1365" (Examination of specific characteristics of female employment in Iran, 1976–1986) (Tehran: Plan and Budget Organization, 1990), 75–76.

34. *Zan-e rooz,* no. 1235, 8 Mehr 1368 (29 Sept. 1989); and no. 1236, 15 Mehr 1368 (6 Oct. 1989), 14–15, 54–55.

35. For statistics and sources, see Moghadam, "Iran's New Home Economics," 352.

36. Markaz-e amar-e Iran, *Iran dar ayineh-ye amar* (Iran in a mirror of statistics) (Tehran, 1989), 11.

37. Markaz-e amar-e Iran, *Salnameh amari-ye sal-e 1370* (Annual statistics 1991) (Tehran, 1992), 34.

38. Markaz-e amar-e Iran, *Gozideh-ye mataleb-e amari* (Selected statistical topics) (Tehran, 1992), 4.

39. Homa Hoodfar, "Devices and Desires: Population Policy and Gender Roles in the Islamic Republic," *MERIP Reports* 24 (5) (1994): 11–17.

40. Ibid., 13.

41. *Iran Times,* no. 1027, 19 July 1991.

42. Personal observations and comparisons during my visits to Iran in 1989, 1992, and 1994.

43. For example, the agricultural development bank had an excellent daycare system, and right after the revolution it was closed.

44. *Zan-e rooz,* no. 1304, Esfand 1369 (1990), 6–10.

45. *Zan-e rooz,* no. 1286, Mehr 1369 (1990).

46. *Zan-e rooz,* no. 1440, 26 Day 1372 (1993), 14–15.

47. *Zan-e rooz,* no. 1444, 24 Bahman 1372 (1993), 10–11.

48. For statistics and sources, see Moghadam, "Iran's New Home Economics," 359.

49. Hammed Shahidian, "The Education of Women in the Islamic Republic of Iran," *Journal of Women's History* 2 (3) (1991): 6–38, 12–14, 17–20.

50. In general, women's work in agriculture is underestimated in Iran. For census data, the question asked is whether women were active in agriculture during the past ten days. While active labor should measure part-time workers, depending on the

time of the interview part-time active female labor may or may not be counted as active. This is in contrast to practices used by some other countries in which the interviewers go to the same household three or four times each year. In the case of the data for 1976, an additional problem arises. According to population census data, total employed women in agriculture was 227.9 thousand persons. According to *ILO Year-book of Labor Statistics* (1982, 58), total active female labor in agriculture was 824.3 thousand persons. While there are definitional differences between employed and active labor and the two numbers should not be identical, the discrepancy appears to be too large.

51. For statistics and sources, see Fatemeh E. Moghadam, "Winners and Losers: Women and Labor-Force Participation in the Islamic Republic of Iran," in *Earnings Inequality, Unemployment, and Poverty in the Middle East and North Africa*, ed. G. Dibeh and W. Shaheen (Westport, Conn.: Greenwood Press, 2000), 217.

52. Baqerian, "Bar-rasi," 74–76.

53. Ibid.

54. Moghadam, "Winners and Losers."

55. *ILO, International Labor Statistics.*

56. For statistics and sources, see Moghadam, "Winners and Losers," 220.

7 ## Labor-Force Participation of Women in Contemporary Iran

AMIR MEHRYAR, GHOLAMALI FARJADI, AND MOHAMMAD TABIBIAN

LABOR-FORCE PARTICIPATION is commonly acknowledged as one of the main pillars of women's status and empowerment. Its importance lies in the fact that it enables women to have access to and control over financial resources and to attain economic independence. Economic independence in turn can help women achieve a more equitable position in household decision making. Working in the nondomestic labor market also enables women to have access to the wider world outside the home, to come into contact with people other than their immediate family, and thus to develop interests and aspirations other than those of a homemaker.[1]

In addition to these personal advantages, labor-force participation of women is also considered essential for national development. Women constitute half of the population of each country, and no nation can afford to keep one-half of its labor force and human resources outside the formal labor market. The conviction that women's participation in the formal labor market can help national development has been largely responsible for increased investment in women's education as part of national development plans. Education is considered important not only for improving women's performance in their traditional reproductive (as mothers) and care-giver roles (as homemakers) but also for enabling them to function as better citizens and to enter the increasingly sophisticated formal job market. More often than not, the main justification for investing in women's education (particularly at secondary and higher levels) is to prepare them to enter the labor market and to make their proportional contribution to economic growth and national development.

If education does not lead to labor-force participation (that is, when there is no or little change in the labor-force participation rate of women following considerable investment in their education), policy makers may have a valid excuse to assign a lower priority to investment in women's education. Yet women's labor-force participation is a complex phenomenon and does not depend solely on their education. Availability of jobs in general and jobs meeting the particular interests, preferences, needs, and abilities of women are also important. The latter aspect will be partly determined by cultural values and traditions concerning gender-appropriate roles and women's status in society. Cultural factors governing the division of labor in society, the relative role of men and women in household structure, and the perceived acceptability of certain occupations for women may also curtail women's ability to participate in formal labor markets.

Because of these complexities, female economic-activity rates vary considerably from one country to another. According to a United Nations report, in 1998 economic-activity rates of women aged fifteen and above varied from 67.9 percent (Sweden) to 35.9 percent (Ireland) among the world's most developed countries.[2] Its highest rates belonged to such low-income African countries as Rwanda (83.1 percent), Mozambique (83.0 percent), Burundi (82.6 percent), and Tanzania (82.1 percent). Nevertheless, even the latter group included countries with much lower female labor-force participation rates (Yemen 29.9 percent, Sudan 34.0 percent, Côte d'Ivoire 43.8 percent, and Sierra Leone 44.2 percent). Developing countries as a whole have a higher mean female economic-activity rate (55.5 percent) than developed countries belonging to the Organization for Economic Cooperation and Development (OECD) (50.8 percent). Among developing countries the highest female economic-activity rate belongs to east Asia (including China) (72.3 percent) followed by the least developed countries (64.9 percent), sub-Saharan Africa (62.0 percent), and southeast Asia and the Pacific (60.6 percent). Although most countries with a Muslim majority have low female economic-activity rates, this rule does not apply to such populous Muslim-majority countries as Bangladesh (65.8 percent), Indonesia (54.5 percent), and Nigeria (48.0 percent). For the Muslim-majority countries of the Middle East, female economic-activity rates range from as low as 17.8 percent (Iraq) to as high as 48.7 percent (Turkey). The rate for Iranian women aged fifteen and above given by a World Bank report is 27.6 percent, which falls in the middle of the range.[3]

The main objective of this chapter is to document the trend of labor-force participation of Iranian women since 1956 and to explore how it has been affected by drastic social changes taking place in Iranian society since 1979.

The chapter continues with a discussion of the major characteristics of economically active women as revealed by the 1996 national census, including a detailed consideration of variations across different regions and districts. Such an analysis contributes to the identification of socioeconomic variables underlying such variations and cultural characteristics that may tend to impede or enhance women's labor-force participation.

Data used in this study come from decennial national censuses conducted by the Statistical Center of Iran from 1956 to 1996.[4] While data from earlier censuses are used mainly for identifying trends and changes in female labor-force participation and employment rates, the results of the latest (1996) census will be analyzed in more detail to portray the current situation and shed light on regional variations.

In the terminology of the Statistical Center of Iran, the "economically active" population refers to "currently employed" plus "currently unemployed but seeking work." In the 1966 and 1976 censuses, those who worked eight hours or more a week were considered as employed while in 1986 and 1996 those who worked at least two days a week were regarded as employed. All persons who were not considered employed and who had not been looking for work during the seven-day period preceding the enumeration were considered as economically non-active. The seasonally unemployed (who were not seeking work) were classified as unemployed in the 1966 and 1976 censuses but as employed in the 1956, 1986, and 1996 censuses.

The "general activity rate" refers to the economically active population aged 10+ years and is calculated by dividing the total number of the employed population plus the unemployed population by the number of people aged 10+ years. A "crude activity rate" can also be derived by dividing the number of the economically active population aged 10+ by the total population. The "employment ratio" is calculated by dividing the number of the currently employed population by the number of the economically active (that is, employed plus unemployed). The "economically non-active population" is in turn divided into three main groups: homemakers, students, and income recipients without work. The majority of Iranian women usually fall into the first group.

Historical Background

Current emphasis on the importance of labor-force participation of women may give the false impression that in societies such as Iran women were totally excluded from economic activity and made little contribution to national production. In reality, Iranian women like women in most other societies have always been actively involved in traditional productive activities in their society. They have played a particularly significant role in their family's economic life. In Iran, like most other Muslim countries, however, the traditional segregation of women from men has led to a more clearly defined, gender-based division of labor.

Within their culturally defined area of activity, women's specific responsibilities have traditionally covered the gamut of social, economic, and educational tasks needed for bearing and rearing children, looking after the family's well-being, and ensuring the survival of the household as a primary production and consumption unit. In rural and tribal communities, women's contributions to household economy and production have usually extended beyond household walls. They have embraced a significant share of outdoor agricultural activities, almost exclusive responsibility for home-based dairy production and poultry raising, and handicrafts and cottage industries. The internationally renowned carpets and rugs for which Iran is famous have been produced mostly by rural and tribal women. Even today, the carpet industry, generally regarded as one of the most important sources of foreign-exchange earnings in the Iranian economy, almost exclusively depends on women's labor.

Most traditional activities undertaken by women are either entirely ignored by or simply counted as "unpaid family labor" in official statistics. As a result, the extent of women's involvement in economic activities and their contribution to the Gross Domestic Product are grossly underestimated. It can indeed be argued that the general title of "homemaker" under which the majority of Iranian women are usually classified is a major economic and occupational category with enormous contributions to both household and national income as well as the nation's general health and well-being. Women classified as housewives are known to make major contributions to their household's earnings and welfare. The opportunity cost of women looking after the household and rearing children, although not easy to express in pecuniary terms, is probably even more significant. Since the revolution of 1978–79, religious leaders ruling Iran have given publicity to some prophetic traditions (hadith/*ravayat*) indicating that women engaging in such household activities, even breast-feeding and nursing children, are entitled to cash reimbursement by their husband if they decide to demand it.

During the revolution Iranian women played an active role and significantly contributed to its quick and relatively nonviolent success. Their massive participation in public demonstrations along with their symbolic gesture of giving flowers to soldiers went a long way in psychologically disarming the latter and undermining Mohammad Reza Shah's ability to repress the revolution by use of force. Yet the period immediately after the revolution's triumph witnessed measures aimed at accommodating Iranian society with Islamic laws (shari'a), which had clearly regressive implications for certain segments of the population. Many of these changes called for more drastic adjustments in the social participation and public appearance of women than men. The decision to enforce Islamic dress codes (hejab Islami), for example, was interpreted and applied more rigorously in the case of women than men and for a while threatened to interfere with their normal schooling and participation in social and economic functions.

Partly because of women's active participation in the revolution and the enlightened views of the revolution's founder, the constitution of the Islamic Republic of Iran did not exclude Iranian women from any basic rights, privileges, and entitlements specified for other citizens. This drastic change in attitudes in Ayatollah Khomeini and the coalition of religious leaders supporting him surprised observers who remembered that he had explicitly objected to the shah's decision in the early 1960s to extend voting rights to women. Some of Khomeini's early supporters went out of their way to warn him against giving women the right to stand as candidates for parliamentary elections.[5]

Thus, according to the constitution, Iranian women enjoy as many rights to public education, health, and social security as men do. Women are entitled to vote in parliamentary and other national and local elections and can stand as candidates for almost all elected positions. In addition to their theoretically unlimited entitlement to active participation in the private job market, they can apply for and hold all positions and functions offered by the public sector. Moreover, public-employment laws adopted in the mid-1980s have been exceptionally gender-blind, and no disparity in wages and salaries of men and women doing the same job in the formal sector of the economy exists. The only public-sector job that Iranian women were officially barred from for some time after the revolution was the legal system where, according to the dominant interpretation of Islamic jurisdiction, only men could act as judges. This ban led to the exclusion of women from law schools for several years. The situation then changed, and by 2001 not only were women allowed to study law and act as private lawyers but also the doors of the judiciary system were gradually reopened to women lawyers who became regarded as indispensable in recently reestablished special family tribunals.

The gender-segregation program implemented since the revolution has in effect resulted in the creation of new job opportunities for women. Because all girls attending middle and high schools were expected to be taught by female teachers, more space and resources were devoted to training women as teachers. This change was particularly important in the area of training women as science teachers where men had been favored by the previous regime. Similarly, to ensure that female patients would not have to be examined and treated by male doctors and nurses, more resources were allocated to training women as medical doctors, nurses, and health workers. For a while this development necessitated the adoption of an affirmative-action policy by medical schools. Almost half of all places in the predominantly government-operated medical universities were earmarked for girls regardless of their relative standing in entrance examinations. Even in the private sector, the gender-segregation policy has resulted in increased employment of women in areas such as giving driving lessons, selling women's intimate attire, and training women as hairdressers and tailors.

General Trends of Economic Activity

The three censuses conducted before the revolution indicated a steady but slight rise in the number and relative share of women in the labor force. In 1956 only 576,000 of the 6.24 million women aged 10+ years (or 9.2 percent) were identified as economically active. Ten years later, the number of women aged 10+ years had risen to 8.2 million, and 1,033,000 (or 12.6 percent) of them were classified as economically active. By 1976 about 1.15 million (12.9 percent) of the 11.21 million women aged 10+ were in the formally defined labor force.

Ten years later, according to the 1986 census, the number of women aged 10+ had risen to over 16 million, of which only 1.31 million were defined as economically active. Thus, eight years after the revolution, the labor-force participation rate of Iranian women had declined to 8.2 percent, about two-thirds (64.0 percent) of the figure for 1976 (12.9 percent). The decline was noticeable in both urban (from 9.0 percent to 8.4 percent) and rural (from 16.6 percent to 7.9 percent) areas but was particularly marked in the case of rural women. Overall, while the number of the economically active population aged 10+ years had increased at an average rate of 2.26 percent per year between 1976 and 1986, the number of economically active women had *declined* at an average annual rate of 2.15 percent over the same period.

This decline was no doubt partly due to general stagnation in the Iranian economy during this period and partly due to social barriers to labor-force participation of women that prevailed for a few years following the revolution. The male economic-activity rate also dropped slightly (from 70.8 percent to 68.0 percent) during this period. Nevertheless, the number of men in the labor force in the 1986 census (11.51 million) was considerably higher than its 1976 value (8.35 million), while the number of economically active women had actually declined (from 1.45 million to 1.31 million), despite the number of women aged 10+ rising by almost five million (from 11.21 to 16.03 million). Thus, unlike similar experiences in the West, the long war against Iraqi aggression (1980–88) had not led to any increase in the labor-force participation rate of Iranian women.

The situation changed gradually during the second half of the period so that by 1991 the number of economically active women (1.63 million) had surpassed its 1976 level (1.45 million), and women's labor-force participation rate had risen to 8.7 percent. By 1996 there were about 2.03 million economically active women, and women's labor-force participation rate had risen to 9.1 percent, which was still considerably lower than its 1976 value (12.9 percent). Nevertheless, the average annual growth rate of economically active women between 1986 and 1996 (6.11 percent) was more than twice that of men (2.48 percent).

Urban-Rural Differences

Throughout the prerevolutionary period, rural women had enjoyed a higher labor-force participation rate than their urban counterparts. The situation changed in favor of urban women in 1986 and remained so until the 1991 combined survey/census. By 1996 rural women had regained their higher labor-force participation rate.

Nevertheless, the steady increase in the number of economically active women is particularly evident in the case of the urban population. It rose from 187,000 to 489,000 between 1956 and 1976, stood at 741,000 by 1986, and reached 1,133,000 by 1996. In rural areas the number of economically active women, which rose markedly (from 387,000 to 960,000) between 1956 and 1976, declined markedly (from 960,000 to 562,000) between 1976 and 1986. It rose slightly (to 662,000) by 1991 but rose markedly afterward to reach the figure of 894,000 by 1996.

Despite this apparent rise in the activity rate of rural women, because of the overall decline of the rural population since 1976, the number of rural women classified as economically active in 1996 (894,000) is lower than its 1976 equivalent (960,000). Even the increased number of economically active rural women enumerated in the 1996 census amounts to no more than 10.7 percent of rural women aged 10+ years, as compared with an economic-activity rate of 64.5 percent for rural men. Corresponding economic-activity rates for urban women and men were 8.1 percent and 58.5 percent, respectively. Nevertheless, 43.9 percent of all economically active women enumerated in 1996 were from rural areas, while rural women accounted for no more than 37.4 percent of all women aged 10+ years.

Relative Share of Women of the Economically Active Population

In 1956 women accounted for 9.5 percent of the total labor force. Over the next decade, the figure rose to 12.1 percent. By 1976 the overall share of women of the economically active population reached 13.8 percent. Of every one hundred economically active people aged 10+, about 13.8 were women. During the next decade, it fell to 8.9 percent. Five years later, according to the 1991 census/survey, the share of women of the economically active population had risen slightly to reach 9.4 percent. This rise would seem to have continued at a faster rate over the ensuing five years so that by 1996 the share of women of the economically active population had risen to 12.1 percent. The decline in the share of women of the economically active population was even more striking in rural areas where it had fallen from 16.04 percent to 9.08 percent between 1976 and 1986 and had gone down to 8.77 percent between 1986 and 1991. By 1996 the share of women of the economically active population had climbed back to 13.41 percent in rural areas while that of urban women was 11.26 percent. In terms of the actual numbers, however, the number of economically active urban women enumerated in 1996 (991,000) was over twice the figure for 1976 (460,000) while that of rural women had increased by only 14,000.

Unemployment Rates of Men and Women

Comparing the number of employed and unemployed women, there was a sharp upturn in the unemployment rate (from 10.17 percent to 14.19 percent) between 1976 and 1986, which was particularly conspicuous in urban areas where the unemployment rate would seem to have risen from as low as 5.42 percent in 1976 to a record high of 15.27 percent in 1986. This situation was partly due to the economic dislocations caused by the revolution and the eight-year war and partly a result of the sudden influx of large numbers of migrants from urban and rural areas of war-torn provinces who moved to other urban centers in search of work and shelter. With the war's end in 1988, the unemployment rate of urban areas immediately improved, which is clearly reflected in the findings of the 1991 census/survey and the 1996 census. In rural areas the period between 1976–86 was actually marked by a decline in the unemployment rate (from 14.17 percent to 12.91 percent), which continued at a much reduced tempo over the ensuing five years but took a sharper upward turn between 1991 and 1996.

Comparing men and women, it would appear that the overall unemployment rate of women (16.4 percent) was higher than that of men (9.1 percent) in 1976. The difference is noticeable in both rural and urban areas and continued during the following two decades. Although the overall unemployment rate of women also fell sharply (from 25.5 percent to 13.4 percent) between 1986 and 1996, it was still considerably higher than that for men in both urban (12.5 percent vs. 8.4 percent) and rural (14.3 percent vs. 8.6 percent) areas. Despite their lower share of the labor market, Iranian women have had to bear a relatively heavier burden of unemployment. In 1996, for example, the share of women of the unemployed population (18.7 percent) was over one-and-a-half times their share of the total labor force (12.7) and the employed (12.1 percent).

Main Fields of Economic Activity and Employment

The various fields of employment of the economically active population are usually divided into three major areas: agriculture, industry, and services. Over the twenty-year period between 1976 and 1996, the relative share of agriculture of the economically active population declined steadily. In contrast, the proportion of the economically active population engaged in the services sector of the economy rose markedly. The rise in the proportion of the workforce employed by the services sector was particularly impressive between 1976 (23.4 percent) and 1986 (42.4 percent), but it grew only slightly (from 42.4 percent to 44.5 percent) between 1986 and 1996. The share of the industrial sector of the employed population dropped sharply (from 37.6 percent to 25.3 percent) between 1976 and 1986 but rose noticeably after that (from 25.3 percent to 27.6 percent between 1986 and 1991 and to 30.4 percent between 1991 and 1996).

In the case of working women, the share of agriculture had gone up markedly between 1976 (19.04 percent) and 1986 (27.86 percent). By 1996 it had dropped to below its 1976 level (16.68 percent). The share of work in industry by working women had dropped by more than half (from 54.47 percent to 23.97 percent) between 1976 and 1986 but improved noticeably after 1986. By 1996 just over one-third (34.5 percent) of all working women were employed in the industrial sector. The share of the services sector of working women had also increased noticeably (from 26.49 percent to 48.17 percent) between 1976 and 1986. By 1996 it had fallen slightly (to 45.86 percent). In 1996 close to three-quarters of working women in urban areas were employed by the services sector, mostly social services provided by the government. In contrast, just over 10 percent of working women in rural areas were employed in this sector.

A comparison of patterns of female employment in 1986 and 1996 indicates that the relative share of women in the agricultural sector had decreased by 37.2 percent over this period while their rate of employment in the industrial sector had risen by 50.7 percent. Their share remained unchanged in the services sector. These changes were mainly due to drastic shifts in the fields of employment of women in rural areas where the proportionate rate of employment of women in the agricultural sector had fallen by 35.8 percent, while it had risen by 51.6 percent and 15.6 percent in the industry and services sectors, respectively. The relative rate of employment of women in the industrial sector had risen by one-and-a-half times in both urban and rural areas between 1986 and 1996. The second decade after the revolution witnessed a shift in women's main field of employment to the industrial sector in both urban (from the services sector) and rural (from agriculture) areas.

Female Employment by Major Occupational Groups

Considering the nine major occupational groups used by the Statistical Center of Iran, in 1996 the majority of working women were employed in the following three major occupational groups: skilled industrial workers and related professions (31.6 percent), experts or specialists (28.0 percent), and skilled workers in agriculture, forestry, and fisheries (14.4 percent). As expected, the main fields of occupation of urban and rural women were quite different. While close to half of urban working women were employed as specialists (46.0 percent) and lawmakers/high-level managers (3.9 percent), only 5.3 percent of working rural women were classified under these categories. And while 50.1 percent of working rural women were classified as artisans or skilled industrial workers, only 17.3 percent of urban working women were classified this way. This marked disparity would seem to be caused by including carpet weaving and similar cottage-based textile industries in the list of skilled industrial workers. Close to one-third (30.7 percent) of rural women as compared with only 1.7 percent of urban women were classified as skilled workers in agriculture.

Public-Sector and Private-Sector Employment

Considering the number of women employed by the public and private sectors of the economy, the proportion of the total labor force employed by the private sector declined sharply (from 80.5 percent to 64.4 percent) between 1976 and 1986. This change reflected the widespread nationalization of all major industries and financial institutions after the revolution. Despite the emphasis put on the need for the private sector's revitalization by the government's first and second development plans implemented since 1989, by 1996 the share of the private sector of the employment market had not risen beyond 67.2 percent.

The period between 1976 and 1986 saw a sharp rise (from 19.01 percent to 31.39 percent) in the share of the public sector of the employment market. This trend continued, albeit at a reduced rate, between 1986 and 1991 by which time almost a third of the total labor force was employed by the public sector. The following five-year period saw a slight decrease in the share of the public sector (from 33.2 percent to 29.2 percent). Despite the emphasis that the constitution put on the cooperative sector as a major pillar of the Islamic economy, the share of this sector remained below 0.4 percent of the labor force.

Comparing the number of women employed by the private sector in 1976 and 1986, it appears that the main reason for the sharp drop in the activity rate of women immediately following the revolution was the huge decrease (from 953,920 to 508,593) in the number of women employed by the private sector. In contrast, the number of women employed by the public sector almost doubled (from 246,000 to 408,000) over the same period. Within the private sector too the decline in the number of economically active women was mainly due to a sharp drop in the number of women classified as wage earners (from 322,146 to 99,838) and family workers (from 495,723 to 213,850). Even by 1996 the number of women employed under these two categories (249,783 and 366,507) had not attained its 1976 levels.

Nevertheless, by 1996 over half (55.5 percent) of working women were employed by the private sector. The overwhelming majority of women employed in agriculture (97.0 percent) and as skilled industrial workers (92.5

percent) belonged to the private sector, as did the large majority of women employed as unskilled workers (74.5 percent), general services/sales workers (63.8 percent), and machine operators (58.2 percent). Although less than 40 percent of women were employed by the public sector, the majority of women occupying high-level positions such as specialists (88.9 percent), legislators/managers (82.9 percent), technicians/assistants (78.3 percent), and office workers (74.0 percent) belonged to this sector.

Categories of Economically Non-Active Women

As economic-activity rates are calculated for the population aged 10+, many of whom are 10–24 years old and expected to be enrolled in schools and universities, any improvement in formal-education opportunities and school-enrollment rates is bound to affect the rate. Thus, the observed decline in the economic-activity rate of the Iranian population from 1986 to 1996 was partly due to the fact that a larger proportion of young women and men aged 10–24 was able and inclined to continue as full-time students far beyond age 10, the lower limit used in defining economic activity. Indeed, the relative share of the nonworking population identified as students of the population aged 10+ increased from 5.4 percent to 27.8 percent between 1956 and 1996. Corresponding figures for men and women were 7.6 percent to 29.0 percent and 3.0 percent to 26.6 percent, respectively.

In the case of urban areas, the share of students in the population aged 10+ rose from 16.1 percent to 30.9 percent for men and from 8.4 percent to 30.9 percent for women. The rise in the share of students in the population aged 10+ was even more impressive for rural men (from 3.4 percent to 25.9 percent) and rural women (from 0.4 percent to 19.7 percent). These trends are welcome reflections of the increased opportunities for education beyond the primary level for females, particularly in rural areas. As a consequence of the relative increase of the share of students of the economically non-active population, the proportion of non-active women classified as homemakers dropped remarkably in both urban (from 77.0 percent to 56.3 percent) and rural areas (from 80.8 percent to 61.9 percent).

Nevertheless, the overwhelming majority (58.4 percent) of all economically non-active women (62.0 percent in urban and 71.0 percent in rural areas) were still classified as homemakers in 1996. Given the variety of direct and indirect productive functions implied by the latter term, such women can hardly be regarded as economically nonproductive. Thus, the practice of the Statistical Center and other official bodies that groups all women working at home as homemakers and classifies them as economically non-active may have resulted in the gross underestimation of the contribution of women to economic activity and production in Iran.

Correlates of Female Labor-Force Participation

Of all women aged 10+ enumerated in 1996, 9.1 percent were economically active, 26.6 percent were students, and 58.4 percent were homemakers. Another 1.6 percent were not economically active but had their own source of income. The economic-activity status of 4.3 percent was not specified. Of women defined as economically active, 86.8 percent were employed and 13.2 percent unemployed. Of the unemployed group, 92.4 percent had never been employed before.

Age and Economic Activity

As expected, the economic-activity rates of both men and women varied considerably with age. Men reached their highest rate of economic activity (95.8 percent) between ages 35 and 39, over 90 percent being economically active in the age group 25–49. Women reached their highest rate of economic activity (14.15 percent) between ages 25 and 29, over 12 percent being economically active in the age group 20–44. The economic-activity rate of women aged 45–49 years (10.01 percent) was also higher than the overall activity rate of all ages (9.10 percent).

In urban areas men reached their highest rate of economic activity (95.56 percent) between ages 35 and 39, over 90 percent being economically active in the age group 30–49. Urban women reached their highest rate of economic activity (14.73 percent) between ages 25 and 29, just over 10 percent being economically active in the age group 20–49. In rural areas men reached their highest rate of economic activity (96.32 percent) between ages 35 and 39, over 90 percent being economically active in the age group 25–59. Rural women reached their highest rate of economic activity (16.21 percent) between ages 20 and 24, over 11 percent being economically active in the age group 15–34.

The child-labor rate, in the sense of economic activity by those below age 14 (4.05 percent), was low. It was much higher among boys (5.15 percent) than among girls (2.92 percent). It varied from 5.15 percent to 8.64 percent for boys and from 1.84 percent to 6.03 percent for girls. The figure was much higher for adolescents aged 14–19 years. Over one-quarter (26.9 percent) of urban and almost one-half (46.5 percent) of rural boys aged 15–19 were classified as economically active. Corresponding economic-activity rates for urban and rural girls of this age were 4.5 percent and 14.9 percent, respectively. On the other extreme, economic-activity rates dropped sharply after age 49 among both men and women in urban areas but remained at a high level for both sexes in rural areas until age 64. Over half (54.3) of all men (44.6 percent in urban and 65.8 percent in rural areas) continued to be economically active beyond age 65, the statutory age of retirement for workers covered by the social security program. The corresponding figure for women aged 65+ was 2.7 percent (1.5 percent in urban and 4.5 percent in rural areas).

A comparison of age-specific economic-activity rates of women in 1976 and 1986 reveals a sharp decline in activity rates of all age groups. After 1986 the decline continued only among the youngest (ages 10–14). In all other age groups but 55–64, not only did the downward trend stop but some increase in activity rates was seen so that in all age groups between 25 and 64 the female-activity rates for 1996 were higher than those seen in 1986 and 1991. Nevertheless, age-specific female activity rates for age groups 10–24 and 45+ in 1996 were still considerably lower than their prerevolutionary, 1976, levels. The difference was much smaller in the age group 25–44 and to some extent among those aged 45–54.

Comparing age-specific activity rates of women in 1986 and 1996, it appears that the activity rate of women below age 20 decreased over this period. The decrease amounts to a fall of 35.6 percent for the age group 10–14 and a fall of 8.5 percent for the age group 15–19. The highest activity rate of women in 1986 and 1996 belonged to age groups 20–24 (12.0 percent) and 25–29 (14.1 percent). Activity rates of women increased in all age groups between 20 and 64, the largest rates of increase being related to age groups 40–44 (65.4 percent), 45–49 (61.3 percent), 35–39 (37.9 percent), and 50–54 (33.3 percent). The evidence thus indicates the relative aging of the female labor force in 1996 as compared with 1986.

A comparison of the age structure of economically non-active women reveals that in the age range 10–19, school enrollment accounted for the largest share (over 50 percent) of economic non-activity among women. After age 20, women identified as homemakers constituted the majority of economically non-active women. The relative share of economically non-active women rose sharply between age groups 10–14 and 15–19 (from 9.3 percent to 35.1 percent) and 15–19 and 20–24 (from 35.1 percent to 67.4 percent) to reach its height (87.5 percent) among those aged 50–59.

Among economically non-active women, the overwhelming majority of those identified as students belong to the age group 10–19. In 1996 women classified under this category accounted for 83.2 percent, 48.1 percent, and 13.2 percent of nonworking women aged 10–14, 15–19, and 20–24 years, respectively. The proportion of nonworking women classified as students was less than 5 percent among the group aged 25–39 and less than 1 percent among those aged 40+. The proportion of non-active women classified as homemakers rose precipitously between ages 10 and 54 but declined after age 55. In 1996 the proportion of non-active women identified as homemakers was only 9.3 percent among those aged 10–14. It rose to include over one-third (35.1 percent) of nonworking women aged 15–19 and over two-thirds (67.4 percent) of those aged 20–24 years. Its highest rate (87.5 percent) was seen among women aged 50–54. Among nonworking women aged 65+, almost three-quarters (76.9 percent in urban and 62.1 percent in rural areas) were identified as homemakers.

The relative proportion of women identified as recipients of income without work was below 1 percent in age group 10–39, rose slowly (from 1.2 percent to 4.4 percent) between ages 40 and 59, increased markedly to 7.4 percent at age group 60–64, and reached its highest level (13.8 percent) among those aged 65+. From this trend it would appear that women classified under this category were mostly retired workers or dependents of retired men. Thanks to an employment-related retirement scheme for the aged population of rural areas launched in the early 1980s, a much larger proportion of non-active women aged 65+ were classified under this category in rural areas (20.0 percent) than in urban areas (9.6 percent).

Economic Activity and Marital Status

Just over half (54.6 percent) of economically active women, as compared with 75.0 percent of economically active men, were married at the time of the 1996 census. The rate was much higher for currently employed women (61.1 percent) and men (78.2 percent) than their unemployed counterparts (12.5 percent of unemployed women vs. 40.6 percent of unemployed men). Conversely, currently unemployed women had a much higher chance (84.0 percent) of never being married than their employed counterparts (32.8 percent). Economically active women also had a much higher chance of never being married (39.7 percent) than economically active men (23.8 percent), despite women in general having a lower chance (39.5 percent) of never being married than men (47.1 percent). At the same time, economically active women were more likely to be widowed (4.0 percent) or divorced (1.3 percent) than economically active men (0.7 percent and 0.3 percent).

Nevertheless, economically non-active women as a group had a slightly lower current nuptiality rate (53.4 percent) than economically active women (54.6 percent). The rate was particularly high for women classified as homemakers (79.2 percent) but low for women described as income recipients without work (21.2 percent) or students (4.2 percent). While the overwhelming majority (94.0 percent) of nonworking women identified as students had never been married, the majority (65.3 percent) of women described as income recipients without work were widows. They also had the highest chance of being divorced (2.45 percent). This applied in both urban (3.27 percent) and rural areas (1.62 percent).

Economic Activity and Literacy

In 1996 the literacy rate of economically active women (80.9 percent) was markedly higher than that of economically non-active women (70.7 percent). The difference was noticeable in both urban (92.9 percent vs. 78.7 percent) and rural areas (66.4 percent vs. 57.3 percent). Among economically non-active women who were not students, those classified as recipients of income without work had a much lower literacy rate (28.6 percent) than those classified as homemakers (59.4 percent). Among economically active women, a larger proportion of the currently unemployed (87.7 percent) than the employed (79.9 percent) were literate. The literacy rates of both currently employed and unemployed urban women (92.7 percent and 94.0 percent) were considerably higher than those of rural women (63.8 percent and 81.6 percent). The overall economic-activity rate of literate women aged 10+ years was 14.03 percent, as compared with 10.90 percent for illiterate women. Despite the overall higher economic-activity rate for literate women, over 85 percent of literate women remained economically non-active.

Level of Education and Economic Activity

The higher economic-activity rate of literate women was mainly due to a higher labor-force participation rate of women with secondary and higher education. Economic-activity rates of women with primary (9.3 percent) and middle-school (7.11 percent) education were lower than that of illiterate women (10.9 percent). The rate rose markedly in the case of women with full secondary education (16.7 percent) but reached its highest level (77.96 percent) in the case of women with higher education. Nevertheless, in terms of absolute numbers, of the 2,227,284 women with secondary-school diplomas enumerated in 1996, only 372,411 were economically active. The enormous investment made in the secondary education of the majority of women does not seem to have resulted in economically productive activity. The magnitude of this wastage may be inferred by comparing the economic-activity figure for women with that of men, which reveals that of the 2,825,032 men with secondary-school diplomas, 2,255,704 or 79.8 percent were economically active.

Nonetheless, over half of economically active women (54 percent of the currently employed and 47 percent of the currently unemployed) had secondary or higher education. Among economically active women, 27.6 percent of the employed and 8.0 percent of the unemployed had a university degree. In contrast, only 1.4 percent of women classified as homemakers, 5.8 percent of those defined as students, and 12.9 percent of the group with non-work-related income had a university degree. Thus, encouragingly strong evidence demonstrates the contribution of higher education to the labor-force participation of women in Iran.

To underline further the significance of higher education for labor-force participation of women, it can be noted that while women with a university degree accounted for under 5 percent of all nonstudent women aged 10+ years, they constituted no less than 19 percent of economically active women. As the overwhelming majority (93.8 percent) of university-educated women lived in urban areas, the share of women in urban areas (36.8 percent) was spectacularly higher than that of university-educated women in rural areas (3.2 percent). The majority of working women in rural areas were in fact either totally illiterate (36.2 percent) or had primary-school (30.7 percent) or adult-literacy (15.6 percent) certificates only. Comparable figures for the share of university-educated men among literate working men were 13.2 percent and 3.7 percent in urban and rural areas, respectively. In 1996 illiterate women accounted for about one-fifth (20.1 percent) of all working women: 7.3 percent of urban working women and over one-third (36.2 percent) of rural working women. Comparable figures for the share of the illiterate among working men were 21.6 percent, 13.4 percent, and 34.1 percent, respectively.

Rising Unemployment Rates

The economically active population consists of two major subgroups: currently employed and currently unemployed (but looking for a job). A marked increase in the number and ratio of the latter group is seen since the revolution. In 1956 only 159,000 (out of a total of 6.07 million) were reported to be unemployed. By 1976 the number had risen to 997,000 (out of a population of 34.8 million and a workforce of 9.8 million). The 1986 census revealed a doubling of the number of the unemployed during the first eight years after the revolution. Since then the number of the unemployed population and the rate of unemployment have gradually fallen. By 1996 the number of the unemployed had reached 1,456,000, of which 272,000 (18.68 percent) were women.

Literacy, Education, and Unemployment

With rising levels of literacy and education since 1979, the composition of the unemployed population also changed markedly. Not only was a larger proportion of the unemployed literate, but there were also disturbingly clear signs of an increase in the rate of unemployment among the better educated, particularly among university graduates. This change was to some extent due to the economy's poor performance in the 1980s and 1990s and to an immense expansion of the higher-education system through both public and private initiatives.

Moreover, the rising unemployment rate of university graduates was not limited to the traditionally over-supplied arts and humanities graduates. It applied to engineering and medical school graduates as well. For the first time in Iran's history, lack of employment opportunities for university-trained medical and paramedical personnel had become a national problem forcing the ministry of health and medical education to impose limits on the admission of new students to medical universities.

Provincial Variations

Although generally low for the country as a whole, the economic-activity rate of women varied considerably across provinces. For the 28 provinces included in the 1996 census, female labor-force participation rates varied from as low as 4.6 percent in the southern province of Bushehr to as high as 18.6 percent in the northern province of Gilan. In 7 of the 28 provinces, the economic-activity rate of women was below 6.4 percent while in another 7 provinces it was above 10.3 percent.

Closer examination reveals that the majority (4 out of 7) of provinces with the lowest female economic-activity rates are hot, southern provinces bordering the Persian Gulf. They include Bushehr (4.6 percent), Sistan and Baluchistan (4.7 percent), Hormozgan (4.9 percent), and Khuzistan (5.1 percent). The remaining 3 provinces with the lowest female economic-activity rates are the north-central provinces of Qazvin (5.6 percent), Loristan (6.3 percent), and Qom (6.4 percent). Two of the latter (Qom and Qazvin) are near Tehran and until the early 1990s were part of Tehran province. On the other extreme, the 7 provinces with the highest female-activity rates are Gilan (18.6 percent), Yazd (16.5 percent), Chaharmahal and Bakhtiyari (14.7 percent), Golestan (12.9 percent), Khorasan (12.1 percent), Isfahan (10.9 percent), and East Azarbayjan (10.3 percent). The middle group includes such well-developed provinces as Tehran (7.3 percent), Semnan (8.1 percent), Markazi (9.6 percent), Mazandaran (9.2 percent), Fars (9.4 percent), and Kerman (9.1 percent) along with such less-developed provinces as Kurdistan (8.1 percent), Ilam (7.7 percent), Kohgiluyeh and Boirahmad (7.0 percent), Ardabil (7.8 percent), and West Azarbayjan (8.7 percent).

What are the reasons for these variations in female labor-force participation rates? To answer this question, the three groups of provinces with low, middle, and high female-activity rates were compared according to many geographic, demographic, social, and economic variables. Comparing the three groups of provinces with respect to many demographic characteristics reveals some consistent differences. The high female activity-rate group consisted of provinces with a larger area and population size than the other two groups. The group of seven provinces with the highest female activity rates accounted for over one-half of Iran's total land area and almost one-third (31 percent) of its total population. It had a lower sex ratio than the other two groups, and a much smaller proportion of its population was young (below age 15), compared with the other two groups. Conversely, it had a higher share of the other two age groups (15–64 and 65+). Consequently it had a smaller mean household size and dependency ratio than the other two groups. It also had the lowest crude birth and total fertility rates as compared with the other two groups, and its population grew at a much lower rate than the other two groups between 1991 and 1996.

Considering socioeconomic indicators, the high female activity-rate group differed consistently from the low and medium female activity-rate groups. They appeared as superior to the other two groups on all educational (eight) and health indicators (three) and the total human-development index. They were also superior to the other two groups with respect to access to electricity, piped natural gas, and telephones. The low female-activity group of provinces had a slight edge on the other two groups in terms of urbanization, while the middle female-activity group occupied the highest place with regard to access to piped water.

Comparing labor-related characteristics of the provinces with low, middle, and high female-activity rates, it would appear that provinces with the highest female activity rate also enjoyed a higher rate of male labor-force participation in both urban and rural areas. Provinces with medium female-activity rates too had higher male activity rates than those with low female-activity rates in all but one instance. The mean activity rate of rural women of these provinces (8.30 percent) fell below that of the low female-activity rate provinces (9.10 percent). Provinces with the highest female-activity rate demonstrated higher rates of employment in industry (36.5 percent) and the private sector (72.9 percent) than those with lower female-activity rates. In contrast, provinces with the lowest female activity rate had the highest rate of employment in the services (46.3 percent) and the public sector (33.3 percent). Provinces with a medium-level female activity rate had the highest rate of employment in the agricultural sector (28.0 percent). They also had a higher rate of employment in the private sector (67.6 percent) than the low female activity-rate group of provinces (63.1 percent).

Conclusion

The economic-activity rate of Iranian women has not changed much over the past sixty years. After some slight rise in the 1960s and 1970s, it fell sharply during the first decade after the revolution. The decline was particularly noticeable in rural areas. It rose again beginning in 1986 but still remained below its prerevolutionary level. While the substantial investment in women's education during this period resulted in a significant rise in the literacy rate and educational attainment of Iranian women, it seems to have had little impact on their labor-force participation rates.

The main reason for the low labor-force participation rates of Iranian women seems to lie in cultural beliefs and traditions that did not approve of women engaging in many of the activities and jobs that the economy offered. The types of outdoor activities not regarded as suitable for a decent, middle-class woman and her family were mostly occupations requiring close interaction with men, particularly in situations that exposed women to sexual harassment and exploitation. Thus, Iranian women were distinguished by their almost total absence in the sales sector. Even in modern cities such as Tehran, saleswomen could be found only in a few large government-operated department stores, women's apparel shops in wealthy urban neighborhoods, and handicraft shops catering to internal and foreign tourists.[6] Similarly, the catering industry, a major employer of women in most developed and developing countries, failed to attract women in Iran. Almost no women could be seen acting as cooks or waitresses in restaurants, hotels, and popular sandwich shops, a common feature of modern areas of Tehran and other large cities.

In contrast, Iranian women (and their families) seemed to have no hesitation to accept employment as white-collar workers in the public sector. The gender-segregation policy adopted since the revolution ironically led to the creation of more employment opportunities of this kind for Iranian women. As these jobs usually required a secondary-school or higher level of formal education, the economic-activity rate of women with secondary-school diplomas or university degrees rose substantially. Thus, in 1996, while only 9 percent of all women were economically active, the activity rate of women with a secondary-school diploma (16 percent) or a university degree (78 percent) was substantially higher. Yet the fact that only 16 percent of women with secondary education were economically active is a clear sign of the limited employment opportunities available for such relatively well-educated women. With the growing number of young women completing their university studies, it is highly likely that in a few years the country will face the serious problem of providing employment opportunities for its better-educated women. If the recent trend continues, if families continue to encourage their female children to study at secondary and higher levels, and if these children have improved chances of entering the labor market, then the already high unemployment rate of Iran is likely to rise further. Even at their meager labor-force participation rate of 9 percent in 1996, Iranian women faced a much higher unemployment rate than their male counterparts.

To overcome this problem, Iranian women (and their families) will no doubt have to adopt a more flexible and realistic definition of the types of jobs that they consider suitable for women. This transformation will certainly take time and require drastic changes in cultural stereotypes of gender-appropriate activities and roles. Data available on provincial variations in female labor-force participation may be useful in indicating the type of socioeconomic variables that are likely to facilitate and promote the cultural changes needed for further and fuller participation of Iranian women in the formal labor force. Among these factors education seems to occupy a particularly important position. Given the basically democratic nature of the Islamic Republic's constitution and the equal voting rights enjoyed by Iranian women, they have a high chance of overcoming social obstacles to labor-force participation that may be created by the more conservative factions of the society. The surprisingly active role played by women voters in the 1997 and especially 2001 presidential elections has already demonstrated the immense political power of Iranian women as well as their ability to identify and support reformist candidates.

NOTES

1. See Ester Boserup, *Women's Role in Economic Development* (New York: St. Martin's, 1970); K. O. Mason, "The Status of Women: Conceptual and Methodological Issues in Demographic Studies: The State of Women, Indicators for 25 Countries," *Sociological Forum* 1 (2) 1986: 284–300; Valentine M. Moghadam, *Modernizing Women: Gender and Social Change in the Middle East* (Boulder: Lynne Rienner, 1993); M. K. Whyte, *Status of Women in Preindustrial Societies* (Princeton: Princeton University Press, 1978); Sunta Kishor and K. Netzel, "Women's Work and Workload," in *DHS Comparative Studies: The State of Women, Indicators for 25 Countries* (Calverton, Md.: Macro International, 1996).

2. Human Development Report, United Nations Development Program, 2000, table 29.

3. World Development Report 2000/2001: Attacking Poverty, World Bank, 2000.

4. *General Census of Population and Housing,* various volumes 1956–96 (Tehran: Statistical Center of Iran); *Demographic Indicators of Iran, 1956–1996* (Tehran: Statistical Center of Iran); "Socioeconomic Characteristics of Women in Iran, 1986–96" (Tehran: Statistical Center of Iran, 2000).

5. Ayatullah Mohammad Hossein Hosseini Tehrani, "Resaleh nekahiyeh: kahesh jam'iyat, zarbeh sangin bar paykar-e Muslimin" (Treatise on marriage: population decline, a heavy blow to the body of Muslims) (Tehran: Hekmat, 1994).

6. In early 2002 I saw women working in sales in small boutiques in the so-called free-market zones of Kish, Qeshm, and Chahbahar, places that the government allowed to appear more Westernized than other sectors of Iranian society. I also noted young and apparently formally educated women working in hotels in these areas. By 2001 women were also working in the tax-free shops of Mehrabad airport in Tehran, even in the middle of the night. In all airports since the revolution, "Islamic sisters" have been solely responsible for the security checking of female passengers. All of these facilities are more or less owned by the government. Lois Beck (personal communication, 2002) notes that these types of female employment seem at odds with Western views of Iran. Westerners often assume that the Islamic government and not the private sector prohibits such labor participation. In these and other areas, the government seems actually to support relatively high rates of female employment, despite all of these women coming into frequent contact with male strangers.

8 Sexuality, Rights, and Islam: Competing Gender Discourses in Postrevolutionary Iran

ZIBA MIR-HOSSEINI

THE REVOLUTION OF 1978–79 in Iran led to the convergence of religious and political authority in the Islamic Republic and inevitably changed the dynamics of the struggle for women's rights. For a decade, talk of gender equality was politically unacceptable, a taboo subject that "good" Muslims could not raise or address. By the early 1990s, this restriction was no longer the case, and voices of dissent began to be heard, known as the "new religious thinking" (*nau-andishi-yi dini*). Gradually space was opened for addressing gender inequality within an Islamic framework. This change occurred by historicizing the construction of gender rights in religious law (shari'a). The election of President Mohammad Khatami in 1997 gave birth to a reformist movement and shifted major political alignments; from that point people talked of reformists versus conservatives rather than moderates versus hard-liners. The way was open for the emergence of a new Islamic discourse on women, radically different from the official Shi'i one.[1]

In this chapter I trace the textual genealogy of this new religious discourse. I argue that it was made possible by severing the implicit link in Islamic law between constructions of gender rights and theories of male and female sexuality. To show the working of this link and the process of severance, I examine a literature that I categorize as "*fiqh*-based" (based on Islamic jurisprudence). These texts do not contain legal reasoning or argument and are not necessarily produced by *fuqaha* (jurists). This makes them more accessible to the general public than fiqh texts proper. I have chosen to focus on them because, in my view, they reveal the rationale for the unequal construction of gender in Islamic law; they expose many of the underlying and unspoken assumptions that shape the fuqaha's understandings and readings of primary sources of Islamic law (that is, the Qur'an and the hadith). It is also through this literature that gender inequality has been propagated and reproduced in the Muslim consciousness.

Broadly speaking, this literature is of three different genres, each with its own gender perspective. I call the first genre "traditionalist" and its perspective "gender inequality." The second genre, which I call "neotraditionalist," advocates "gender balance." The third, the "modernist" genre, argues for "gender equality." Each genre has its own distinct style, mode of address, audience, themes, and language. Thus, the first is preoccupied with certain terms and themes relating to sexuality—such as conduct during coitus and purification rules following sex—on which the others are almost silent, while focusing instead on themes such as love or women's legal rights. Likewise, each genre is identified with a political tendency. Writers of the first and third genres are generally identified with the conservative and reformist camps respectively, while those of the second genre tend to have one foot in each camp.[2]

The boundaries between these three genres and gender perspectives are far from rigid and clear-cut. There are many overlaps, but a gradual shift or progression can be discerned. The more a text is rooted, for example, in the first genre, the more candid it is in its references to sexuality and the more it is opposed to gender equality. The opposite is the case with texts of the third genre.

Women's Sexuality in Traditionalist Discourse

The traditionalist genre comprises a whole range of texts, which can perhaps be best defined as marriage guides,[3] with titles such as *The Union of Two Flowers or Bride and Groom*,[4] *Guide to Marital Relations from Islam's View*,[5] *Marriage in Islam*,[6] *Family Ethics*,[7] *Ethics in the Family*,[8] and *Ethics at Home*.[9] Produced by religious publishing projects in Qum or Tehran, these texts are written by men for men and aim to advise them of their Islamic rights and duties in marriage. The only exception is *The Way of Happiness and Advice to Believing Sisters*,[10] written by Banu Amin Isfahani, a female *mujtahid* (jurist). Some of these texts were written by well-known personalities and politicians. The writer and translator of *Marriage in Islam* are both high-ranking political clerics: the former, Ayatollah Mishkini, is head of the Assembly of Experts (*majlis khubragan*), which is charged with the election and supervision of the supreme jurisconsult (*vali-yi faqih*); the translator, Ayatollah Jannati, is head of the Guardian Council (*shura-yi nigahban*), charged with ensuring that the laws passed by parliament are not in contradiction with shari'a. Akbar Husaini, author of *Ethics in the Family*, is a cleric. He was a member of parliament from 1988 to 2000 and had a regular television program.[11]

Although they never state it explicitly, the authors in this genre hold that men and women are created differently and have different destinies and that men are created superior to women and so it is natural for men to dominate. They consider the model of family and gender relations manifested in fiqh rules to be divine and immutable, and they make no attempt to engage with nonreligious sources of knowledge about the family or to consider women's position in contemporary society. The most they do is to interrupt their texts with an anecdote, warning, or piece of advice to keep away from the evils of family life as lived by others.

They see their mission as informing the believer how to live a "proper Islamic family life," which to a large extent reflects the worldview and lifestyle of a certain class of Iranians: urban merchants and artisans known as *bazaari*. They ignore the fact that this lifestyle is no longer the dominant one in Iran and is alien to the majority of Iranians. Likewise, many Iranians are unaware of the existence of this genre of literature or of fiqh rules relating to sexuality and sexual conduct.[12]

Texts in this genre have a similar format. They are written in a conversational style and are primarily based on hadith, sayings of the Prophet Mohammad or the twelve Shi'i imams. The books all include chapters or discussions on "the virtues of marriage" and "the rights and duties of each spouse in marriage." Some also contain discussions of "sexual etiquette," which cover matters such as the time, manner, and frequency of sexual intercourse, permissible and nonpermissible positions, states of purity and impurity, and menstruation. Their language is sexually explicit and uses terms such as *shahvat* (sexual desire, lust, passion) and *jama'* (intercourse). These chapters appear to be based on an implicit theory of sexuality: God gave women greater shahvat than men, but this is mitigated by two factors: men's *ghairat* (sexual honor and jealousy) and women's *haya* (modesty, shyness). The working of the theory and its key concepts—ghairat, haya, and shahvat—can be found in the following three passages.[13]

> Sexual desire (shahvat) in women is nine parts and in men is one part. God has chained women's shahvat with modesty and chastity (*haya va 'iffat*). If

their modesty is taken away, it is possible that every man will be followed by ten women wanting to make love with him. In *Lali al-akhbar* it is quoted that Imam Ali said, What motivates the beasts of prey is their hunger and what motivates women and draws them to men is to extinguish the fire of their desire (shahvat).[14] Modesty (haya) has ten parts of which nine parts are in women and one part in men. Then when a woman is asked for in marriage, one part of her modesty goes; when she is contracted in marriage, another part goes; when she gives birth, another part goes; when her husband has intercourse with her, another part goes; she is left with five parts, and if she commits the hideous act of fornication (*zina*), all her haya is removed. Pity the people, when all haya is taken from women.[15]

Imam Baqir said, God has not intended ghairat for women but for men, because for men he has made licit four permanent wives and slave girls but for women only one husband. If a woman shows affection for another man, she is considered *zina-kar* (fornicator) in the eyes of God. Women who show ghairat (when their husbands are polygynous) are those who are faithless, not those who believe in the rules of God.[16]

In another hadith he said that women's ghairat is in reality jealousy, and jealousy is the root of heresy; when a woman's ghairat is aroused, she becomes angry, and when she becomes angry she tends toward heresy. Of course, such women are not Muslim.[17]

While a theory of difference in men's and women's sexuality finds support in the sayings of Shi'i imams, control over women's sexuality finds its legitimacy in the fuqaha's conception of marriage. One of the most prominent Shi'i jurists, Muhaqqiq Hilli, defines marriage this way: "a contract whose object is that of dominion over the vagina, without the right of possession."[18] What the contract entails for each party is dealt with under the rubric of rights and duties in fiqh, and these texts reproduce them. They all revolve around the twin themes of sexual access and compensation, embodied in the concepts of *tamkin* (submission) and *nafaqa* (maintenance). Tamkin, defined as unhampered sexual access, is a man's right and thus a woman's duty. Nafaqa, defined as shelter, food, and clothing, is a woman's right and a man's duty.

These passages contain no argument and no discussion, only commands and warnings. A woman is told that she should keep herself covered so that her beauty is not seen by anyone apart from her husband and that she should satisfy her husband's sexual needs and his other wishes. If not, her place will be in hell, as one hadith has it. According to another one, if she refuses her husband at night, she will be cursed all night by angels. A man is told to make sure that his wife observes the rule of hijab (Islamic dress code, modest dress) and to have mercy on her. In the minds of the authors of these texts, these rules are divinely ordained, and their truths are so self-evident that they see no need to provide rational arguments for them. A woman's duty is to be sexually at her husband's disposal. She cannot leave the house without her husband's permission, because her unapproved absence would infringe on his right of access to her.

Ayatollah Mishkini, a powerful political cleric opposed to the reformists, views women's right to work this way: "Islam has not openly forbidden women from work and commerce, but its program is such that she is automatically prevented from these activities. We know that Islam does not approve it because a woman, according to God's command, cannot leave the house without her husband's permission, and the best work for her is taking care of her husband and raising children—the more the better—which takes all her time, so she has no 'opportunity' to do work outside the home."[19]

Other writers in this genre employ the same tone and logic. They make no allusion to issues of women's rights and gender equality, not even paying lip service to them. They see no need to engage with contemporary social realities or nonreligious sources.

Women's Sexuality and the Neotraditionalist Discourse

The neotraditionalist genre is quite different, for its writers are aware of and sensitive to current discussions of gender and criticisms by both secular and religious women of patriarchal biases in shari'a legal rules. Women's education and employment, divorce laws, and the question of hijab are the main themes through which the issue of gender equality is addressed, and a range of positions are defined. It is common to find a single text arguing for gender equality on one issue (for example, women's employment and education) but rejecting it on another (for example, divorce rights). Women's magazines are the main forum for publication of these texts, which also find their way into scholarly journals and periodicals or appear as books. Likewise, unlike the traditionalist genre, these texts are written for women and some of them by women, with titles indicative of their concerns: *An Examination of Women's Rights in Divorce*[20] and *Women's Rights in Islam and the Family.*[21] Others are written by clerics: *The Face of Women in the Mirror of Islam and the Qur'an*[22] and *Women in the Mirror of Glory and Beauty.*[23] These texts vary in style, approach, and degree of sophistication, and they range from fairly conventional Islamic apologias on the place of women to more novel reassessments, but on gender issues they argue for complementarity rather than equality. All adhere to a perspective of gender balance.

This perspective is aired in almost all Iranian women's journals (*Zan-i ruz, Payam-i zan, Payam-i hajar, Huquq-i zan, Mahjuba, Nida*). Its neotraditionalist adherents attempt to introduce "balance" into patriarchal interpretations and differ from traditionalists in both the sources they use and their mode of argumentation. They refer to the Qur'an rather than hadith and quote Western psychological and sociological studies for "scientific" proofs for their positions. Their language is less explicit on sexuality, and in their writings, *ishq* (love) replaces shahvat (sexual desire) as a focus. Prescriptions of purification rules related to sex and menstruation are replaced by discussions on women's status in society, women's legal rights, and the philosophy of hijab. The tone and the argument become moral and abstract. Fiqh rules, which engender social and psychological harmony, are justified as the best means to regulate sexual dynamics. In these texts biology is still destiny.

The most coherent (and influential) argument of this genre is found in Ayatollah Murtaza Mutahhari's *Rights of Women in Islam*.[24] Rooted in the decisive debates in the 1960s between traditionalists and secular modernists over reforms in shari'a family laws, this text reflects the position of neotraditionalist clerics on the eve of the 1979 revolution. It has its origins in a series of articles in *Zan-i ruz* (Today's woman), the popular women's magazine of the Pahlavi era. The journal was supporting a campaign for the reform of family laws. Mutahhari responded, putting forward the neotraditionalist Islamic position; he dismissed gender equality in rights and duties as a Western notion with no place in Islam and proposed, as a new justification for shari'a family law, the notion of complementarity in gender rights and duties, both in marriage and in society.

Mutahhari takes issue with both traditionalist texts and secular modernists. On the one hand, he rejects the thesis that underlies all traditionalist texts ("women are created of and for men") and contends that, in the Islamic view, women are equal to men in creation and do not depend on men for attaining perfection (but attain their perfection independently). On the other hand, he takes issue with the secularists and argues that the roles assigned to men and women in creation are different and that shari'a laws reflect this difference. It is here that Mutahhari puts forward the theory of the naturalness of Islamic law and argues that differences in rights and duties between the sexes do not mean inequality or injustice; if properly understood, they are the very essence of justice. The theory of the naturalness of shari'a laws was first advanced by the most renowned Shi'i philosopher of the twentieth century, Allamah Tabataba'i, in his monumental, twenty-volume Qur'anic commentary commonly known as *al-Mizan*,[25] but it was Mutahhari who developed it systematically and turned it into a powerful argument in defense of fiqh conceptions of family and gender relations.

Mutahhari modifies the traditionalist theory of sexuality to eliminate its conflict with the naturalness of shari'a law. The central contradiction is that if women's sexual desire (shahvat) is nine times greater than men's (as Imam Ali's saying has it) and if shari'a laws work with, not against, the grain of nature, then why do they allow men but not women to contract more than one marriage at a time? In his defense of polygyny, Tabataba'i in effect contradicts Imam Ali: "Women's religious education in an Islamic society teaches them modesty and chastity (hava va 'iffat). Contrary to the common belief that women's desire (shahvat) is greater than men's, for which women's desire for beauty and ornaments is taken as proof, [proper religious education] makes women's desire much less than men's, and this is what Muslim men who have wives trained in Islamic ways know well. Therefore, a man's desire on average requires him to have more than one woman and even two and three."[26]

Evidently Tabataba'i sees sexual desire not as fixed and innate but as malleable and social, hence his advocacy of the proper Islamic education of women in society, which enhances men's sexual desire and contains that of women. While concurring with this objective, Mutahhari adds a psychological twist and contends that men and women desire in different ways: "A man is the slave of his own desire (shahvat), and a woman is a prisoner of a man's love (*muhabbat*). . . . A man wants to take possession of the person of a woman and to wield power over her; a woman wants to conquer the heart of a man and prevail upon him through his heart. . . . A man wants to embrace a woman, and a woman wants to be embraced. . . . A woman is better able to control her desire than a man. A man's desire is primitive and aggressive, and a woman's desire is reactive and responsive."[27]

This area remains the only one in which neotraditionalist texts depart from the traditionalist notion of sexuality. In arguing for his notion, Mutahhari does not look to Islamic sources but to Western ones, namely psychological and sociological studies. His reading of these sources is quite selective, and he cites as "scientific evidence" only those that are in line with fiqh definitions of marriage: "The association of married life rests upon the pillar of spontaneous attachment and has a unique mechanism. Creation has given the key to strengthening it, and also the key to bringing it down and shattering it, into the hand of man. Under the command of creation, every man and woman has a certain disposition and certain characteristics, when compared with each other, which cannot be exchanged and are not the same."[28]

In line with the logic of the fiqh conception of marriage, women's sexuality, now defined as passive, is subordinated to that of men. "Nature has devised the ties of a husband and a wife in such a form that the part of a woman is to respond to the love of a man. The affection and love of a woman that is genuine and stable can only be that love which is born as a reaction to the affection and admiration of a man toward her. So the attachment of a woman to a man is the result of the attachment of a man to a woman and depends upon it. Nature has given the key of love of both sides to a man, the husband. If he loves his wife and is faithful to her, the wife also loves him and remains faithful to him. It is admitted that a woman is naturally more faithful than a man, and that a woman's faithfulness is a reaction to the unfaithfulness of a man."[29]

This, Mutahhari contends, is why fiqh gives the right of divorce and polygamy to men. "Nature has deposited the key of the natural dissolution of marriage in the custody of a man. In other words it is a man who by his own apathy and unfaithfulness toward his wife makes her cold and unfaithful. Conversely, if the indifference begins on the side of a wife, it does not affect the affection of her husband; rather, incidentally, it makes the affection more acute."[30]

Thus, there is no need for any change or reform of the divorce laws or even in the form of divorce (*talaq* or repudiation of the wife by the husband). "Sometimes these people ask: 'Why does divorce take the form of a release, an emancipation? Surely it should have a judicial form.' To answer these people it should be said: 'Divorce is a release in the same way that marriage is a state of dominance. If you can possibly do so, change the natural law of seeking a mate in its absoluteness with regard to the male and the female and remove the natural state of marriage from the condition of dominance; if you can, make the role of the male and female sexes in all human beings and animals identical in their relations and change the law of nature. Then you will be able to rid divorce of its aspect of release and emancipation.'"[31]

In the early 2000s, Mutahhari's arguments were still the most eloquent and refined among those who held the concept of gender equality to be contrary to the shari'a. They provided the Islamic Republic in its early years with a much-needed validation of its gender policies. His book has been reprinted many times, and the bulk of the vast postrevolutionary literature on women, especially that produced by the official Islamic Propagation Organization, not only follows Mutahhari but usually reproduces his arguments verbatim.

The Modernists: Gender Equality

By the early 1990s, the notion of complementarity of rights had begun to be questioned, even by those who once subscribed to Mutahhari's position and helped to translate it from rhetoric into state policy. A growing number of women started to see no contradiction between fighting for equal rights and remaining good Muslims, and they argued that no inherent or logical link stands between patriarchy and Islamic ideals. These views—found in a variety of forums—were first aired in the journal *Zanan* (Women), which is a part of a modernist and reformist tendency known as "new religious thinking" (nau-andishi-yi dini). This tendency has its roots in a rift that occurred in the Kayhan Publishing Institute when one of its publications—*Kayhan-i farhangi*—featured Abdolkarim Soroush's controversial articles on the historicity and relativity of religious knowledge. Separating religion from religious knowledge, Soroush in these articles argues that, while the first is sacred and immutable, the second is human and evolved in time as a result of forces external to religion itself.[32]

Soroush's theory angered conservatives in the clerical establishment, who saw it as a direct challenge to their religious authority. A heated debate followed, which led to the closure of *Kayhan-i farhangi* in June 1990 and the departure from *Kayhan* of a group of Muslim intellectuals who were sympathetic to Soroush's theory. Two key figures among them were Mashallah Shamsolvaezin, who later became editor of the reformist daily newspapers *Jami'a, Tus, Nishat,* and *Asr-i azadagan,* all closed in succession,[33] and Shahla Sherkat, who as editor of *Zan-i ruz* from 1982 had played a role in the Islamization of the women's press. Both now became editors of important new journals: Shamsolvaezin of *Kiyan* (Foundation), launched in October 1991, and Sherkat of its sister paper *Zanan,* launched in February 1992.

Armed with Soroush's theory of the relativity of religious knowledge, these two journals in the 1990s became magnets for those whose ideas and writings formed the intellectual backbone of the reformist movement that emerged in 1997.[34] Those who wrote for *Kiyan* and *Zanan* showed a genuine willingness to reassess old positions. Whereas in the 1980s these men and women saw their brief as the Islamization of culture and society, in the 1990s they wanted to create a worldview reconciling Islam and modernity, and they argued for a demarcation between state and religion. They argued that the human understanding of Islam is flexible, that Islam's tenets can be interpreted to encourage both pluralism and democracy, and that Islam allows change in the face of time, space, and experience.

While advocating a brand of feminism that takes Islam as the source of its legitimacy, *Zanan* makes no apologies for drawing on Western feminist sources and collaborating with Iranian secular feminists. Two of its regular contributors in the 1990s were a secularist female lawyer, Mehrangiz Kar, and a male cleric, Sayyid Muhsin Sa'idzada, who in their articles took issue with the very premises of the official Islamic discourse on women and laid bare their inherent gender bias.[35] Sa'idzada's articles, written in the language and mode of argumentation of fiqh, transported *Zanan*'s message to the heart of the clerical seminaries.[36]

Sa'idzada called his approach the "equality perspective" and contended that it had always existed in fiqh alongside what he called the "inequality perspective" and that some eminent jurists had adhered to it. He saw his achievement to be in articulating it coherently and shaping it to accord with twentieth-century realities. He grounded his arguments in a commentary on theological and jurisprudential issues, with the premise that theologians and jurists, in understanding doctrines and inferring shari'a rulings, cannot detach themselves from their own worldview, which in turn reflects the state of knowledge, politics, and social customs of the age and milieu in which they operate. In all this he was clearly influenced by thinkers outside the seminaries such as Soroush. Sa'idzada went on to argue that, apart from some minor religious rules (relating to biological differences), Islam regards men and women in the same way.[37] He also argued that a substantial number of hadith and fiqh theories obstruct the way to equality between the sexes. A majority of jurists and all hadith specialists have sacrificed the principle of equality in Islam in order to endorse a set of theories resting on assumptions that are no longer valid.

Sa'idzada had set himself the task of demolishing untenable theories and argued that this process should be done from within fiqh by using its own language and mode of argumentation. Where Mutahhari, the most articulate proponent of the neotraditionalist discourse, relied on Western scholarship to explain the disparity between men's and women's rights in the shari'a, Sa'idzada, so far the most radical protagonist of the new line, relied on Islamic scholarship to argue for the necessity of a new feminist reading of these texts in line with changed conditions. In so doing, he turned the classical texts on their heads by using their own style of reasoning and arguments to argue for radical change. His perspective made him one of the victims of the struggle between reformists and conservatives, which took a new turn following the 1997 presidential elections. He was detained in June 1998 after the publication of an article in the now-closed liberal daily *Jami'a*, in which he compared religious traditionalists in Iran to the Taliban in Afghanistan. Although he was never officially charged, his "offense" was to extend debates and arguments belonging to the seminaries to the world outside. He was released five months later but was defrocked; he lost his clerical position and became "forbidden pen" (that is, his writings cannot be published). In late 2003 Sa'idzada was still deprived of his clerical robe and unable to publish.

Yet neither *Zanan* nor Sa'idzada (who remains the only cleric to have come out openly in favor of gender equality) has yet addressed the issue of sexuality as opposed to gender. In fact, while reformists now openly discuss many aspects of women's rights in society and the family, they have not touched on any topic involving the issue of sexuality.[38]

The silence of the proponents of the gender-equality perspective is significant and needs further attention. It is strategic in the sense that it is a conscious effort to carve out a space within fiqh where women can be treated as *social* beings. In classical fiqh texts, gender rights and women are discussed only in terms of sexuality and only in chapters on marriage and divorce. Only by diverting the focus away from women's supposed nature to their social experience can the modernists move the debate on sexuality onto new ground. The silence is also epistemological in the sense that constructing women's sexuality as defined and regulated by familial and social circumstances suggests that it is not determined by nature or the divine, that Islam as a religion has nothing to say on the subject, and that people may claim that certain aspects are Islamic when they may be only the views and perceptions of Muslims, which are neither sacred nor immutable but human and changing.

Conclusion

It is perhaps too early to say how and when the emerging Islamic modernist discourse on women in Iran will make its impact and redress the inequalities inherent in earlier interpretations of Islamic law. Both the new discourse and the reformist movement of which it is a part are still in formation, and their fortunes are tied to political developments in Iran. Two remarks can be made at this stage.

First, the emerging discourse on women has the potential, in my view, to shift the old and tired debate on "women in Islam" onto new ground and to bring about a paradigm shift. This has been achieved by disconnecting the existing link between sexuality and gender rights, which underlies the inability of earlier Islamic discourses to deal with the issue of women's legal rights, despite the growing debate on women's rights and the emergence of so-called Islamic feminism.[39] The disconnection both freed its advocates from taking a defensive position and enabled them to go beyond old fiqh wisdoms in search of new questions and new answers.

Second, the emerging discourse can challenge the hegemony of earlier interpretations and question the legitimacy of the views of those who until now have spoken in the name of Islam. Such a challenge has been made possible, even inevitable, by their ideological construction of Islam and the very methods and sources that their ideologues—neotraditionalists—used in their defense and rationalization of fiqh constructions of gender rights. By appealing to the believer's logic and reasoning and relying on arguments and sources outside religion, they have opened a Pandora's box. It remains to be seen what else will come out.

NOTES

1. See Ziba Mir-Hosseini, *Islam and Gender: The Religious Debate in Contemporary Iran* (Princeton: Princeton University Press, 1999).

2. In the following notes, whenever possible I point out the political sympathies of the writers in this genre.

3. These titles are a sample of materials obtained during my research in Qum in 1995. They are sold on newsstands in Tehran although not in high-brow bookshops. They belong to a popular genre of religious literature usually recommended to and consulted by would-be spouses.

4. *Paivand-i du gul ya 'arus va damad,* written and published by Haj Shaikh Ali Qarani Gulpaygani, printed in Qum by Alhadi, 9th edition, Esfand 1370 (March 1991).

5. *Rahnama-yi zana-shu'i az nazar-i Islam,* written and published by Hasan Maujudi, printed in Tehran by Gauhar, 13th edition, summer 1370 (1991).

6. *Izdivaj dar Islam,* written in Arabic by Ayatollah Ali Mishkini and translated into Persian by Ayatollah Ahmad Jannati, published in Qum by Alhadi, 8th edition, Mordad 1366 (August 1987).

7. *Akhlaq-i khanavada,* written by Ahmad Sadiq Ardistani, published in Tehran by Khazar Publishing House, 41st edition, winter 1363 (1964).

8. *Akhlaq dar khanavada,* written by Sayyid Ali Akbar Husaini, published by Islamic Publishing House in Tehran, 1st edition, Murdad 1369 (August 1990).

9. *Akhlaq dar khana,* written by Ayatollah Husain Mazahiri, published in Qum by Akhlaq Publishers. The book contains the first series of sermons delivered in Qum

during Ramadan 1368 (1989) after the public prayers at noon and in the evening. These sermons were popular with clerics' wives who commented on them frequently to me during my research in Qum in 1995.

10. *Ravish-i khushbakhti va tausiya bi khaharan-i imani,* written by Banu Amin Isfahani, published by Amir Publishers in Qum, 6th edition, 1369 (1980).

11. Husaini lost his seat in the February 2000 elections for the sixth majlis, won by the reformists by a landslide. Soon after the elections, he was the subject of a rumor with a sharp gender irony indicative of the popular challenge to the official gender discourse: Husaini has two wives whom he angers by marrying a third, a young girl. The first two decide to teach him a lesson, and one day when he visits the toilet, they turn off the water in the house. When he asks for a ewer (*aftaba*) to clean himself, he is handed one full of acid. His genitals severely corroded, he is hospitalized and unable to enjoy his new marriage. The rumor became so strong that Husaini had to deny it, both in the press and in parliament, saying that he was in the hospital for other reasons. He accused the reformist newspapers of damaging his reputation and threatened to sue them.

12. At the time of the revolution, a selection of Ayatollah Khomeini's writings relating to fiqh regulations for sexual conduct was translated as part of *The Little Green Book;* see *Sayings of the Ayatollah Khomeini: Political, Philosophical, Social and Religious* (New York: Bantam Books, 1980). Secularists found such writings both ridiculous and obscene and used this volume as propaganda against the Islamic Republic.

13. Translations of these passages are mine.

14. The saying (*ravayat*) of Imam Ali to which the author refers is: "Almighty God created desire in ten parts and then gave nine parts to women and one to men."

15. Gulpaygani, *Paivand-i du gul,* 53–54.

16. Mishkini, *Izdivaj dar Islam,* 100.

17. Ibid., 101.

18. Muhaqqiq Hilli, *Sharayi' Islam* (Laws of Islam), vol. 2. Persian translation by Abolqasim Yazdi, compiled by Mohammad Taqi Danish-Pazhuh (Tehran: Tehran University Press, 1364/1985), 428.

19. Mishkini, *Izdivaj dar Islam,* 75.

20. *Bar-rasi-yi huquq-i zanan dar mas'ala talaq,* written by Zahra Gavahi (close to the reformist camp), published by Sazman-i tablighat-i Islami, Tehran, 1st edition, 1373 (1994).

21. *Huquq-i zan dar Islam va khanava,* written by Maryam Savaji (close to the reformists), published by Mujarrid, Tehran, 2nd edition, 1371 (1992).

22. *Chihra-yi zan dar a'ina Islam va Qur'an,* written by Murtaza Fahim Kirmani (a middle-ranking cleric close to the reformist camp), published by Daftar nashr-i farhang-i Islami, 5th edition, 1373 (1994).

23. *Zan dar a'ina jalal va jamal,* written by Ayatollah Javadi-Amuli (a high-ranking cleric close to the conservative camp), published by Nashr-i farhang-i rija, 3rd edition, 1372 (1993).

24. First published in 1974, this book has gone through many reprints, and an English translation appeared in 1980. The Persian and English editions to which I refer are: Ustad Murtaza Mutahhari, *Nizam-i huquq-i zan dar Islam,* 15th ed. (Qum: Mul-

la Sadr, 1370/1991); and *The Rights of Women in Islam,* 4th ed. (Tehran: World Organization for Islamic Services, 1991).

25. The gist of Tabataba'i's theory is found in his *Ta'dud-i zaujat va maqam-i zan dar Islam* (Polygamy and the status of women in Islam) (Qom: Azadi, n.d.).

26. Ibid., 52.

27. Mutahhari, *Nizam-i huquq,* 1370, 207. For this passage, I supply my own translation because the published translation renders shahvat variously as "sexual drive" and "passion." I take later quotations from the published translation.

28. Mutahhari, *Rights of Women in Islam,* 297.

29. Ibid., 274.

30. Ibid.

31. Ibid., 298–99.

32. For Soroush's theory and its impact on gender discourses, see Mir-Hosseini, *Islam and Gender,* chapter 7.

33. Shamsolvaezin was jailed in July 2000 for a term of five years.

34. *Kiyan* and *Zanan* played a role in Iran in the 1990s similar to that of the Husainiyya Irshad (the popular religious lecture hall) in Iran in the 1970s, in the sense that they both became forums for new religious thinking. The most important Muslim intellectuals in Iran were associated with them: Ali Shari'ati with Husainiyya Irshad and Abdolkarim Soroush with *Kiyan.*

35. By winter 2001 neither wrote for *Zanan* any longer. Both were victims of the antireformists' wrath and were imprisoned, Sa'idzada in June 1998 as described below and Kar in April 2000 following parliamentary elections.

36. In many ways the 1992 launch of *Payam-i zan,* a women's magazine published by the Qum seminaries, was a neotraditionalist response to *Zanan.* For discussion, see Ziba Mir-Hosseini, "Rethinking Gender: Discussions with Ulama in Iran," *Critique: A Journal of Middle East Studies* 13 (Fall 1998): 45–59.

37. Sayyid Muhsin Sa'idzada, "Correspondence between Feminism and Islamic Religious Issues" (Tatbiq-i feminizm ba masa'il-i dini-i Islam), in *Women, Gender, and Islam,* proceedings of the Sixth Seminar of the Iranian Women's Studies Foundation, 1995, 34.

38. In my 1995 discussions with the clerics of *Payam-i zan,* I also avoided raising such issues. I criticized their gender discourse, which is a modified version of Ayatollah Mutahhari's, and questioned many underlying assumptions, but when it came to his conception of sexuality, I kept silent. The topic was still very much taboo. See *Islam and Gender,* 277–78.

39. For a discussion of this debate in the Iranian context, see Val Moghadam, "Islamic Feminism and Its Discontents: Notes on a Debate," *Iran Bulletin,* <http://www.iran-bulletin.org/islamic_feminism.htm>.

9 Rural Women's History: A Case Study from Boir Ahmad

ERIKA FRIEDL

ILLITERATE VILLAGE WOMEN leave few records of their lives: tools, some anonymous creations such as carpets, stories and songs passed down through generations, and observations that outsiders have occasionally found note-worthy enough to write down or photograph.[1] These sources speak mostly to women's work and conditions of life. What women in the past may have thought about themselves, their work, and others is hardly accessible at all. Women's memories and retrospective evaluations of life in the past are the focus of this chapter.

Most scholarly literature on historical aspects of Iranian women concen-trates on urban settings and the middle and upper classes.[2] Rural women are discussed, if at all, in the framework of topics other than their history.[3] From these dispersed accounts, a picture of rural women's lives and patterns of change in the wake of so-called modernization and economic development in Iran emerges that resembles, in its outlines, those of women elsewhere.[4] Generalizing broadly, in traditional agricultural as well as agricultural/pas-toral communities in Iran, the sexual division of labor kept men and wom-en dependent on each other's services; women's labor input was intensive and essential for the group's survival and well-being and was recognized as such; reproduction and social services (childbearing and child rearing, tak-ing care of sick and elderly family members) were only a small part of wom-en's work; women's work involved special skills and produced not only sub-sistence items but also valuable surplus such as butterfat and textiles; their work included heavy physical exertion such as gathering and transporting foodstuffs, water, and firewood; and women kept up a flow of information and reciprocal services that facilitated economic and political enterprises by men of the group.[5]

In the course of fast integration of rural communities into national administrative structures and into the cash-based markets of the expanding modern economy since the mid-twentieth century, women's traditional jobs became obsolete or at least much curtailed. Women's energies were idled or turned to the elaboration of new homemaking activities, to schooling, and in a few cases to white-collar jobs. At the same time, the availability of low-paid wage work for men in towns, cities, and Persian Gulf states took husbands and fathers out of villages, often for months or years at a time, thus leaving women to cope at home with managerial problems and chores that traditionally had been men's responsibility. Unprecedented population growth after 1950 made it increasingly necessary for men in rural areas to abandon traditional farming and pastoral enterprises for lack of suitable agricultural and pastoral land and rights to water. The shortages were exacerbated by the landlord-privileged management of land, relentless division of land among heirs, and spread of fast-growing villages and towns into former fields and pastures. (Such developments are typical for most parts of Iran.) Part of the rural population was thus squeezed out of rural economies, thus swelling towns and cities or, in earlier times, settling elsewhere in villages with available arable land. The remaining communities grew nevertheless, developing nonfarming segments that stratified villagers along urban/national lines. Men with too little land for survival opened shops, worked for wages locally, became teachers, or found clerical jobs through formal education that was becoming available in the 1960s. Their wives, daughters, and sisters had dramatically fewer options in small traditional communities. Blue-collar jobs were not readily available for women and were considered unsuitable for them, as were positions in trading, such as in retail sales. Teaching, midwifery, school administration, and a few clerical jobs such as in local banks offered job opportunities to only a few rural women, and all required higher education that was much harder to obtain for women than for men. Whether women worked in the new jobs or not, the household changed from an economically productive unit to a consumption unit increasingly dependent on goods, services, and income from outside. This process changed interpersonal relationships, patterns of power and authority, and the ways men and women thought of themselves and of each other.

These broad changes in the division of labor and in gender relationships in the course of economic development seem to be universal, at least for patrilineal, androcentric societies. Their effects can be interpreted to mean that the loss of the traditional economic importance of women brought about a loss of self-worth, authority, and social standing vis-à-vis men, because women became dependent for even the most basic livelihood on resources provided solely by husbands, fathers, or the state. The effects of modern economic development can also be interpreted to mean the opposite for women, especially rural women, namely less drudgery and less hard physical labor, some options for work outside the home, access to formal education, and thus an improvement of their condition. Adverse conditions can be seen as a transitory phase from one type of unpaid female labor in the traditional, rural/agricultural community to one in which women may eventually achieve social and economic parity with men at some time in the future.

These different interpretations reflect different assumptions about how societies operate. The first—critical or Marxist—approach is based on the assumption that capitalist economic and social development unrestrained by corrective measures has a price that is paid by those who have the fewest resources: the poor, the illiterate, the unskilled, and women. Gender inequalities will be reproduced. Various ideologies such as homemaker-ideals, glorification of motherhood, and gender attributes are said to mystify women's exploitative conditions. Where women are figured into planned development, they either are considered an expensive hindrance because of illiteracy, lack of skills, and purported clinging to traditions, or else they are seen as a cheap source of labor.[6] Jobs that are made available to women in a developing capitalist economy thus will not speedily change unequal, exploitative gender relations.

The second—liberal—approach is based on the assumption that linear growth, aided by rational technological changes, increases efficiency and the standard of living. In the pursuit of efficiency, some inequality is inevitable, but it is a small price to pay for the overall betterment of social conditions. In this approach, any loss of economic power and benefits by a social group such as women is seen as temporary and thus of little consequence. As development progresses, more educational opportunities and jobs will open for women, enabling them not only to regain lost traditional status but also to transcend it. This change will lead to a decline in births, which will make paid labor easier for women and will lead to higher status and economic well-being in a spiral toward emancipation and economic autonomy.[7]

Both approaches reflect outside, Western, socioeconomic philosophies. A third approach is the Islamic Republic's own gender philosophy as expressed in laws, scriptural interpretations, school curricula, and labor politics.[8] It is based on the traditional local assumption that biological sexual differences determine hierarchical male-female relationships. It lends itself easily to support androcentric, paternalistic, and authoritarian practices that, in rural areas, accelerate the dependency of most women on men. But it also gives some rural and lower-class women the absolutely novel opportunity to rise to middle-class status through higher education in professional fields covering women's needs in a sex-segregated society. For example, the need for female physicians and teachers in Iran is satisfied with quotas for admission to university programs explicitly for urban and rural women. A "true Islamic society" is not meant to provide individual freedom in the liberal sense and total socioeconomic equality for women but depends on every individual's fulfillment of duties and responsibilities in the God-ordained male-female hierarchy on earth. Until this situation is realized, hardships are to be expected. Protesting women ought to be educated into understanding their correct position in society, or else their just grievances ought to be addressed.

In all three modes of looking at women, what women have to say about themselves and their work seems largely immaterial. The women's point of view does not count much. In the Marxist model, a subordinated woman satisfied with her situation as a housewife, for example, is suspected to be mystified. She cannot critically appraise her situation because she has been enculturated in the ideology that makes agreeing to her subordination seem reasonable to her. In the liberal model, women's satisfaction or dissatisfaction is indicative of progress in development (or the lack of it) and of individual women's willingness to make choices. In the third model, dissatisfied women easily appear as unreasonable, although in practice many people in Iran in the late 1990s recognized women's hardships as legitimate concerns and advocated change in the name of Islam.

Depending on the viewpoint the observer takes, the women under observation emerge in seemingly contradictory historical dynamics. I suggest that the contradictions do not pose the question of right or wrong, for different interpretations are equally valid as long as their premises are explicit. Rather, they pose the question of historiographic relevance. In the case of rural Iranian women, all three models tend to deny women the opportunity for a valid appraisal of their own condition and thus make it hard to construct a woman-centered history. One can arrive at a woman-centered history only by taking into account macro-conditions and macro-processes and also the view from below, that is, what women themselves made of their world at different times and by taking their interpretations as valid historical data.

Here I sketch part of such a history for women in a large tribal village in the province of Kohgiluye-Boir Ahmad in southwestern Iran which I call Deh Koh, where I have worked as an anthropologist since 1965.[9] I look at the village from below, as seen from women's position, and focus on how women remembered and evaluated some facets of their past and on what they had to say about the changes they experienced.

Methodology

I rely on what women of Deh Koh told me over many years of close, cordial association. I talked with women of all social strata, from the poorest to members of the former chiefs' families, illiterate and educated ones alike. I listened carefully to what they said to one another about the past. Several attempts at a more formal oral historical collection of data were successful only with some high-ranking women; most others, when asked directly about the past, dismissed my questions with short answers or jokes. Indeed, women did not talk much about the past even among themselves, other than telling an occasional story by way of comparison to more recent events.[10] Comments on the past were not a genre of stories, of conversation, or of conceptualizing oneself. The reminiscences were realistic rather than romanticizing, more likely critical of past conditions than nostalgic. But they also emphasized earlier warm, close relationships with relatives and neighbors. They expressed pride in women's endurance and strength in previous hard times when women had to carry heavy loads during migrations, fetch water from faraway wells and streams, give birth along the road if need be, and get hardly any sleep for weeks during peak milking times in the herding outposts. Indirectly, while talking about topics of immediate concern, women commented on all conditions in their world, from material circumstances to social relationships, from fun and pain to politics, as far back as seemed relevant to them when they wanted to put their present condition into perspective.

A short case study cannot possibly deal with all aspects women deemed relevant. For reasons of clarity and space, I concentrate on describing how the dramatic economic changes in this village during the twentieth century were evaluated and integrated in the women's own perceptions of their history. Economic changes were by far not the only factors women compared and contrasted, but they provide a convenient and, for women, obvious line that linked successive generations.

The village shared many features with rural transhumant communities in the Zagros mountains generally.[11] Archeological evidence suggests considerable cultural continuity in the area since prehistoric times.[12] How local developments compare with those in other rural Iranian communities we will not know until we have many more reports about women's histories from other areas.

Political History

Deh Koh was founded around 1880 in the former summer pastures of a small transhumant group of Luri-speaking people in the southern Zagros mountains. Under the leadership of a tribal chief, some twenty households moved there from an earlier settlement, reportedly for strategic reasons of defense and for need of expansion of agricultural production and good water resources.[13] The village prospered and grew from fewer than a hundred people around 1890 to nearly four thousand in 2000 and changed from a purely pastoral/agricultural, transhumant way of life of largely illiterate peasants to one with a diversity of jobs and socioeconomic groups and a high level of literacy. Women constituted slightly less than half of the total population. Nearly 50 percent of the population was under the age of seventeen.

The political history of the area was one of strife, violence, and instability.[14] Chiefs were leaders of retinues of armed men in wars and raids. Although women rarely seem to have been fighters or targeted victims, they described how they had suffered when they lost sons, husbands, and fathers, and they recounted how they had lived in fear of attacks on villages, especially in the vulnerable herding outposts. One Deh Koh woman was widowed three times when her successive husbands, who were brothers, were killed in fights. Another woman lost her mind when her husband and a son were killed in one day.

The destruction of the traditional local power structure by the government after 1963, when the last paramount tribal chief of the area was assassinated, meant for women a decided shift toward a quieter life. The fear of attacks and of losing male relatives in fights was gone, and moving between villages or in fields and gardens became safer. Women told tales of violence in the frame of "those were the bad old times." In these accounts a class bias became apparent. High-ranking women from the chiefs' families remembered the violence in terms of bravery in a heroic past. By mediating between feuding chiefly families and voicing their opinions in political matters, a few of these women had even been politically engaged as counselors of their husbands and sons. Indeed, one can get different pictures of rural political life depending on whether one is listening to women from a rich, influential chief's family or from a non-influential, poorer one. A foreign visitor is more likely to be able to talk to the former than to the latter, if for no other reason than the former's hospitality and social skills, and is thus more likely to be exposed to the views of life of chiefs' women and their constructions of the past than to those of other women. The memories and stories of women of noninfluential families about intertribal and inter-village hostilities in earlier times were colored by their perception of the past as filled with fear, grief, and danger.[15] A middle-aged woman remembered how, as children, she and her playmates would hide in barns and up in trees if someone shouted, "The chiefs are coming!" For women, the end of raids and fights and of the chiefs' economic oppression after 1963 marks the most memorable positive consequence of a political event. An elderly woman summed it up as, "The young ones who complain about life now have no idea how much fear and grief we had then."

Women's Work

Carrying water home in goatskin bags, washing wheat, leaching acorn-meal, and washing clothes were women's work as far back as women could remember. All these tasks required reliable sources of water. In this regard the move to Deh Koh in the late nineteenth century benefited women directly, although the decision to move there had not been made for the sake of easing women's work. Convenient access to abundant water (springs and, later, irrigation channels) significantly cut time and effort spent on water-dependent activities without changing work patterns and their social frame. Women congregated at springs and channels, combining socializing with washing and fetching water as they had done earlier but now with much less exertion.[16] In addition, a bathhouse in the village made possible a level of hygiene that earlier it and other villages in the area could not afford. Women's own assessment of changes is important for my argument. The move to water-rich Deh Koh was advantageous because it made their grandmothers' work easier and provided the amenity of a bathhouse.[17] Further developments of local water resources that brought water to every house by 1985 made it unnecessary for most women to leave home to procure the resource. Although this arrangement was even more convenient, and women appreciated it as such, it deprived them of the earlier most-compelling reason for leaving the house several times a day and of regular occasions to socialize with women they otherwise did not meet easily. Propriety made it difficult for women to leave their compounds in the absence of what were seen as legitimate tasks. Most women said they missed casual contacts with other women. Piped water was also said to be less tasty and cold than water in earlier times, when it was stored in skin bags. Nevertheless, and although women were aware of the isolating effects of indoor plumbing, they would not want to return to carrying water bags on their hips. "Who needs it?" a woman asked rhetorically. "How often during winter did I come home from the channel with the water bag frozen to my skirt!"

Oak forests surrounding Deh Koh in the past provided wood, game, and acorns. In the old village, the gathering of firewood had been women's work as it still is in other areas in Iran. In Deh Koh, as men extended fields into the woods by burning or felling trees, they also took over the transport of heavy oak logs to the village on donkeys. By 1960 men had to travel long distances to gather firewood, and from the mid-1970s, off and on, logging was curtailed somewhat by the government. Oil and natural gas largely replaced wood for heat energy, a change that meant that women moved from expending heavy labor for fuel to nearly no labor at all, but also that they moved from having control over fuel for cooking and keeping warm in winter to total dependence on men and the state to provide fuel. Men had to organize the timely filling of canisters with propane gas, which the government provided for cash. Yet women saw their dependency on having to be provided with gas and oil as a great improvement over former times when they had to carry wood and brush home on their own backs. As far as they were concerned, the daily lives of women in Deh Koh greatly improved.

Housekeeping in the past was not elaborated beyond cooking and washing, and not much of that was done in the absence of resources, which was what women talked about when mentioning their former activities. People were often hungry then; they were cold, and hardly anyone possessed shoes. Children were often sick, and many died. People slept tightly packed in small houses, often together with some animals. Packed-earth floors were covered with felt mats, if at all, and a heavy knotted wool rug served as a cover for sleepers. In winter the air in the overcrowded rooms was filled with smoke. Women had to make do with little. Yet life then was uncomplicated because possessions were few and simple. No one was fussy about homemaking, for more important and pressing chores needed to be done. "I have spent all morning washing curtains," complained a woman in 1994. "Twenty years ago I would have had something good to show for my time—at least a ball of spun yarn!"

Subsistence

The hunting of birds and wild sheep and goats was exclusively men's work. Women had no part in it save provisioning a hunting expedition. Game was high-status food, taxed by the village chief, and one of the few sources of meat.[18] Game was distributed according to a social hierarchy that located men above women. Until the late 1940s, game was plentiful, though, and women remembered it as an important part of the local diet then. Rapid environmental degradation since the late 1940s, and later the disarmament of people by the rural police meant the loss of this source of meat, meager as it was for women at the best of times. Meat was in the firm control of men. For example, a woman who pledged a lamb in a vow to a saint had to wait to fulfill her pledge until her husband decided he could afford to give up one of his lambs. In fact, women's access to all but the lowest-ranking foodstuffs had always been rather limited, especially if it involved a cash expense. Where villagers were nourished poorly, women suffered malnutrition more than men did. In Deh Koh, anemia and signs of protein deficiency in women were endemic according to local doctors, even after food became more plentiful after 1965. Dairy products were consumed sparingly because they could be sold for cash. In the value system of most women, providing men and guests with the best available food took precedence over feeding themselves and their children, especially females.[19] Thus, whenever the village suffered famines—quite frequently, women remembered—women and children were hit the hardest. They did have access to alternative sources of food such as locusts and other occasional gathered foodstuffs that, because of their low status, did not have to be shared with people in higher social positions, but it is not clear to what extent these occasional foods influenced women's and children's nutrition. In talking about these times, women placed collecting and eating locusts into the context of hunger in the past, a time they were glad to have left behind. No severe food shortage in Deh Koh has occurred since the early 1960s, but, in the later times of plenty, women moaned and groaned about aches and pains, weakness and ill health, and contrasted their ailments with the strength they said all people possessed in the past. In their opinion, modern, "weak," "artificial" food such as bakery bread, vegetable shortening, mass-produced "factory" chickens, and imported rice, together with lack of mobility and physical exertion, made them weak and sickly. They obviously felt, and occasionally emphatically said, that something had gone awry over the years.

Women at the fringes of a net of social support on which they were totally dependent were the most likely to perceive their marginal, exposed position as a result of a loss of self-sufficiency and autonomy when compared to the past. For example, a young woman, whose husband was working abroad and had left her financially at the mercy of his parents and brothers, bemoaned her precarious situation of dependency on tightfisted in-laws. She said she did not have even the few coins needed to see a doctor when she was ill or to buy cookies for guests, and she wished she could at least go out to collect almonds as in the old times to have some item to serve to visitors. Unlike in some other parts of the Middle East, many rural women in Iran did not easily gain control over the money of their absent husbands beyond what they may have needed for a basic livelihood. In Deh Koh it was unheard of for a married woman to buy property or start a business with her absent husband's savings. Only in exceptional cases did married women manage or inherit property. Upon return from abroad, men used their savings to build houses or start businesses and provided their wives with a better life, but the wives would have no more control over money than they had in the past. Women were aware of both consequences of this kind of property ownership and management and commented on them. The most important reason for sending a girl to school and university was to make it possible for her to get a job with an income. "Without money in their own pockets, women have no freedom and are servants like our grandmothers were," said a mother of three daughters.

Acorns were the single most important food resource gathered by women in the past. Properly leached, ground, made into dough, and baked on convex iron griddles over open fires, acorns formed the staple until yields from irrigated fields replaced acorn bread with wheat bread and, to a lesser degree, with rice.[20] During frequent times of shortages, mostly due to lack of land, crop failures, or over-taxation by the village chiefs, various types of acorn bread were eaten until the 1960s. From the gathering of acorns to the baking of acorn-meal bread, all acorn-related work was women's. Gathering was done in women's work groups that formed spontaneously along lines of kinship and neighborhoods. The elderly, the sick, young children, women in advanced stages of pregnancy, and those with young infants stayed home. What women brought home stayed under their control in the women's hierarchy within the household (mother over daughters, mother-in-law over her son's wives, older women over younger) but was shared by all household members. Women remembered the acorn expeditions fondly, even though harvesting acorns and carrying them home in heavy bags was hard work, processing acorns was cumbersome, and acorn bread was not a favorite food because it tasted bitter and caused constipation.[21] Obviously, in women's opinion the social aspects of a work party out in the open, away from everyday routines and the constraints of life in the village, amply compensated for the hardships. When reliable domestic and outside foods became readily available locally, and women no longer had to leave the house to obtain staple food, they said that life became easier. But in the same breath they mentioned the loss of the experience of community, freedom, and space. "The loads were heavy but our hearts were light," said an elderly woman. Going into the woods just for the fun of it, though, was considered improper for women and thus not a realistic activity.

Similarly organized parties of women gathered wild vegetables, nuts, and herbs in the mountains. They used these plants fresh or dried and stored them for winter consumption. Women expressed great satisfaction with this kind of work. They remembered these outings fondly and looked forward to them; such trips involved not only climbing and hiking in beautiful (labeled as such by people) surroundings rarely ever visited otherwise, but also a picnic of sorts and much socializing among women. Despite some objections to this activity in the name of propriety after the 1978–79 revolution and despite the absence of dire necessity for foodstuffs collected this way, such gathering parties continued to be organized occasionally.

These activities were almost completely sex-segregated: men hunted, women gathered. I did not hear of any woman hunter, and no such motif is found in folktales or songs either. Although shepherds or men in the woods and mountains occasionally brought home herbs, wild almonds, or mushrooms, men did not identify with gathering activities.

The hunting/gathering complex historically links the villagers to the oldest known form of subsistence in the Zagros mountains.[22] In small nomadic communities such as existed in earlier times in a rich environment with plentiful game and edible plants for most of the year, hunting and gathering can safely be assumed to have been less time-consuming than it was after 1950, when available wild foodstuffs were found only in increasingly remote areas because the growing population destroyed native vegetation and wildlife by deforestation, building, cultivating, and overgrazing. Gathering was steady but not hard work then and could be accomplished by just about all but the youngest, oldest, and sickest women. Women's gathering seems to have been essential to the dietary well-being of households from the earliest times until within living memory of adult women in the 1990s. The way women talked about it, gathering was also a source of pleasure and self-worth, especially so because they retained control over the distribution of their food.

The people who settled Deh Koh were transhumant farmers with strong traditions of a tribally organized, pastoral nomadic way of life in terms of political organization, material culture, lifestyle, and folklore. Under the leadership of the founder and his heirs, irrigation channels were dug, fields prepared, enemies warded off, and schools established. Fields provided staple foods such as wheat and barley for the growing population and the increasingly demanding chief's family. Pasture camps in various environmental niches in the mountains up to half a day's journey away from Deh Koh served as seasonal centers for the herding of sheep, goats, and cattle. Mules, donkeys, and the people themselves provided transport services. Eventually vineyards (for raisin and syrup production) and fruit orchards were established. In the long run, these provided the highest and most stable income. At various times during the twentieth century, labor-intensive cash crops were tried and abandoned, such as poppies (for opium), tobacco, and sugar beets. Irrigated and dry-field grain production was almost exclusively men's work, as was the harvesting in the high mountains of fodder for the winter. Herding was done by boys and occasionally by young girls. Women helped with weeding and at the tail end of harvesting but otherwise were not supposed or encouraged to participate in field work involving grain production. They labored in other agricultural areas, such as weeding and harvesting legumes, opium producing, tobacco growing, sugar-beet cultivating, and grape, apple, and walnut harvesting. Of these, only legume growing and grape, apple, and walnut harvesting involved women regularly in the early 2000s. Opium was outlawed, and tobacco and sugar beets were abandoned by the late 1970s.

Women did not remember their work in cash crops with any enthusiasm. It was, in their words, not only hard work but drudgery. They worked long hours in cramped positions for products they could not use themselves and had no control over in any way. Men, including chiefs and state officials, managed these products and siphoned off all but the most paltry profits. But most legumes were grown for household consumption, weeded, harvested, washed, dried, stored, cleaned, and cooked by women, and although women complained about the work involved, about the heat, dust, and long walk to the field, they did not demean or deplore this work. They saw it as part of what it takes to keep a good house. For the same reason, they rarely complained about their labor input in grape products such as raisins and syrup or about the exhausting work of harvesting and hulling walnuts. "Today my back aches," a woman commented about walnut collecting, "but tomorrow we will have good things to eat."

In animal husbandry, women's involvement was the most steady the year around and the most indispensable. Like gathering, this work was the same in transhumant villages and in nomadic camps throughout the region. While men owned and managed the herds, organized shepherds and pasture rotations, arranged for cooperative herding, took care of the animals' health and fodder, and marketed the end products, women milked and processed milk into yogurt, butterfat, buttermilk, and dried curds; washed, cleaned, and carded fleece and goat hair; spun yarn on the drop-spindle; and wove pile rugs and flat weaves on horizontal, transportable looms, from floor-coverings and a dozen different kinds of bags to goat-hair tent panels. A woman's skills, ability, and willingness to work hard were prime criteria for a "good" wife. When animal husbandry declined in the early 1970s, women eventually lost all of these activities. Looking back at those times twenty years later, women admired themselves for their endurance, strength, and skills then, but hardly a woman bemoaned the loss of the unending long hours of toil these activities meant.

Weaving

In the past, spinning on the drop-spindle and weaving on the horizontal loom, which required women to sit on the woven fabric on the ground or floor, were considered female housekeeping skills. "The spindle follows a woman wherever she goes," women said. If a woman had her hands free she would spin, sitting, standing, or walking. Spinning was the first women's skill a girl learned. It was "good" work, easy on the legs and back, rewarding as she saw the ball of yarn grow, a companion in quiet hours or while socializing. In the past all women wove for their household's needs, and many spun and wove a surplus. In 1965 all women were still spinning yarn, but most of the fiber goods needed in the village were imported or made and bartered by only a few local weavers. Even this activity had almost ceased by 1995 when elderly women weavers were slowly giving up this work while none of the young women were taking it up, despite demand and relatively good income and despite favorable working conditions. A weaver worked at home at her own pace, between her other chores, and used traditional patterns she knew by heart. Frequently needing to interrupt her weaving, she also gave her legs and back much-needed rest and was able to run her household with minimal disruption. A woman at the loom was also an invitation for others in the compound to gather and socialize. Looking back, women in 2002 remembered activities around looms almost with nostalgia but showed no inclination to weave as their grandmothers had done. Weaving had become a sign of rural/tribal backwardness, and all services performed by women for a patron in Deh Koh carried the stigma of servitude and were undertaken only under economic stress.[23] Elsewhere in the region and nation, women wove for export on large, upright, factory-type looms. These women likely spent much time at the loom and relied on other household members to perform most chores. Generally these women worked for a state agency promoting cottage wage work for homebound women and paying little (less than 10 percent of what an unskilled male worker made), or they worked for an urban entrepreneur for a small wage or to pay off debts or, in nomadic communities, for a chief or his wife who might have treated the weavers as servants. Women working under these conditions made little money and rarely had control over it. Such weaving was hard work, women in Deh Koh said, work that made one's back and legs "lame" and ruined one's hands—for yarn is coarse—especially so if one had to spend many uninterrupted hours at the loom. Young women working in a government-sponsored weaving workshop in Deh Koh complained about unhealthful work conditions, aches and pains caused by sitting still in front of the vertical loom for many hours, low wages, bad management, and lack of time for household tasks. Never more than about ten women worked on such looms at home in any given year. Thus, seemingly similar work—weaving—was regarded differently by women, depending on what kind of control they had in decision making and management and over the products of their labor. In earlier times, women said, weaving was a necessary chore, on a level with all the others women performed to keep a household going and thus did not have the connotation of either servitude or business.

Recent Economic Developments

After about 1970, as men increasingly found work outside the traditional farm economy, transhumant pastoralism in Deh Koh declined and with it migrations to and from herding outposts, dairy products produced by female labor, and weaving. Thus, women lost their most important economic activities as well as their most significant reason for spatial mobility. Women commented on this loss both negatively and positively. Those who had been active in the transhumant economy remembered, first and foremost, the hard work that kept them on their feet all day long and even at night, for butter was churned during the wee hours regardless of illness, pregnancy, and birth. But they also commented on the sense of well-being and on the camaraderie and mutual support among women in the open spaces of the high-mountain outposts, which they missed in the isolating conditions of life in the village. Nevertheless, rarely did a woman protest when her husband sold their animals and settled the family permanently in the village. The amenities of village life such as convenient water, electricity, gas ranges, television, and access to stores and schools outweighed the drawbacks, especially for younger women who held educational aspirations or liked the urban lifestyle. The immediate interests of women in an "easy" life colluded with their economic marginalization. Whether one calls this process liberating or subordinating for women is beside the point. The women I talked with were not totally blind to the price they paid for the easier life, nor did they see much of a chance or advantage in resisting "progress" (*pishraft*). It happened no matter what they said; it was outside their influence. They were aware that their activities now were confined to the home and revolved around food preparation and childcare. Housekeeping became more elaborate when women took on needlework, managed new household tools, and elevated chores including cleaning and washing into long drawn-out processes. They also realized that for just about all their needs they had come to depend on men.[24] In this context, women reported depression, fatigue, loss of meaning, and feelings of loneliness, while for the past they remembered overwork, mistreatment, poverty, and hunger. They said that suffering always was part of life but that now life was easier and that therefore they did not want the old times back.

Children

Without exception women remembered that they had learned to work at a young age.[25] Even in the mid-1990s, toddlers were sent to fetch items, shoo chickens, and rock cradles. Three- and four-year-olds were expected to carry a younger sibling on their backs if need be, run errands, wash pots, pick grapes, and hull walnuts. Traditional games for girls stressed the acquisition of skills such as baking bread, cooking, washing, and spinning. By the age of six, girls were working alongside their mothers for a good part of the day, only a generation or two ago. By age nine or ten, they were supposed to be able to perform all essential household chores including dairy production and caring for animals and were expected to take over the household in their mother's absence.[26] Although school attendance changed this schedule somewhat, for girls the pressure to work at home remained much stronger than for boys. By the time a girl was seen as "mature" and "ready," between ten and thirteen years of age, she was likely married and had to know how to work for her mother-in-law "like a servant," women said. Her usefulness to her husband's family largely consisted of her contributions to work and her ability to bear and raise children, especially males.[27] Having cared for her younger siblings or the children of a married older brother since she was young herself, she would have learned childcare along with other women's duties while she was growing up in her father's house. She also learned to think that most work was burdensome and unpleasant and that she was better off delegating it whenever possible—mostly to young girls. Thus, she likely taught the same skills and expectations to her own daughters. Although the age at which work was expected rose and the kind of work asked of girls changed, expectations of labor and patterns of interactions for adults and young female children did not change substantially over the past few generations. Modern children, especially females, were said to have a much better and healthier life than those in earlier generations, and this change was all to the good, but women nevertheless complained because they did not have the kind of help from their daughters that they themselves had rendered their own elders.

For as far back as women remembered, and until the 1960s, most female children were married off at the onset of puberty or even earlier, which meant they were handed over to their mothers-in-law as children for further care and instruction. It was not uncommon for a young woman to be pregnant before her first period came, women said.[28] Sexual relations might or might not have started right away. In any case, women remembered the transfers as traumatic almost without exception, and the custom of giving female children away at an early age was deplored. Women told of their or their sisters' resistance violently broken when, as "mere children who knew only how to play," as one woman said, they were taken to live in another house, made to sleep with people they barely knew, required to work hard, were beaten frequently, and had sex forced on them before they even knew what it was all about. Several suicides by young women were remembered in this context. The only women who saw an advantage in the traditional child-bride arrangements were mothers-in-law frustrated by the insubordination of their daughters-in-law or their lack of domestic skills. "In my time," such a woman said, "we learned how to behave in the husband's father's house when we were young enough and scared enough to learn. The older, educated girls our sons now marry have no respect." Not a minute later, however, she said that she firmly opposed her own daughter marrying young because it was "bad" for her. Women discussed the hardships or the advantages of child-bride marriages depending on whether they identified with their daughters as brides or with their sons' interests or whether they looked back at themselves being dragged from their fathers' houses or at a pitiable "old" unmarried girl of twenty-two. It was quite clear to women that child-bride marriages worked to the advantage of the husband's family, just as bringing up a female child was beneficial to her future husband's family rather than to her own. To this day a daughter is proclaimed "lost" to her family upon marriage.

In 1992 the government launched a birth-control campaign to curb population growth in Iran. In Deh Koh it was an unqualified success. Small families with only two or three children became the ideal. This change colored the opinion young people expressed about their elders. "In the past, women had children like cows, one a year," a young woman said. And a young man, one of seven children, complained, "Our grandmother, who had ten children, did not know any better. But my father and mother—I cannot understand why they had to have seven children. People in the past were just like animals." Older women said that to become pregnant in the bridal chamber was expected. Ten or more pregnancies were quite common for women while childlessness was considered a terrible misery. "One was a real woman only if she had children," said a mother of six. Another older woman noted, "In the past, being a youth meant being healthy and strong, working hard, and bearing one child after another. We had no choice. Our daughters have a choice, and this is good." The same argument of choice was made in regard to options for jobs for women. Although for village women the number of available jobs was small, seeing some young women "getting out," as people said, raised hopes for the future.

Conclusion

By 1995 women in Deh Koh were looking back over a hundred years of changes in their way of life, changes taking them from a transhumant existence to one in a market-oriented, stratified village. Comparing their own to their elders' lives, women romanticized neither the past nor the present. Rather, they applied two sets of criteria for the interpretation and evaluation of their history. One pertained to conditions of survival such as availability of food and creature-comfort amenities, health, conduct of chiefs and government agencies, and work loads and other demands on them. On this count, they found women's lives in the past rather deplorable and the socioeconomic developments to their advantage. The other set of criteria consisted of emotions: closeness to other women; support of children, family, and other women; pride in skills and accomplishments; and feelings of peace and contentment as well as pain and sorrow. And on this count the past looked better than the present. Women said that improvements in the material conditions of life were achieved at the price of boredom and loss of meaning as well as the devaluation of women's traditional skills in the increasingly cash-based economy to which only a few women gained direct access. In discussing development, women subscribed to a linear model of change. Just as living conditions for most of them have eased compared to their own mothers' and grandmothers', so modern society might open doors to a better life for their children. Women defined this better life by the attainment of a materially secure middle-class existence that eventually would entail good health and contentment. Mothers expected their daughters to benefit from life in a brighter future either through education and jobs or at least indirectly through their husbands and, later, their sons. Realistically, chances for the quick attainment of this improved life were scant for most villagers and especially for women. But nostalgic moments and anxieties about the future notwithstanding, there was no looking back when it came to women's wishes for the future of their daughters. Despite all hardships, the success of some women inspired hope in many others. Besides, hardships had always been part of women's own gender philosophy and thus of women's reality of life. It informed their memories of the past as well as their expectations for the future.

NOTES

1. For western Iran, see Merian Cooper and Ernest Schoedsack, *Grass* (film), Paramount Pictures, 1925; Arthur Christensen, *Persische Märchen* (Düsseldorf-Köln: Eugen Diederichs Verlag, 1958); Erika Friedl, "Women in Contemporary Persian Folktales," in *Women in the Muslim World,* ed. Lois Beck and Nikki Keddie (Cambridge: Harvard University Press, 1978), 629–50; Erika Friedl, "The Meaning of Life in Boir Ahmad Folksongs," unpublished paper; Manuchehr Lam'e, *Farhang-e ami-ane-ye asha'ir-e Boir Ahmadi va Kohgiluye* (Tehran: n.p., 1349/1970); Inge Demant Mortensen, "Women after Death: Aspects of a Study on Iranian Nomadic Cemeter-

ies," in *Women in Islamic Societies,* ed. Bo Utas (New York: Olive Branch Press, 1983), 26–47.

2. See other contributions in this book and its companion volume (*Women in Iran from the Rise of Islam to 1800,* ed. Guity Nashat and Lois Beck [Urbana: University of Illinois Press, 2003]) and also Janet Afary, "The Debate on Women's Liberation in the Iranian Constitutional Revolution, 1906–1911," in *Expanding the Boundaries of Women's History,* ed. Cheryl Johnson-Odim and Margaret Strobel (Bloomington: Indiana University Press, 1992); Mahnaz Afkhami, "Women in Post-Revolutionary Iran: A Feminist Perspective," in *In the Eye of the Storm: Women in Post-Revolutionary Iran,* ed. Mahnaz Afkhami and Erika Friedl (London: I. B. Tauris, 1994); Haleh Afshar, "The Emancipation Struggles in Iran: Past Experiences and Future Hopes," in *Women, Development, and Survival in the Third World,* ed. Haleh Afshar (London: Longman, 1991), 11–21; Janet Bauer, "Poor Women and Social Consciousness in Revolutionary Iran," in *Women and Revolution in Iran,* ed. Guity Nashat (Boulder: Westview, 1983); Valentine Moghadam, *Modernizing Women: Gender and Social Change in the Middle East* (Boulder: Lynne Rienner, 1993), 171–206; Hamideh Sedghi and Ahmad Ashraf, "The Role of Women in Iranian Development," in *Iran: Past, Present and Future,* ed. Jane Jacqz (New York: Aspen Institute for Humanistic Studies, 1976), 201–10.

3. For western Iran, see Lois Beck, *Nomad: A Year in the Life of a Qashqa'i Tribesman in Iran* (Berkeley: University of California Press, 1991); Lois Beck, "Women among Qashqa'i Nomadic Pastoralists in Iran," in *Women in the Muslim World,* ed. Lois Beck and Nikki Keddie (Cambridge: Harvard University Press, 1978), 351–73; Daniel Bradburd, *Ambiguous Relations: Kin, Class, and Conflict among Komachi Pastoralists* (Washington: Smithsonian Institution Press, 1990); Mary Elaine Hegland, "'Traditional' Iranian Women: How They Cope," *Middle East Journal* 36 (4) (1982): 483–501; Soheila Shahshahani, "The Four Seasons of the Sun: An Ethnography of Women of Oyun, A Sedentarized Village of Mamasani Pastoral Nomads of Iran," doctoral dissertation, New School of Social Research, University Microfilm International, 1982; Susan Wright, "Prattle and Politics: The Position of Women in Doshman-Ziari," *Journal of the Anthropological Society of Oxford* 9 (2) (1978): 98–112. Also Nancy Tapper, "The Women's Subsociety among the Shahsevan Nomads of Iran," in *Women in the Muslim World,* ed. Lois Beck and Nikki Keddie (Cambridge: Harvard University Press, 1978), 374–98. Two articles on rural women's recent history are Mary Elaine Hegland, "Political Roles of Aliabad Women: The Public-Private Dichotomy Transcended," in *Women in Middle Eastern History,* ed. Nikki Keddie and Beth Baron (New Haven: Yale University Press, 1991), 215–30; Erika Friedl, "The Dynamics of Women's Spheres of Action in Rural Iran," in *Women in Middle Eastern History,* 195–214; and Erika Friedl, "Tribal Enterprises and Marriage Issues in Twentieth-Century Iran," in *Family History in the Middle East: Household, Property, and Gender,* ed. Beshara Doumani (Albany: State University of New York Press, 2003), 151–70.

4. Growing documentation and discussion of this process exist. See Haleh Afshar, ed., *Women, Development, and Survival in the Third World* (London: Longman, 1991); Ester Boserup, *Women's Role in Economic Development* (New York: St. Martin's, 1970); Ruth B. Dixon, *Rural Women at Work* (Baltimore: Johns Hopkins University Press, 1978); Hilda Kahne and Janet Giele, eds., *Women's Lives and Women's Work: The Con-*

tinuing Struggle (Boulder: Westview, 1992); Patricia Maguire, *Women in Development: An Alternative Analysis* (Amherst: University of Massachusetts Press, 1984); Mira Zussman, *Development and Disenchantment in Rural Tunisia* (Boulder: Westview, 1992).

5. For the range of women's work, see Erika Friedl, "Women and Division of Labor in an Iranian Village," *MERIP Reports* 11 (3) (1981): 12–18; Hegland, "Political Roles"; see also Maguire, *Women in Development*, 23.

6. Afshar, "Emancipation Struggles"; Rae Lesser Blumberg, *Stratification: Socioeconomic and Sexual Inequality* (Dubuque, Iowa: William Brown, 1978); Barbara Rogers, *The Domestication of Women* (New York: St. Martin's, 1979).

7. For example, see Fatemeh Moghadam, "Commoditization of Sexuality and Female Labor Participation in Islam: Implications for Iran, 1960–90," in *In the Eye of the Storm*, 80–97.

8. See contributions in *In the Eye of the Storm*; Hisae Nakanishi, "Power, Ideology, and Women's Consciousness in Postrevolutionary Iran," in *Women in Muslim Societies*, ed. Herbert Bodman and Nayereh Tohidi (Boulder: Lynne Rienner, 1998), 83–100; Nikki Keddie, *Iran and the Muslim World* (New York: New York University Press, 1995).

9. The research on which this chapter is based was conducted at various times between 1965 and 2000 for a total of nearly seven years. I am grateful to all funding agencies who have made different stages of my research possible: the Social Science Research Council, the Wenner-Gren Foundation for Anthropological Research, the National Endowment for the Humanities, the University of Chicago, and Western Michigan University.

10. For this type of remembering apropos of something else, see Friedl, "Dynamics of Women's Spheres," 142–59.

11. Descriptions are found in Beck, *Nomad;* Jacob Black-Michaud, *Sheep and Land* (Cambridge: Cambridge University Press, 1986); Bradburd, *Ambiguous Relations;* C. G. Feilberg, *Les Papis* (Kobenhavn: Nordisk Forlag, 1952); Erika Friedl, *Women of Deh Koh* (New York: Penguin, 1991); Carol Kramer, "An Archaeological View of a Contemporary Kurdish Village: Domestic Architecture, Household Size, and Wealth," in *Ethnoarchaeology,* ed. Carol Kramer (New York: Columbia University Press, 1979); Patty Jo Watson, *Archaeological Ethnography in Western Iran* (Tucson: University of Arizona Press, 1979). For a visual illustration of the pastoral nomadic lifestyle, see the film *Grass*.

12. Linda Jacobs, "Tell-i Nun: Archaeological Implications of a Village in Transition," in *Ethnoarchaeology;* Watson, *Archaeological Ethnography*.

13. In this chapter I use the generic term "chief" to connote leaders in Deh Koh. For problems surrounding tribal leadership, including the attempts of tribal leaders to become landlords after founding Deh Koh, see Reinhold Loeffler, "The Representative Mediator and the New Peasant," *American Anthropologist* (73) (5) (1971): 1077–91.

14. Ibid.; Reinhold Loeffler, *Encyclopaedia Iranica,* s.v. "Boir Ahmadi," 320–25.

15. To some extent, especially since the 1978–79 revolution, a fear of stranger-rapists has replaced the earlier type of fear. It is manipulated to keep women, especially young ones, from venturing out alone. Fears of rape and attack are used by some men,

women, and government agents to add the weight of reason to restrictive demands in the name of propriety. No doubt the same reasoning—avoidance of danger—kept women stationary in the past too. In the early 2000s, hiking became fashionable, and groups of mountain climbers attracted young local women. The gathering of wild fruits and vegetables was popular again among women and some men as an activity that combined usefulness and leisure, although security was no better than it was twenty years previously.

16. Where women have to draw water from a reservoir, river, or irrigation channel, they may spend several hours a day fetching water. Such water is used sparingly, especially for washing. Walter Koelz comments on the "dirty" appearance of Lur people; *Persian Diary, 1939–1941* (Ann Arbor: University of Michigan Press, 1983), 86. Drawing on their own experience, Deh Koh women pity people who do not have enough water to keep comfortably clean and to perform the ablutions required by Islam.

17. Eventually the new village also provided more space and bigger, warmer, and better-built houses. See Erika Friedl and Agnes Loeffler, "The Ups and Downs of Dwellings in a Village in West Iran: The History of Two Compounds," *Archiv für Völkerkunde* 48 (1994): 1–44.

18. A family's sheep, goats, cows, and chickens were slaughtered only for a guest or a feast or if injured or sick. Women were in charge of poultry, but the chicken population did not even keep up with the demand for eggs, let alone for meat. Most meat consumed was bought from a butcher. Chickens from farm enterprises were bought in food stores.

19. See Akbar Aghajanian, "The Status of Women and Female Children in Iran: An Update from the 1986 Census," in *In the Eye of the Storm,* 44–60. His research was based in part on detailed work in the city of Shiraz.

20. Reinhold Loeffler, Erika Friedl, and Alfred Janata, "Die Materielle Kultur von Boir Ahmad, Südiran," *Archiv für Völkerkunde* 28 (1974): 69.

21. Erika Friedl, "Dynamics of Women's Spheres," 201. After the revolution of 1978–79, when the economic situation in Deh Koh deteriorated, some women took to the oak woods again to augment their larder with acorn meal.

22. See Frank Hole, *The Archaeology of Western Iran: Settlement and Society from Prehistory to the Islamic Conquest* (Washington: Smithsonian Institution Press, 1987); Henry Wright, *Archaeological Investigations in Northeastern Xuzestan, 1976* (Ann Arbor: University of Michigan, Museum of Anthropology, 1979). For a description of the wealth of edible plants and wildlife in the area until the 1940s, see Koelz, *Persian Diary.*

23. Manual wage work "for others" in contrast to "for my family" was easily considered a sign that a woman and her children were not taken care of properly by their menfolk. It was a negative social comment on the whole family. See Hegland, "Political Roles," 224, 230, about another village in Iran; and Zussman, *Development,* 152, about Tunisian women.

24. Some women cared for a cow or two and/or some goats and a few chickens. They sold milk, yogurt, butter, and eggs locally. Most retained control of the money, little as it was, and spent it mostly on household necessities.

25. For a discussion of childhood and children in Deh Koh, see Erika Friedl, *Children of Deh Koh* (Syracuse: Syracuse University Press, 1997).

26. Erika Friedl, "Moonrose, Watched through a Sunny Day," *Natural History* 101 (8) (1992): 34–45.

27. So-called benign neglect of female infants and children was widespread in Iran and led to gender imbalances in favor of males at all ages and to gender scripts that devalued women's work and well-being. This situation was especially apparent in rural areas and among the poor. See Aghajanian, "Status of Women."

28. According to Islamic law, it is permissible to give a girl in marriage when she reaches nine years of age. Until recently, chronological age was often not even known and in any case much less important for determining the "right" age for marriage than were signs of "maturity" as measured in physical strength, skills, and responsibility in work habits.

Qashqa'i Women in Postrevolutionary Iran

LOIS BECK

> On the following morning I discovered that here . . . were domiciled
> multitudes of tribesmen on their way to their summer quarters. On the
> road, which wound through beautiful grassy valleys bedecked with sweet
> spring flowers, we met many more, all bound for the highland pastures
> which we were leaving behind us, and a pretty sight it was to see them
> pass; stalwart, hardy-looking men, with dark, weather-beaten faces; lithe,
> graceful boys clothed in skins; and tall, active women with resolute faces,
> not devoid of a comeliness which no veil concealed. They were accom-
> panied by droves of donkeys bearing their effects, and flocks of sheep
> and goats, which paused here and there to nibble the fresh grass.
>
> —E. G. Browne, traveling from Isfahan to Shiraz in the spring of 1888

IN THIS CHAPTER I examine four topics (politics, economics, social change, and Islam and culture) as they each pertain to the ways that Qashqa'i wom-en—as nomadic pastoralists, villagers, and town residents; as members of a tribally organized society; and as part of a politicized, national, ethnic mi-nority—responded to the establishment of the Islamic Republic of Iran in 1979. The discussion here differs from that usually presented about "women in Iran" because other authors usually consider only urban, middle- and up-per-class Persian women. The locations in and circumstances under which Qashqa'i women lived, their tribal and ethnic-minority identities, and their notions of political autonomy and economic self-reliance help to explain how and why they carved out a unique position for themselves in Iran after 1979.

Most published accounts of women in Iran after the revolution in 1978–79 pertain to urban Persian women of the middle and upper classes, usually residents of Tehran. Most of them were formally educated and expressed attitudes and demonstrated behaviors reflecting Western orientations. These were also the women about whom many Iranians abroad and many non-Iranian writers expressed concern, and the issues they raise relate largely to them: restrictive dress codes (oddly enough, still the primary issue for many

Qashqa'i women and children at a wedding. Photo by Lois Beck.

people, despite more debilitating problems), higher education, professional training, salaried work outside the home, discrimination in the law, constraints on social life (including entertainment and sports), and freedom to travel abroad.

Before the revolution, most anthropologists focused on detailed, local-level studies of tribal, rural, and lower-class urban women. Both before and after the revolution, political scientists, sociologists, and historians whose methodologies differ fundamentally from those of anthropologists conducted another kind of research. They stressed the effects on and implications for women of state laws and policies and the ruling elite's attitudes. Such laws and policies, and the attitudes underlying them, assume a universal application for the country as a whole, but the category of women most aware of and influenced by them were middle- and upper-class urban residents.[1]

The majority of women in Iran have not been, and were not in the early 2000s, urban Persians of the middle and upper classes, and few writers have yet discussed their circumstances after the revolution.[2] Until the early 1980s, at least half of Iran's people lived in rural areas,[3] and many urban Iranians were recent migrants from there and often experienced conditions that replicated rural life to some extent. Lower-income households and neighborhoods in Tehran and other cities differed from those in middle- and upper-class areas, and the lives of women varied accordingly.

Further, the majority of women in Iran are not ethnolinguistically identified as Persians. Half of all Iranians are Persians, people whose first language
is Persian and whose primary identity is with a broadly defined notion of
Persian culture. (Persian is the official language in Iran.) The other half are
not Persians; they do not speak Persian as a first language, and their primary identity is with other cultures and ethnolinguistic groups. They include
Azeri Turks, Kurds, Baluch, Lurs, Bakhtiyari, Qashqa'i, Turkmans, Arabs, and
many others (perhaps including many Gilakis and Mazandaranis).[4] Some
Iranians are tribally organized; their primary sociopolitical and sociocultural
ties are not to the nation-state or its dominating political groups but to their
own extended lineages, subtribes, tribes, and tribal confederacies. Almost all
of these tribal people are not Persians; they include Baluch, Lurs, Bakhtiyari,
Qashqa'i, Turkmans, many Kurds and Arabs, some Turks (excluding the nontribal Azeri Turks), and others. Shi'i Muslims constitute approximately 93
percent of Iran's population, Sunni Muslims 5 percent, and Christians,
Baha'is, Zoroastrians, Jews, and others 2 percent. While some members of
these religious minorities consider themselves Persians as their primary identity, others consider their primary identity as Armenians, Assyrians,
Chaldeans, Jews, Sunni Arabs, Sunni Kurds, and so forth.[5]

Most published studies, even otherwise excellent analytical writings, gen-
eralize for all women in Iran after the revolution without including these and
many other critical distinctions. Few of them address the complex socioeconomic, cultural, ethnic, linguistic, tribal, religious, and regional diversity there
or explain how attributes of this diversity relate to and affect gender.[6] State
laws and policies as they affect urban, middle-class, and upper-class Persian
society—the explicit or implicit subject matter of almost all writings on
women—do not adequately or necessarily explain the situation for other
women in Iran.

Background on the Qashqa'i

I offer here one example of such diversity. I discuss Qashqa'i women in terms
of their own society as well as in the context of the wider Iranian society. I
consider only non-elite women unless I note otherwise. The socioeconomic
and political situation of elite Qashqa'i women, women in families of the
tribal khans (leaders), is different from that of the vast majority of Qashqa'i
women who live as nomads and villagers. By necessity and for contrast and

comparison, I also include information about Qashqa'i men because women do not live isolated or in all-female groups but rather form an intrinsic part of a larger community. Many studies on Iran (and other parts of the world) neglect to place women in the contexts where they actually live and to account for the impact of such contexts on their lives.

This chapter is based on my anthropological research among the Qashqa'i in Iran in 1979, 1991, 1992, 1995 (two separate trips), 1996, 1997, 1998, 1999, 2000–2001, and 2001–2. It also benefits from my earlier research there in 1969–71 and 1977 (two separate trips). During the eleven visits since the revolution in 1978–79, I resided with members of one of the many Qashqa'i subtribes in their winter and summer pastures, and I also traveled widely in Qashqa'i territory and interviewed many other Qashqa'i in seasonal camps, villages and towns, and Shiraz, Isfahan, and Tehran. My general remarks about the Qashqa'i reflect these broad contacts, and yet I also comment about specific individuals, families, and small groups (whose names I do not include here, not for reasons of anonymity, but because of the chapter's scope).[7]

The Qashqa'i are members of a tribal confederacy of more than 800,000 people (2003), most of whom live dispersed throughout the mountainous areas of southwestern Iran. Their paramount political leaders played important roles in nineteenth- and especially twentieth-century Iranian politics. The Qashqa'i speak a Central-Asian-derived Turkish language, are Shi'i Muslims, and are one of Iran's many ethnic and national minorities. The low-altitude winter pastures and the high-altitude summer pastures of Qashqa'i nomadic pastoralists are separated by hundreds of kilometers across the southern Zagros mountains, and the migrations of spring and autumn each last from one to three months. Some Qashqa'i reside part-time or full-time in villages in or near Qashqa'i territory and often combine agriculture with pastoralism. Some live in towns and in Shiraz, Isfahan, and other cities where men and some women engage in wage or salaried work. No necessary diminution of Qashqa'i cultural and tribal identity occurs when people adopt more permanent residences and new livelihoods and lifestyles. In fact, many of them develop a heightened sense of themselves as Qashqa'i, in part because of their increased awareness of cultural differences and their greater contact with others. People in local (residential), kinship, and tribal groups are closely intermarried. Marriage outside these groups, especially for women, is rare.

The Qashqa'i share some broad political, economic, social, and cultural patterns with other groups of tribally organized nomadic pastoralists and former nomadic pastoralists in Iran, particularly other Turkic groups such

Qashqa'i bride on the spring migration. Qashqa'i women do not cover their faces, but this woman was temporarily guarding her mouth and nose from the dust. Photo by Lois Beck.

as the Shahsevan and Turkmans. Varying geographical, ecological, and historical circumstances help to account for their differences.[8]

Information in the rest of this chapter is presented in the past tense because of the ongoing nature of change. After a brief statement about recent history, I examine four topics as they each pertain to Qashqa'i women: politics, economics, social change, and Islam and culture. Implicitly and explicitly I compare their roles and statuses with those of other Iranian women and attempt to explain differences and similarities.

Mohammad Reza Shah's attempts to modernize Iran in the 1950s, 1960s, and 1970s affected Qashqa'i society in different ways.[9] His programs for land reform and the nationalization of pastures undermined nomadic pastoralism, and government-subsidized prices for meat and dairy products undercut the Qashqa'i economy. Like many other rural Iranians during this period, most Qashqa'i lacked access to modern services and infrastructural improvements. Some boys and girls did receive formal, elementary education under an innovative program for nomads begun in 1953. Some aspects of Qashqa'i society and culture (including family structure, gender roles and attitudes, kinship and tribal organization, customs, and beliefs) were not much affected by changes in government policy during these three decades, and most women's roles and activities were similar to what they had been in previous decades. Extended families, kinship groups, the tribal system, and the relative remoteness and isolation of most Qashqa'i territories served to insulate and protect women from many outside incursions and influences. To a lesser degree, men were also protected in this way. Other than some urban residents, few Qashqa'i women played any direct role in revolutionary activities in 1978 and 1979.

The interrelated effects of the revolution, the Islamic Republic's formation in 1979, the devastating war with Iraq (1980–88), and national economic problems help to explain circumstances for the Qashqa'i in the 1980s, 1990s, and early 2000s. Many carry-over effects from the sometimes-repressive regimes of Reza Shah (1925–41) and especially Mohammad Reza Shah (1941–79) are also explanatory factors. The Qashqa'i perceived most changes occurring in Iran from 1978 through the early 1980s as political in nature, as a political revolt followed by a change in state leaders. They did not explain them in simplistic terms relating to Islam, unlike some Western accounts. They also downplayed the so-called revolutionary aspects of these changes, because, from their perspective, life as members of a minority group under any kind of central government held many common features such as alternating patterns of oppression and neglect. For them initially, the new government meant not much more than state rule passing from one segment of urban, Persian, Shi'i Muslim society to another. Most Qashqa'i were as alienated from the shah's Pahlavi regime as from the emerging Islamic one; they viewed the first as corrupt and abusive of power, the second as rigidly ideological with negative political, social, and cultural ramifications. They had benefited little from the shah's modernizing policies; they did not expect to prosper under the rule of hard-line conservative clergymen.[10] (Later they saw that they would benefit by new state policies favoring nomads and other sectors of Iranian society considered to have been "deprived" and exploited by the Pahlavi shahs. Some government officials viewed them as part of "the oppressed," the *mustaz'afin*.) In their two-hundred-year history as a tribal confederacy, the Qashqa'i experienced many changes in state rule, and they viewed the most recent one as one in a long succession. Their tribal system—its institutions, groups, leaders, customs, ideologies, moral codes, and symbols—responded to the wider instability and provided people with the means to maintain some degree of autonomy, defend their own interests, and cope with and adapt to changing political conditions.

Politics

The Islamic Republic soon brought about political changes for the Qashqa'i at the confederacy and local levels, which affected men and women differently. In the early 1980s, new state rulers tried to eliminate the top and secondary levels of the Qashqa'i confederacy's political hierarchy: the *ilkhani* (paramount khan) and other members of the leading Janikhani lineage at the top and khans of the component Qashqa'i tribes beneath them. Through political edicts and manipulation of the media, the government discredited the Qashqa'i tribal khans because of their supposedly feudal practices and their ties with the paramount Qashqa'i khan and the defensive resistance he led in 1980–82 against the state's military attacks. Using political and military sanctions, the government forced the virtual elimination of the khans as the mediators for the tribespeople. Some young Qashqa'i men, many formally educated, also opposed the khans' leadership and influenced opinions within their local communities. Some of them also disapproved of the new government. Popular sentiment throughout Iran inveighed against the former national political elite, which included some Qashqa'i khans.

At the local level—the nomadic camps, seasonal pastures, villages, and towns—some non-elite Qashqa'i men who had exercised power and authority before 1979 retained their positions by adapting customary patterns of leadership to the new situation, while others were replaced by Qashqa'i men who quickly allied with the new government.

Most Qashqa'i women played a relatively minor role in the new alignments of local political forces. Those who did create a role did so initially as the kinswomen of politically active men. People at the local, lineage, and subtribal levels intermarried, and, as in the past, women—representing both their natal and affinal families—mediated between political factions. Some gained stature in the process. Women tended not to be split by the political divisions found among some men, and many often independently expressed their own opinions. People did not necessarily identify them based on the political affiliations and sentiments of their fathers, brothers, husbands, and older sons. These men's political interests sometimes differed, in part because they belonged to potentially opposing kinship and residential groups. While some men within local and larger groups engaged in political disagreements, women rarely did so and in fact often mediated between disputing men by deploying their multiple connections in various kinship and residential groups.

After the revolution, a small minority of young Qashqa'i men became *hezbollahis,* following a trend throughout Iran. Perceived to be the Islamic Republic's staunch supporters, these "partisans of the party of God" marked this affiliation by expressing religious piety and a solemn public demeanor, dressing conservatively, wearing a beard, and trying to impose changes in people's behavior. No Qashqa'i women I met or heard about defined themselves as hezbollahis or were considered by others to be so (unless in joking). ("With your headscarf worn down across your forehead like that [and hiding your hair], you could practically be a hezbollahi," someone would jest.) The label was applied to women, in a minority of cases, only in their roles as the mothers, wives, and daughters of hezbollahis, largely because these men insisted on certain behavior and attire from women tied closely to them. Women married to hezbollahis, for example, did not dance at weddings or wear customary Qashqa'i headgear, despite many of them desiring to do so. A village woman who held no special status before 1979, but whose husband became a determined hezbollahi, acquired some local political stature—but not necessarily respect—because of her ties with him and influenced local decision making. People sometimes approached her, rather than him, on issues concerning changes in state bureaucracy or links with local government officials and hoped that she would relay their queries to him. Some hezbollahis were government-paid revolutionary guards (*pasdars*) who exercised power and caused apprehension in the wider Iranian society. While some Qashqa'i women married to hezbollahis and revolutionary guards seemed to exploit their husbands' positions for their own social and economic benefit, many others distanced themselves from, or did not concern themselves with, their husbands' political stances. To my knowledge, no Qashqa'i women were employed as revolutionary guards. By 1995 men formerly identified as hezbollahis had lost most of the power they had earlier exerted within Qashqa'i communities, and some no longer demonstrated hezbollahi traits. Hardly any younger men, those born just before or after the revolution, chose to adopt the hezbollahi role and identity. Hezbollahis no longer existed in many local groups, unlike during the 1980s.

Placing a heavy personal burden on virtually all Qashqa'i women and having mixed social and economic repercussions, the eight-year Iran-Iraq war was the most significant political event affecting them after the revolution.[11] Female kin of the war's many conscripts, volunteers, and casualties suffered emotional pain and economic hardship because of their kinsmen's absence and loss. Members of kinship and tribal groups—especially those people being drawn away by new livelihoods and lifestyles (see below)—came together in grief and as an expression of solidarity. The war's calamitous impact demonstrated the importance of renewing and strengthening their own kinship and tribal ties; they saw how quickly they had been swept up in and harmed by a national disaster that was not of their own making. A woman whose son was captured and held as a prisoner of war by Iraq for eight years received frequent visitors who hoped to assuage her grief and calm her uncertainties. From these visits, she emerged as an influential figure associating with many people and disseminating information and advice through her widening networks. The mothers of those considered as "martyrs" (*shahids*), men killed in or because of the war, gained respect and a special social status in the community and especially the wider Iranian society where many people valued martyrdom. Condolence visits of relatives and acquaintances drew attention to them and their families and reconfirmed wider kinship and tribal ties. The martyrs' parents, wives, and children received death benefits, monthly stipends, and other special state privileges and used the new income to buy land and vehicles and increase investments in agricultural production, formal education, and occupational training. A few Qashqa'i women who were university students served near the war front as auxiliary personnel, but to my knowledge none were martyred there.[12]

Some Qashqa'i women voted in national parliamentary and other elections in 1979 and 1980 but soon became disillusioned when hard-line conservatives expelled from parliament their most prominent and successful candidate, a Qashqa'i khan, and later executed him. Some women remarked that they might as well have been denied the right to vote. Fewer numbers of them were said to have voted in subsequent national elections, for which many expressed little interest. In 1996, when at least ten non-elite Qashqa'i men ran for parliamentary seats against non-Qashqa'i candidates, many Qashqa'i women participated again in the national political process by voting in the primary and runoff elections, sometimes traveling quite a distance to cast their votes. Five of the ten Qashqa'i candidates won four-year terms, the second time in history that any non-elite Qashqa'i individuals had been elected to national office. Several of these elections were quite close, and some women, attributing the success of the Qashqa'i candidates to their own votes, stated that men's votes alone would never have elected these men. Non-Qashqa'i women were apparently not as mobilized as Qashqa'i women to vote for their own candidates in these contests, which were marked by explicit ethnic and linguistic distinctions. Many Qashqa'i commented that they hoped that parliamentary representation would benefit their community, and their expectations were partly fulfilled in the legislative successes of the five electees. All Qashqa'i women and men with whom I spoke noted that they had voted in 1997 and again in 2001 for Mohammad Khatami, the moderate (and winning) candidate, as Iran's president.

Soon after its inception, the Islamic Republic adopted a policy of hiring formally educated tribal people (Qashqa'i and others) to dispense services to their own and other tribal groups. Under the last shah's regime, almost all state agents with whom the Qashqa'i came into contact were superior-acting urban Persians who were said to be corrupt. The new policy brought to camps and villages men of tribal background who were sympathetic and responsive to nomads' and villagers' needs. They interacted comfortably with Qashqa'i women, who previously had avoided and been suspicious of Persian agents. As a result, these women sought and received beneficial state services more directly than before.

Economics

Qashqa'i women of all economic levels actively participated in the work of their households (which entailed much more than chores relating to the home), and hence any local and wider economic changes affected them directly. After the revolution, rapidly rising inflation took its toll on them, as it did on many Iranians, but in some ways these women also benefited from a changing market economy that increasingly valued the essential commodities they and their households produced, including meat, dairy products, fruit, wool, yarn, and woven carpets and blankets. More self-sufficient economically than many other rural and especially urban people, they consumed their own products, traded such products for others locally available, relied on gathering and hunting, constructed necessary items from locally available resources, and hence relied less on the market economy and could often avoid its inflationary prices.

As part of a policy to assist "deprived" sectors of Iranian society, the Islamic Republic's ministries and agencies brought services to nomads and to a lesser extent villagers, often through the efforts of formally educated, state-employed tribal people. The Organization for Nomads' Affairs, staffed by tribal men and part of the new Ministry of Rural Reconstruction (Jihad-e sazandegi), was the main vehicle for these services.[13] General modernization from the 1980s through the early 2000s, not always directed by the new government's specific policies, also affected nomads and villagers. Both sets of changes included projects the shah's regime could also have implemented

Qashqa'i mother and daughter churning butter in front of their tent. Photo by
Lois Beck.

(especially because of oil revenue and readily available foreign technical assistance) but had refused to do, and some of them addressed problems caused
by that regime.

The new government initiated the construction of new and improved
roads (especially in remote areas), additional primary and secondary schools,
and public bathhouses. It facilitated house building through low-interest
bank loans and subsidized construction materials, and it introduced or improved access to water, veterinary and agricultural services, health services,
modern medicine (especially vaccinations, antibiotics, and birth control),
formal education beyond the primary level (including many new universities in towns near tribal territory), occupational training, and subsidized
market commodities. In the 1980s wealthy urban Iranians complained about
the state's rationing of basic commodities, but nomads and some villagers
were glad to receive coupons for price-subsidized goods otherwise expensive
at open- or black-market prices. All these changes directly and immediately
improved the quality of women's work, health, and well-being. Life, as many
women stated, was more comfortable now than before, and some credited
the new government and its reliance on tribal people as state agents.

Under the shah, many nomads had lost or were losing control of their pastoral and agricultural land and were forced to settle in villages and assume new livelihoods, in their view demeaning, as low-paid agricultural and other wage laborers at the bottom of the nation's socioeconomic hierarchy. In contrast, the new government permitted nomads through land leases and purchases to cultivate crops and plant orchards on or adjacent to their pasturelands, a practice previously forbidden or restricted by the shah's regime. In this way, nomads could diversify their economies according to their own choices and meet new market demands, while at the same time remaining nomadic and residing (seasonally) on their cherished tribal lands. They could continue to migrate seasonally with their sheep and goats and yet increase their reliance on agriculture without jeopardizing their use of land in either winter or summer areas. The new government also allowed nomads to build houses in their seasonal pastures, another activity prohibited or restricted by the shah's agents. Many nomads continued to pitch their black goat-hair tents nearby and used their new, often small and rudimentary, houses and huts for storage and for residence during inclement weather. Provincial officials of the Ministries of Agriculture and Rural Reconstruction (merged into one ministry in 2000) facilitated the nomads' efforts to secure legal land deeds and grazing permits, a process often prevented or impeded by the shah's regime. In the 1990s and early 2000s, many nomads exerted greater control over the land on which they depended than they had in the 1960s and 1970s.

The arduous work of nomadic pastoralism decreased for women in the 1980s, 1990s, and early 2000s. Many were glad to live in houses, even simple huts, instead of tents during harsh weather. In many locations where water was scarce, the new government donated water tanks, built reservoirs, and regularly filled them for nomads, and many women no longer needed to spend hours every day traveling with pack animals to and from distant springs and wells. Although women who now migrated by truck said they missed not being able to gather wild plants and other natural resources along the migratory routes (for use as essential foods, medicines, and dyes), they did appreciate the decreased labor. A more equitable division of labor resulted when men used machines to perform work that men and women formerly did manually, sometimes assisted by pack and draft animals, such as migrating, transporting goods, cultivating, harvesting, and hauling fuel and water. Women tended fewer such animals. Many now used propane gas for lanterns and some cooking, thereby decreasing the wood, brush, and dung they gathered for fuel. Men produced and purchased more food, particularly fruits and vegetables, and diet was substantially improved for all family members. Women used commercial soaps to assist in laundry and other washing. Inexpensive plastic containers of all sorts lightened their chores. Men built new or more substantial pens to shelter and protect the sheep and goats and constructed barriers to hold the ewes and does for milking, both easing women's tasks.[14]

Qashqa'i women increased their economic production after the revolution, primarily because their goods had become scarce in the market economy, held high value, and brought in needed income. Meat and dairy prices rose rapidly in Iran, and nomads and villagers received a share of the increase.[15] Before 1979 many women had woven primarily to meet domestic and social needs, but after the revolution they increasingly wove for the commercial market because of rising prices there, new family demands for cash income, and more time. Freed from months of migrating and from some other chores they used to perform, they now had more time available for weaving, a process they controlled and enjoyed.[16] Because of government restrictions on the export of Iranian hand-knotted pile carpets in the 1980s and 1990s and the resulting fluctuations in prices, Qashqa'i women wove fewer carpets for sale and instead produced other items for the market, including gelims and other blankets, prayer mats, cushion covers, and fabric for urban women's purses, some of which they had not constructed for themselves in the past. They did continue to weave knotted pile carpets for their own family's use, for dowries and gifts, and for local market sale where demand was still great. Many Iranians in villages, towns, and cities outfitted their homes with knotted pile carpets, often their most valued possessions. They regarded Qashqa'i carpets with high esteem. Continuing to export carpets abroad illegally, smugglers reported that Qashqa'i ones were particularly appreciated in the Arab states of the Persian Gulf and in Europe.

Differences in levels of wealth decreased among nomads and, to a lesser extent, villagers, a change caused largely by national economic trends and policies and the nomads' diversifying livelihoods, sometimes including more permanent residence and wage and salaried labor. Women in many formerly poor and moderate-income families benefited the most. The state provided stipends to people its agents perceived as economically vulnerable, including widows, fatherless children, the elderly, and families with war casualties. In the 1990s many nomads owned herds of roughly the same size, unlike during the 1960s and 1970s. Most of them now cultivated grain and fodder crops for their own use instead of having to purchase most or all of the supplies they needed, and some planted orchards and sold fruit commercially. In the 1980s fewer of them hired shepherds, unlike past decades, and those who sold their camels and adopted vehicular transport no longer needed to hire camel herders. Many of the poor—the former shepherds and camel herders—found better-paying jobs as agriculturalists and wage laborers, and some became viable herd owners themselves. In the 1990s and early 2000s many families were again hiring shepherds because their increasingly diversifying economies meant shortages in household labor, a situation exacerbated by more of their children attending school, continuing beyond the primary level, and seeking employment in the larger society. Willing to work for low wages, many new shepherds including Afghan refugees of nomadic, tribal backgrounds were not Qashqa'i.

Social Change

Patterns of gender segregation found in much of the wider Iranian society—both before and especially after the revolution—were noticeably absent in Qashqa'i society, especially for nomads. Nomadic pastoralism required intensive, interrelated labor from all family members, women included. Men and women moved freely in and around their open tents and open camps. Remarking that they exercised little or no choice in the matter after the revolution, Qashqa'i villagers and especially town residents adopted some patterns of segregation found in their locales. A new form of gender separation among the nomads appeared only during large funeral and memorial gatherings for which people pitched separate reception tents for men and women. They explained these new practices by their obligations to accommodate nontribal outsiders who might attend these events and expect segregated seating. Men and women, however, moved between these tents to welcome attendees, receive condolences, and provide hospitality. Smaller gatherings where outsiders were unlikely were not segregated. For villagers holding funeral and memorial services in local mosques, either men attended alone or men and women sat separately.

Qashqa'i women had never been secluded or much restricted in movement, and after the revolution they were more mobile than before because of new roads, more motorized vehicles, expanded patterns of visiting caused by the dispersal of their wider kin groups throughout and beyond Qashqa'i territory, and increased reliance on markets and modern medicine available only in towns and cities. Women had always visited the many tents and camps in their large seasonal pastures, and they now also traveled by vehicle beyond these territories. Many tribal weddings, funerals, and memorials drew hundreds of women from all over Qashqa'i territory and its environs. They traveled with male kin, not necessarily just their fathers, brothers, husbands, or older sons—women's customary guardians in much of Iran.

The expansion of formal education affected many Qashqa'i women. In the 1960s and 1970s, a small percentage (0–20) of nomadic girls attended the tribal tent schools that moved seasonally between winter and summer pastures. In the 1990s a much larger percentage (60–80+) was in school. In several large tribal groups with which I am well acquainted, all girls of primary-school age attended school in the 1990s and early 2000s, and many schools I visited held equal numbers of girls and boys. Tribal schools were coeducational, unlike urban and many village schools. Some nomadic girls, a minority of female students, continued their education in town schools after completing the five elementary grades offered by tribal schools. According to parents, housing for daughters studying away from home was the main obstacle. They preferred the girls to stay with relatives if possible. Girls' dormitories were available in some towns. Some female students attended high-standard, tribal, boarding, middle and high schools in towns and in Shiraz and, until it closed in 1982, a tribal teacher-training facility in Shiraz. (Beginning in 1982, the government created or expanded many other teacher-training programs in the region for both women and men.) A woman in one Qashqa'i group was a government-paid schoolteacher, the only woman there in 1991 who received wages for work performed outside the home. In 1996 several of her cousins, young women who graduated from town high schools and passed qualifying examinations, attended university, and by 2001 they had earned degrees and located salaried jobs. Unprecedented, another female relative began study in an urban religious seminary. Beyond becoming teachers, office workers, nurses, and midwives, most young women found few other practical applications for their years of formal study, but they were encouraged by the opportunities newly open to them. They also served as role models for younger girls in their determination to continue schooling despite difficulties, and they noted that they would assist in their own children's education.

Another social change for Qashqa'i women was the rising age for marriage. Some girls used to marry soon after puberty, usually to boys several years older, and the rest married shortly thereafter. In the 1990s and early 2000s, many women in their late teens, early twenties, and even middle to late twenties were not yet married. Mothers stressed certain advantages in keeping their daughters at home longer or even permanently. Girls were marrying later or not at all because of many factors, including the following: changing family and household demographic and economic patterns, time needed for formal education beyond primary school and for occupa-

Qashqa'i girls and boys in elementary school. Photo by Lois Beck.

tional training, paying jobs away from home, rising expectations for suitable husbands, a sex-ratio imbalance, their personal choice to delay or avoid marriage, and the reluctance of parents to part with them (partly because of their economic role, especially in weaving).

Increasing opportunities for young men in formal education, job training, and wage and salaried labor in locations beyond their camps and villages caused them also to delay marriage (while at the same time enhancing their marital prospects). Their now-obligatory, two-year national military service was another factor.[17] The many young men who were killed, injured, or captured and held as prisoners in the eight-year Iran-Iraq war created a shortage of men and temporarily altered marriage patterns. The death of each one meant a year or more of mourning during which his family, kin group, and others postponed weddings out of grief and respect.

The greater likelihood that men, not women, would marry outside their immediate kin, tribal, and local groups created a sex-ratio imbalance that left some women without prospects for marriage. Because of preferred patterns of patrilocal residence after marriage, parents kept sons nearby regardless of the bride's origin. By contrast, parents suffered the devastating and usually permanent loss of daughters who married outside kin, tribal, and local groups.

Parents often scheduled weddings for their daughters and sons close to-gether in order to address anticipated changes in their household's labor force. When a daughter married, she (and her labor) left home; when a son married, his wife (and her labor) were added to his parents' household. When one marriage was delayed, often so was the other. One father said he post-poned his daughter's marriage because he needed her assistance during her brother's wedding celebration, which he and his wife hosted for hundreds of guests.

Many people complained about the rising costs of weddings owing to inflation and escalating notions about expected goods and services. Most weddings, even for nomads, now featured many recent innovations includ-ing printed invitations, hired cooks, rented supplies, and chartered transpor-tation. Kinspeople used to contribute the food consumed at weddings, but by the 1990s the groom's family purchased most items from markets. Hav-ing lived for years as a university student in Tehran, one groom insisted on chicken as well as red-meat stew, salad, and carbonated bottled beverages, unprecedented additions to wedding celebrations in his large tribal group. As a result of new economic pressures, families were often forced to postpone weddings until their financial circumstances improved. Although a son's marriage was more expensive than a daughter's because his parents provid-ed economic resources to the bride and her family and financed the celebra-tion, a daughter's marriage required her to assemble an often-expensive dowry. Marriages of daughters and sons were often paired for this reason too; incoming wealth helped to compensate for outgoing wealth and for the cer-emony. The cost of forming new households also rose, thereby delaying marriage further and causing many newly married couples to live with the groom's parents for a longer period than in the past so that they could accu-mulate necessary equipment.[18]

Uncertain political and economic conditions in Iran in the 1980s, espe-cially during the war with Iraq, were also a factor in changing marriage pat-terns and in delaying women's marriage. People postponed major decisions such as marriage until they understood better how national events and cir-cumstances would affect them locally. The war was especially unsettling be-cause parents were unsure about their sons' participation and ultimate fate. Decisions to decrease or increase their efforts in nomadism, house building, agriculture, formal education, job training, and paid labor directly affected plans for the marital alliances families wanted to form. A nomadic family planning to reside part-time in a village weighed the benefits of choosing, for a daughter or son, a spouse from the village (in order to create new ties there) or a spouse from seasonal pastures (in order to maintain access to pastureland and continue the family's contacts with the nomads there). Until the late 1970s, most nomads who were selecting a son-in-law knew that the young man, whoever he was, would be a nomadic pastoralist, but after the revolution rapidly changing politics and the wider range of choices in education and occupation for young men complicated the process of selection. Before making a final decision, parents wanted to know where their daughter would live, how the new family would subsist, and what chores she would have, especially if they differed from those she performed at home. Formerly these issues had often been taken for granted because sons had followed in their fathers' footsteps.

Women, especially those living in villages and towns, often complained about having too many children, and they wanted to learn about and use modern forms of birth control (which both state agencies and private clinics provided free or at low cost). Most nomads said they could support more children but now viewed them in financial terms because of rising costs for food, clothes, healthcare, and education. As nomadic pastoralists, all children performed essential tasks. As village or town residents, extra children were a financial burden and a nuisance, especially in small, crowded houses and during inclement weather.[19]

A nomad woman with ten children commented with some resignation, "I have been breast-feeding without respite for more than twenty years" (twenty-three, in fact). Her eldest child was enrolled in university, another served in the army, and others attended school, herded the family's animals, cultivated, and wove. She noted that her family was currently coping economically, but she did worry about the future and the expense of further formal education, ten weddings, new daughters-in-law, and many grandchildren. She wondered about livelihoods for her six sons, for only two were needed at home to support and eventually replace her husband's labor. For Qashqa'i nomads, the average number of surviving children for couples married at least fifteen years dropped from seven in the early 1970s, to four in the mid-1990s, and to three in 2002. Use of modern forms of birth control facilitated the decrease.[20]

Islam, Politics, and Culture

Sentiments about Qashqa'i cultural, tribal, and national-minority identity deepened with the revolution and the Islamic Republic's formation and intensified during the following twenty-some years. Women were somewhat less involved in this process than men because their contacts with the surrounding Persian-dominated Iranian society were fewer. They did not interrelate with outsiders as regularly and intensively as men did, who experienced a stronger sense of the Qashqa'i as a minority group and were more subjected to political and social discrimination. Yet women's own contacts and mobility had also expanded since the 1970s, and they too were more aware of the Qashqa'i as a distinct group than they were previously. Their own heightened sense of identity after the revolution included the following: preserving their Turkish language in the face of increased Persian and Arabic incursions, retaining customary Qashqa'i dress despite state prohibitions, expanding enthusiasm for Qashqa'i customs (especially music, dance, and rituals), emphasizing styles and designs used in the past for weaving, and perpetuating what they regarded was a Qashqa'i lifestyle (including seasonal migrating, living in the mountains, dwelling in black goat-hair tents, relying on customary technologies and natural resources, and separating themselves from non-Qashqa'i people).[21] Here I examine Qashqa'i culture as people expressed it through attire, religious belief and practice, and ritual and ceremony.[22]

Attire

A potent symbol of Islam and revolutionary change in Iran was women's dress. One way to determine the Islamic Republic's power and influence and the Qashqa'i people's degree of integration in the wider Iranian society is to examine how Qashqa'i women adhered to new national standards of modest Islamic dress. Since the late 1920s, the Pahlavi shahs had prohibited or condemned some features of men's ethnic dress in Iran but not women's.[23] By contrast, the Islamic Republic did not forbid or discourage people from wearing ethnic dress per se unless the attire violated what state officials defined as Islamic values.[24] Still, Qashqa'i women asserted—and were allowed—certain freedoms of dress unavailable to most other Iranian women and for reasons having little or nothing to do with Islam.

Until 1979 most Qashqa'i women and girls had worn a thin diaphanous headscarf pinned loosely under the chin and exposing the hair around the face. After the revolution, state enforcers and supporters—especially non-Qashqa'i members of local revolutionary committees (*komitehs*)—insisted that girls nearing puberty and all women should conceal their hair, in line with what became national law.[25] Many Qashqa'i women and girls, especially those in frequent contact with the wider Iranian society, responded in part by donning an opaque scarf to cover much of their hair, often worn in long braids. Now wearing a scarf knotted under the chin like many other women in Iran, they complained that they could no longer don the multicolored silk headband, a distinctive feature of Qashqa'i attire, which they had tied loosely at the back of the head, over the diaphanous scarf, its long ends trailing down the back. The new style of scarf also conflicted with the rest of their customary dress, which consisted of multiple skirts gathered at the waist, a loose tunic slit up the sides to the waist, and a short form-fitting jacket, all in vibrant, often sparkling fabrics and all adorned with sequins, beads, metallic embroidery, and other kinds of trim. "We are Turks [Qashqa'i] only from the neck down. We are Tats from the neck up." (Tat was a deprecatory term that the Qashqa'i used for any Tajik, by which they meant anyone who was not a Turk or who did not follow a Qashqa'i Turkish way of life.)

Qashqa'i women did insist on wearing brightly multicolored, boldly patterned scarves, a choice that many urban women, pressured or forced by state agents to wear somber, solid colors (black, navy blue, dark gray, dark brown), were unable to make for themselves, especially during the first decade of Islamic rule. Qashqa'i women still did not cover the hair around their face, as the government required of urban women during the first decade, nor did they conceal their body in the ways demanded of urban women, even when they went to town. The state compelled urban women to wear an enveloping head-to-toe veil-wrap (chador) or a lengthy loose overcoat and hair-concealing hood or scarf fitting closely around the face. Some institutions such as universities and state agencies (especially in provincial towns) required women to wear a chador over their overcoat and hood or scarf, for travel to and from school and work, and some other women adopted this style when in public. By the mid-1980s most Qashqa'i women donned a chador, usually patterned, when they visited town but did not wrap it fully around their head and body, and it did not cover them or the vibrant clothes they wore underneath, especially the voluminous skirts. Qashqa'i women living in cities commented to me that they admired the freedom of expression these other Qashqa'i women were determined to maintain.[26]

At a state-sponsored Qashqa'i cultural festival in Tehran in 1996, middle-class urban Persian women viewing the clothes of the female Qashqa'i participants and spectators complained bitterly to me about their own restrictive attire. "Why are we forced to be so concealed when these women are so free? Do we have to join a tribe in order to escape the government's harsh clothing regulations?" Using the term "tribe" derogatorily, they grumbled that they could gain freedom only if they demeaned themselves by joining a tribe. (Many urban Iranians viewed tribes as primitive polities threatening their modern society [while others romanticized tribes and their customs].) Apparently, wearing state-mandated modest dress was worse than being a tribal person (not that acquiring such an identity would have been possible). Hearing these women's complaints, a Qashqa'i man angrily proclaimed, "Let these Persians fight for their own rights! We [the Qashqa'i] are living under restrictions because of *them! They* brought us this government, so let *them* figure out a way to change its policy!"

The Islamic state required Qashqa'i girls to wear certain forms of modest attire while attending their tribal elementary schools, and some had little choice but to abandon most or all of the features of customary Qashqa'i dress, at least on schooldays. Their teachers, almost all of them Qashqa'i and the rest members of other tribal groups, exercised some discretion in this matter and could relax the requirements if they so chose. Wearing plain trousers, full-skirted overdresses, overcoats or long jackets, and headscarves, most commonly unadorned in drab, solid colors, some schoolgirls became virtually indistinguishable from non-Qashqa'i village girls. Others adapted Qashqa'i dress to meet the new standards. (Required to wear concealing monochrome uniforms, urban schoolgirls were even more restricted in their style and color of clothing.) Qashqa'i girls did continue to attend tribal schools with boys, however, unlike urban and many village girls. When they completed their formal education, which for some girls meant finishing the fifth grade, many resumed wearing customary Qashqa'i dress full-time, sometimes including the translucent scarf. A Qashqa'i schoolteacher dressed in full compliance with ministerial and provincial regulations, all her body except for her face and hands covered with layers of black cloth. If she had taught in a tribal elementary school in seasonal pastures or in an all-Qashqa'i village, she could have dressed less severely, but she served a large village where other female teachers and her students were not Qashqa'i. At home with her family, she substituted a multicolored patterned scarf for her other head coverings and displayed the hair around her face.

Formerly nomadic, an elderly village woman stopped wearing the full version of customary Qashqa'i dress shortly after the revolution in order to adopt a version of Islamic dress as defined by the state and as stipulated by her many sons who were said to be extremist hezbollahis. Then her daughter's son was killed in the war against Iraq. Full of anguish for this cherished boy, she immediately resumed wearing full Qashqa'i attire. "I wore Islamic dress," she told her family, "but what difference did it make? Did it keep my grandson safe? Now, dressed in black, I mourn." Blaming the government for the boy's death, she withdrew her support, despite entreaties from her sons. Many middle-aged and virtually all elderly women maintained their customary style of clothing including the diaphanous scarf, and the only change they allowed was to darken the colors. Elderly women, often widows, always wore black or other dark, often solid, colors both before and after the revolution.

Qashqa'i women did not attribute their changes in attire to Islam per se but rather to the demands of those who had seized state power. They noted that, during the 1980s, government enforcers, particularly revolutionary guards, had threatened sanctions against their closest kinsmen, including physical coercion and denial of state services, if they did not comply. (State agents rarely administered such punishments; instead they usually issued stern reprimands and threats.) Some women also blamed the inflationary economy for changes in their young daughters' attire because "village" clothes (often loose pants, an overdress, and a headscarf) were cheaper to sew and easier to maintain than Qashqa'i clothing, which required dozens of meters of expensive, often imported, sometimes fragile fabric and decorative trim.

Many Qashqa'i women escaped the state's fluctuating attempts to enforce dress codes in the 1980s, 1990s, and early 2000s because their locations were usually remote and often isolated. For many urban women, a particular appearance—such as visible hair, visible toes, evidence of cosmetics, or revealing or inappropriate attire—that one week provoked assaults by revolutionary guards, hezbollahis, or mobile morals squads might not provoke them the next week. These fluctuations were said to correlate with political struggles in Iran. Often, when the dominance of hard-line conservatives was threatened, urban women were subjected to increased surveillance, coercion, and control.

By the mid-1990s revolutionary guards and other state enforcers focused less on Qashqa'i women's clothing, and women now enjoyed even more freedom in choice of style and color. Attending wedding celebrations, many now dressed in full Qashqa'i attire including the transparent scarf, even if non-Qashqa'i outsiders were present. Thousands of glittering sequins and beads, often arranged in the elaborate designs women also used in weaving, decorated many scarves, a means by which women proclaimed their freedom to reassert their cultural heritage and to feature their fully visible hair, now often worn loose and flowing down their chest and back. Increasingly, Qashqa'i women resumed wearing full Qashqa'i dress on a daily basis, especially while residing in or visiting winter and summer pastures.

Renewed national, often state-sponsored, interest in (even fascination with) Iran's ethnic minorities—especially nomads and others perceived as picturesque and exotic—contributed to the resumption of full Qashqa'i dress. (Almost all of these ethnic minorities were Muslim, and many were also Shi'i. Several of Iran's religious minorities received a less charitable response.) Cultural festivals, statewide celebrations of the annually observed Day of the Nomad, television programs, films (such as *Gabbeh*), the popular print media, photography books, and even postcards displayed in streetside kiosks and airport gift shops prominently featured customarily attired Qashqa'i women and legitimized the images they presented. Still forced to wear restrictive, conservative attire, middle- and upper-class urban women complained resentfully about the double standard. Why, they wanted to know, were Iran's ethnic minorities able to dress as they wished, regardless of so-called Islamic notions of decency, while the Persian "majority" was still forced to observe strict standards? It was not that urban women wanted these minorities to dress like them, to be more covered; rather, they too wanted to escape the restrictions.

Mounted in Shiraz's and Isfahan's airport terminals and available in handicraft shops and bookstores, a popular photograph (rendered as posters and postcards) of three young Qashqa'i women at a wedding shows them standing with their backs to the camera, faces not visible. Initially I saw the image as one simply displaying the vibrant, exotic clothing but then realized that certain proprieties were still maintained by not showing any faces. I was reminded of a scene in an Iranian film of the mid-1990s, in which an urban Persian woman returning home from work makes the initial gestures of removing her scarf as she enters a bedroom. Viewers imagine her inside the room completing the act, without the filmmakers risking censorship by actually showing her scarfless. Likewise, those seeing the Qashqa'i women could imagine them turning around and showing their faces and their only partially covered hair.

Public appropriation of Qashqa'i women's dress took some bizarre forms when people who were not Qashqa'i were inspired by these apparently alluring and yet liberating images. In one case, an upper-class Persian woman wore Qashqa'i dress to hide her "ever more ample figure."[27] Another upper-class Persian woman wore "a traditional tribal costume" (possibly Baluch or Qashqa'i dress) when she received a government award at a public ceremony, apparently in order to escape wearing the dark concealing attire that the state mandated and to demonstrate her disapproval of it.[28] Handicraft shops sold Qashqa'i and other ethnic attire, and such articles of clothing were also prominently displayed and readily available in urban bazaars for tourists as well as the Qashqa'i themselves. Even outside Iran, Qashqa'i dress was perceived as appealing, also for peculiar reasons. In Orange County, California, a "Persian" cultural festival in 1998 featured dances performed by non-Qashqa'i Iranian women wearing elaborate Qashqa'i attire. For some enthusiastic participants and spectators, many in involuntary exile, Qashqa'i dress symbolized Iran before it succumbed to the Islamic Republic's restrictions. Some even noted, incorrectly, the anti-Islamic message offered by the attire.[29] To celebrate the Iranian New Year, some Iranians living in the United States encouraged their children to wear indigenous Iranian ethnic dress, including distorted Qashqa'i versions, despite having no connection with and being ignorant about the groups represented by the attire. At one event, "children wearing traditional dress are to receive prizes, and here and there a child is dressed in the colorful, flowing skirts of Iranian tribal women. . . . [A] little girl in native dress goes up for a prize. The master of ceremonies asks her a question in Farsi [Persian], but she does not understand. 'Well, at least she is wearing native dress,' the emcee says with an awkward laugh."[30]

Religious Belief and Practice

The basic religious faith, as expressed in love of God and ethical behavior, of the Qashqa'i as Shi'i Muslims was strong. Many resented or disapproved of the new government's efforts to exploit Islam for political purposes, however, and the Islamic beliefs and practices most reiterated by the state became tainted in their view.[31] Nomads viewed cynically the state's attempts to provide an Islamic explanation or justification for every circumstance, from a scarcity of chickens for sale in the bazaar to prohibitions against wedding music but not military music. Town residents, less explicit in their skepticism, worried that their Persian and Lur neighbors, especially the merchants and state agents on whom they depended, would criticize them if they spoke their minds. Many nomads and some town dwellers explicitly distinguished between their religious faith and the Islamic government's politics. They resisted the politics, not the basic faith.

Tribal codes and customs rather than Islamic law (shari'a) regulated the lives of nonurban Qashqa'i women and girls. Of course such codes and customs were influenced in a general sense by Islamic law and its underpinnings during the past centuries, just as Islamic law affected the wider Iranian society, but most Qashqa'i were unaware of the details. Some stated that certain rules came from Islam even though they were not apparently connected. They claimed that other customs were tribal and specific to the Qashqa'i, when indeed they were compatible with Islamic values and might have derived from or been influenced by Islam. As elsewhere in Iran and in Muslim society in general, codified Islamic (and secular) laws may not have affected how people actually lived, an issue often unacknowledged in the literature on women and Islam.[32] Dissemination of religious information through schools and modern technology in Iran, particularly via the state-controlled media, was gradually changing the ways that many Qashqa'i viewed Islam.

The Islamic Republic's formation altered the public and personal religious lives of only some Qashqa'i women. Before 1979 few nomad women had performed the five daily prayers (often combined in Iran in three prayer sessions), and few began to pray after the revolution. A nomad explained that women in his community were unable to pray because of multiple factors: their hard work and many children did not allow them any free time, they lacked access to bathing facilities (and hence could not carry out required ablutions), and they did not understand Arabic (the required language of prayers, which was also not understood by most men who prayed). After the revolution some women, new residents of villages, began to pray (occasionally) because of pressure exerted by their husbands and older sons who were influenced by nearby towns and who also began to pray. (Compulsion in matters of religious practice is forbidden by Islamic law, yet such behavior still occurs.) For nomads, the term *hezbollahi* identified men who became religious after the revolution, "the ones who now pray." (The term primarily signified a government supporter.) The closest kinswomen of hezbollahis were also the ones most likely to pray (occasionally). Qashqa'i villagers and town residents, especially those with access to electricity, were influenced by religious instruction and programming in the media, particularly television. All children in school received lessons in Islam, the Qur'an, and Arabic. Some nomads and most village and town dwellers held funeral and memorial rites at the nearest mosque, and women sometimes attended these gender-segregated services if space was provided for them.

Few nomad women fasted during the month of Ramadan, either before or after the revolution. Some village and town women did fast, or at least they behaved publicly as if they did. Before the revolution, few nomads went as pilgrims to the eighth Shi'i imam's tomb in Mashhad in northeastern Iran, and hardly any went as pilgrims to Mecca. After the revolution, more men, although still a small minority, ventured on these trips, and women occasionally accompanied them. In one tribal group, several women traveled by bus to Mashhad with kinsmen, and one journeyed by plane to Mecca with her father. These participants seemed more enthusiastic about the adventure than about any accruing religious merit.

Before 1979 nomads, women more than men, had invoked the names of historical figures in Islam in their daily speech (as in, "Oh Ali, help me to lift this load"), but in the 1990s and early 2000s they rarely did. Some noted that they still revered these individuals but did not appeal to them as they used to do. Their formally educated sons sometimes chided them for these exclamations. Muslim clergy in Iran discouraged people from calling upon these figures for mundane purposes, a practice they labeled as improper.

Islamic beliefs and practices also related to healthcare, and changes in people's attitudes toward the issue reflected not just scientific medical developments in the late twentieth century but also the influences of the Islamic state. Seeking what passed in Iran as modern medical care, men and women alike traveled to towns and cities to visit doctors, hospitals, clinics, and pharmacists. They used to rely more heavily on their own herbalists, curers, and bone setters and on non-Qashqa'i itinerants who visited Qashqa'i camps and villages to dispense prayers, prepare amulets, counteract the evil eye, and assist people in making and fulfilling vows. After the revolution, some urban clergymen declared that those practitioners who asserted enhanced legitimacy in Islam because of their status as dervishes and *sayyids* (reputed descendants of the Prophet Mohammad) acted out of ignorance and superstition and that their treatments were not part of Islam and hence forbidden. For some years these healers no longer practiced openly. Relying on them more than men, Qashqa'i women were the most affected. The symptoms they expressed for themselves and their children often defied any proper diagnosis from the deliverers of modern medicine. Fewer women placed protective, Islam-related amulets on their young children as they had always done before 1979, because, they said, they were not sure if these objects were efficacious anymore. Saying that the clergy condemned the use of such religious symbols, they explained that they now expressed their beliefs in Islam differently than they had done in the past. Their use of indigenous—or what they considered non-Islamic—amulets, particularly auspicious shapes carved from special wood, increased. Although people's knowledge about illness and its causes had changed because of formal education and exposure to the media, modern medicine was still distant from their camps and villages, often expensive, and usually improperly and even dangerously applied. By the

mid-1990s most Qashqa'i, while still seeking treatments from modern doctors and medicines, were once again relying on traditional methods and practitioners, Qashqa'i and others. External pressures against these individuals
had relaxed, and people once again sought their services.

Ritual and Ceremony

Soon after the revolution, the Islamic Republic banned activities its ruling
clergy considered immoral or un-Islamic.[33] The state's regional enforcers and
local supporters prohibited Qashqa'i music, dancing, and the stick-fighting
game (an aggressive yet choreographed dance performed to music), activities that had helped in the past to define the Qashqa'i as a distinctive group
in Iran.[34] Women experienced the loss of these expressive forms as sharply
as men. For more than a decade, they were forbidden to include these socially
and symbolically meaningful performances in their wedding celebrations,
one of only two occasions when the Qashqa'i gathered in large groups. The
other occasion was funerals and memorials.[35]

Qashqa'i music was played by specialized Qashqa'i musicians on oboes
and large and small skin drums, and its distinctive rhythmic sounds carried
long distances. Revolutionary guards and committees declared that drums

Qashqa'i dancers at a wedding. Photo by Lois Beck.

stirred up illicit passions and that drums combined with the oboe were particularly incendiary to men's and women's smoldering desires. Hence they prohibited their playing. Outsiders—Westerners as well as some non-Qashqa'i Iranians—might view these amusements as trivial, but they were vital expressions of cultural identity.

These restrictions, imposed primarily from outside, began to relax in 1990. A few Qashqa'i groups began to feature the oboe, without drums, at weddings. Men seeking close ties to the government, however, did not permit the oboe at their groups' weddings. In one group only one man objected to the instrument on what he claimed were religious grounds. His motivations were, in fact, political. Acquiescing to his attempts to exert control, the other men held a wedding without music. In another group, a ten-year-old girl born after the revolution ran to her mother to report that she had just heard the most captivating music. As the mother accompanied her back to the musicians, she realized that the girl had never heard Qashqa'i music played live.

According to reports circulating rapidly throughout Qashqa'i territory in 1990, some men had performed without incident or interference the competitive stick-fighting game, accompanied by the oboe, at several weddings. People responded enthusiastically. In some places in 1991 and spreading everywhere in Qashqa'i territory in 1992, musicians were again performing at many such gatherings, a response to decreased state surveillance and control and increased local, Qashqa'i demands. They played drums along with the oboe without major incident, and men reveled in being able to compete after a hiatus of fourteen years. Practicing on the sidelines, boys eagerly learned the choreographed sport.

From 1979 until 1991 or 1992, women could dance privately if no men were present. But, as some nomads joked, women lacked any privacy, owing to the open terrain and open tents. Also, dancing required music, and that too was forbidden during this period. Women in villages could dance within closed rooms to tape-recorded music played at low volume.

During a wedding celebration in a small Qashqa'i village in 1991, women danced on a porch within a high-walled courtyard while their kinsmen chatted inside an adjoining room. Coming from a nearby town to watch, Persian revolutionary guards stood for several hours in the lane outside the courtyard and peeked through gaps in the door frame. Relaxing, they tapped out the rhythm of the music issuing from an audiocassette player. When the men in the room were served a meal of meat and rice, the guards were invited to join them, as rules of hospitality required. When the guards left the room after eating heartily, one of them sternly instructed the women, still on the porch, that they were forbidden to dance and must stop immediately. The celebrants later laughed about the hypocrisy.

Many Qashqa'i struggled with the conflicting pressures on them in 1991 and 1992 and were uncertain about consequences if they took matters into their own hands. Almost all of them wanted to celebrate as they had done before the revolution, but they still feared possible government reprisals, especially because they depended on services from state agents. When they saw that some groups increasingly ignored the state's restrictions without being punished, they became more willing to act on their own behalf.

At a wedding in 1992, men performed games of stick fighting accompanied by musicians playing the oboe and drums, while women sitting in an open reception tent watched the players and entertained themselves with talk. At another wedding a week later, while men competed in stick fighting to live music, women danced in a semi-secluded spot behind the bridal tent accompanied by music from a cassette player. Two young Qashqa'i men out of the hundreds present objected vehemently on religious grounds (actually political ones) when the musicians switched from stick-fighting music to dance music. An intense verbal, nearly physical, fight ensued among the men before anyone had a chance to dance, and the celebration ended abruptly and prematurely when all the guests departed angrily. And at a third wedding a few days later, the musicians alternated equally between stick-fighting and dance music. Men competed at their game, and men and women danced in separate but adjoining circles in full view of one another and the large, surrounding, attentive audience. People there laughed about the pretense of gender segregation and predicted that within a year men and women would dance together in a single circle, a prediction that indeed came true. The musicians playing at these three weddings were the same three men, who had adjusted their performances in tune with local decisions.

From 1992 through 2002 practically all weddings featured live music, stick fighting, and men's and women's dancing. (On occasion the recent death of a distant relative meant a simpler, less exuberant, ceremony out of respect. The death of a close relative forced a wedding's postponement.) Qashqa'i hezbollahis did not permit their immediate families to engage in these festive activities, still forbidden or condemned by the state. As some of them became less strict by 2000, they began to tolerate live music but only for men's stick fighting and certainly not for women's public dancing. Changing their ideological message in order to support their changing behavior, they justified the music and sport on the grounds of the integrity of the Qashqa'i culture, which they now said was not historically or inherently un-Islamic.

At a large jubilant wedding held by a wealthy Qashqa'i kin group in an orchard in 1997, the hosts boasted that a cash bribe to the Persian revolutionary guards assigned to a nearby village allowed them to celebrate with music and dance without interference. Even throughout the 1980s, a period of strictly enforced state restrictions, elite Qashqa'i families holding wedding celebrations in urban hotels and restaurants routinely delivered payoffs to local state enforcers so that the celebrants could enjoy live music, men's and women's dancing, and no restrictions on women's hair, dress, cosmetics, and interactions with men. On these occasions, most women wore customary Qashqa'i dress with translucent headscarves, their hair fully visible. Other Qashqa'i women, their hair completely uncovered, wore tight Western-style dresses and danced provocatively like urban Persians they had seen.[36]

Through the 1980s, 1990s, and early 2000s Qashqa'i women understood that the state's restrictions on music, dancing, certain attire, and male-female interaction affected all Iranians and were not aimed solely at the Qashqa'i. They did note that their society and culture were harmed nonetheless and that their children were growing up without understanding the full meaning of being Qashqa'i. These children were simultaneously bombarded by Persianizing, Islamizing, and Arabizing pressures and influences through their schools, the media, and their intensified contact with the wider Persian-dominated society. In their parents' opinion, this wider context made their own efforts to enhance Qashqa'i culture, especially through symbolic means, more immediate and essential. They explained the prohibitions against certain forms of music, dance, dress, appearance, and intergender contact as examples of the state's coercion and its attempts to control citizens and further integrate them in a more unified, complacent whole.[37]

Conclusion

The formation of the Islamic Republic affected Qashqa'i men and women differently. Men, not women, were the most likely to express support for or grievance against the government because they were more directly in contact with and affected by the state's apparatus and agents. Some changes caused by the new government, facilitated by tribal people who were now its employees, benefited many Qashqa'i. People credited not religion but the forced removal of the shah and a new political climate that, at least for the time being, favored groups (such as nomadic tribes) that the Pahlavi regimes had oppressed and deprived.[38] Men were often opinionated about the new government and together discussed what they considered to be its positive and negative features. Women talked primarily about other issues (which also drew men's attention), such as kinship and marriage ties, household econo- mies, the fate of their sons as nomadic pastoralists or as workers in the wid- er Iranian society, and the fate of their daughters who would marry and leave home despite any formal education they may have received.

The position of Qashqa'i women in postrevolutionary Iran was not what either the proponents or the opponents of the current government wanted it to be. Certain aspects of their lives had obviously changed since 1979, some by specific state policies, others by the era's general transformations, and still others by individual, family, and group decisions. Also of utmost importance were the continuities in their tribally organized society, a significant part of which still remained largely unaffected by external events. Factors explain- ing the context of both change and continuity include the following: process- es of modernization, hold-over effects from half a century of often repres- sive Pahlavi rule, implementation of new state policies (including special services for nomads), greater integration in the Iranian state and society, continuing consequences of national-minority status, and the impact of state enforcers and supporters on people at the local level. Remarking about the gradual decrease in government restrictions affecting them in the mid-1990s, Qashqa'i men and women said they hoped that the trend would continue. They were enthusiastic about the election in 1997 of Iran's new, moderate president and the climate of greater individual freedom it promised. Al- though disappointed by the president's inability to implement many of the reforms he proposed, they said they supported and voted for him once again in 2001. As before the revolution, women were sheltered and insulated by their family and kinship groups, the tribal system, and the relative remoteness and isolation of most Qashqa'i territories. They enjoyed barriers of protection that many other Iranian women lacked.

NOTES

My research in Iran in the 1990s and early 2000s was assisted by many Iranian offi- cials; they include those at the Permanent Mission of the Islamic Republic of Iran to the United Nations; Interests Section of the Islamic Republic of Iran at the Embassy of Pakistan in Washington, D.C.; Ministries of Foreign Affairs, Jihad Sazandegi, and

Islamic Guidance; and national and regional offices of the Organization for Nomads' Affairs. Given the lack of official ties between the governments of Iran and the United States, I especially appreciate the efforts of these and other officials on my behalf. I thank my hosts in Iran, including several special extended families: the Qermezi family and tribe in Qashqa'i winter and summer pastures and the Solat Ghashghaie and Bayat families in Tehran. I acknowledge supportive grants from the National Endowment for the Humanities, Joint Committee on the Near and Middle East of the American Council of Learned Societies and the Social Science Research Council, American Philosophical Society, and Washington University in St. Louis. I received helpful comments on earlier drafts of this chapter from Erika Friedl, Shahla Haeri, Leonard Helfgott, Julia Huang, Val Moghadam, Philip Salzman, and Eliz Sanasarian. Julia, ja-ye tu dar en ketab khali ast. The chapter's epigraph comes from Edward Granville Browne, *A Year amongst the Persians: Impressions as to the Life, Character, and Thought of the People of Persia* (1893; reprint, London: Century, 1984), 259.

1. Shahla Haeri reminds me of these important distinctions (personal communication, 6 April 2002).

2. Only several writers describe rural women during the revolutionary period: Erika Friedl, *Women of Deh Koh: Lives in an Iranian Village* (Washington: Smithsonian Institution Press, 1989), and *Children of Deh Koh: Young Life in an Iranian Village* (Syracuse: Syracuse University Press, 1997) (on Boir Ahmad Lur village women); Mary Hegland, "'Traditional' Iranian Women: How They Cope," *Middle East Journal* 36 (4) (1982): 483–501, and "Aliabad Women: Revolution as Religious Activity," in *Women and Revolution in Iran,* ed. Guity Nashat (Boulder: Westview, 1983) (on Persian village women near Shiraz); Janet Bauer, "Poor Women and Social Consciousness in Revolutionary Iran," in *Women and Revolution in Iran* (on lower-class migrant women in Tehran and on women in the migrants' villages of origin). Only Friedl (*Women of Deh Koh, Children of Deh Koh,* her chapter in this volume) and Julia Huang (*Weaving Memories: Five Tribeswomen in Iran* [forthcoming, 2004] focus on rural women after the revolution. Like some other scholars making a similar decision, Val Moghadam explains why she excludes rural women from her study of women's work in postrevolutionary Iran; "Women, Work, and Ideology in the Islamic Republic," *International Journal of Middle Eastern Studies* 20 (2) (1988): 241–42. Haleh Afshar comments briefly on Lur and Shahsevan village women near Qom, apparently in 1980; "The Position of Women in an Iranian Village," in *Women, Work, and Ideology in the Third World,* ed. Haleh Afshar (London: Tavistock, 1985). Parvin Ghorayshi offers general remarks about women in an agricultural village in Mazandaran but does not state when she visited there; "Women and Social Change: Towards Understanding Gender Relations in Rural Iran," *Canadian Journal of Development Studies* 18 (1) (1997): 71–92. When other writers on Iran do occasionally mention rural women after the revolution, their comments are usually brief and general and may not be widely representative. See, for example, Nayereh Tohidi, "Modernity, Islamization, and Women in Iran," in *Gender and National Identity: Women and Politics in Muslim Societies,* ed. Valentine Moghadam (London: Zed Books, 1994), 115, 116–18. Asef Bayat includes some comments about women as part of poor people's movements in postrevolutionary urban Iran; *Street Politics: Poor People's Movements in Iran* (New

York: Columbia University Press, 1997). Three studies on religious expression among lower- and middle-class urban women are Azam Torab, "Piety as Gendered Agency: A Study of *Jalaseh* Ritual Discourse in an Urban Neighbourhood in Iran," *Journal of the Royal Anthropological Institute* 2 (2) (1996): 235–51; Torab, "The Politicization of Women's Religious Circles in Post-Revolutionary Iran," in *Women, Religion, and Culture in Iran,* ed. Sarah Ansari and Vanessa Martin (Surrey, Great Britain: Curzon Press, 2002); and Zahra Kamalkhani, *Women's Islam: Religious Practice among Women in Today's Iran* (London: Kegan Paul, 1998). Studies on women in prerevolutionary rural, tribal Iran include Nancy Tapper, "The Women's Subsociety among the Shahsevan Nomads of Iran," in *Women in the Muslim World,* ed. Lois Beck and Nikki Keddie (Cambridge: Harvard University Press, 1978); and Soheila Shahshahani, *Chahar fasl-e aftab: Zendegi-ye ruzmarreh-ye zanan-e eskan yafteh ashayer-e Mamassani* (Four seasons of the sun: Daily lives of settled women of the Mamassani tribe) (Tehran: Toos, 1987).

3. Iran's population was (approximately) 46.9 percent urban in 1976, 54.2 percent in 1986, 57 percent in 1991, and 61 percent in 1996; Bernard Hourcade et al., *Atlas d'Iran* (Paris: Reclus, La Documentation Française, 1998), 34.

4. Some people disagree with these statements, especially the notion that Persians are possibly a minority in Iran, and stress the common (according to them, Persian) cultural characteristics of all Iranians. Many authors, in fact, equate Persian and Iranian culture. Iranians who are not Persians, however, often stress their own cultural traits, their difference from and exclusion by Persians, and their minority status. Of course identity, being dynamic, multifaceted, and contextual, is more complicated than a single label. General statements cannot cover all the complexities, such as issues of intermarriage and the identity of any resulting children. The process of acculturation and assimilation as it relates to people who are not Persians is another complex issue. Persian culture—especially as disseminated through government agencies and schools and the national media—influences the lives of many non-Persians in Iran, and hence the issue is further complicated. Cultural features that many Iranians do share include celebrating the beginning of the New Year, but even No Ruz is observed differently by diverse cultural groups. For discussions of identity in contemporary Iran, see three chapters in *Le Fait ethnique en Iran et en Afghanistan,* ed. Jean-Pierre Digard (Paris: Centre National de la Recherche Scientifique, 1988): Richard Tapper, "Ethnicity, Order, and Meaning in the Anthropology of Iran and Afghanistan"; Nouchine Yavari-d'Hellencourt, "Ethnies et ethnicité dans les manuels scolaires iraniens"; and Bernard Hourcade, "Ethnie, nation et citadinite en Iran." See also Lois Beck, "Tribes and the State in Nineteenth- and Twentieth-Century Iran," in *Tribes and State Formation in the Middle East,* ed. Philip Khoury and Joseph Kostiner (Berkeley: University of California Press, 1990). For historical perspectives, see Firoozeh Kashani-Sabet, *Frontier Fictions: Shaping the Iranian Nation, 1804–1946* (Princeton: Princeton University Press, 1999); Kashani-Sabet, "Cultures of Iranianness: The Evolving Polemic of Iranian Nationalism," in *Iran and the Surrounding World: Interactions in Culture and Cultural Politics,* ed. Nikki Keddie and Rudi Matthee (Seattle: University of Washington Press, 2002); and Afsaneh Najmabadi, *Women with Moustaches and Men without Beards: Gender and Sexual Anxieties of Iranian Modernity* (Berkeley: University of California Press, 2004). The Kurds are a

major ethnic and national minority in Iran (and in other states) whose sense of distinctiveness is highly developed; for documentary including photographic evidence, see Susan Meiselas, *Kurdistan: In the Shadow of History* (New York: Random House, 1997). The issue of ethnolinguistic diversity is especially important because of the increasing tendency of many scholars to assume—or to imagine—a homogeneity in Iran as a whole. Some of them acknowledge what they consider to be exotic cultural anomalies in remote regions, near borders, and on society's fringes. Even those who do recognize ethnic diversity sometimes still equate Persian and Iranian culture. For example, David Menashri (*Post-Revolutionary Politics in Iran* [London: Frank Cass, 2001]) notes "Iran's unique identity—ethnic (Persian) and religious (Shi'i)" (179) and comments that "being Shi'i by faith . . . and Persian in language and culture . . . fostered the unique national character of Iran" (231). The editorial policy of an authoritative encyclopedia on Iran always to use the term "Persia" for Iran and to consider all residents of "Persia" to be "Persians," regardless of their language, culture, and self-identity, is misleading and inaccurate and appears to be an attempt to further notions of Persian supremacy for political and other reasons. Scholars and others visiting Iran, including Iranians who reside abroad, often see only certain sections of Tehran (and perhaps one or two other major cities) and may not understand how much cultural variation actually exists in the country. Recent literature on identity and ethnicity among Iranians abroad sheds new perspectives on these topics. Ali Akbar Mahdi notes the difficulty in characterizing the content of Iranian identity and ethnicity in the United States, especially in the second generation. He tends to equate Persian and Iranian culture, however, like many other authors; "Ethnic Identity among Second-Generation Iranians in the United States," *Iranian Studies* 31 (1) (1998): 77–95. Some Iranians abroad may identify with Persian and perhaps Shi'i Islamic culture despite their other ethnic and religious identities, but my discussion in this chapter refers to women *in* Iran. Also discussing ethnicity among Iranians in the United States, Mehdi Bozorgmehr includes only religious minorities; "From Iranian Studies to Studies of Iranians in the United States," *Iranian Studies* 31 (1) (1998): 17–19.

5. Eliz Sanasarian discusses issues relating to religious minorities; "State Dominance and Communal Perseverance: The Armenian Diaspora in the Islamic Republic of Iran, 1979–1989," *Diaspora* 4 (3) (1995): 243–65; and *Religious Minorities in Iran* (Cambridge: Cambridge University Press, 2000).

6. For example, Haideh Moghissi begins an article: "This chapter tries to throw some light on the lives of women in the Islamic Republic of Iran. . . . It examines the changes in the Islamization policies of the Iranian government over the past 15 years, and studies their effects on the conditions of life and work of the female population of Iran"; "Public Life and Women's Resistance," in *Iran After the Revolution: Crisis of an Islamic State,* ed. Saeed Rahnema and Sohrab Behdad (London: I. B. Tauris, 1995), 251. Nowhere does she mention the complex diversity of Iran and its relation to different patterns of gender. Only at the end (264) does she note the dispossessed, the poor, and the impoverished lower-middle classes but without any specific connection to gender. She does indicate another basis for difference (258): "women in Iran form three distinct groups: conservative Muslims, reformist Muslims and secular women." The editors (above) place the volume's sole contribution on women

at the collection's very end, as if the issue of women—whether diverse or not—is an afterthought and not of major concern compared with the other topics included.

7. My book, *Nomads Move On: Qashqa'i Tribespeople in Post-Revolutionary Iran*, detailing the activities of a Qashqa'i subtribe, is forthcoming.

8. For comprehensive anthropological and historical information on the Turkic Shahsevan, see Richard Tapper, *Pasture and Politics: Economics, Conflict, and Ritual among Shahsevan Nomads of Northwestern Iran* (London: Academic Press, 1979); and *Frontier Nomads of Iran: A Political and Social History of the Shahsevan* (Cambridge: Cambridge University Press, 1997). For comparative material on the Baluch, see Philip Carl Salzman, *Black Tents of Baluchistan* (Washington: Smithsonian Institution Press, 2000).

9. For different dimensions of this history, see Lois Beck, "Women among Qashqa'i Nomadic Pastoralists in Iran," in *Women in the Muslim World*, ed. Lois Beck and Nikki Keddie (Cambridge: Harvard University Press, 1978); *The Qashqa'i of Iran* (New Haven: Yale University Press, 1986); *Nomad: A Year in the Life of a Qashqa'i Tribesman in Iran* (Berkeley: University of California Press, 1991); "Qashqa'i Nomads and the Islamic Republic," *Middle East Report* 22 (4) (1992): 36–41; "Use of Land by Nomadic Pastoralists in Iran, 1970–1998," Bulletin Series, *Yale School of Forestry and Environmental Studies* 103 (1998): 58–80; "Local Histories: A Longitudinal Study of a Qashqa'i Subtribe in Iran," in *Iran and Beyond: Essays in Middle Eastern History in Honor of Nikki R. Keddie*, ed. Rudi Matthee and Beth Baron (Costa Mesa, Calif.: Mazda, 2000); and "Qashqa'i Nomadic Pastoralists and Their Use of Land," in *Yeki Bud, Yeki Nabud: Essays on the Archaeology of Iran*, ed. Naomi Miller and Kamyar Abdi (Los Angeles: Cotsen Institute of Archaeology, UCLA, 2002).

10. Authors on Iran often tend to approve of one regime and to criticize the other, sometimes because of personal experiences. Iranians who reside in the country often complain about both regimes and argue about the relative merits of each, but such more-balanced perspectives do not always enter into the scholarly literature.

11. For discussion of the war's impact on women in Shiraz, see Kamalkhani, *Women's Islam*, 71–85. Reliable numbers of the war's participants and casualties are not publicly available in Iran but are generally acknowledged to be high. In one Qashqa'i subtribe of approximately 2,500 individuals, 150 men volunteered or were conscripted, 13 were killed or presumed killed, and others were wounded or suffered from chemical attacks. Some families held out hope until April 2003 that men whose bodies had not been returned were among the many prisoners of war still being held by Saddam Hossein in Iraq. Eric Hooglund reports 26 war deaths from a village of 2,500 people; "Letter from an Iranian Village," *Journal of Palestine Studies* 27 (1) (1997): 79. Fereydoun Safizadeh notes several deaths but also 125 draft dodgers and deserters for an Azerbaijani village of 1,689 people; "Peasant Protest and Resistance in Rural Iranian Azerbaijan," in *Peasants and Politics in the Modern Middle East*, ed. Farhad Kazemi and John Waterbury (Miami: Florida International University Press, 1991), 322, 323.

12. Leftists consider as martyrs the few female Qashqa'i leftists killed in struggles during the revolution or against the new Islamic government.

13. Richard Tapper discusses some activities of the Organization for Nomads' Affairs in 1992–93; "Change, Cognition and Control: The Reconstruction of Nomad-

ism in Iran," in *When History Accelerates: Essays on Rapid Social Change, Complexity, and Creativity,* ed. C. M. Hann (London: Athlone Press, 1994). For a brief comparative description of changes in a Persian village near Shiraz from 1979 to 1997, see E. Hooglund, "Letter from an Iranian Village."

14. For accounts of socioeconomic change affecting women in pastoral societies in the Middle East and elsewhere, see *Ethnos* 52 (1–2) (1987), a special issue devoted to the topic; Erika Friedl's chapter in this volume; and Friedl, "The Dynamics of Women's Spheres of Action in Rural Iran," in *Women in Middle Eastern History,* ed. Nikki Keddie and Beth Baron (New Haven: Yale University Press, 1991). Dawn Chatty discusses the impact of motorized vehicles, particularly trucks, and other aspects of modernization on bedouin women in Syria and Oman; *From Camel to Truck: The Bedouin in the Modern World* (New York: Vantage Press, 1986); and *Mobile Pastoralists: Development Planning and Social Change in Oman* (New York: Columbia University Press, 1996).

15. Non-Qashqa'i urban merchants and moneylenders, who continued to exploit nomads and villagers, also received a share of increased prices. Despite the Islamic ban on usury, they continued to calculate high interest rates while not always subtly concealing the ways they collected it.

16. Haleh Afshar ("Position of Women") notes what she considers to be the detrimental aspects of weaving for women in a small Lur and Shahsevan village. By contrast, Qashqa'i women regarded most aspects of weaving positively, especially those under their control. Focusing on the lives of individual Qashqa'i women and girls, Julia Huang (*Weaving Memories*) explains the social context of weaving and the attitudes of weavers and their family members about the activity. Leonard Helfgott offers a historical analysis; *Ties that Bind: A Social History of the Iranian Carpet* (Washington: Smithsonian Institution Press, 1994).

17. Military service was said to be obligatory under the shah, but many young Qashqa'i men had avoided it.

18. For a detailed examination of similar and different marriage strategies in Pukhtun tribal society in Afghanistan in the early 1970s, see Nancy Tapper, *Bartered Brides: Politics, Gender, and Marriage in an Afghan Tribal Society* (Cambridge: Cambridge University Press, 1991).

19. The scenes Friedl (*Women of Deh Koh, Children of Deh Koh*) describes for a Boir Ahmad Lur village near Qashqa'i territory tell a tale of poverty, inadequate resources, overcrowding, and the resulting stress placed on women and children.

20. Studies on fertility and family size in the Muslim Middle East demonstrate that these issues are more complicated than simply the availability or lack of effective birth control. See Marcia Inhorn for a review of this literature; *Quest for Conception: Gender, Infertility, and Egyptian Medical Traditions* (Philadelphia: University of Pennsylvania Press, 1994); and *Infertility and Patriarchy: The Cultural Politics of Gender and Family Life in Egypt* (Philadelphia: University of Pennsylvania Press, 1996).

21. The Islamic Republic disseminated Persian—Iran's official language—through its agencies, schools, and the media, but the ruling clergy and its supporters also emphasized Arabic—the language of Islam—in many facets of political, religious, and social life. Iranians became increasingly familiar with Arabic words and phrases, some of which appeared to be replacing Persian ones. Because of changes in the

curriculum of schools and universities directed toward Islamization, students were especially affected.

22. The Qashqa'i regarded themselves as a unique, distinctive group in Iran. Of course their degree of difference from others cannot be quantified. Similar kinds of dress, music, dance, and sport were found among many tribal groups in southwestern Iran, but significant as well as subtle differences among them were also present. If four tribal women—for example a Boir Ahmad Lur, a Bakhtiyari Lur, a Khamseh Arab, and a Qashqa'i Turk —of similar socioeconomic backgrounds and settings were brought together, each would immediately differentiate herself from the others on cultural (including linguistic) grounds. Even within such named tribal groups, cultural and other markers distinguished people.

23. For many women in Iran under Reza Shah, their notions of modest dress were part of, and inseparable from, their customary attire. When Reza Shah condemned women's concealing attire in the 1930s (see Ettehadieh's chapter in this volume), he appeared to have certain urban, Persian styles in mind. When his agents tried to enforce his new policy, they were uncertain about how to handle nonurban, non-Persian women (such as rural Kurds and Baluch), whose own forms of dress were also modest but often unlike urban ones. Many nonurban women of ethnic and tribal groups, including the Qashqa'i, did not alter their attire when Reza Shah enforced strict policies against "veiling," in part because state agents viewed the clothing differently than the urban styles with which they were familiar. For Reza Shah's dress-code law, see Houshang Chehabi, "Staging the Emperor's New Clothes: Dress Codes and Nation-Building under Reza Shah," *Iranian Studies* 26 (3–4) (1993): 209–33.

24. One of the first sets of postage stamps issued by the Islamic Republic in 1979 featured Kurds and other men in Iran in indigenous ethnic dress. Beginning with parliament's first session in 1980, a few male deputies of ethnic-minority backgrounds wore their distinctive dress there. To demonstrate ethnic diversity, government schoolbooks from 1981 through the early 2000s included drawings of Iranian men in varying headgear and Iranian children in regional dress. See Golnar Mehran's discussion of ethnic and other biases and stereotypes in primary-school textbooks published in 1999; "The Presentation of the 'Self' and the 'Other' in Postrevolutionary Iranian School Textbooks," in *Iran and the Surrounding World: Interactions in Culture and Cultural Politics.* In 1996 state-sponsored Islamic dolls featured Sara and Dara in regional ethnic dress including a (distorted) Qashqa'i version.

25. For legal aspects of modest dress in postrevolutionary Iran, see Afsaneh Najmabadi, "Power, Morality, and the New Muslim Womanhood," in *The Politics of Social Transformation in Afghanistan, Iran, and Pakistan,* ed. Myron Weiner and Ali Banuazizi (Syracuse: Syracuse University Press, 1994); and Parvin Paidar, *Women and the Political Process in Twentieth-Century Iran* (Cambridge: Cambridge University Press, 1995). Anne Betteridge discusses its social and religious dimensions; "To Veil or Not to Veil: A Matter of Protest or Policy," in *Women and Revolution in Iran.* Farzaneh Milani draws connections between veiling and literary expression; *Veils and Words: The Emerging Voices of Iranian Women Writers* (Syracuse: Syracuse University Press, 1992). For an analysis of the veiling of Muslim women as a powerful symbol, with examples drawn from Iran, see Homa Hoodfar, "The Veil in Their Minds and on Our Heads: Veiling Practices and Muslim Women," in *The Politics of Culture in the Shad-*

ow of Capital, ed. Lisa Lowe and David Lloyd (Durham: Duke University Press, 1997). Hammed Shahidian offers political analyses of the issue for the first two decades of the Islamic Republic; *Women in Iran: Gender Politics in the Islamic Republic* (Westport, Conn.: Greenwood Press, 2002) and *Women in Iran: Emerging Voices in the Women's Movement* (Westport, Conn.: Greenwood Press, 2002). Azar Nafisi provides a personal view based on her experience teaching and living in Tehran in 1979–97; *Reading Lolita in Tehran: A Memoir in Books* (New York: Random House, 2003).

26. For details about the dress of Qashqa'i women and girls, including those who attended different kinds of rural and urban schools, see Huang (*Weaving Memories*).

27. As shown by Cherry Mosteshar, *Unveiled* (New York: St. Martin's Press, 1995), following p. 170.

28. As recounted by Haleh Esfandiari, *Reconstructed Lives: Women and Iran's Islamic Revolution* (Baltimore: Johns Hopkins University Press, 1997), 109. Esfandiari suggests that the dress may have been Baluch (personal communication, 20 April 2002).

29. Writing about Iranians in the United States, Mahdi ("Ethnic Identity," 87–88) notes, "The Iranian revolution has made many Iranians hostile, suspicious, or indifferent toward religion." The brochure (in the author's possession) advertising this "Persian Festival of Autumn" includes a color photograph of non-Qashqa'i Iranian women performing in Qashqa'i clothes.

30. Gelareh Asayesh, *Saffron Sky: A Life between Iran and America* (Boston: Beacon Press, 1999), 207–8.

31. Researchers in rural southwestern Iran during or after the revolution note the same attitude reported here for the Qashqa'i; Anonymous, "Report from an Iranian Village," *MERIP Reports* 12 (3) (1982): 26–29; Mary Hooglund [Hegland], "Religious Ritual and Political Struggle in an Iranian Village," *MERIP Reports* 12 (1) (1982): 10–17, 23; Mary Hegland, "Islamic Revival or Political and Cultural Revolution?: An Iranian Case Study," in *Religious Resurgence: Contemporary Cases in Islam, Christianity, and Judaism,* ed. Richard Antoun and Mary Hegland (Syracuse: Syracuse University Press, 1987), 205; Erika Friedl, "State Ideology and Village Women," in *Women and Revolution in Iran;* Friedl, *Women of Deh Koh;* Reinhold Loeffler, *Islam in Practice: Religious Beliefs in a Persian [sic] Village* (Albany: State University of New York Press, 1988), 225–44. "As some individuals became disillusioned with the course of the revolution and the activities of the Islamic Republic, I frequently observed a reversal in this increased devotion to Islam, and sensed even a feeling of repugnance towards religion" (M. Hooglund [Hegland], "Religious Ritual," 15). "There appears to be an erosion of the observance of private [Islamic] rituals . . . because of their association with the Islamic regime" (Anonymous, "Report," 28). Religion in one village "is largely stripped of ritual because ritual is linked with the religious powers-that-be, and these are suspected of using the religious idiom to further their own interests. . . . Traditional rituals of the Islamic calendar are boycotted. Prescribed fasts are no longer observed. . . . Many women don't even pray any more. . . . Religious rituals are fast becoming meaningless" (Friedl, "State Ideology," 229).

32. For example, Islamic inheritance rights, stipulating that sons receive full shares and daughters receive half shares of a deceased father's property, are often ignored in all parts of the Muslim world. Haleh Afshar ("Position of Women," 68) notes for Iran: "Even though women are theoretically still entitled to their Islamic rights, in

practice few rural women have the means of enforcing the Islamic law against patriarchal, traditional, social and psychological resistance to it."

33. Condemning music at the beginning of Ramadan in July 1979, Khomeini proclaimed, "The playing of music is an act of treason to this country and our youth;
therefore, musical programs should be entirely stopped"; as quoted in Ali Rahnema
and Farhad Nomani, *The Secular Miracle: Religion, Politics, and Economic Policy in
Iran* (London: Zed, 1990), 222. Later, Islamic and revolutionary martial music was
permitted and then Iranian classical music, but any music thought to stimulate people's sexual desires was forbidden. Some musical instruments were authorized in 1988.
After Khatami was elected president in 1997, popular music sung by males was tol-
erated but female singers continued to be prohibited through 2002.

34. See note 22.

35. The deaths of many men in the Iran-Iraq war also led to internal restrictions
on festivities connected with weddings, due to required rites of mourning. Beginning with the war's first fatalities, some funerals and memorials rivaled weddings in
the numbers of people attending.

36. Qashqa'i people abroad circulated videotapes of these celebrations, and others viewing them received the erroneous impression that women in Iran were no
longer subject to restrictions about their appearance and behavior.

37. Even after the first decade of Iranians being subjected to Islamizing, anti-West-
ern policies, observers increasingly noted their many failures. "A somber dress code,
and a drastic ban on drinking, gambling, and display of affection in public, have been
brutally enforced in order to fight Westernization; but the public's yearning for most
things Western has hardly been dented"; Jahangir Amuzegar, *Iran's Economy under
the Islamic Republic* (London: I. B. Tauris, 1993), 324.

38. Non-Qashqa'i state officials often credited their own religious ideology by saying that, guided by Islamic values, they aimed to help people who had been oppressed.

CONTRIBUTORS

Mahnaz Afkhami was born in Iran. She is president of Women's Learning Partnership and executive director of the Foundation for Iranian Studies in the United States. She was secretary-general of the Women's Organization of Iran and minister-of-state for women's affairs before 1979. She writes on women's human rights; women in leadership; and women, civil society, and democracy. Her publications include *In the Eye of the Storm: Women in Postrevolutionary Iran* (1994, edited with Erika Friedl), *Women in Exile* (1994), *Faith and Freedom: Women's Human Rights in the Muslim World* (1995), *Muslim Women and the Politics of Participation* (1997, edited with Erika Friedl), *Claiming Our Rights: A Manual for Women's Human Rights Education in Muslim Societies* (1998), *Safe and Secure: Eliminating Violence against Women and Girls in Muslim Societies* (1998), *Leading to Choices: A Leadership Training Handbook for Women* (2001), and *Toward a Compassionate Society* (2002).

Lois Beck is professor of anthropology at Washington University in St. Louis. Her books include *Women in the Muslim World* (1978, edited with Nikki Keddie), *The Qashqa'i of Iran* (1986), *Nomad: A Year in the Life of a Qashqa'i Tribesman in Iran* (1991), *Women in Iran from the Rise of Islam to 1800* (2003, edited with Guity Nashat), and *Nomads Move On: Qashqa'i Tribespeople in Post-Revolutionary Iran* (forthcoming). She has conducted anthropological research in Iran on multiple occasions over a span of thirty-five years, including eleven visits during the postrevolutionary period, and she continues to pursue topics related to political, economic, and social change among nomadic and tribal people in Iran.

Haleh Esfandiari is consulting director of the Middle East Program at the Woodrow Wilson International Center for scholars in Washington, D.C. Until 1979 she served as deputy secretary-general of the Women's Organization of Iran. She is the author of *Reconstructed Lives: Women and Iran's Islamic Revolution* (1997), editor of *Iranian Women: Past, Present, and Future* (1977), and coeditor of *The Economic Dimensions of Middle Eastern History* (1990). She is currently researching a book on the cross-cultural encounters of four generations of European and American women who married Iranians and went to live in Iran.

Mansoureh Ettehadieh (Nezam Mafi) is professor of modern history at Tehran University in Iran. She is the author and editor of books in Persian on the nineteenth-century social and political history of Iran, including *Inja Tehran Ast* (concerning the city's social history), an edited biography of Nosrat al-Dowleh Firuz, and a political biography of Reza Qoli Khan Nezam al-Saltaneh. She has published two novels and founded a publishing company, Nashr-e Tarikh-e Iran, that produces historical texts.

Gholamali Farjadi is a labor economist by training and a faculty member of the Institute for Research on Planning and Development in Tehran, Iran. He writes on the labor market in Iran.

Erika Friedl is professor emerita of anthropology at Western Michigan University. She has written on ethnographic issues relating to the people of Boir Ahmad in southwestern Iran and continues her interests in marriage and kinship relationships there. Her books include *Women of Deh Koh* (1991), *In the Eye of the Storm: Women in Postrevolutionary Iran* (1994, edited with Mahnaz Afkhami), *Children of Deh Koh* (1997), and *Muslim Women and the Politics of Participation* (1997, edited with Mahnaz Afkhami).

Shireen Mahdavi was born in Iran and taught and conducted research there on social-welfare programs. She is currently an independent scholar affiliated with the University of Utah. She writes on various aspects of Iranian history, with special emphasis on the nineteenth century and women. She is the author of *For God, Mammon, and Country: A Nineteenth-Century Persian Merchant* (1999). She is writing a book on the social history of Qajar Iran.

Amir Mehryar, a psychologist by training, is a faculty member of the Institute for Research on Planning and Development and the director of the Center for Population Studies and Research of the Ministry of Science, Research, and Technology in Tehran, Iran. He writes on reproductive health and family planning and on government spending on social services in the Islamic Republic of Iran.

Ziba Mir-Hosseini is an independent consultant, researcher, and writer on Middle Eastern issues and specializes in gender, family relationships, Islam, and the law. She is a research associate at the University of Cambridge and the University of London. She is the author of *Marriage on Trial: A Study of Islamic Family Law in Iran and Morocco* (1993, revised ed. 2000) and *Islam and Gender: The Religious Debate in Contemporary Iran* (1999) and the codirector of two documentary films, *Divorce Iranian Style* (1998) and *Runaway* (2001).

Fatemeh Etemad Moghadam is professor of economics at Hofstra University. She writes on the agricultural economy and economic history of Iran, including the book *From Land Reform to the Revolution: The Political Economy of Agricultural Development in Iran, 1960–1979* (1996). She is currently conducting research on middle-class women and informal labor market participation in Tehran, women entrepreneurs, and women and work in rural Iran.

Guity Nashat is associate professor of history at the University of Illinois at Chicago. She is a native of Iran. Her books include *The Beginnings of Modern Reform in Iran* (1983), *Women and Revolution in Iran* (1984, edited), *Women in the Middle East and North Africa* (1999, with Judith Tucker), and *Women in Iran from the Rise of Islam to 1800* (2003, edited with Lois Beck).

Mohammad Tabibian, an economist by training, is a faculty member of the Institute for Research on Planning and Development in Tehran, Iran. He writes on macroeconomics, poverty, and income distribution in Iran.

INDEX

Abbas (or Gulsaz), Madame, 64
Abortion, 132, 174. *See also* birth control
Agha Muhammad Khan (1794–97), xi, 5
Ahmad Shah (1909–25), xii
Alavi, Ghodsieh, 142
al-Ayn, Qurrat, 15
al-Ayn, Tahira Qurat, 78–79
al-Dawla, Furugh, Malika-yi Iran (daughter of Nasir al-Din Shah), 73–74
al-Din, Muzaffar Shah (1896–1907), xii
al-Din, Nasir Shah (1848–96), xi, 8
al-Douleh, Anis, 55, 72–73
al-Douleh, Mirza Husayn Khan, 14
Ali, Fath Shah (1797–1834), xi, 5, 8
Ali, Muhammad Shah (1907–9) xii, 5
al-Saltaneh, Taj (later, Tavus Khanum; daughter of Nasir al-Din Shah), 9–10, 58, 76–78

Bab, xi, 15
Baha'i faith, 9
Baha'ullah, 9
Behrouzi, Mariam, 155
Birth control, 116–17, 257. *See also* Abortion
Boir Ahmad. *See* Deh Koh, rural case study of
Bozorgnia, Sadr al-Malek, 151
Bureau for women's affairs, 159

Chador. *See* Veiling
Childcare, 117, 131

Children: and marriage, 173, 233–34; and work, 194–95, 232–33
Clerical opposition to: election of non-Muslims, 139; Muhammad Reza Shah, 27; women's education, 96; Women's Organization of Iran, 128–29; women's rights, 113, 138, 165; women's sexuality, 205–11
Constitutional period (1905–11), 18

Dabbagh, Marzieh, 155
Danesh (Knowledge) newspaper, 91
Dastghaib, Gowhar Sharieh, 155
Deh Koh, rural case study of, 218–39; acorn gathering work, 225, 227–28; agricultural gender roles, traditional, 218–19; animal husbandry, 230; cash crops, 229; child-bride marriages, 233–34; children and work, 232–33; choice, 234; contacts with other women, 225, 228, 231; control of food, 225, 229–30; ease vs. hardship, 226, 230, 232; economic changes in rural communities, 219–20; feelings about changes in life, 235; hunting vs. gathering, 225, 228; independence of women, 220; Islamic Republic's gender philosophy, 220–21; liberal theory of societal development, 220; methodology, 222–23; rural history sources, 218; socioeconomic bias, 223–24; traditional work, 228–30, 231; weaving, 230–31; weaving for export, 231; women's views of life, 221

de la Marininere, Madame, 64

Dieulafoy, Jane, 69

Dirakhshan, Badruduja, 19

Divorce: in gender discourse, 208, 211; in Islamic Republic of Iran, 30, 33, 40, 146, 167–70; in Pahlavi dynasty, 131; in Qajar dynasty, 7, 25, 40–41, 48, 54–55

Dowlatabadi, Sediqeh, 91–92, 97

Dowlatshahi, Mehrangiz (member of twenty-first *majlis*), 139, 140, 141, 148, 150

Ebadi, Shirin (Nobel Peace Prize winner), xiii, 33

Ebtehaj-Samii, Nayereh (member of twenty-first *majlis*), 141

Ebtekar, Maasoumeh, 159

Education, 197–98, 199; in Islamic Republic of Iran, 175–76; in Pahlavi dynasty, 21, 23, 27; in Qajar dynasty, 14, 16; Qashqa'i, 254; and women's movement, 87, 88, 90, 93, 95

Ettelaat (newspaper), 139

Fahim-Azar, 141

Family planning, 116–17, 257

Family Protection Law, xii, 30, 150–51, 158, 167–68; revision, 132, 153; suspension, 154–55

Fath Ali Shah (1794–97), xi, 5, 8

Fiqh-based literature, 204–5

Franchise for women, 18, 24–25, 87, 112–13, 137–38, 248

Gender discourse in postrevolutionary Iran, 204–17. *See also Fiqh*-based literature; Modernist discourse in postrevolutionary Iran; Neotraditionalist discourse in postrevolutionary Iran; Traditionalist discourse in postrevolutionary Iran

Geramizadegan, Ashraf, 159

Habibi, Shahla, 159

Hallaj, 15–16

Hashemi, Faezeh (daughter of President Rafsanjani), 159

High Council of Women's Organizations of Iran, xii, 113. *See also* Women's Organization of Iran

Iran, Malikeh-yi (daughter of Nasir al-Din Shah), 18

Iranian feminist, first, 15

Islam: European misinterpretations of, 9–10; Shi'i, 5, 263; Sunni, 5

Islamic Republic of Iran (1979–), xiii, 30–34; clerical authority, 30; education for women, 32–33; Family Protection Law, suspension of, 154–55; Iran-Iraq war (1980–88), 31; Khatami, Muhammad (President), 32–34; Khomeini, Ruhollah Ayatullah, 30–32; loss of women's rights, 154–55; women members of Parliament, 33; women's reforms, 30–31, 33

Jahanbani, Showkat Malek (member of twenty-first *majlis*), 141, 143, 145

Kabir, Amir, 14

Kanun-i banuvan (women's center), 21–22, 92

Karbala, center of Shi'i learning, 15

Karrubi, Fatemeh, 159

Kayhan (newspaper), 139

Khan, Agha Muhammad (1794–97), xi

Khanum, Bibi, 44–45, 75–76

Khanum, Galin, 59

Khanum, Gulrukh, 74

Khanum, Malik Jahan, 13–14

Khanum, Maryam, 52

Khanum, Tavus (earlier, Taj al-Saltaneh; daughter of Nasir al-Din Shah), 9–10, 58, 76–78

Khatami, Muhammad (President), xiii, 32–34; women decisive in his election, 159

Khomeini, Ayatulla Ruhollah, xiii, 24, 27–28, 30–32, 173, 186; asks for women's support in Referendum, 139; death, 32; encourages women to support Revolution, 154; exiled, 114; opposes Muhammad Reza Shah, 24, 28; opposes women's right to vote, 114, 138; returns from exile, xiii

Kirmani, Mirza Agha Khan, 9

Kiyan (Foundation) magazine, 212

Labor in contemporary Iran, 182–203; age, 194–95; agriculture, 190–91; cash reimbursements from husbands, 185; categories of economically non-active women, 193–94; catering industry, 202; child labor, 194–95; cooperative sector, 192; correlates of female labor-force participation, 194–201; cultural factors, 183, 184, 201–2; economic factors, 183; education, level of, 197–98, 199; experts or specialists, 191–92; female economic-activity rates in other countries, 183; gender-segregation, postrevolutionary, 186; homemakers, 193–94; industrial workers and related professions, 191; industry, 190–91; legal profession, 186; literacy, 197; marital status, 196–97; national development, 182; private sector, 192–93; provincial variations, 199–201; public sector, 192–93; relative share of economically active population, 189; sales force, 201–2; services, 190–91; Statistical Center of Iran, 184; students, 193; terminology, 184; trends of economic activity, 187–94; unemployed population and levels of education and literacy, 199; unemployment rates, 189–90, 198–99; urban-rural differences, 188–89; white-collar work, 202; women's activities, traditional forms, 185; workers in agriculture, forestry, and fisheries, 191–92. *See also* Labor in the Islamic Republic of Iran

Labor in the Islamic Republic of Iran, 163–81; abortion, 174; agriculture, 176; child marriage law, 173; divorces, increases in, 169; dower (*mahriyeh*), 165; education, 175–76; exclusion from public activities, 164–65; factors impacting employment, 170–71, 173; Family Protection Law, 167–68; govermental policies, 1960s-90s, 163–64, 172–75; household labor (and child raising), 164–65, 168, 178; husband's permission to work needed, 175; ideological changes, 163, 172; Islamic law, 166; legal loopholes in reform laws, 169–70; manufacturing, 176–77; marital duties, 165, 177; "new home economics," 164; other characteristics of female labor, 177; participation in the labor market, women's, 164, 165, 178; percentages of women in labor market, 171–72; reforms, postrevolutionary, 167–70; standardized marriage contract, 168; tradional activities, devaluation of, 164; trends in activity rate, 183–84; upkeep (*nafaqeh*), 165; wage equivalent for household labor (*ojrat olmesi*), 168–70. *See also* Labor in contemporary Iran

Literacy, 146, 199

Malika-yi Iran, Furugh al-Dawla (daughter of Nasir al-Din Shah), 73–74

Manouchehrian, Mehrangiz (member of twenty-first senate), 141, 146–50, 152

Marininere, Madame de la, 64

Marriage in the Qajar dynasty, 50–62. alliances, political and social, 51–53; Fath Ali Shah's wives, 51–54; harems, 50–51, 57–58; Nasir al-Din Shah's wives, 54–57; Qahraman Mirza's wife, 59; temporary wives, 51–57; tribal traditions, 51. *See also* Marriage in the Qajar period

Marriage in the Qajar period, 37–62. advantages of, 48; bridewealth (*mahr*), 39–41; ceremonies, 45–46; children and, 41–42; contract (*aqd*), 39, 46; customs, 47; festivities, 48; influence of families on, 38; and Islamic law, 42–43; Khanum, Bibi, 44–45; and legal empowerment of women, 40–41; matchmaker (*dallaleh*), use of, 45; mullah, role of, 39; Mustoufi family, 42–44; permanent (*nikah*), 38; purposes of, 38; and security for women, 40–41; temporary (*mut'a*), 38; trousseaus, 47–48; women's status in, 39–40. *See also* Marriage within the Qajar dynasty

Marriage, polygymous, 49

Marriage, temporary (*mut'a*), 38, 49–50, 51–57

Members of parliament, 1963–88, 136–62; education expansion, 136; Family Protection Law in twenty-first parliamemt, 150–51; investigative magistrates, 158; issues compatible with Islamic law and teachings, 142; leadership passes to younger women, 153; *majlis* of the Islamic Republic, first and second, 136, 155–56; *majlis*, twenty-first, 136; pressure by non-member women, 157; senate, twenty-first, 136; third *majlis* of Islamic Republic, 156; twenty-first parliament, issues of, 142–51; twenty-second parliament, issues of, 151–53; visibility of women, 159; women heading women's organizations, 159; women's first involvement in referendum, 139–40; women's movement, shift of, 153; women's rights, bills against, 160

Ministry of Rural Reconstruction, 249

Misperceptions of Iranian and European women, 63–84

Modernist discourse in postrevolutionary Iran, 212–14; Islamic scholarship, 213;

Kiyan (Foundation) magazine, 212; religious knowledge, relative theory of, 212; Sa'idzada, Sayyid Muhsin, 213–14; sexuality vs. gender, 214; Soroush, Abdolkarim, 212; *Zanan* (Women) magazine, 212. *See also* Gender discourse in postrevolutionary Iran; Neotraditionalist discourse in postrevolutionary Iran; Traditionalist discourse in postrevolutionary Iran

Mosahab, Shams ol-Moluk (member of twenty-first senate), 141, 143–46, 147, 152

Mostafavi, Zahra (daughter of Ayatollah Ruhullah Khomeini), 159

Muhammad Ali Shah (1907–9), xii, 5

Muhammad Reza Shah (1941–79), xii, 24, 27, 110, 114, 124, 244–45

Muhammad Shah (1834–48), xi, 124

Muhammad, Agha Khan (1794–97), xi, 5

Musaddiq, Muhammad, xii, 24, 29

Mutahhari, Ayatollah Murtaza, 209–12

Muzaffar al-Din Shah (1896–1907), xii

Nafisi, Nezhat (member of twenty-first *majlis*), 141

Nasir al-Din Shah (1848–96), xi, 8

National Front, 29

National Plan of Action, 109, 124–25

Neotraditionalist discourse in postrevolutionary Iran, 208–12; *al-Mizan* (Qur'anic commentary), 210; gender balance, 209; Islamic law, naturalness of, 209–11; Mutahhari, Ayatollah Murtaza, 209–12; primary outlet, 208–9; *Rights of Women in Islam*, 209–11; Tabataba'i, Allamah, 210; traditionalists and modernists, convergence, 209; Western sources, 210; women or men writing for women, 208. *See also* Gender discourse in postrevolutionary Iran; Modernist discourse in postrevolutionary Iran; Traditionalist discourse in postrevolutionary Iran

Organization for Nomads' Affairs, 249

Pahlavi, Ashraf, Princess (sister of Muhammad Reza Shah), xii, 25, 113, 127

Pahlavi, Farah Diba (wife of Muhammad Reza Shah), 126

Pahlavi Dynasty, xii-xiii, 20–30; abdication of Reza Shah, 24; American support of

Reza Muhammad Shah, 24, 27–28; coup d'etat (1921), 20; coup d'etat (1953), 24; education for women, 21, 23, 27; franchise for women, 25; Khomeini, Ruhollah Ayatullah, 24, 28; National Front, 29; nationalism, 27; Patriotic Women's League, 23; reforms benefiting women, 21, 25, 136–37; repression, 22–23; SAVAK (state security agency), 28; secular vs. religious groups, 29; Society for Democratic Women, 24; Tudeh party, 24; ulama, 23; veiling, 22, 137; women activists, 22; women's center (kanun-i banuvan), 21–22

Parsa, Farrokhru (member of twenty-first *majlis*), 141, 146; deputy minister, 151; Iran's first woman minister of education, 151

Patriotic Women's League, 23

Qajar Dynasty, 1794–1925, xi-xii, 4–20; agrarian economy, 10; cultural gap between Europe and Iran, 7–8; education of women, 14–16; Eurocentric view of Muslim women, 7; European misunderstandings of Islam, 6–7; franchise for women, 18; gender roles, 6–8, 16, 18; influence of Europeans, 5–9; invasion, 20; Iranian view of Iranian culture, 9–10; language, 5; literary forms, new, 12; marriage, 16, 37–59; nationalism, rise of, 5, 11; political behavior of women, 12–13, 15–16, 18; rural women, 17, 18; Shi'i Islam, imposition of, on Iranian highlands, 5; Sunni Ottomans, 5; Tudeh party, 24; urban women, 12–13, 16–17; Western Transmutation, 6

Qashqa'i women in postrevolutionary Iran, 240–78; alienation from political groups, 245; attire standards, Islamic, 258–63; basis of study, 243; birth control, 257; ceremony restrictions, 266–69; continuity vs. change, 270; economic diversification, 251; economic self-sufficiency, 249; education, 254; elite vs. majority, 242; ethnic minorities, national interest in, 262; gender segregation, 253–54; government policies, effects of, 249–53; healthcare attitudes, 265–66; *hezbollahis* and revolutionary guards, 247; identity, sense of, 258; Iran-Iraq war, effects of, 247–48; marriage, 254–57; Ministry of Rural Reconstruction, 249; Muhammad Reza Shah's modernization of Iran, 244–45; Organization for Nomads' Affairs, 249; Persian identity vs. other ethnolinguistic groups, 242; political changes from 1978 through the 1980s, 245; public appropriation of Qashqa'i dress, 262–63; religious faith vs. Islamic government's politics, 263–64; religious practice, 264–65; resources on rural women, 240–42; traditional dress, 258–63; tribal characteristics, 244–45; tribal hierarchy, elimination of, 246; tribal people to dispense services, use of, 249, 269; voting, 248

Rafsanjani, President, 159
Rahnavard, Zahra, 159
Rajai, Ateqeh, 155
Referendum, 138–40, xiii
Reuter contract, xi
Revolution, 1978–79, 1, 130; women's participation in, 26–27, 30, 154
Reza, Muhammad Shah (1941–75), xii, 24, 27, 110, 114, 244, 245
Reza Shah (1925–41), xii, 24, 94, 110

Saidi, Nayereh, 151
Sa'idzada, Sayyid Muhsin, 213–14
Sanasarian, Eliz, 88
Sand, George, 78–79
SAVAK (state security agency), 28
Saveh functional literacy project, 120–21
Sexuality, 205–11, 214
Serena, Carla, 69
Sheil, Lady, wife of a British minister, 14, 17; perceptions of Iranian women, 66–69
Shojai, Zahra, 159
Society of Democratic Women, 24
State security agency (SAVAK), 28
Sufi martyr, first, 15–16

Tabataba'i, Allamah, 210
Talbot concession, xii
Taleghani, Azam, 155, 159
Tarbiat, Hajar (member of twenty-first *majlis*), 22, 139–40, 141, 145, 146
Tehran, 37
Tehran University, 136

Traditionalist discourse in postrevolutionary Iran, 205–8; gender inequality, 205–8; language, sexually explicit, 206; men writing for men, 205; men's rights, 207–8; women's duties, 207–8. *See also* Gender discourse in postrevolutionary Iran; Modernist discourse in postrevolutionary Iran; Neotraditionalist discourse in postrevolutionary Iran
Transliteration, system of, ix
Tudeh party, xii, 24, 112, 137; women's reforms, 137

United National First World Conference on Women (1975), 109

Veiling, xii, xiii; in Islamic Republic of Iran, 30, 158–263; in Pahlavi dynasty, 22, 23, 27, 97–100, 137; in Qajar dynasty, 15, 17, 19, 38, 42

Western Transmutation, 6
White Revolution, xii-xiii, 139–40, 143
Women and Elections, 137–38
Women in the nineteenth century: al-Dawla, Anis, 72; diplomatic community, wives of members, 65; education, 65; French Revolution, influence of, 64; higher learning insititution, first secular (Dar al-Funun), 65; "ideal type" under the Qujars, 75; Iranian and European women, contrast of, 78–79; Iranian students in the West, first, 65; missionaries, 65; oppression of Iranian and European women, 80; powerful Iranian women, 72–79; rights for European women, 79–80; status of women, challengers of, 75–78; Western impact on Islamic world, 63–64; Western misperceptions, 66–71
Women's movement in Iran, 1906–41, 85–106; change in emphasis, 92; childcare, 117; controlled by government, 101; education, 87–88, 90, 93, 94, 95, 111; education, opposition to, 93; feelings inspiring the movement, 94–95; *hadith* (the Prophet Mohammad's traditions), 85; health concerns, 90, 100; interests, scope of, 92; Islamic legal code (*shari'a*), 85; law, constitutional and supplementary, 87; newspaper and magazine support,

87, 92; newspapers of women, 91; periodicals, role of, 111; phases, 95; political
societies, 89–90; Reza Shah's aims, 94;
spontaneous origin, 86; unveiling, opposition to, 96–97; urban and educated
class phenomenon, 88; veiling, 97–100;
women activists, 88–89. *See also* Wom-
en's Organization of Iran
Women's Organization of Iran, 107–35;
achievements of, 131–34; Ashraf Pahlavi
(sister of Muhammad Reza Shah), 112,
127; attitudinal changes, 114; Ayatollah
Ruhollah Khomeini, opposition of, 114;
basic structure, 115; budget, 115; charter
approval, 114; *A Comparative Study of
the Socioeconimic Situation of Working
Women in Tehran, Qazvin, and Kashan,*
118; constitution, amendments to, 122–
23; cultural nuances, 107–8; economic
self-sufficiency, 117; empowerment and
organization, 109; family unit, challenge to, 121–22; family welfare centers
(originally called houses of women),
116–17, 127; federation, attempts at, 112;
government, relationship with, 125–28;
High Council of Women's Organizations of Iran, 113; ideological shift, 121–
22; *Images of Women in Elementary-
School Textbooks,* 119; international

connections and support, 109; leftists,
opposition of, 128; men in government,
support of, 109; Muslim clergy, opposition of, 113, 128–29; National Plan of
Action, 124–25; opinion, convergence
needed, 110; Pahlavi, Farah Diba (wife
of Muhammad Reza), 126; participation
in the Revolution, 111; prior organizations, 112; programs, 117; religious establishment, relationship with, 128–30;
research endeavors, 118–20; revolution
of 1978–79, 130–31; role of Muhammad
Reza Shah Pahlavi, 110, 114; Saveh functional literacy project, 120–21; school of
social work, 117; *The Status of Women in
Tribal Society,* 118; Tudeh party and
publications, 112; women and men,
opposition of, 108; women's roles in
1940s, 112; women's roles in 1960s, 113;
World Plan of Action, 109, 123–24. *See
also* Women's Movement in Iran, 1906–
41
Women's suffrage, 24, 87, 112–13, 137
World Plan of Action, 109, 123–24
Writings about women, 1–4

Zaban-e-zanan (Mouthpiece of women)
   newspaper, 91
Zanan (Women) magazine, 159, 212

The University of Illinois Press
is a founding member of the
Association of American University Presses.

———————————————————————

Composed in 10.5/13 Minion
with Minion and Caravan Borders One display
at the University of Illinois Press
Manufactured by Thomson-Shore, Inc.

University of Illinois Press
1325 South Oak Street
Champaign, IL 61820-6903
www.press.uillinois.edu